Learners'
Companion Series
Vocabulary

George Davidson

LEARNERS
PUBLISHING

© 2002 Learners Publishing Pte Ltd

First published 2002 by **Learners Publishing Pte Ltd**
222 Tagore Lane, #03–01 TG Building, Singapore 787603

Reprinted 2002, 2003

Email: learnpub@learners.com.sg
Visit our website: http://www.learners.com.sg

ISBN 981 4070 90 4

Printed by COS Printers Pte Ltd, Singapore

ASSOCIATE COMPANIES

RIC Learners International Limited
PO Box 332
Greenwood
Western Australia 6924

RIC Publications Limited (Asia)
5th floor, Gotanda Mikado Building
2-5-8 Hiratsuka
Shinagawa-ku Tokyo
JAPAN 142-0051
Tel: 03-3788-9201
Fax: 03-3788 9202
Email: elt@ricpublications.com
Website: www.ricpublications.com

Preface

English is now firmly established as the main language of international communication in the modern world. While many of those who are for this reason learning English as a second or foreign language might wish that the world had chosen a less complicated and difficult language to communicate in – one with no irregular verbs perhaps, and with a more consistent spelling system – the choice is now made, for the present at least, and no-one can hope to advance far in business or science without a good knowledge of English.

For a person to speak and write a language well, two things in particular are necessary: a good knowledge of grammar and a good vocabulary. Spelling and pronunciation must not be ignored either, of course. But to cover all these areas thoroughly in one single book would make for a very large book, and the *Learners' Companion to English: Vocabulary* therefore concentrates for the main part on just one aspect of language: vocabulary.

The user will find information on synonyms and antonyms, on prefixes and suffixes, on proverbs and idioms, on phrasal verbs, on words that are often confused, on foreign words and phrases used in English, and much, much more.

There are now two main standard forms of English in use throughout the world: British English and American English. These two forms of English are of course very similar, but differ to some extent in grammar, vocabulary and spelling. While the book focuses mainly on British English, American English has not been ignored, and in Unit 21 the main vocabulary and spelling differences between the two standards are described.

Although the emphasis in the book is on vocabulary rather than grammar, certain areas in which grammar and vocabulary come very close together, such as irregular verbs and the comparison of adjectives and adverbs, are also covered.

The book can be used both as a reference book and as a tool for learning English or improving your knowledge of the language. For this reason, every unit is followed by two or more exercises that provide practice on the information given in the unit. The answers to the exercises are to be found at the end of the book.

Whether by dipping into the book now and again in search of the right word or phrase or by systematic study unit by unit, by using this book every speaker of English can bring more variety and accuracy to their speech and writing.

George Davidson
2002

What you'll find in this book

PRONUNCIATION SCHEME
used in this book

CONSONANTS

phonetic	sound
p	p
t	t
k	k
b	b
d	d
g	g
m	m
n	n
ŋ	ng *as in* si**ng**
θ	th *as in* **th**ing
ð	th *as in* **th**e
f	f
v	v
s	s
z	z, *or voiced* s
ʃ	sh
ʒ	s *as in* plea**s**ure
tʃ	ch *as in* ar**ch**
dʒ	j *or soft* g, *as in* **j**u**dg**e
h	h
l	l
r	r
j	*consonant* y, *as in* **y**et
w	w

VOWELS

phonetic	sound
SHORT VOWELS	
ɪ	i *as in* h**i**t
e	e *as in* b**e**d
a	a *as in* h**a**t
ʌ	u *as in* h**u**t
ɒ	o *as in* h**o**t
ʊ	u *as in* p**u**t *or* b**oo**k
ə	schwa, *as in* **a**live, acr**e**
i	*final* y, *as in* dirt**y**
LONG VOWELS	
iː	*long* e, *as in* h**ea**t
ɑː	*long* a, *as in* h**ar**m
ɔː	o *as in* f**a**ll, br**oa**d
uː	*long* u, *as in* r**u**de, f**oo**d
ɜː	*long vowel like* schwa, *as in* b**ir**d
DIPHTHONGS	
eɪ	a *as in* h**a**te
aɪ	i *as in* b**i**te
ɔɪ	oy *as in* b**oy**, p**oi**nt
aʊ	ow *as in* s**ow**, b**ou**t
oʊ	*long* o *as in* r**oa**d, n**o**te
ɪə	*as in* r**ea**l, p**ee**r
eə	*as in* **air**, p**ear**, sh**are**
ʊə	*as in* s**ure**, p**oor**

1 ► Synonyms

Synonyms are words that have the same, or almost the same, meaning. A list or book of words and their synonyms is called a **thesaurus**.

⚠ Warning

Although the headwords and synonyms in a thesaurus are very close in meaning, there are sometimes slight differences in sense, and also differences in grammar and usage, that make one word more appropriate than another in a particular context. This must always be taken into account when you are selecting a word from the lists of synonyms in this unit. It may sometimes be necessary to refer to a dictionary to check on the exact meaning or grammar of a word you think you want to use.

How to use the lists of synonyms

▶ Where a headword in the following lists belongs to more than one part of speech, the synonyms for each part of speech are listed separately, with the part of speech indicated in *coloured italic* print.

▶ Where a headword has more than one meaning, the synonyms for each meaning are listed separately, with key words in SMALL CAPITALS to indicate which sense is meant.

▶ Words that are *formal*, *informal*, *literary*, *slang* or *offensive* have been labelled as such in the synonym lists. American words have been labelled *US*.

▶ To avoid repetition of word lists, some headwords are not followed by lists of synonyms but by cross-references to other headwords where synonyms can be found. Some entries have both synonyms and cross-references to other headwords.

abandon

LEAVE: desert, forsake, leave, leave behind
GIVE UP: drop, give up, quit, renounce, withdraw from

abandoned

DESERTED: derelict, deserted, empty, unoccupied, vacant
WICKED: depraved, dissipated, dissolute, sinful, wicked

abbreviate

abridge, condense, cut, cut down, reduce, shorten

abduct

carry off, kidnap, run away with

ability *see* capability

able *see* capable

abnormal *see* peculiar, unusual

abolish

do away with, eliminate, end, put an end to, put a stop to, stamp out; *see also* ban

abominable

appalling, awful, despicable, detestable, dreadful, horrible, revolting, terrible

about

preposition BESIDE: around, beside, close to, near, round
preposition ON THE SUBJECT OF: concerning, re (*formal*), regarding, relating to, with regard to, with respect to
adverb see approximately

abrupt

SUDDEN: hasty, quick, rapid, sudden, unexpected
RUDE: blunt, brusque, curt, rude, short

absent

away, gone, left, missing, not here, not there, out

absolute

complete, out-and-out, perfect, pure, thorough, total, sheer, utter

absolutely

completely, definitely, entirely, perfectly, thoroughly, totally, utterly, wholly

absurd

crazy, foolish, idiotic, illogical, laughable, ludicrous, nonsensical, ridiculous, stupid

abundant

ample, considerable, copious, generous, great, large, lavish, plentiful, profuse

abuse

noun WRONG USE: damage, exploitation, ill-treatment, injury, maltreatment, mistreatment, misuse
noun INSULTS: insults, rudeness, rude words, scorn
verb USE WRONGLY: damage, exploit, harm, hurt, injure, maltreat, mistreat, misuse, spoil
verb SCORN: insult, revile, scorn, sneer at, swear at

accept

TAKE: receive, take
AGREE: abide by, accede to, admit, agree to, allow, approve, consent to, submit to
TOLERATE: abide, endure, put up with, stand, stomach, suffer, tolerate

acceptable

adequate, all right, fair, good enough, OK, passable, satisfactory, tolerable

accident

MISHAP: blow, calamity, disaster, misfortune, mishap
ROAD ACCIDENT: bump (*informal*), collision, crash, pile-up (*informal*), smash (*informal*)

acclaim

verb applaud, cheer, clap, commend, praise
noun acclamation, applause, approval, cheers, commendation, praise

accompany
attend, conduct, escort, follow, go with

accomplish
achieve, complete, conclude, effect, execute, finish, fulfil, perform, pull off

accuracy
correctness, exactness, faithfulness, fidelity, precision, truth

accurate
correct, exact, factual, faithful, precise, right, true

accuse
blame, charge, denounce, impeach, indict, reproach, reprove

ache
noun agony, discomfort, pain, soreness, sting, throbbing, twinge
verb be sore, hurt, pound, smart, sting, throb, twinge

achieve
attain, manage, obtain, produce, reach, realize, succeed, win; *see also* accomplish

acknowledge
accept, admit, allow, concede, confess, grant, recognize

acquaint
accustom, advise, familiarize, inform, notify, tell

acquire
buy, gain, gather, get, obtain, procure, purchase

acquit
absolve, clear, discharge, excuse, exonerate, let off, release, reprieve

act
verb behave, officiate, perform, play, pretend
noun ACTION: action, deed, exploit, feat; *see also* action

noun LAW: bill, decree, edict, law, statute
noun PERFORMANCE: item, performance, routine, scene, show, sketch, turn
noun PRETENCE: charade, pose, pretence, sham, show

action
effort, endeavour, manoeuvre, move, movement, performance; *see also* act

active
LIVELY: energetic, enthusiastic, forceful, lively, on the go, vigorous
COMMITTED: committed, dedicated, militant

actual
authentic, concrete, definite, genuine, positive, real, tangible, true

actually
absolutely, as a matter of fact, indeed, in fact, really, truly

acute
CLEVER: astute, bright, clever, perceptive, sharp, shrewd, smart
SEVERE: extreme, intense, serious, severe, sharp, strong

add
ATTACH: affix, append, attach, fasten on, join on, tack on; *see also* include
TOTAL: count up, sum, tally, total, tot up

additional
added, extra, fresh, more, new, spare, supplementary

adequate
ENOUGH: ample, enough, plenty, sufficient
GOOD ENOUGH *see* acceptable

adhere
STICK: cling, hold, stick
OBEY: abide by, comply with, follow, obey, observe, respect, stand by

adjacent
adjoining, close, contiguous, neighbouring, next-door, touching

adjourn
break off, defer, discontinue, interrupt, postpone, suspend

admirable
commendable, creditable, excellent, fine, laudable, praiseworthy

admiration
appreciation, approbation, approval, esteem, liking, regard, respect

admire
applaud, esteem, honour, idolize, like, praise, prize, respect, revere

admirer
FAN: adherent, aficionado, devotee, disciple, enthusiast, fan, follower, supporter
LOVER: boyfriend, girlfriend, lover, suitor, sweetheart

admit
CONFESS: acknowledge, concede, confess, own, own up
LET IN: allow in, let in, receive, take in
ALLOW: allow, permit

adore
cherish, dote on, esteem, idolize, like, love, revere, worship

adorn
beautify, decorate, embellish, garnish, ornament

adult
full-grown, fully grown, grown-up, mature

advance
verb BENEFIT: assist, benefit, foster, further, promote
verb FLOURISH: flourish, progress, prosper, thrive
verb MOVE ON: go ahead, move on, proceed

noun development, growth, headway, increase, progress, rise

advantage
benefit, edge, gain, good, help, lead, profit, start, upper hand

advice
guidance, information, instruction, opinion, recommendation, suggestion, warning

advise
caution, guide, inform, instruct, recommend, suggest, tell, urge, warn

affair
HAPPENING: business, happening, incident, matter, occurrence, operation, project, undertaking
RESPONSIBILITY: business, concern, interest, responsibility
LOVE RELATIONSHIP: liaison, love affair, relationship, romance

affect
INFLUENCE: alter, apply to, change, concern, influence, modify, relate to, transform
DISTURB: disturb, impress, move, touch, trouble, upset, worry

affection
attachment, devotion, fondness, friendliness, goodwill, liking, love, tenderness, warmth

affectionate
attached, cordial, devoted, fond, kind, loving, tender, warm, warm-hearted

affirm
assert, declare, maintain, say, state, swear, testify

afraid
alarmed, anxious, apprehensive, frightened, nervous, scared, terrified

agent

deputy, envoy, go-between, intermediary, representative

aggravate

ANNOY: anger, annoy, enrage, exasperate, harass, irritate, provoke, tease, vex
WORSEN: exacerbate, heighten, increase, intensify, worsen

aggression

antagonism, belligerence, hostility, provocation; *see also* **attack**

agile

lithe, lively, nimble, quick, sprightly, spry

agitate

alarm, disturb, excite, fluster, perturb, trouble, unsettle, upset, worry

agony

anguish, distress, misery, pain, suffering, torment, torture

agree

accede, allow, assent, comply, concur, consent, permit, see eye to eye

agreeable

PLEASANT *see* **pleasant**
WILLING: happy, prepared, ready, willing

agreement

arrangement, bargain, contract, deal, pact, settlement, treaty, understanding

aid

noun assistance, donation, grant, help, sponsorship, support
verb aid and abet, assist, ease, encourage, facilitate, help, promote, sponsor, support

aim

noun ambition, aspiration, dream, goal, intention, object, objective, purpose, target, wish

verb INTEND: aspire, dream, intend, plan, propose, seek, strive
verb POINT A WEAPON: direct, point, target, train

alert

verb forewarn, inform, notify, signal, tip off (*informal*), warn
adjective attentive, awake, on the ball (*informal*), vigilant, wary, watchful

alike

adjective comparable, corresponding, equivalent, identical, parallel, similar
adverb equally, fairly, similarly, together, uniformly

alive

LIVING: animate, breathing, live, living
LIVELY: active, animated, lively, spirited

alliance

association, coalition, federation, league, partnership, union; *see also* **friendship**

allow

agree to, approve, authorize, grant, let, permit, sanction; *see also* **tolerate**

ally

noun accessory, accomplice, collaborator, confederate, helper, supporter; *see also* **colleague, friend**
verb affiliate, associate, combine, join, join forces, team up, unite

almost

about, approaching, approximately, more or less, nearly, practically, virtually

alone

lone, lonely, single, single-handed, sole, solitary, unaccompanied, unaided, unassisted

also

additionally, as well, besides, furthermore, in addition, likewise, moreover, to boot, too

alter

adapt, adjust, amend, change, modify, reshape, revise, transform, vary

always

consistently, constantly, continually, endlessly, forever, perpetually, unfailingly, without exception

amazed *see* astonished

amazement *see* astonishment

amazing

breathtaking, fantastic, magnificent, marvellous, remarkable, wonderful; *see also* astonishing, impressive

ambiguous

confused, equivocal, uncertain, unclear, vague

amiable

agreeable, charming, friendly, genial, pleasant

amount

extent, mass, number, quantity, size, sum, total, whole

ample

abundant, enough, generous, plentiful, sufficient

amuse

charm, cheer, delight, divert, entertain, tickle (*informal*)

amusing *see* funny

ancient

antiquated, antique, obsolete, old, outdated, outmoded, out of date, prehistoric; *see also* primitive

anger

noun exasperation, displeasure, fury, indignation, rage, temper, wrath; *see also* annoyance

verb antagonize, displease, enrage, exasperate, incense, infuriate, offend; *see also* annoy

angry

blazing, cross, exasperated, fuming, furious, infuriated, livid, mad, outraged, wild; *see also* annoyed

announce

advertise, broadcast, declare, disclose, proclaim, report, reveal, say, state, tell

annoy

aggravate, bother, disturb, harass, hassle, irritate, pester, provoke, tease, try one's patience; *see also* anger, trouble

annoyance

BEING ANNOYED: aggravation, displeasure, irritation; *see also* anger

SOMETHING ANNOYING: bother, hassle, inconvenience, irritation, nuisance, pest

annoyed

cross, displeased, irritated, miffed (*informal*), peeved (*informal*); *see also* angry

annoying

aggravating, exasperating, infuriating, irritating, provoking, tiresome, troublesome, trying

anonymous

incognito, nameless, unidentified, unnamed, unsigned

answer

noun REPLY: acknowledgement, reaction, rejoinder, reply, response, retort

noun SOLUTION: explanation, key, solution, way out

verb acknowledge, react, rejoin, reply, respond, retort

anticipate

await, bank on, count on, expect, forecast, foresee, look forward to, predict, wait for; *see also* prevent

antique

ancient, antiquated, archaic, dated, obsolete, old, out of date; *see also* primitive

anxiety

apprehension, disquiet, dread, foreboding, misgiving, nervousness, unease, uneasiness, worry; *see also* fear

anxious

WORRIED: afraid, apprehensive, concerned, fearful, troubled, uneasy, worried; *see also* frightened, nervous

KEEN: desperate, eager, impatient, keen, yearning

apology

confession, excuse, explanation, justification, plea

appalling *see* awful

apparently

evidently, manifestly, obviously, ostensibly, plainly, seemingly, unmistakably

appealing *see* attractive

appear

SEEM: act, behave, look, seem

ARRIVE: arrive, come, emerge, materialize, occur, show up, surface, turn up

appease

calm, humour, mollify, pacify, placate, propitiate, satisfy, soothe

applaud

acclaim, approve, cheer, clap, commend, compliment, praise

applause

acclaim, cheers, clapping, commendation, compliments, praise, a standing ovation

appropriate

applicable, apposite, apropos, fitting, proper, relevant, right, suitable, timely, well-chosen

approval

PRAISE: admiration, commendation, esteem, favour, praise, respect

AGREEMENT: agreement, assent, blessing, consent, the go-ahead, the green light (*informal*), permission, sanction, support

approve

PRAISE: applaud, commend, esteem, favour, like, praise, recommend

AGREE TO: accept, agree to, allow, authorize, back, consent to, endorse, permit, sanction, support

approximately

about, almost, around, close to, in the region of, more or less, nearly, roughly

aptitude *see* capability, gift

area

PLACE: district, locality, neighbourhood, place, region, surroundings, territory, zone

SIZE: breadth, expanse, extent, size, width

TOPIC: department, field, province, sphere, topic

argue

bicker, debate, disagree, discuss, dispute, fight, quarrel, squabble

argument

controversy, debate, disagreement, discussion, dispute, fight, quarrel, row, squabble

arrange

ORDER: adjust, group, move, order, organize, place, plan, position, set out

CLASSIFY: class, classify, group, order

FIX: contrive, devise, fix, organize, plan, prepare, set up

arrangement

POSITION: distribution, grouping, layout, order, organization, placement, placing, position, positioning

AGREEMENT: agreement, compromise, terms

arrest
apprehend, capture, catch, detain, nick (*informal*), seize

arrive
appear, come, enter, reach, show up, turn up

arrogant *see* vain

ascend
climb, fly up, go up, mount, rise, scale, soar

ashamed
abashed, apologetic, embarrassed, humiliated, mortified, red-faced, shame-faced, sheepish

ask
appeal, beg, enquire/inquire, entreat, implore, interrogate, invite, plead, query, question

ask for
beg, demand, request, summon

aspire
aim, desire, dream, hanker, hope, intend, long, seek, wish, yearn

assemble
accumulate, collect, congregate, gather, group, meet, rally

assert
affirm, certify, declare, maintain, say, state, swear, testify

assist
HELP: aid, aid and abet, back, collaborate with, co-operate with, help, support
BOOST: advance, boost, facilitate, further, promote

assistance
aid, backing, collaboration, co-operation, help, support

assistant
accessory, accomplice, aide, associate, collaborator, colleague, confederate, helper, mate, partner

assume
believe, guess, presume, suppose, take for granted, take as read, think

astonish
amaze, astound, bowl over, dumbfound, shake, stagger, stun, surprise; *see also* shock

astonished
amazed, astounded, bowled over, dumbfounded, shocked, speechless, staggered, stunned, surprised

astonishing
amazing, astounding, breathtaking, extra-ordinary, fantastic, incredible, staggering, stunning, surprising, unbelievable

astonishment
amazement, incredulity, surprise, wonder; *see also* shock

atrocious *see* awful

attach
add, affix, connect, fasten, fix, join, link, secure, stick on, tie on

attack
noun ASSAULT: assault, blitz, bombardment, invasion, offensive, onslaught, raid, strike
noun CRITICISM: blame, censure, criticism
verb ASSAULT: assault, bombard, invade, raid, storm
verb CRITICIZE: abuse, berate, blame, censure, charge, criticize, lay into (*informal*)

attain
accomplish, achieve, arrive at, gain, get, obtain, reach, win

attempt

noun bash (*informal*), bid, effort, endeavour, go, shot, try

verb have a bash (*informal*), endeavour, have a go, have a shot, try, undertake, venture

attractive

appealing, charming, cute, delightful, fetching, inviting, lovely, pretty, sweet; *see also* **pleasant**

author

creator, inventor, originator, novelist, writer

automatic

instinctive, involuntary, mechanical, reflex, unconscious, unthinking

avoid

dodge, escape, evade, get out of, prevent, refrain from, shirk, shun, steer clear of

awful

abysmal, appalling, atrocious, dreadful, ghastly, horrendous, horrific, shocking, terrible; *see also* **horrible**

awfully

badly, dreadfully, exceedingly, extremely, greatly, immensely, quite, terribly, very

awkward *see* **difficult**

backbone

PART OF BODY: spinal column, spine

COURAGE: courage, determination, grit, mettle, moral fibre, nerve, pluck, resolve

bad

UNPLEASANT: atrocious, awful, disagreeable, distressing, nasty, painful, sad, unpleasant

UNSATISFACTORY: awful, atrocious, defective, faulty, hopeless, incompetent, inferior, pathetic, poor, unsatisfactory

HARMFUL: adverse, damaging, dangerous, detrimental, disastrous, harmful, injurious

EVIL: corrupt, criminal, dishonest, evil, immoral, sinful, vile, wicked

NAUGHTY: disobedient, mischievous, naughty, unruly

MOULDY: addled, decayed, mouldy, off, putrid, rancid, rotten, sour, spoilt

SEVERE: harsh, serious, severe, terrible

SORRY: conscience-stricken, contrite, guilty, remorseful, rotten, sad, sorry, upset

ILL: awful, ill, rotten, sick, unwell

badly

NOT WELL: abysmally, atrociously, carelessly, disastrously, imperfectly, inadequately, incompetently, mischievously, unsatisfactorily

UNKINDLY: harshly, unfairly, unkindly, unpleasantly

NOT HONESTLY: dishonestly, immorally, improperly

VERY: awfully, dreadfully, extremely, hopelessly, immensely, quite, severely, terribly, very, very much

baffled *see* **bewildered, confused**

ballot

election, poll, referendum, show of hands, vote

ban

verb bar, disallow, exclude, forbid, outlaw, prohibit, proscribe, veto

noun bar, embargo, prohibition, veto

barren

arid, bleak, desert, desolate, dry, infertile, parched, waterless

barrier

bar, barricade, blockade, fence, obstacle, obstruction

base

FOUNDATION: bottom, foundation, support

HEADQUARTERS: camp, centre, headquarters, post

bashful

coy, diffident, hesitant, modest, reluctant, reserved, shy, timid

bathe

WASH: bath, clean, cleanse, immerse, purify, rinse, soak, wash
SWIM: paddle, swim

bear

TOLERATE: abide, accept, endure, put up with, stand, stomach, suffer, tolerate
CARRY *see* **carry**
PRODUCE: breed, generate, give birth to, produce, yield

beast

CRUEL PERSON: barbarian, brute, devil, fiend, monster, savage, swine
ANIMAL: animal, creature

beat

HIT: batter, flog, hit, knock, pound, punch, strike, thrash, thump
DEFEAT: conquer, defeat, hammer (*informal*), outdo, overcome, slaughter (*informal*), thrash, trounce, vanquish
VIBRATE: flutter, patter, pound, pulsate, race, throb, thump, vibrate

beautiful

elegant, exquisite, fine, gorgeous, handsome, lovely, ravishing, splendid, stunning; *see also* **attractive**

become

COME TO BE: get, grow, turn
SUIT: befit, embellish, suit

beg

ask, beseech, crave, desire, entreat, implore, plead, pray, request, solicit

begin

commence, inaugurate, initiate, set in, set out, start

beginner

apprentice, learner, novice, recruit, starter, trainee

behave

act, function, operate, perform, run, work

behaviour

actions, conduct, manners, performance

belief

CONFIDENCE: assumption, assurance, confidence, conviction, faith, impression, trust; *see also* **hope**
OPINION: creed, doctrine, dogma, faith, persuasion, teaching, tenet, theory; *see also* **opinion**, **principle**, **view**

believe

THINK: accept, consider, gather, guess, hold, imagine, presume, reckon, suppose, think; *see also* **understand**
TRUST: rely on, trust

bend

verb bow, buckle, curve, incline, lean, stoop, turn, twist
noun angle, arc, corner, curve, loop, turn, twist, zigzag

beneficial

advantageous, helpful, favourable, profitable, useful

benefit

advantage, gain, good, help, profit, service, use, value, welfare

best

adjective choice, finest, foremost, greatest, pre-eminent, select, supreme, unsurpassed
noun FINEST: choice, cream, elite, finest, flower, pick
noun GREATEST EFFORT: utmost

bewildered

baffled, confused, disconcerted, disorientated, muddled, mystified, nonplussed, perplexed, puzzled

big *see* **great**, **large**

big-headed *see* vain

bit

    chunk, fragment, morsel, part, piece, portion, scrap, segment, slice

blame

    verb accuse, censure, condemn, criticize, reprimand, reproach, scold
    noun ACCUSATION: accusation, censure, condemnation, criticism, reprimand, reproach
    noun FAULT: fault, guilt, liability, responsibility

blend

    verb amalgamate, coalesce, combine, fuse, merge, mingle, mix, unite
    noun alloy, amalgam, combination, compound, fusion, mixture, union

block

    noun bar, brick, cake, chunk, cube, ingot, lump, piece
    verb bar, choke, clog, close, halt, hinder, impede, obstruct, stop

blockage

    barricade, barrier, closure, obstruction, restriction, road block, stoppage

boastful

    big-headed, conceited, proud, swollen-headed, vain

boost

    noun encouragement, enhancement, help, improvement, increase, jump, lift, push, rise
    verb bolster, encourage, enhance, foster, further, help, improve, increase, lift, promote

border

    boundary, brim, brink, circumference, edge, fringe, frontier, margin, perimeter

boring

    dreary, dry, dull, humdrum, monotonous, tedious, uneventful, unexciting, unimaginative, uninspiring

bottom

    BASE: base, basis, bed, floor, foot, foundation, ground, origin, root, seat
    PART OF BODY: arse (*slang*), backside (*informal*), behind (*informal*), bum (*slang*), buttocks

box

    carton, case, chest, container, crate, pack, package, packet, trunk

brave

    bold, courageous, daring, fearless, heroic, intrepid, plucky, unafraid, valiant

bravery

    courage, daring, fearlessness, fortitude, guts (*informal*), heroism, nerve, pluck (*informal*), valour

break

    verb burst, crack, disintegrate, fracture, fragment, shatter, smash, snap, split, tear
    noun HOLE: crack, fracture, gap, gash, hole, opening, split, tear
    noun PAUSE: halt, interlude, intermission, interruption, let-up, pause, recess, respite

breakable

    brittle, delicate, flimsy, fragile

brief

    concise, cursory, fleeting, momentary, passing, short, short-lived, succinct, transient; *see also* quick

bright

    SHINING: dazzling, gleaming, glistening, glittering, glowing, luminous, polished, shining, shiny, sparkling
    SUNNY: cloudless, sunny
    CLEVER: astute, brainy, clever, intelligent, quick-witted, sharp, smart
    CHEERFUL *see* cheerful

broad

LARGE: ample, extensive, large, roomy, spacious, vast, wide

COVERING MANY THINGS: comprehensive, extensive, general, sweeping, wide, wide-ranging

NOT EXACT: approximate, ballpark (*informal*), imprecise, inexact, loose, rough, round

brutal

barbarous, callous, cruel, heartless, merciless, pitiless, rough, ruthless, vicious, violent

build

assemble, construct, erect, make, raise

building

construction, edifice (*formal*), house, hut, shed, structure

burst

break, crack, disintegrate, fragment, puncture, shatter, split, tear; *see also* explode

business

COMMERCE: commerce, industry, manufacturing, selling, trade

EMPLOYMENT: calling, career, employment, job, occupation, profession, trade, vocation, work

COMPANY: company, concern, corporation, enterprise, establishment, firm, organization

RESPONSIBILITY: affair, assignment, concern, duty, function, job, responsibility, task

busy

ACTIVE: active, assiduous, diligent, energetic, hard-working, industrious

OCCUPIED: employed, engaged, engrossed, occupied, working

buy

acquire, get, obtain, pay for, procure, purchase

calamity

catastrophe, disaster, misfortune, mishap, ruin, tragedy

calm

NOT WORRIED: composed, cool, laid back (*informal*), peaceful, placid, relaxed, unflappable, unflustered, unperturbed, untroubled

NOT STORMY: balmy, mild, peaceful, smooth, still, tranquil, windless

cancel

abolish, annul, countermand, delete, erase, repeal, rescind, revoke

capability

ability, capacity, competence, expertise, facility, means, potential, power, talent; *see also* gift, intelligence

capable

COMPETENT: able, clever, competent, efficient, proficient, skilful, skilled, talented

LIKELY: liable, likely, susceptible

capacity

SIZE: dimensions, extent, size, space, volume

JOB: job, function, office, position, post, responsibility, role

ABILITY *see* capability

captivity

custody, detention, enslavement, gaol/jail, imprisonment, internment, prison, slavery

capture

verb apprehend, arrest, catch, grab, seize, take

noun apprehension, arrest, detention, seizure

care

noun PROTECTION: control, direction, guardianship, keeping, management, protection, supervision

noun CAUTION: caution, circumspection, forethought, heed, prudence, vigilance, wariness, watchfulness *noun* WORRY: anxiety, hardship, stress, trial, tribulation, trouble, worry

noun CAREFULNESS: attention, carefulness, concentration, conscientiousness

verb WORRY: bother, mind, worry

verb CARE FOR: guard, look after, mind, protect

careful

CAUTIOUS: alert, cautious, chary, circumspect, prudent, vigilant, wary, watchful

ACCURATE: accurate, attentive, conscientious, meticulous, painstaking, scrupulous, thorough

careless

NOT ATTENTIVE: casual, inaccurate, inattentive, lackadaisical, negligent, off-hand, perfunctory, slap-dash (*informal*), slipshod, sloppy

NOT WORRIED: heedless, nonchalant, rash, reckless, thoughtless, unconcerned, unthinking

carry

bear, bring, conduct, convey, haul, lift, relay, shoulder, take, transport

catastrophe *see* disaster

catch

arrest, capture, grab, grasp, grip, seize, snatch, take hold of

cause

noun basis, grounds, motivation, motive, reason, stimulus

verb create, generate, give rise to, induce, occasion, precipitate, produce, provoke

caution

WARINESS: care, circumspection, prudence, wariness, watchfulness

WARNING: admonition, advice, caveat (*formal*), counsel, warning

cautious

careful, chary, circumspect, prudent, vigilant, tentative, wary, watchful

cease *see* stop

centre

bull's-eye, core, focus, heart, middle, mid-point, nucleus

certain

SURE: confident, convinced, definite, positive, satisfied

CONVINCING: conclusive, convincing, irrefutable, known, reliable, true, undeniable

SOME: a few, individual, one or two, particular, some, specific

chance

POSSIBILITY: likelihood, occasion, opportunity, possibility, probability, prospect, risk, scope

LUCK: accident, coincidence, destiny, fate, fortune, luck, providence

change

verb adapt, adjust, alter, convert, modify, revise, transform, vary

noun adaptation, adjustment, alteration, conversion, modification, revision, revolution, transformation, variation

chaos

bedlam, confusion, disorder, disorganization, havoc, mayhem, pandemonium, shambles

charity

alms, assistance, benevolence, gift, hand-out, philanthropy; *see also* generosity, kindness

charming

appealing, attractive, captivating, cute, delightful, inviting, lovely, pretty, sweet

cheap

NOT EXPENSIVE: cut-price, dirt-cheap, economy, inexpensive, low-cost, reasonable, reduced

OF POOR QUALITY: inferior, poor, second-rate, shoddy, tawdry

cheat

verb defraud, double-cross, dupe, fool, hoax, hoodwink, rip off (*informal*), swindle, trick; *see also* **deceive**

noun charlatan, con man (*informal*), double-crosser, fraud, impostor, swindler

cheerful

bright, carefree, cheery, happy, jolly, jovial, light-hearted, merry, sunny

chief

noun boss (*informal*), commander, director, head, leader, manager, master, principal, ruler, supremo (*informal*)

adjective see **main**

chiefly

especially, essentially, for the most part, generally, mainly, mostly, predominantly, principally, usually

childhood

adolescence, boyhood, girlhood, infancy, schooldays, teens, youth

choice

noun alternative, decision, option, pick, preference, say, selection, variety

adjective best, elite, exclusive, hand-picked, prime, prize, select, special, superior; *see also* **excellent, rare**

choose

adopt, designate, elect, opt for, pick, prefer, select, settle on, single out, vote for

clean

adjective fresh, hygienic, immaculate, pure, spotless, sterile, uncontaminated, unpolluted, washed; *see also* **tidy**

verb bath, bathe, cleanse, disinfect, dust, purify, rinse, scrub, sweep, wash; *see also* **tidy**

clear

DEFINITE: definite, distinct, evident, explicit, obvious, plain, unambiguous, unmistakable, well-defined

CERTAIN: certain, convinced, definite, positive, satisfied, sure

ABLE TO BE SEEN THROUGH: crystalline, diaphanous, limpid, see-through, transparent

DESCRIBING WEATHER: bright, cloudless, fair, fine, sunny

clearly

IN A CLEAR WAY: distinctly, legibly, neatly

OBVIOUSLY: evidently, manifestly, markedly, notably, noticeably, obviously, plainly, undeniably, undoubtedly, visibly

clever

astute, brainy, bright, ingenious, intelligent, knowledgeable, perceptive, talented, wily, wise; *see also* **capable, cunning**

client

consumer, customer, patient, patron

climb

ascend, clamber, go up, mount, scale, shin up

close

adjective NEARBY: adjacent, adjoining, near, nearby, neighbouring

adjective ACCURATE: accurate, exact, faithful, literal, minute, precise, word-for-word; *see also* **thorough**

adjective APPROXIMATE: approximate, ballpark (*informal*), loose, rough

verb SHUT: bar, block, choke, lock, obstruct, plug, seal, secure, shut, stop

verb END: conclude, discontinue, end, finish, shut down, terminate, wind up; *see also* **stop**

noun closure, completion, discontinuation, end, ending, finale, finish, shutdown, stop, termination

clothes

apparel (*formal*), attire (*formal*), clothing, costume, dress, garments, get-up (*informal*), outfit, wardrobe, wear

cloudy

NOT SUNNY: dark, dim, dismal, dull, gloomy, leaden, overcast

NOT CLEAR: blurred, hazy, indistinct, muddy, murky, obscure, opaque, translucent

coarse

crude, foul-mouthed, immodest, improper, indelicate, offensive, ribald, rude, vulgar; *see also* impolite

cold

NOT WARM (OF WEATHER): arctic, biting, bitter, chilly, freezing, frosty, glacial, icy, wintry

NOT WARM (OF PERSON): chilly, freezing, frozen, shivery

NOT FRIENDLY: aloof, chilly, cool, formal, frosty, lukewarm, stand-offish, stony, unfeeling, unfriendly

colleague

assistant, associate, collaborator, co-worker, partner, team-mate; *see also* ally

collect

accumulate, amass, assemble, congregate, converge, gather, pile up, stockpile

college

academy, institute, polytechnic, school, university

colour

complexion, dye, hue, paint, pigmentation, shade, tinge, tint, tone

combination

alloy, amalgam, amalgamation, blend, compound, fusion, merger, mix, mixture, union

combine

amalgamate, coalesce, blend, fuse, merge, mingle, mix, pool, unify, unite; *see also* join

command

verb ORDER: bid, compel, decree, dictate, direct, enjoin, order, require; *see also* demand

verb CONTROL: control, direct, govern, lead, manage, rule, supervise

noun ORDER: bidding, decree, directive, edict, fiat, injunction, instruction, order, ultimatum; *see also* demand

noun CONTROL: authority, charge, control, direction, government, lead, management, power, rule, supervision

common

EVERYDAY: average, common-or-garden, commonplace, conventional, everyday, familiar, frequent, general, prevalent, regular; *see also* normal, usual

INFERIOR: hackneyed, humdrum, inferior, low, stale, trite, vulgar

compassion

charity, clemency, fellow-feeling, humanity, kindness, mercy, pity, sympathy

compel *see* force

competent *see* capable

competitor

adversary, challenger, contender, contestant, entrant, opponent, participant, rival

complain

carp, criticize, grouse, grumble, lament, moan, protest, whine, whinge (*informal*)

complaint

criticism, grievance, gripe, grouse, grumble, lament, moan, protest, whinge (*informal*); *see also* illness

complete

ENTIRE: all, all-inclusive, entire, full, intact, integral, total, undivided; *see also* whole

THOROUGH: comprehensive, deep, detailed, exhaustive, extensive, full, plentiful, thorough

VERY MUCH A: absolute, out-and-out, perfect, pure, thorough, thoroughgoing, total

UNCUT: intact, unabridged, unabbreviated, uncut, unedited, unexpurgated

FINISHED: accomplished, concluded, ended, finished

completely

altogether, entirely, perfectly, quite, thoroughly, totally, utterly, wholly; *see also* definitely

complicated

complex, detailed, difficult, elaborate, intricate, involved, tangled, tortuous

comprehend

appreciate, conceive, discern, fathom, grasp, perceive, see, tumble to, understand

conceal

bury, camouflage, cloak, cover, disguise, hide, mask, obscure, screen, veil

conceited *see* vain

conclude

END: cease, close, complete, end, finish, stop, terminate

THINK: assume, decide, deduce, infer, judge, reckon, suppose, surmise, think

condemn

blame, censure, damn, disparage, pan (*informal*), reproach, reprove, revile, slam (*informal*), slate (*informal*)

confused

BAFFLED: all at sea, disconcerted, disorganized, disorientated, flummoxed, flustered, muddled, nonplussed, perplexed, puzzled; *see also* bewildered, dazed

IN DISORDER: chaotic, disorderly, disorganized, higgledy-piggledy, jumbled, muddled, topsy-turvy, untidy

consider

HAVE AN OPINION: believe, judge, rate, regard, think

THINK ABOUT: contemplate, deliberate, examine, mull over, ponder, reflect, study, think, weigh, weigh up

construct

BUILD: assemble, build, erect, fabricate, fashion, knock up (*informal*), make, put up, raise

CREATE: create, form, formulate, frame, make

contest

noun battle, combat, conflict, debate, encounter, fight, struggle; *see also* dispute, game

verb challenge, compete, contend, debate, deny, dispute, fight, oppose, question, struggle against; *see also* dispute

continual

constant, continued, frequent, perpetual, recurrent, regular, repeated

continuous

ceaseless, constant, endless, incessant, interminable, perpetual, prolonged, unbroken, unremitting

contract

noun agreement, arrangement, bargain, deal, commitment, pact, treaty, understanding

verb become smaller, condense, narrow, shrink, shrivel, tighten

control

verb BE IN CHARGE: command, direct, dominate, govern, guide, lead, manage, oversee, rule, supervise

verb OPERATE: determine, drive, manipulate, operate, regulate, steer

verb RESTRICT: constrain, curb, limit, repress, restrain, subdue, suppress

noun COMMAND: authority, command, direction, government, guidance, leadership, jurisdiction, management, oversight, supervision *noun* RESTRICTION: brake, check, constraint, curb, limitation, restraint, restriction, suppression

conversation

chat, dialogue, discussion, exchange, talk, tête-à-tête

convince

assure, confirm, dissuade, persuade, prove, reassure, satisfy, sway, win over

copy

verb DO THE SAME AS: ape, echo, emulate, follow, imitate, mimic, mirror, parrot, repeat, simulate
verb MAKE A COPY OF: counterfeit, forge, photocopy, plagiarize, reproduce, transcribe
noun duplicate, facsimile, forgery, imitation, likeness, photocopy, print, replica, reproduction, transcription

correct

adjective ACCURATE: accurate, exact, faithful, faultless, flawless, precise, right, spot on (*informal*), true, word-perfect
adjective APPROPRIATE: appropriate, fitting, just, proper, right, seemly
verb SCOLD: admonish, chasten, chastise, chide, discipline, punish, reprimand, reprove, scold, warn
verb IMPROVE: adjust, amend, cure, debug, improve, mark, rectify, reform, remedy, right

country

NATION: fatherland, homeland, kingdom, land, motherland, nation, realm, region, state; *see also* people
COUNTRYSIDE: countryside, farmland, outback, outdoors
LANDSCAPE: landscape, terrain

courage *see* bravery

courageous *see* brave

courteous *see* polite

cover

coat, dress, envelop, protect, screen, shade, shelter, shield, veil; *see also* conceal

cowardly

faint-hearted, fearful, scared, soft, spineless, timid, timorous, weak, weak-kneed

crazy *see* impractical, mad, ridiculous

crowd

GROUP: army, bunch, horde, host, mass, mob, multitude, pack, swarm, throng; *see also* group
AUDIENCE: audience, spectators

crude

NOT POLITE: coarse, dirty, indecent, lewd, obscene, rough, rude, tasteless, vulgar
NOT WELL MADE: amateurish, makeshift, primitive, rough, rudimentary, sketchy

cruel

barbaric, barbarous, brutal, callous, cold-blooded, hard-hearted, harsh, heartless, vicious; *see also* ruthless, severe, unkind

cunning

astute, clever, crafty, devious, ingenious, sly, sneaky (*informal*), wily

cure

noun antidote, healing, medicine, panacea, remedy, treatment
verb alleviate, correct, ease, fix, heal, help, mend, relieve, restore, treat

curious

ODD *see* unusual
WANTING TO KNOW: inquisitive, interested, nosy, prying, questioning

custom

convention, etiquette, fashion, policy, practice, procedure, ritual, rule, tradition, usage, wont (*literary*); *see also* habit

customer
buyer, client, consumer, patron, shopper

cut
verb DIVIDE: chop, divide, halve, intersect, part, segment, sever, slice, split

verb CUT OFF: carve, chop, clip, mow, pare, prune, sever, shave, shear, trim

verb DECREASE: abbreviate, abridge, condense, curtail, decrease, prune, reduce, shorten, trim, truncate; *see also* delete

noun WOUND: gash, groove, incision, nick, rip, scratch, slash, slit, tear, wound

noun DECREASE: cutback, decrease, diminution, economy, fall, lowering, reduction, saving, slash (*informal*)

damage
verb deface, destroy, harm, hurt, impair, injure, mutilate, ruin, spoil, wreck

noun destruction, detriment, devastation, harm, hurt, impairment, injury, loss, mutilation, ruin

damp
clammy, dank, humid, moist, rainy, sodden, soggy, sopping, wet

dance
verb caper, frolic, hop, prance, skip, spin, whirl

noun ball, disco, knees-up (*informal*), rave (*informal*); *see also* party

danger
hazard, jeopardy, menace, peril, risk, threat

dangerous
critical, hazardous, insecure, menacing, perilous, precarious, risky, threatening, treacherous, unsafe

daring
adjective adventurous, audacious, bold, fearless, game, intrepid, plucky, reckless; *see also* brave

noun audacity, boldness, bottle (*informal*), fearlessness, grit (*informal*), guts (*informal*), nerve, pluck (*informal*), spirit; *see also* bravery

dazed
baffled, bewildered, confused, stunned, stupefied

deadly
baneful, devastating, fatal, lethal, malignant, mortal, poisonous, venomous

dear
NOT CHEAP: costly, expensive, pricey (*informal*)

LOVED: beloved, cherished, darling, esteemed, favourite, precious, prized, treasured, valued

deceive
con (*informal*), delude, dupe, fool, mislead, take for a ride (*informal*), take in, trick; *see also* cheat, lie, trick

deception
deceit, deceitfulness, duplicity, false pretences, feint, fraud, hoax, illusion, subterfuge; *see also* lie, trick

declare
affirm, announce, assert, certify, claim, maintain, proclaim, pronounce, state, testify; *see also* say

decorate
adorn, beautify, do up (*informal*), embellish, garnish, ornament, paint, paper, renovate

decoration
ORNAMENT: adornment, beautification, embellishment, frill, ornament, ornamentation, trimming

MEDAL: award, badge, crown, emblem, garland, laurel, medal, ribbon

decrease
verb BECOME LESS: decline, drop, dwindle, ease off, fade away, fall, peter out, shrink, slacken, subside

verb MAKE LESS: curtail, cut down, diminish, ease, lessen, lower, reduce

noun abatement, contraction, cutback, decline, diminution, downturn, reduction, shrinkage

deduce

calculate, conclude, estimate, infer, judge, work out; *see also* **guess, think**

defect

blemish, deficiency, flaw, imperfection, inadequacy, mistake, shortcoming, weakness

definitely

absolutely, categorically, decidedly, positively, truly, unquestionably

delay

noun hold-up, postponement, setback, stoppage, wait

verb defer, hinder, hold back, hold up, impede, postpone, put off, set back

delete

cancel, cross out, erase, remove, rub out, score out

delicious

appetizing, mouthwatering, scrumptious (*informal*), tasty

delighted

ecstatic, elated, enchanted, joyful, jubilant, overjoyed, over the moon (*informal*), thrilled; *see also* **happy**

delightful

agreeable, attractive, captivating, congenial, enchanting, enjoyable, heavenly, ravishing, sweet; *see also* **charming**

demand

verb ask, ask for, call for, insist on, need, order, request, require; *see also* **command**

noun call, claim, necessity, need, order, request; *see also* **command**

describe

characterize, define, depict, explain, outline, portray, recount, report, sketch; *see also* **tell**

desert

verb abandon, defect, forsake, leave, leave in the lurch, quit

noun wasteland, wilderness

adjective arid, bare, barren, desolate, dry, infertile, parched, waterless

desire

verb aspire to, covet, fancy (*informal*), hanker after, hunger for, long for, want, wish for, yearn for; *see also* **ask**

noun WISH: appetite, aspiration, craving, hankering, longing, wish, yearning, yen

noun PASSION: ardour, lust, passion

desperate

daring, dire, drastic, frantic, frenzied, furious, hopeless, panicky, reckless, wild

die

breathe one's last (*literary*), expire (*formal*), kick the bucket (*informal*), pass away (*formal*), perish (*literary*), snuff it (*informal*)

different

OF SEVERAL TYPES: assorted, diverse, miscellaneous, several, sundry, various

OTHER: contrasting, dissimilar, other, unlike

difficult

NOT EASY: arduous, awkward, baffling, demanding, hard, intractable, knotty, onerous, problematic, tough; *see also* **complicated**

NOT CO-OPERATIVE: awkward, demanding, fussy, obstinate, perverse, stubborn, troublesome, trying, unco-operative

dirty

NOT CLEAN: filthy, grimy, grubby, messy, mucky, muddy, scruffy, soiled, squalid
RUDE: blue, indecent, obscene, pornographic, risqué, rude, smutty (*informal*), vulgar

disagreeable

difficult, disgusting, nasty, objectionable, obnoxious, offensive, repugnant, repulsive, unfriendly, unpleasant

disappear

depart, dissolve, escape, evaporate, fade, flee, pass, vanish

disaster

calamity, catastrophe, misfortune, mishap

disease *see* illness

dislike

verb abhor, despise, detest, disapprove of, hate, loathe
noun abhorrence, antipathy, aversion, distaste, hatred, loathing, repugnance, resentment, revulsion

disorder

MUDDLE: chaos, clutter, commotion, confusion, disarray, disorganization, mess, muddle, untidiness
ILLNESS *see* illness

display

demonstrate, exhibit, expose, flaunt, flourish, manifest, parade, present, reveal, show

dispute

verb cast doubt on, challenge, contest, contradict, deny, fight, question
noun argument, contest, controversy, debate, disagreement, fight, quarrel

distant

far, faraway, far-flung, far-off, out-of-the-way, remote

distress

agony, anguish, distress, misery, pain, suffering, torment, torture, woe

divide

bisect, cut, halve, intersect, part, partition, segment, separate, split

dreadful

appalling, atrocious, awful, ghastly, horrible, shocking, terrible

dream

PICTURE IN MIND: daydream, delusion, hallucination, fantasy, nightmare, trance, vision
AIM *see* aim

drink

verb gulp, knock back (*informal*), lap, sip, suck, swallow
noun LIQUID: beverage (*formal*), potion
noun QUANTITY OF LIQUID: glass, gulp, sip, swallow

dull

NOT LIGHT: cloudy, dark, dim, drab, gloomy, leaden, overcast
NOT INTERESTING *see* boring
NOT INTELLIGENT: dense, dim, dimwitted, slow, stupid, unintelligent
NOT SHARP: blunt

eager

anxious, ardent, avid, earnest, enthusiastic, fervent, intent, keen

easily

comfortably, effortlessly, readily, simply, standing on one's head, with one arm tied behind one's back

eat

chew, consume, devour, feed on, gobble, munch, nibble, scoff (*informal*), swallow

eat away

corrode, decay, erode, rot, rust

edge

border, boundary, brim, brink, fringe, margin, perimeter, rim, threshold, verge; *see also* side

educate

coach, instruct, school, teach, train, tutor

elaborate *see* complicated

elegant

artistic, beautiful, chic, fashionable, fine, graceful, refined, stylish, tasteful; *see also* noble

embarrassed

abashed, discomfited, disconcerted, humiliated, mortified, red-faced, shamed, shamefaced

emotion

excitement, feeling, fervour, passion, reaction, sensation, sentiment, vehemence, warmth

emphasis

accent, accentuation, force, insistence, intensity, prominence, strength, stress, weight

emphasize

accentuate, dwell on, feature, highlight, insist on, spotlight, stress, underline

end

noun FINISH: cessation, close, closure, completion, conclusion, culmination, expiry, finale, finish; *see also* result

noun DESTRUCTION: annihilation, death, demise, destruction, doom, downfall, extermination, extinction, ruin, termination

noun PURPOSE: aim, design, goal, intent, intention, object, objective, purpose, reason

noun BOUNDARY: boundary, edge, extremity, limit

verb FINISH: cease, close, complete, conclude, culminate, finish, stop, terminate, wind up

verb PUT A STOP TO: abolish, close, destroy, finish, stop, terminate, wind up

enemy

adversary, antagonist, foe (*literary*), opponent, rival

energetic

active, dynamic, forceful, lively, spirited, strong, tireless, vigorous

energy

drive, fire, get-up-and-go (*informal*), liveliness, spirit, stamina, steam, vigour, vim and vigour, vitality; *see also* power, strength

enlarge

add to, broaden, expand, extend, increase, widen

enormous *see* huge

enough

adequate, ample, plenty, sufficient

ensure

guarantee, make certain, make sure

enthusiasm

devotion, eagerness, fervour, keenness, passion

enthusiastic

avid, devoted, eager, fervent, keen, passionate

entire

all, complete, full, intact, total, unabridged, uncut, whole

entirely *see* completely

environment

ambience, background, conditions, habitat, medium, milieu, scene, setting, situation, surroundings

envious *see* jealous

envy

noun see envy
verb begrudge, be jealous of, grudge, resent

error

MISTAKE *see* mistake
WRONGDOING: fault, offence, oversight, sin, slip, slip-up, wrong, wrongdoing

escape

verb GET AWAY: abscond, bolt, break loose, break out, flee, fly, get away, slip through; *see also* run away
verb AVOID: avoid, circumvent, dodge, duck, elude, evade, get out of
verb LEAK OUT: drain out, emanate (*formal*), flow out, gush, issue, leak, pour out, seep out, spurt out, trickle out
noun GETAWAY: bolt, break, break-out, evasion, flight, getaway, jail-break
noun AVOIDANCE: avoidance, circumvention, evasion
noun LEAK: discharge, effluence, emission, gush, leak, leakage, seepage, spurt

essential

basic, crucial, fundamental, indispensable, key, necessary, much-needed, required, vital; *see also* important

eventually

at last, at length, finally, in the end, lastly, sooner or later, ultimately

evil

noun corruption, depravity, immorality, sin, sinfulness, villainy, wickedness, wrong, wrongdoing
adjective bad, corrupt, criminal, cruel, depraved, immoral, iniquitous, sinful, wicked

exact

accurate, correct, detailed, faithful, faultless, flawless, meticulous, precise, strict, true

excellent

brilliant, fabulous, fantastic, magnificent, marvellous, outstanding, phenomenal, splendid, superb, wonderful

excited

animated, breathless, elated, enthusiastic, exhilarated, frenzied, inspired, thrilled, wild; *see also* eager

exciting

breathtaking, electrifying, enthralling, exhilarating, impressive, inspiring, sensational, stunning, thrilling; *see also* amazing

exhausted

TIRED: all in, dead-beat (*informal*), dog-tired (*informal*), done in (*informal*), tired, tired out, weary, whacked (*informal*), worn out
FINISHED: consumed, depleted, finished, gone, spent, used up

expertise see ability

explode

blow up, burst, detonate, erupt, go off, set off

extend

broaden, enlarge, expand, increase, lengthen, prolong, spin out, spread, stretch, widen

extensive

broad, far-reaching, huge, large, massive, sweeping, swingeing, wide-ranging

extra

added, additional, fresh, more, new, spare, supplementary

fable

allegory, fairy tale, legend, myth, story, tale

fair

JUST: disinterested, equitable, even-handed, honest, impartial, just, legitimate, unbiased, unprejudiced

ADEQUATE: acceptable, adequate, all right, not bad, OK, passable, reasonable, satisfactory, so-so, tolerable

BEAUTIFUL: beautiful, handsome, pretty

fall

verb BECOME LESS: decline, decrease, drop, dwindle, lessen, plunge, sink, slump, subside

verb FALL OVER: stumble, topple, trip, tumble

noun LESSENING: collapse, decline, decrease, diminution, dip, dive, drop, reduction, slump

noun DOWNFALL: death, defeat, destruction

false

NOT TRUE: erroneous, inaccurate, incorrect, invalid, misleading, mistaken, unfounded, unreliable, untrue, wrong

NOT GENUINE: artificial, bogus, counterfeit, dummy, fake, fictitious, forged, imitation, phoney

NOT FAITHFUL: dishonourable, disloyal, faithless, perfidious (*formal*), unfaithful, unreliable, untrustworthy

famous

acclaimed, celebrated, distinguished, eminent, legendary, noted, prominent, renowned, well-known; *see also* infamous

fan

addict, admirer, aficionado, buff (*informal*), devotee, enthusiast, freak (*slang*); *see also* supporter

fantastic

STRANGE *see* peculiar

VERY GOOD *see* excellent

far *see* distant

fascinating

amazing, astonishing, captivating, compelling, enchanting, enthralling, gripping, interesting, intriguing, riveting

fashion

MANNER: form, look, manner, method, pattern, style, way

CRAZE: convention, craze, cult, custom, fad, habit, rage, trend, usage, vogue

fast

brisk, hasty, hurried, quick, rapid, speedy, swift

fasten

anchor, attach, chain, clamp, fix, link, moor, nail, rivet, secure, tie, tie up

fatal

baneful, calamitous, catastrophic, deadly, destructive, disastrous, lethal, mortal, terminal

fate

chance, destiny, fortune, karma, kismet, providence, the stars

fatigue

exhaustion, lethargy, overtiredness, tiredness, weariness

fault

noun ERROR: blunder, inaccuracy, lapse, mistake, negligence, oversight, shortcoming, slip, slip-up

noun FLAW: defect, deficiency, flaw, imperfection

noun BLAME: blame, culpability, liability, responsibility

verb blame, censure, criticize, find fault with, impugn, pick holes in

fear

noun alarm, consternation, dismay, distress, dread, foreboding, fright, panic, phobia, terror; *see also* anxiety

verb be afraid, dread, panic, tremble at, worry about

fearful

AFRAID: afraid, alarmed, faint-hearted, frightened, jittery, jumpy, nervous, panicky, scared, timid; *see also* anxious
VERY BAD *see* awful

fearless *see* brave

feeble

NOT STRONG: delicate, faint, flimsy, frail, ineffective, ineffectual, powerless, weak
NOT GOOD: inadequate, incompetent, inefficient, insufficient, mediocre, pathetic, poor, weak

ferocious

bloodthirsty, bloody, brutal, fierce, merciless, murderous, savage, vicious, violent, wild; *see also* ruthless

fertile

fruitful, lush, productive, rich

fetch

bring, carry, convey, get, take

fierce

FEROCIOUS *see* ferocious
STRONG: intense, powerful, raging, relentless, stormy, violent

few

a couple of, a handful, hardly any, one or two, some; *see also* rare

fight

noun BATTLE: battle, brawl, clash, conflict, contest, duel, feud, skirmish, struggle, war
noun ARGUMENT: argument, battle, clash, dispute, quarrel, squabble
verb HAVE COMBAT: battle, brawl, clash, feud, skirmish, spar, struggle, tussle
verb ARGUE: argue, battle, bicker, clash, quarrel, skirmish, squabble

finish *see* end, result

firm

adjective HARD: hard, set, solid, stiff, rigid
adjective FIXED: anchored, embedded, fastened, fixed, secure, stable, steady
adjective adamant, determined, dogged, resolute, staunch, steady, unshakable, unwavering
noun see business

fit

HEALTHY: in good shape, healthy, strong
SUITABLE: capable, competent, prepared, qualified, ready, suitable

fix

FASTEN: attach, anchor, connect, fasten, glue, join, nail, pin, secure, tie; *see also* place
SET: agree on, arrange, decide, finalize, set, settle, specify
MEND *see* mend

flag

banner, colours, ensign, pennant, pennon, standard

flavour

FEELING: character, essence, feel, hint, property, quality, suggestion, tinge
TASTE: piquancy, savour, seasoning, tang, taste, tastiness

fond

LOVING: affectionate, attached, caring, doting, loving
KEEN: addicted, attached, keen, mad, partial

fool

noun ass, buffoon, clot (*informal*), clown, dope, fathead, half-wit, idiot, nitwit, twit (*informal*), wally (*informal*)
verb bamboozle, con (*informal*), deceive, delude, dupe, hoax, hoodwink, mislead, trick; *see also* cheat

foolish

daft (*informal*), idiotic, ill-advised, imprudent, rash, reckless, senseless, silly, stupid, unwise; *see also* mad

foolishness

absurdity, folly, idiocy, imprudence, madness, nonsense, rashness, recklessness, senselessness, stupidity

force

verb bully, coerce, compel, drive, impel, intimidate, lean on, oblige, pressurize, push

noun aggression, coercion, compulsion, constraint, duress, intimidation, might, muscle, pressure, violence; *see also* energy, power, strength

foreigner

alien, immigrant, incomer, newcomer, outsider, refugee, stranger

foretell

augur, bode, forecast, foreshadow, forewarn, predict, presage, prophesy

forever

always, constantly, continually, endlessly, eternally, incessantly, interminably, perpetually, persistently

forgetful

absent-minded, inattentive, oblivious, scatterbrained

forgive

absolve, acquit, excuse, let off, overlook, pardon

fortunate

auspicious, convenient, favourable, helpful, lucky, opportune, providential, successful, timely, well-timed

fortunately

happily, luckily, providentially

fortune

LUCK: chance, circumstances, destiny, fate, good luck, luck, providence

MONEY: assets, a mint (*informal*), a packet (*informal*), a pile (*informal*), prosperity, riches, treasure, wealth

fragrance

aroma, bouquet, odour, perfume, savour, scent, smell

free

verb disentangle, emancipate, let go, liberate, loose, release, rescue, set free, unchain, untie

adjective AT NO COST: complimentary, extra, for nothing, free of charge, gratis, on the house, unpaid, without charge

adjective NOT ATTACHED OR RESTRICTED: at large, at liberty, independent, liberated, loose, off the hook, on the loose, unimpeded, unrestricted

adjective NOT IN USE: available, empty, idle, spare, unattached, uncommitted, unemployed, unoccupied, unused, vacant

friend

chum (*informal*), companion, comrade, mate (*informal*), pal (*informal*), side-kick (*informal*), soul mate, supporter; *see also* ally

friendly

affable, amiable, amicable, approachable, cordial, pleasant, sociable, warm, welcoming; *see also* kind, loving

friendship

affection, brotherhood, brotherly love, camaraderie, companionship, comradeship, fellowship, harmony, love; *see also* alliance

frighten

alarm, intimidate, panic, petrify, scare, shock, startle, terrify, unnerve, worry

frightened

alarmed, intimidated, panic-stricken, petrified, scared, startled, terrified, timid; *see also* anxious, nervous

frightening

blood-curdling, dreadful, hair-raising, hideous, horrible, horrific, horrifying, spine-chilling, terrifying, unnerving; *see also* worrying

full

COMPLETE *see* **complete**

LEAVING NO ROOM: chock-a-block, chock-full, crammed, crowded, jammed, jam-packed, loaded, overcrowded, packed, stuffed

funny

ODD *see* **peculiar, suspicious**

AMUSING: amusing, comic, comical, droll, entertaining, facetious, hilarious, humorous, witty

furious

ANGRY: angry, blazing, enraged, fuming, infuriated, livid, mad, wild

INTENSE: fast, fierce, frantic, frenzied, intense, stormy, turbulent, vehement, wild

gain

achieve, acquire, attain, earn, get, make, obtain, realize, win

game

AMUSEMENT: amusement, distraction, diversion, entertainment, fun, joke, pastime, recreation, sport

MATCH: competition, contest, match, tournament

gap

HOLE: break, chink, cleft, crack, crevice, hole, opening, space

INTERVAL: break, interlude, intermission, interruption, interval, pause

gather

GET: accumulate, acquire, amass, assemble, collect, get, harvest, obtain, procure, reap

BRING TOGETHER: accumulate, assemble, build up, collect, group, round up, stockpile

COME TOGETHER: accumulate, assemble, collect, congregate, flock, form, group, grow, pile up

LEARN: conclude, deduce, hear, infer, learn, surmise, understand

gay

CHEERFUL *see* **cheerful**

HOMOSEXUAL: homosexual, lesbian, queer (*offensive*)

general

COMMON: common, everyday, normal, ordinary, prevalent, regular, typical, usual, widespread

VAGUE: broad, loose, sweeping, vague

generally *see* usually

generosity

benevolence, kindness, munificence, philanthropy; *see also* **charity, kindness**

generous *see* ample, kind

genuine

actual, authentic, bona fide, pure, real, sincere; *see also* **true**

get

ACQUIRE: acquire, amass, attain, collect, earn, gain, make, obtain, receive, win; *see also* **catch**

FETCH: fetch, go for, send for

get off

alight (*formal*), disembark, dismount, leave

get out

alight (*formal*), disembark, escape, leave

ghost

apparition, phantom, shade, spectre, spirit, spook (*informal*)

gift

PRESENT: bequest, contribution, donation, grant, offering, present

TALENT: aptitude, flair, knack, talent

give

PRESENT: award, bestow, contribute, deliver, donate, hand over, present

PROVIDE: produce, provide, supply, yield

IMPART: impart, lend

give in

capitulate, collapse, comply, concede, submit, surrender, yield

give up

STOP: cease, quit, resign, stop
SURRENDER *see* give in

glad *see* delighted, happy

go

MOVE: advance, drive, journey, make one's way, move, proceed, progress, travel, walk
LEAVE: abscond, beat it (*informal*), depart, exit, leave, push off (*informal*), shove off (*informal*), take one's leave
DISAPPEAR: die, disappear, fade, fade away, pass away, perish, vanish

good

WELL DONE, ADEQUATE: acceptable, adequate, admirable, commendable, fair, fine, praiseworthy, satisfactory, satisfying, worthy; *see also* excellent
THOROUGH: extensive, full, thorough
SUITABLE: appropriate, handy, helpful, ideal, suitable, useful
SKILLED: able, accomplished, adept, capable, competent, efficient, expert, proficient, skilful, talented
PLEASANT: agreeable, congenial, enjoyable, friendly, nice, pleasant, pleasing
FAVOURABLE: advantageous, auspicious, beneficial, convenient, favourable, fitting, opportune, profitable, propitious
BEHAVING WELL OR HONESTLY: honest, honourable, moral, noble, obedient, pious, polite, trustworthy, virtuous, well-behaved
KIND: benevolent, benign, charitable, considerate, dutiful, humane, kind, kindly, merciful, nice
ACCURATE, REAL: accurate, authentic, correct, exact, faithful, precise, real, reliable, true, valid
NOURISHING: choice, eatable, edible, nourishing, nutritious, safe, wholesome

goodbye

bon voyage, bye (*informal*), bye-bye (*informal*), bye for now (*informal*), cheerio (*informal*), cheers (*informal*), farewell (*formal*), see you later (*informal*), so long (*informal*)

gorgeous *see* beautiful, splendid

govern

RULE: command, control, direct, guide, lead, manage, master, oversee, rule, supervise
DETERMINE: control, decide, determine, influence, regulate

gradually

bit by bit, gently, gingerly, inch by inch, little by little, piece by piece, slowly, step by step

gratitude

appreciation, gratefulness, recognition, thankfulness, thanks

grave

adjective WORRYING: acute, critical, dangerous, momentous, perilous, serious, severe, significant, threatening, worrying
adjective SOLEMN: gloomy, preoccupied, quiet, sad, serious, solemn, sombre, unsmiling, worried
noun catacomb, crypt, mausoleum, sepulchre, tomb, vault

greasy

oily, slimy, slippery, waxy

great

IMPORTANT: distinguished, eminent, famous, illustrious, important, leading, major, outstanding, pre-eminent, prominent
ENJOYABLE: excellent, fabulous, fantastic, marvellous, superb, terrific, tremendous, wonderful
SKILFUL: accomplished, adept, expert, fabulous, fantastic, fine, proficient, skilful, skilled, talented

LARGE *see* **large**

VERY MUCH OF: big, colossal, considerable, huge, massive

grief

anguish, distress, heartache, misery, pain, sadness, sorrow, suffering, woe (*literary*)

grounds

base, basis, cause, excuse, justification, motive, premise, rationale, reason

group

band, body, bunch, crowd, gang, mob, number, set, squad, team

grow

DEVELOP: develop, evolve, expand, flourish, mature, prosper, thrive

INCREASE: expand, increase, multiply, proliferate, rise, spread, sprout, swell, widen

CULTIVATE: breed, cultivate, farm, nurture, produce, propagate, raise

BECOME: become, get, turn

guard

verb defend, escort, look after, patrol, police, preserve, protect, shelter, shield, watch over

noun custodian, defender, escort, lookout, picket, protector, sentry, warder, watchman

guess

verb estimate, hypothesize, imagine, judge, reckon, speculate, surmise, work out; *see also* **assume, deduce, think**

noun conjecture, deduction, feeling, hypothesis, judgement, opinion, reckoning, speculation, supposition, theory

guide

verb TAKE: accompany, conduct, convey, direct, escort, lead, manoeuvre, steer, take

verb ADVISE: advise, counsel, direct, instruct, lead, manage, teach, train, tutor

noun ADVISER: adviser, authority, counsellor, director, escort, instructor, mentor, teacher, trainer, tutor

noun EXAMPLE: clue, criterion, example, guideline, indication, key, model, paradigm, standard, template

noun BOOK: ABC, A to Z, catalogue, companion, directory, guidebook, handbook, instructions, manual

habit

convention, custom, inclination, nature, practice, routine, rule, second nature, usage, way

habitual

DONE AS A HABIT: accustomed, constant, established, familiar, fixed, frequent, ingrained, recurrent, regular, routine; *see also* **normal**

DOING SOMETHING AS A HABIT: confirmed, inveterate, persistent, regular

halt

verb call a halt, call it a day, end, pack it in (*informal*), pause, put a stop to, quit, rest, stop, terminate

noun break, close, end, interruption, pause, rest, standstill, stop, termination

handle

COPE WITH: cope with, deal with, manage

MANAGE: administer, control, direct, guide, manage, manipulate, manoeuvre, operate, steer, supervise

TOUCH: feel, finger, fondle, grasp, hold, pick up, touch

happen

arise, come about, crop up, occur, take place, transpire

happy

carefree, cheerful, cheery, content, contented, glad, jolly, light-hearted, pleased, satisfied; *see also* **delighted**

hard

DIFFICULT: complex, complicated, difficult, intricate, knotty, perplexing, puzzling, tough

TIRING: arduous, backbreaking, exhausting, fatiguing, laborious, strenuous, tiring, wearisome, wearying

SOLID: firm, rigid, set, solid, stiff

STERN: demanding, fierce, hard-hearted, harsh, heartless, severe, stern, strict, tough; *see also* cruel, ruthless

hardly

barely, by no means, faintly, just, not much, not very, rarely, scarcely, with difficulty

hardworking

assiduous, careful, conscientious, diligent, energetic, industrious

harm

noun abuse, damage, detriment, hurt, ill, ill-treatment, injury, ruin, ruination

verb damage, hurt, ill-treat, impair, injure, maltreat, mistreat, ruin, spoil, undermine

harmful

damaging, dangerous, destructive, detrimental, hurtful, injurious, noxious, poisonous, toxic

harmless

gentle, innocent, innocuous, non-toxic, safe, unexceptionable, unobjectionable

haste

alacrity, hastiness, hurry, impetuosity, rapidity, rush, speed, urgency

hastily

hurriedly, impetuously, impulsively, in double-quick time, precipitately, promptly, quickly, rapidly, rashly, speedily

hasty

hurried, precipitate, quick, rapid, rushed

hate

noun HATING: abhorrence, animosity, antipathy, distaste, enmity, hatred, hostility, loathing, resentment, spite; *see also* dislike

noun SOMETHING HATED: aversion, bête noire, dislike, pet hate

verb abhor, despise, detest, dislike, loathe, resent

hateful

abhorrent, despicable, distasteful, horrible, horrid, loathsome, nauseating, obnoxious, odious, offensive, repugnant; *see also* wicked

hatred *see* hate

healthy

fine, fit, good, in good shape, well

heap

accumulation, collection, hoard, mass, mound, mountain, pile, stack

heaven

HAPPY CONDITION: bliss, ecstasy, happiness, joy, seventh heaven

PLACE: the afterlife, the hereafter, the next world, nirvana, paradise

heavy

bulky, cumbersome, hefty, large, massive, substantial, weighty

height

STATE OF BEING HIGH OR AMOUNT OF HEIGHT: altitude, elevation, loftiness, stature, tallness

TOP: climax, culmination, limit, maximum, peak, summit, top, ultimate, utmost

hell

UNHAPPY CONDITION: agony, anguish, misery, nightmare, ordeal, suffering, torment, torture

PLACE: Hades, the inferno, the underworld

help

noun advice, aid, assistance, collaboration, co-operation, guidance, support

verb aid, aid and abet, assist, collaborate with, co-operate with, facilitate, further, lend a hand, promote, support

hidden

camouflaged, concealed, covered, disguised, secret

hide

bury, camouflage, conceal, cover, disguise, mask, obscure, secrete, shelter

hinder

arrest, check, delay, hamper, handicap, hold back, hold up, impede, slow down

hit

bump, collide with, kick, knock, punch, slap, smack, strike, thump, wallop

hobby

diversion, interest, pastime, recreation

hold

verb HAVE IN HAND, ETC: clasp, cling to, clutch, cradle, embrace, grasp, grip, have, keep

verb HAVE ROOM FOR: accommodate, carry, contain, seat

verb APPLY: apply, be in force, be valid, hold good

verb BELIEVE: believe, consider, deem, judge, reckon, regard, think, view

verb ARREST: arrest, confine, detain, imprison

noun GRIP: embrace, foothold, footing, grasp, grip

noun INFLUENCE: authority, control, dominance, dominion, influence, leverage, power, sway

hole

NATURAL OR INTENDED HOLE: aperture, cavity, crack, crater, excavation, fissure, gap, hollow, opening, outlet

ACCIDENTAL HOLE: pot-hole, puncture, tear

holy

DEVOUT: devout, god-fearing, pious, pure, religious, righteous, saintly, spiritual, venerable

SACRED: blessed, consecrated, divine, sacred, sacrosanct

home

abode (*formal*), birthplace, dwelling (*literary*), dwelling-place (*literary*), fireside, home town, pad (*informal*), residence (*formal*); *see also* **house**

honest

RELIABLE, LAW-ABIDING: honourable, just, law-abiding, reliable, reputable, scrupulous, trustworthy, trusty, upright, virtuous

TRUTHFUL, ACCURATE: accurate, candid, frank, impartial, objective, sincere, straight, true, truthful

GENUINE: authentic, bona fide, genuine, legitimate, sincere, true

honour

verb applaud, celebrate, commemorate, commend, compliment, pay homage to, praise, remember, respect; *see also* **worship**

noun PRAISE: admiration, commendation, compliment, credit, esteem, homage, praise, regard, respect, tribute; *see also* **worship**

noun DECENCY: decency, dignity, fairness, good name, honesty, integrity, morality, principles, virtue

hope

verb anticipate, aspire, await, contemplate, dream, expect, rely, trust; *see also* **intend, want**

noun ambition, anticipation, aspiration, confidence, dream, expectation, faith, promise, prospect, trust; *see also* **belief, wish**

horrible

atrocious, dreadful, frightful, grim, gruesome, horrific, nasty, repulsive, revolting; *see also* **awful, frightening, ugly**

house

abode (*formal*), apartment, dwelling (*formal*), flat, habitation (*formal*), residence (*formal*); *see also* **home**

hug

verb clasp, cling to, cuddle, embrace, grip, hold, squeeze

noun clasp, cuddle, embrace, squeeze

huge

VERY LARGE: colossal, enormous, giant, gigantic, immense, massive, monumental, mountainous, tremendous, vast; *see also* large

AFFECTING MANY THINGS: extensive, massive, sweeping, swingeing

humble

MEEK: deferential, docile, meek, modest, obsequious, respectful, submissive, unassuming

POOR: common, commonplace, insignificant, lowly, obscure, poor, simple

humorous *see* funny

hurry

verb bustle, dash, fly, get a move on (*informal*), jump to it (*informal*), rush, speed up, step on it (*informal*)

noun bustle, haste, rush, speed, urgency

hurt

verb HARM: abuse, damage, harm, impair, injure, maltreat, spoil, torture, wound

verb ACHE: ache, pound, smart, sting, throb, tingle, twinge

verb DISTRESS: afflict, annoy, distress, grieve, offend, pain, sadden, upset

noun HARM: damage, detriment, disadvantage, harm, injury, loss, wound, wrong

noun ACHE: ache, discomfort, pain, soreness, sting, throbbing, twinge

noun DISTRESS: annoyance, distress, grief, heartache, misery, pain, sadness, sorrow, upset

adjective DAMAGED: bruised, damaged, injured, maimed, wounded

adjective DISTRESSED: aggrieved, annoyed, displeased, miffed (*informal*), offended, piqued, sad, saddened, upset

hut

booth, cabin, chalet, garage, garden hut, lean-to, shack, shanty, shed

idea

THOUGHT: concept, impression, inkling, notion, opinion, suspicion, theory, thought, view, vision; *see also* belief, guess, suggestion

AIM: aim, design, dream, end, goal, intention, object, plan, point, purpose

ill

ailing, indisposed (*formal*), off-colour, out of sorts, poorly, sick, under the weather, unwell

illegal

banned, criminal, forbidden, illicit, outlawed, prohibited, proscribed, unauthorized, unlawful

illness

affliction, ailment, complaint, disability, disease, disorder, epidemic, ill-health, indisposition (*formal*), infirmity

illusion

deception, error, fallacy, hallucination, mirage, misapprehension, misconception

illustration

DRAWING: drawing, image, photograph, picture, plate, representation, sketch

EXAMPLE: case, clarification, demonstration, example, exemplification, instance, specimen

imagine

THINK: conceive, conjecture, envisage, infer, judge, presume, suppose, surmise, suspect, think; *see also* assume, guess

THINK UP: conceive, dream up, picture, think up, visualize

DREAM: dream, fantasize

imitate
copy, duplicate, emulate, impersonate, mimic, mirror, parody, send up, simulate, take off

imitation
noun copy, impersonation, impression, likeness, parody, reproduction, send-up, simulation, take-off
adjective artificial, dummy, man-made, mock, phoney, pseudo, sham, synthetic

immediate
instant, instantaneous, prompt, unhesitating, urgent

immediately
at once, instantaneously, instantly, now, promptly, right away, straight away, straight off, unhesitatingly

impatient
anxious, eager, hasty, impetuous, keen, restless

imperfection
blemish, crack, defect, dent, failing, fault, flaw, inadequacy, shortcoming, weakness

impolite
bad-mannered, boorish, discourteous, disrespectful, ill-mannered, insolent, rough, rude

important
SIGNIFICANT: basic, crucial, fundamental, key, momentous, newsworthy, noteworthy, serious, significant, valuable; *see also* **essential, extensive**
FAMOUS: foremost, high-ranking, influential, leading, notable, outstanding, powerful, pre-eminent, prominent, weighty; *see also* **famous**

impossible
absurd, hopeless, impracticable, inconceivable, ludicrous, preposterous, ridiculous, unattainable, unworkable

impractical
cock-eyed (*informal*), half-baked (*informal*), impossible, mad, ridiculous, unrealistic, unworkable

impressive
awe-inspiring, awesome, breathtaking, effective, imposing, magnificent, powerful, striking, stunning, stupendous; *see also* **amazing**

imprisonment
custody, detention, gaol/jail, internment, prison

improbable
absurd, doubtful, far-fetched, implausible, questionable, ridiculous, unbelievable, unconvincing, unlikely

improve
BECOME BETTER: get better, look up, perk up, pick up, rally, recover, recuperate,
MAKE BETTER: amend, correct, enhance, mend, polish, rectify, reform, touch up

incident
affair, episode, event, happening, occurrence

include
comprise, contain, cover, embrace, incorporate, involve, subsume, take in

increase
verb add to, expand, grow, heighten, intensify, soar, spread, strengthen, swell
noun escalation, expansion, extension, growth, intensification, rise, spread, upsurge

incredible
UNBELIEVABLE: extraordinary, fantastic, far-fetched, inconceivable, ludicrous, ridiculous, unbelievable, unconvincing, unlikely, unthinkable; *see also* **amazing, impossible**

EXCELLENT: brilliant, excellent, fantastic, great, outstanding, phenomenal, splendid, stunning, superb, wonderful

indicate

denote, designate, express, imply, point to, prove, register, reveal, show, signify; *see also* state

inexpensive *see* cheap

infamous

disreputable, evil, notorious, outrageous, scandalous, shocking, wicked; *see also* famous

inferior

OF POOR QUALITY: imperfect, low-grade, mediocre, poor, second-rate, shoddy, substandard, unsatisfactory

OF LESSER RANK: humble, junior, lesser, lower, subordinate, subsidiary

information

data, facts, gen (*informal*), info (*informal*), knowledge, low-down (*informal*), news, report, word

injure

abuse, damage, deface, harm, hurt, maim, maltreat, mistreat, spoil, wound

injury

abuse, damage, harm, hurt, impairment, maltreatment, mistreatment, wound, wrong

innocent

NOT GUILTY: blameless, faultless, sinless, spotless, stainless

NAÏVE: childlike, credulous, gullible, ingenuous, naïve, trustful, trusting

inquire

ask, explore, inspect, interrogate, investigate, look into, probe, query, question

inquisitive

curious, inquiring, nosy (*informal*), prying

insane *see* mad

intelligence

ability, brains, capacity, cleverness, common sense, genius, intellect, sense, understanding, wit

intelligent

brainy, bright, brilliant, clever, gifted, intellectual, quick, quick-witted, sharp, smart

intend

aim, aspire, dream, have a mind to, mean, plan, propose, seek, strive; *see also* hope

intense

deep, fierce, great, powerful, profound, severe, strong, terrific

intention

aim, ambition, aspiration, goal, motive, object, objective, plan, purpose, target

interesting

absorbing, entertaining, enthralling, fascinating, gripping, intriguing, stimulating, thought-provoking

intricate

complex, complicated, convoluted, difficult, elaborate, involved, tangled, tortuous

invasion

aggression, assault, attack, blitz, foray, incursion, offensive, raid, strike

irritable

bad-tempered, cantankerous, crabby (*informal*), cross, crotchety (*informal*), irascible, prickly, short-tempered, tetchy, touchy

irritating *see* annoying

jealous

envious, green with envy, resentful

jealousy

covetousness, envy, resentment, spite

job

OCCUPATION: business, calling, career, employment, livelihood, occupation, post, profession, trade, work

TASK: activity, assignment, batch, chore, errand, task

ROLE OR RESPONSIBILITY: business, concern, duty, function, lot, mission, place, responsibility, role

join

CONNECT: combine, connect, fasten, glue, link, merge, splice, tie, unite

BE WITH OR PART OF: affiliate, combine, enlist, enrol, enter, merge, sign up, team up, unite

journey

noun course, excursion, expedition, outing, pilgrimage, tour, trip, visit, voyage

verb go, hitch-hike, roam, sail, tour, travel, trek, voyage, wander

joy

bliss, delight, ecstasy, elation, gladness, glee, happiness, joyfulness, pleasure, pride

judge

verb ASSESS: adjudicate, appraise, arbitrate, assess, evaluate, examine, rate, referee, try

verb CRITICIZE: blame, censure, condemn, criticize, damn, denounce, reproach, reprove

verb MAKE A RULING: conclude, decide, decree, determine, rule, sentence

verb THINK: conclude, decide, estimate, find, guess, reckon

noun adjudicator, arbiter, arbitrator, assessor, critic, evaluator, magistrate, referee, umpire

judgement

ASSESSMENT: appraisal, assessment, conclusion, deduction, diagnosis, estimate, finding, ruling, verdict; *see also* opinion

CRITICISM: blame, censure, condemnation, criticism, damnation, denunciation, reproach, retribution

WISDOM: acumen, common sense, discernment, discrimination, intelligence, prudence, sense, taste, wisdom

jump

verb bounce, bound, gambol, hop, leap, pounce, prance, skip, spring, vault

noun bounce, bound, hop, leap, pounce, prance, skip, spring, vault

just

UNBIASED: disinterested, equitable, even-handed, fair, impartial, unbiased, unprejudiced; *see also* accurate

PROPER: appropriate, deserved, due, fair, justified, legitimate, proper, reasonable, rightful; *see also* legal

HONEST: blameless, honest, honourable, righteous, virtuous

keen

ENTHUSIASTIC: ardent, avid, dedicated, devoted, earnest, enthusiastic, fanatical, fervent, passionate; *see also* anxious

SHARP: sharp

keep

GUARD: defend, guard, look after, mind, protect, preserve, safeguard, shelter, take care of, watch

HOLD: control, hang on to, hold, hold on to, maintain, manage, possess, preserve, retain

HAVE: have, stock, store

kill

annihilate, butcher, do away with (*informal*), execute, exterminate, massacre, put down, put to death, slaughter, wipe out; *see also* murder

killing

bloodshed, destruction, execution, extermination, massacre, slaughter; *see also* murder

kind

noun brand, breed, category, class, genre, nature, sort, species, type, variety

adjective affectionate, charitable, considerate, generous, gentle, gracious, kind-hearted, sympathetic, thoughtful; *see also* **friendly**, **nice**

kindness

benevolence, compassion, generosity, goodness, kind-heartedness, sympathy, thoughtfulness

king

caliph, emperor, maharajah, monarch, pharaoh, prince, rajah, sovereign, sultan, tsar; *see also* **queen**, **ruler**

knock

verb HIT: hit, jolt, nudge, poke, push, shove, strike, thump

verb TAP: bang, rap, tap

noun HIT: blow, hit, jolt, nudge, poke, push, shove, thump

noun TAP: bang, rap, tap

knowledge

education, experience, gen (*informal*), information, know-how (*informal*), learning, understanding; *see also* **wisdom**

lack

absence, dearth, deficiency, insufficiency, need, poverty, shortage

large

big, broad, bulky, economy-size, extensive, generous, great, king-size, wide; *see also* **ample**, **huge**, **spacious**

last

verb carry on, continue, endure, hold on, hold out, persist, remain, survive

adjective closing, concluding, final, hindmost, latest, rearmost, ultimate

lavish

abundant, copious, extravagant, generous, liberal, luxurious, plentiful, prodigal, profuse, sumptuous

law

act, code, commandment, decree, edict, principle, regulation, rule, statute

lazy

idle, indolent, lethargic, slothful, work-shy

leader

boss (*informal*), captain, commander, controller, director, guide, head, ringleader, ruler

lean

adjective emaciated, gaunt, scrawny, skinny, slim, thin, wiry

verb RELY: count, depend, rely

verb SLOPE: incline, list, slant, slope, tilt, tip

leap

verb bounce, bound, hop, jump, pounce, skip, spring, vault

noun bounce, bound, hop, jump, pounce, skip, spring, vault

least

fewest, lowest, merest, minimum, slightest, smallest, tiniest

leave

depart, desert, disappear, go away, move, move out, pull out, quit, set out, withdraw

legal

above-board, authorized, constitutional, lawful, legalized, legitimate, permissible, statutory

let

agree to, allow, authorize, consent to, enable, grant, permit, sanction, tolerate

lie

verb fib (*informal*), perjure oneself (*formal*), tell lies

noun fabrication, falsehood, fib (*informal*), invention, little white lie, untruth, whopper (*informal*)

like

adjective alike, identical, resembling, same, similar

verb admire, adore, approve of, care for, enjoy, fancy, love, relish, take to; *see also* want

likely

believable, feasible, plausible, probable, reasonable

liking

affection, fondness, love, partiality, soft spot, taste, weakness; *see also* desire

limit

noun border, boundary, edge, end, extent, frontier, perimeter, periphery, rim, threshold

verb check, constrain, control, curb, hinder, lessen, ration, restrain, restrict

line

ROW: column, file, row, queue, procession, rank, series

BAR: band, bar, dash, streak, strip, stripe, stroke

ROPE: cable, rope, string, thread, wire

WRINKLE: crease, furrow, groove, wrinkle

BUSINESS *see* business

little *see* short, small, young

lively

active, agile, alert, animated, bright, brisk, energetic, keen, nimble, vigorous

loathe

abhor, despise, detest, dislike, hate

look

verb GLANCE: gape, gaze, glance, observe, ogle, peek, peep, view, watch; *see also* see

verb EXAMINE OR INVESTIGATE: examine, inspect, investigate, observe, reconnoitre, scan, scout around, scrutinize, survey

verb SEEM: appear, look like, seem

noun GLANCE: gape, glance, glimpse, peek, peep, squint, view

noun EXAMINATION OR INVESTIGATION: examination, inspection, investigation, once-over, reconnoitre, scan, scrutiny, squint, survey

noun APPEARANCE: air, appearance, effect, expression, guise

loose

NOT FASTENED: baggy, free, movable, slack, unconfined, unfastened, untied, wobbly

NOT PRECISE: imprecise, inaccurate, indefinite, inexact, rambling, vague

lose

drop, forget, leave, mislay, misplace

loss

bereavement, debt, defeat, destruction, disadvantage, disappearance, ruin

loud

blaring, deafening, ear-piercing, noisy, piercing, raucous, rowdy, strident, vociferous

love

noun ENJOYMENT: enjoyment, fondness, liking, partiality, soft spot, taste, weakness; *see also* desire

noun LOVING FEELING: affection, attachment, devotion, fondness, friendship, liking, passion, regard, tenderness, warmth; *see also* worship

verb adore, cherish, dote on, enjoy, fancy, like, relish, take pleasure in, think the world of, treasure; *see also* desire

lovely

adorable, attractive, beautiful, delightful, enchanting, enjoyable, pleasant, pretty; *see also* nice

loving

affectionate, caring, devoted, doting, fond, passionate, tender, warm, warm-hearted; *see also* friendly, kind

lower

adjective inferior, junior, lesser, minor, secondary, subordinate, subsidiary

verb LESSEN: cut, decrease, diminish, drop, fall, lessen, minimize, moderate, prune, reduce

verb LOWER ONESELF: condescend, deign, demean oneself, stoop

loyal

dependable, devoted, faithful, patriotic, staunch, steadfast, true, trustworthy, trusty

luck

CHANCE: accident, chance, coincidence, destiny, fate, fluke, providence, serendipity

GOOD LUCK: blessing, break, fluke, godsend, good fortune, providence, windfall

BAD LUCK: act of God, misfortune

luxury

affluence, comfort, extravagance, indulgence, opulence, riches, splendour, sumptuousness

mad

INSANE: absurd, berserk, crazy, daft, delirious, deranged, eccentric, foolish, idiotic, insane; *see also* reckless, stupid

ANGRY *see* angry

KEEN: avid, devoted, enthusiastic, fanatical, fervent, keen, passionate

magnificent *see* impressive, marvellous

main

cardinal, central, chief, foremost, leading, predominant, pre-eminent, premier, principal, supreme

mainly

above all, as a rule, chiefly, for the most part, in general, largely, mostly, on the whole, overall, predominantly; *see also* usually

majority

bulk, greater part, mass, preponderance

make

CREATE: assemble, build, construct, create, erect, fashion, manufacture, mould, put together, shape

CAUSE: accomplish, bring about, cause, engender, generate, induce, lead to, occasion, produce, render

FORCE: bully, coerce, compel, drive, force, impel, induce, oblige, pressurize

APPOINT: appoint, designate, elect, install, nominate, ordain

manage

ACHIEVE: accomplish, achieve, arrange, bring about, contrive, effect, engineer, succeed

CONTROL: administer, control, direct, guide, handle, lead, oversee, run, steer, supervise; *see also* rule

COPE: cope, get along, get by, make do, muddle through, survive

management

MANAGING: administration, command, conduct, control, direction, guidance, handling, operation, running, supervision; *see also* rule

MANAGERS: administration, bosses (*informal*), directors, employers, executive, governors, managers, supervisors

manner

air, appearance, bearing, behaviour, conduct, demeanour, habit, nature, style, way; *see also* method

manners

GOOD MANNERS: courtesy, decorum, etiquette, good behaviour, morals, politeness, protocol, p's and q's, refinement

BAD MANNERS: coarseness, discourtesy, rudeness, uncouthness, vulgarity

many

countless, lots of, numerous, several, umpteen (*informal*), various

mark

noun TRACE OF SOMETHING: fingermark, fingerprint, footprint, impression, sign, trace, trail, vestige

noun DIRT OR DAMAGE: blemish, blot, bruise, dent, scar, scratch, smudge, spot, stain, streak

noun FEATURE, INDICATION: badge, characteristic, emblem, feature, hallmark, indication, label, sign, symbol, token

noun SCORE: grade, points, result, score, total

verb LEAVE OR GET A TRACE: blot, blotch, bruise, dent, nick, scar, scratch, smudge, stain, streak

verb ASSESS: appraise, assess, correct, evaluate, grade

marvellous

brilliant, fabulous, fantastic, magnificent, remarkable, sensational, splendid, super, superb, wonderful; *see also* excellent, impressive, incredible

mass

AMOUNT: batch, block, chunk, heap, load, lot, lump, pile, quantity, stack; *see also* majority

CROWD: body, bunch, collection, crowd, group, horde, host, mob, number, throng

master

noun COMMANDER: boss (*informal*), chief, commander, controller, director, lord, overlord, owner, ruler, superintendent

noun TEACHER: guru, mentor, schoolmaster, schoolteacher, teacher, tutor

noun ADEPT: ace (*informal*), adept, dab hand, expert, genius, maestro, virtuoso, wizard

verb LEARN: acquire, get the hang of, grasp, learn

verb BEAT: beat, conquer, control, defeat, overcome, subdue, subjugate, tame, vanquish

match

bout, competition, contest, game, set, test, trial

material

cloth, constituents, elements, fabric, stuff, substance

maximum

biggest, greatest, highest, largest, most, utmost

maybe *see* perhaps

mean

verb denote, indicate, imply, represent, signify, stand for, symbolize

adjective NOT GENEROUS: miserly, niggardly, selfish, stingy (*informal*), tight-fisted

adjective UNKIND: cruel, nasty, spiteful, unkind, vicious

meaning

explanation, interpretation, point, sense, significance

medicine

cure, drug, medication, nostrum, pill, remedy

meet

COME TOGETHER: assemble, collect, come together, congregate, convene, converge, gather, muster, rally, unite

TOUCH: abut, adjoin, come in contact, intersect, join up, link up, touch

ENCOUNTER: bump into, chance on, come across, encounter, happen on

FACE: encounter, endure, experience, face, go through, suffer, undergo

mend

correct, cure, darn, fix, heal, patch, rectify, renovate, repair, restore

mention

allude to, bring up, broach, divulge, make known, name, refer to, reveal, speak of, touch on

merciful
compassionate, forgiving, generous, gracious, humane, kind, lenient, mild, sympathetic, tender-hearted

merciless
callous, cruel, hard-hearted, heartless, inhuman, inhumane, pitiless, relentless, remorseless, ruthless

mercy
benevolence, clemency, compassion, forbearance, forgiveness, grace, kindness, leniency, pardon, pity

method
approach, manner, procedure, process, programme, routine, scheme, system, technique, way

middle
adjective central, halfway, inner, intermediate, mean, medial, mid
noun centre, halfway mark, halfway point, heart, midpoint

minimum
least, lowest, slightest, smallest, tiniest

minor
insignificant, negligible, petty, secondary, slight, small, trifling, trivial, unimportant

minority
handful, subgroup

mischievous
impish, naughty, playful, teasing

miserable
UNHAPPY: dejected, depressed, desolate, despondent, disconsolate, grief-stricken, heart-broken, mournful, sorrowful; *see also* sad
NOT GOOD: abject, contemptible, deplorable, disgraceful, dismal, lamentable, pathetic, pitiful, poor

misery
agony, anguish, desolation, despair, hardship, heartache, pain, suffering, torment, torture

mistake
blunder, error, faux pas, howler (*informal*), inaccuracy, misprint, oversight, slip, slip-up

mix
amalgamate, blend, coalesce, combine, fuse, intermingle, join, merge, mingle, shuffle

mixture
BLEND: alloy, amalgamation, blend, combination, compound, fusion, mix, synthesis
ASSORTMENT: assortment, medley, miscellany

modest
humble, self-effacing, unassuming, unpretentious

money
bread (*slang*), capital, cash, change, coins, currency, dough (*slang*), funds, wealth, the wherewithal

most
biggest, greatest, largest, maximum

motionless
at rest, fixed, frozen, immobile, paralysed, stationary, still, unmoving

motive
incentive, inducement, inspiration, motivation, plan, purpose, rationale, reason, stimulus

movement
ACTION: action, gesture, manoeuvre, motion, move, operation, progress
GROUP: campaign, crusade, faction, front, group, organization, party

murder

verb assassinate, bump off (*informal*), massacre; *see also* kill

noun assassination, homicide, manslaughter; *see also* killing

murderer

assassin, hit-man (*informal*), homicide, killer

mysterious

abstruse, arcane, cryptic, enigmatic, esoteric, inexplicable, inscrutable, mystical, occult, puzzling; *see also* strange

mystery

enigma, problem, puzzle, question, riddle, secrecy, secret

myth

allegory, fable, fairy tale, legend, old wives' tale, parable, story, superstition, tale

naked

bare, in the altogether, in the buff (*informal*), in the nude, nude, stark-naked, undressed

nasty

UNPLEASANT: disagreeable, disgusting, distasteful, objectionable, obnoxious, odious, offensive, repugnant, repulsive, unpleasant; *see also* horrible

SEVERE: bad, serious, severe

natural

INBORN: inborn, inherent, innate, instinctive

NORMAL: characteristic, normal, regular

NOT AFFECTED: characteristic, spontaneous, unaffected, unsophisticated

nature

character, disposition, mood, outlook, style, temper, temperament

nearly

about, almost, approaching, approximately, more or less, practically, towards, virtually

neat

DAINTY: adroit, dainty, deft, dexterous, precise

TIDY: elegant, orderly, smart, tidy

necessary

crucial, essential, imperative, indispensable, mandatory, much-needed, obligatory, required, vital

necessity

essential, need, obligation, prerequisite, requirement, sine qua non

need

verb call for, demand, lack, require; *see also* want

noun DEMAND OR LACK: demand, lack, insufficiency, necessity, obligation, requirement, shortage, urgency, want, wish

noun SOMETHING NEEDED: essential, necessity, requirement, requisite

noun POVERTY: deprivation, destitution, distress, penury, poverty

negligent

careless, cursory, forgetful, inattentive, lax, offhand, remiss, slack, thoughtless, unthinking

nervous

apprehensive, flustered, hesitant, jittery, jumpy, on edge, tense, timid, uptight; *see also* anxious, frightened

new

MODERN: contemporary, latest, modern, newfangled, novel, recent, topical, trendy, up to date, up-to-the-minute

NOT KNOWN OR SEEN BEFORE: different, fresh, original, unfamiliar, unknown, unusual

YOUNG: newborn, young

NOT EXPERIENCED: inexperienced

news

gossip, hearsay, information, intelligence, the latest, report, revelation, rumour, scandal, story

next

NEIGHBOURING: adjacent, adjoining, closest, nearest, neighbouring

FOLLOWING: following, forthcoming, subsequent, succeeding

nice

ENJOYABLE: agreeable, attractive, delightful, enjoyable, lovely, pleasant, pleasing, satisfying

FRIENDLY: agreeable, amiable, charming, congenial, courteous, friendly, likeable, pleasant; *see also* **kind, polite**

PRETTY: attractive, charming, delightful, lovely, pretty

noble

adjective ARISTOCRATIC: aristocratic, distinguished, grand, highborn, majestic, titled, upper-class; *see also* **elegant**

adjective HONOURABLE: generous, honourable, kind, magnanimous, public-spirited, unselfish, virtuous

noun aristocrat, lady, lord, nobleman, noblewoman, peer, peeress

noise

blare, clamour, clash, clatter, commotion, din, racket, row, sound, uproar

noisy

boisterous, deafening, loud, rowdy, strident, vociferous

nonsense

FOOLISH WORDS: baloney (*informal*), bunkum (*informal*), codswallop (*informal*), drivel, piffle (*informal*), rubbish, twaddle (*informal*)

FOOLISH BEHAVIOUR: foolishness, silliness, stupidity

normal

USUAL: average, natural, ordinary, regular, routine, run-of-the-mill, standard, typical, unexceptional, usual; *see also* **common, habitual**

SANE: compos mentis, rational, sane, well-adjusted

normally

as a rule, commonly, habitually, ordinarily, regularly, routinely, typically, usually

notable

FAMOUS: celebrated, distinguished, eminent, famous, illustrious, notorious, outstanding, prominent, renowned, well-known

NOTICEABLE: conspicuous, evident, marked, memorable, noteworthy, noticeable, pronounced, remarkable, striking; *see also* **unusual**

nothing

nought, zero, zilch (*informal*)

notice

noun ad (*informal*), advert, advertisement, announcement, notification, poster, sign

verb detect, discern, note, observe, perceive, remark, see, spot

obey

abide by, adhere to, carry out, comply with, follow, honour, keep, observe, take orders from, toe the line

observe

SEE: detect, keep an eye on, look, monitor, notice, see, spot, watch, witness

SAY: comment, declare, mention, note, remark, say, state

OBEY *see* **obey**

CELEBRATE: celebrate, commemorate, keep, remember

obstinate

determined, dogged, firm, headstrong, intransigent, pig-headed, stubborn, tenacious, wilful

obtain

achieve, acquire, attain, come by, earn, gain, get, procure, secure

obvious

CLEARLY VISIBLE: conspicuous, distinct, glaring, noticeable, prominent, pronounced, recognizable, unmistakable, visible

EASILY UNDERSTOOD: apparent, clear, evident, plain, self-explanatory, undeniable, unmistakable

occupation

business, calling, employment, job, post, profession, trade, vocation, work

occur

arise, chance, come about, crop up, happen, take place, transpire, turn up

odd   *see* peculiar

odour

aroma, bouquet, fragrance, perfume, scent, smell, stench, stink

offend

affront, annoy, antagonize, disgust, displease, insult, outrage, provoke, upset, vex

often

again and again, frequently, repeatedly, time after time, time and again

old

ELDERLY: aged, elderly, over the hill, venerable

FROM LONG AGO: age-old, ancient, antediluvian, antiquated, antique, archaic, prehistoric, primitive

OUT OF DATE: antiquated, antique, dated, obsolete, outdated, outmoded, out of date, passé

NOT CURRENT: former, last, out of date, previous

LONG-ESTABLISHED: long-established, long-standing, traditional

NOT FRESH: stale

SAID OF CARS: veteran, vintage

open

adjective NOT SHUT: agape, ajar, uncovered, unfastened, unlocked, unsealed

adjective NOT PROTECTED: exposed, unconcealed, undefended, unfenced, unprotected, unsheltered, vulnerable

adjective RECEPTIVE, ACCESSIBLE: accessible, approachable, available, receptive, uncommitted, unrestricted, willing

adjective LIABLE: exposed, liable, prone, susceptible, vulnerable

adjective FRANK: above-board, candid, frank, honest, natural, sincere, upfront (*informal*)

adjective CLEAR: blatant, clear, downright, evident, flagrant, manifest, obvious, plain, public, undisguised

verb BEGIN: begin, commence, inaugurate, initiate, launch, start

verb UNSEAL: unblock, undo, unfasten, unlock, unseal

verb BREAK: break, come apart, crack, rupture, separate

opinion

belief, feeling, idea, point of view, position, stance, theory, thought, view, viewpoint; *see also* judgement

opponent

adversary, antagonist, challenger, competitor, enemy, foe (*literary*), rival

opportunity

break, chance, occasion, opening, scope, shot, time, turn

option

alternative, choice, possibility, preference, selection

oral

spoken, verbal

order

noun ARRANGEMENT: arrangement, array, classification, grouping, layout, line-up, pattern, sequence, series *noun* ORGANIZATION: organization, system, tidiness

noun COMMAND: command, decree, directive, instruction, law, regulation, rule, ruling, stipulation

noun REQUEST: application, booking, request, reservation

verb ARRANGE: arrange, classify, group, lay out, organize, place, set out, sort out

verb COMMAND: command, decree, direct, instruct, ordain, prescribe, require, tell

verb REQUEST: apply for, book, request, reserve

ordinary

average, conventional, general, regular, run-of-the-mill, standard, typical; *see also* common, habitual, normal

organize

PLACE: catalogue, classify, lay out, marshal, set out, set up, sort out, systematize, tabulate, tidy; *see also* arrange

MAKE HAPPEN: arrange, co-ordinate, run, see to, set up, sort out, stage-manage

origin

ancestry, beginnings, birth, cause, creation, derivation, foundation, parentage, roots, source

other

EXTRA: added, additional, extra, fresh, more, new, spare, supplementary

DIFFERENT: alternative, different, new

outstanding

distinguished, eminent, excellent, exceptional, extraordinary, memorable, superb, superlative; *see also* impressive

own

verb have, hold, keep, possess, retain

adjective individual, particular, personal, private

pack

box, bundle, carton, case, package, packet, parcel

pain

noun PHYSICAL PAIN: ache, agony, discomfort, headache, pang, soreness, spasm, throb, twinge

noun MENTAL PAIN: anguish, distress, grief, heartache, misery, pang, suffering, torment, torture, woe

verb CAUSE PHYSICAL PAIN TO: hurt, torture, wound

verb CAUSE MENTAL PAIN TO: aggrieve, annoy, distress, grieve, hurt, sadden, vex, wound

painful

SORE: aching, agonizing, excruciating, sore, tender

UNPLEASANT: disagreeable, distasteful, distressing, grievous, hard, sad, unpleasant

paradise

bliss, heaven, nirvana, seventh heaven

parcel

bundle, carton, case, pack, package, packet

parched

arid, barren, dry, waterless, withered

pardon

verb absolve, acquit, condone, excuse, exonerate, forgive, let off, overlook, reprieve

noun absolution, acquittal, amnesty, excuse, exoneration, forgiveness, indulgence, mercy, reprieve

part

noun SMALL AMOUNT: bit, chunk, fragment, morsel, piece, portion, scrap, segment, slice

noun FRACTION: fraction, portion, share

noun ELEMENT OF SOMETHING MORE COMPLEX: bit, component, constituent, department, division, element, ingredient, piece, section, unit

verb break, break up, come apart, separate, sever, split, tear

particular
distinct, especial, individual, notable, peculiar, personal, private, special, unique

party
celebration, dinner, do (*informal*), gathering, get-together, house-warming, social, soirée; *see also* **dance**

pastime
activity, amusement, game, hobby, interest, recreation, relaxation, sideline

path
FOOTPATH: alley, avenue, footpath, lane, pathway, pavement, road, track, trail, way
ROUTE: channel, course, passage, pathway, route, track, trail

pathetic
abject, deplorable, dismal, feeble, inadequate, lamentable, pitiful, poor, sorry, worthless

patient
calm, even-tempered, forbearing, long-suffering, persistent, philosophical, restrained, tolerant, uncomplaining

pause
noun break, delay, halt, interruption, interval, lull, respite, rest, stoppage, suspension
verb break, halt, hesitate, rest, stop, take a break, take a breather (*informal*)

peace
calm, calmness, harmony, quiet, quietness, rest, silence, stillness, tranquillity

peaceful
NOT AGGRESSIVE: friendly, gentle, harmonious, non-violent, peace-loving
NOT WORRIED: calm, placid, serene, undisturbed, untroubled
SAID OF WEATHER, SITUATION, ETC: calm, restful, still, tranquil

peculiar
ODD: bizarre, curious, eccentric, extraordinary, funny, odd, queer, strange, unconventional, weird; *see also* **unusual**
PERSONAL: individual, personal, private, special, unique

penalty
fine, forfeit, punishment, retribution, sentence

people
NATION: clan, folk, nation, race, tribe
CITIZENS: citizens, the community, the general public, inhabitants, the masses, the public, society
PERSONS: folk, human beings, humanity, humans, individuals, persons

perceive
SEE: discover, distinguish, make out, observe, see, spot
UNDERSTAND: comprehend, gather, grasp, learn, realize, recognize, sense, understand

perfect
ACCURATE: accurate, exact, faithful, precise, true, unerring
FLAWLESS: faultless, flawless, ideal, immaculate, impeccable, masterly, polished, spotless, unblemished, untarnished; *see also* **splendid**
PURE: absolute, complete, full, sheer, unadulterated, unalloyed, unmitigated, utter

perform
ACT: act, play, put on, stage
DO: achieve, act, carry out, complete, do, execute, function, manage, produce, work; *see also* **accomplish**

performer
actor, actress, artist, artiste, entertainer, player

perhaps
conceivably, feasibly, maybe, possibly

permission

approval, assent, authorization, consent, dispensation, the go-ahead, the green light, leave

permit *see* allow

person

bloke (*informal*), chap, character, customer (*informal*), fellow, guy, individual, man, sort (*informal*), woman

persuade

PERSUADE: coax, convince, entice, induce, inveigle, lean on, prevail upon/on, sweet-talk, talk into, win over; *see also* **urge**
PERSUADE NOT TO: dissuade, talk out of

pick

verb choose, decide on, elect, opt for, select, settle on, single out
noun best, choice, cream, crème de la crème, elect, elite, flower, pride, selection

picture

ILLUSTRATION: drawing, illustration, image, likeness, painting, photograph, portrait, representation, sketch
DESCRIPTION: account, depiction, description, portrayal, report
FILM: film, motion picture, movie (*informal*)

pile

accumulation, heap, hoard, mass, mound, stack

pity

charity, clemency, compassion, kindness, mercy, sympathy, understanding

place

noun AREA: area, district, locality, neighbourhood, region, spot, surroundings, territory
noun POSITION: location, niche, point, position, site, situation, venue, whereabouts

verb deposit, install, lay, locate, position, put, situate, stand, station, stick (*informal*)

plain

CLEAR: apparent, clear, evident, obvious, visible
SIMPLE : simple, straightforward, unadorned

plan

noun PICTURE: blueprint, chart, design, diagram, draft, drawing, layout, map, outline, sketch
noun AIM: aim, ambition, goal, intention, object, purpose
noun SUGGESTION: plot, proposal, scheme, suggestion
verb aim, conspire, devise, draft, envisage, intend, mastermind, plot, propose; *see also* **organize**

pleasant

agreeable, attractive, delightful, enjoyable, genial, kindly, lovely, nice, pleasing, welcome; *see also* **friendly**

please

amuse, charm, delight, enchant, gladden, satisfy, suit

pleasure

amusement, comfort, delight, enjoyment, gratification, happiness, satisfaction

point

verb aim, direct
noun POSITION: location, place, position, site, spot
noun PURPOSE: aim, end, goal, intention, object, objective, purpose, reason, sense, use

point out

draw attention to, indicate, show, signal

polite

civil, courteous, genteel, gracious, polished, refined, respectful, well-behaved, well-mannered

poor

NOT RICH: badly off, bankrupt, broke (*informal*), destitute, hard up (*informal*), impoverished, needy, penniless, poverty-stricken

NOT GOOD: deplorable, dismal, feeble, inadequate, inferior, lamentable, mediocre, miserable, pathetic, pitiful; *see also* **unsatisfactory**

position

PLACE: arrangement, location, place, site, situation, spot, whereabouts

CONDITION: circumstances, condition

JOB: capacity, employment, place, post, rank

OPINION: belief, idea, outlook, perspective, point of view, stance, theory, view, viewpoint; *see also* **opinion**

possess

have, hold, keep, own

possessions

assets, belongings, effects, estate, goods, goods and chattels, property, worldly goods (*literary*)

possibly

maybe, perhaps

post

appointment, employment, job, place, position, situation

poverty

BEING POOR: deprivation, destitution, hardship, pennilessness, privation

LACK: dearth, deficiency, insufficiency, lack, scarcity, shortage

power

ENERGY: capacity, energy, force, intensity, might, muscle, strength, vigour

AUTHORITY OR CONTROL: authority, clout (*informal*), control, dominance, influence, rule, sovereignty, supremacy, sway

powerful

MUSCULAR: athletic, brawny, muscular, robust, strapping, strong, sturdy, vigorous

ACTING STRONGLY: energetic, potent, robust, strong, vigorous

IMPORTANT: important, influential, leading, prominent

CONVINCING: compelling, convincing, impressive, persuasive, telling, weighty

practice

CUSTOM: convention, custom, habit, routine, rule, tradition, way, wont (*literary*)

REHEARSAL: dry run, dummy run, exercise, rehearsal, run-through

practise

exercise, rehearse, run through, train

praise

noun acclaim, applause, approval, cheers, clapping, commendation, compliments, ovation, tribute

verb acclaim, applaud, cheer, clap, commend, compliment, pay tribute to, speak well of

precious

COSTLY: costly, dear, expensive, priceless, valuable

LOVED: beloved, cherished, darling, dear, dearest, favourite, prized, treasured, valued

precise

accurate, correct, definite, distinct, exact, explicit, faithful, meticulous, word-for-word

prefer

choose, favour, go for, opt for, pick, plump for, select, would rather, would sooner; *see also* **support**

prepare

GET ONESELF READY: practise, rehearse, steel oneself, train, warm up

GET SOMEONE READY: brief, coach, groom, instruct, prime, psych up (*informal*), ready, rehearse, train

MAKE PLANS: anticipate, plan

MAKE: concoct, construct, contrive, cook, develop, devise, draw up, make, produce

pretty

appealing, attractive, beautiful, charming, cute, lovely, nice, sweet

prevent

avert, forestall, head off, impede, obstruct, stave off, stop, thwart, ward off

priceless

costly, expensive, invaluable, irreplaceable, precious

pride

BEING PROUD: arrogance, big-headedness, conceit, conceitedness, self-importance, snobbery, snobbishness, superciliousness, vanity

BEST: best, cream, elite, flower, jewel, pick

primitive

crude, elementary, rough, rudimentary, savage, uncivilized, unsophisticated; *see also* ancient, simple

principal

chief, dominant, foremost, highest, leading, main, major, pre-eminent, primary

principle

axiom, criterion, formula, golden rule, law, maxim, moral, proposition, rule, tenet; *see also* belief

MORALITY: decency, honesty, honour, integrity, morality, scruples, virtue

private

SECRET: confidential, exclusive, secluded, secret, unofficial

SEPARATE: exclusive, individual, own, particular, personal, separate

probable

apparent, likely, plausible, possible, reasonable

probably

as likely as not, doubtless, in all likelihood, in all probability, likely, presumably

procession

cavalcade, cortège, march, motorcade, parade

produce

CAUSE: cause, create, generate, give rise to, occasion, provoke, result in

MAKE: bear, breed, create, make, manufacture, supply, yield

profession

JOB: business, calling, employment, job, occupation, post, trade, work

CLAIM: affirmation, assertion, claim, confession, statement, testimony

profit

advantage, benefit, earnings, gain, interest, proceeds, return, revenue, surplus, takings

profitable

advantageous, beneficial, cost-effective, fruitful, lucrative, productive, remunerative, rewarding, valuable, worthwhile; *see also* useful

prohibit

ban, bar, disallow, forbid, outlaw, prevent, put a stop to, rule out, veto; *see also* stop

prominent

IMPORTANT: celebrated, eminent, high-ranking, important, influential, leading, notable; *see also* famous

NOTICEABLE: conspicuous, eye-catching, noticeable, obtrusive, obvious, pronounced

STICKING OUT: bulging, jutting, projecting, protruding

promise

verb agree, assure, commit oneself, give one's word, guarantee, pledge, state, swear, undertake, vow *noun* GUARANTEE: agreement, assurance, commitment, guarantee, oath, pledge, undertaking, vow, word, word of honour

noun POTENTIAL: ability, capability, capacity, flair, the makings of, potential, talent

prompt

adjective early, immediate, instant, instantaneous, punctual, quick, rapid, speedy, swift, unhesitating

verb CAUSE: cause, elicit, evoke, give rise to, induce, instigate, occasion, provoke, result in, stimulate

verb MOTIVATE: cause, impel, incite, induce, influence, inspire, motivate, move, stimulate; *see also* urge

proof

attestation, authentication, confirmation, corroboration, demonstration, documentation, evidence, verification

property

POSSESSIONS: assets, belongings, estate, goods, goods and chattels, possessions, real estate, resources, riches, wealth

FEATURE: attribute, characteristic, feature, hallmark, mark, peculiarity, quality, trait

proposal

manifesto, offer, outline, plan, project, proposition, recommendation, scheme, suggestion

propose

intend, move, nominate, plan, put forward, recommend, submit, suggest, table, tender

prosper

boom, flourish, grow, progress, succeed, thrive

prosperity

affluence, the good life, luxury, riches, success, wealth

prosperous

affluent, in the money (*informal*), opulent (*formal*), rich, successful, wealthy, well-heeled (*informal*), well-off, well-to-do

protect

defend, guard, keep, look after, preserve, safeguard, save, shelter, shield

protection

armour, care, cover, defence, refuge, safekeeping, screen, security, shelter

protest

noun complaint, demonstration, disagreement, dissent, objection, outcry

verb COMPLAIN: complain, demonstrate, disagree, dissent, object, remonstrate

verb SAY: assert, contend, declare, insist, maintain

proud

CONCEITED: big-headed, conceited, haughty, high and mighty, overbearing, self-important, stuck up (*informal*), toffee-nosed (*informal*), vain

PLEASED: gratified, honoured, pleased

prove

attest to, authenticate, bear out, confirm, corroborate, demonstrate, establish, show, substantiate, verify

provide

arrange for, bring, contribute, furnish, lend, present, produce, supply, yield

pull

drag, draw, haul, jerk, stretch, tow, trail, tug, wrench, yank

purchase

acquire, attain, buy, get, obtain, pay for, procure

pure

CLEAN: clean, clear, spotless, uncontaminated, unpolluted, unsoiled, untainted; *see also* real

ABSOLUTE: absolute, arrant, complete, out-and-out, perfect, sheer, thorough, total, utter

BLAMELESS: blameless, chaste, innocent, spotless, stainless, virtuous

purpose

aim, end, goal, idea, intention, motive, object, plan, point, reason

pursue

chase, dog, follow, hunt, shadow, stalk, track, trail

push

verb SHOVE: butt, elbow, press, prod, propel, ram, shoulder, shove, squeeze, thrust; *see also* **knock**

verb FORCE: browbeat, bulldoze, bully, coerce, dragoon, drive, force, impel, pressurize; *see also* **persuade**

verb PROMOTE: advertise, boost, encourage, hype, peddle, plug, promote, publicize

noun SHOVE: butt, prod, shove, squeeze, thrust; *see also* **knock**

noun ENERGY: application, drive, dynamism, effort, energy, impetus

noun PROMOTION: boost, encouragement, hype, plug, promotion, publicity

put

PLACE: fit, fix, lay, place, position, post, rest, set, situate, station

SAY: couch, express, phrase, say, state, word, write

SUGGEST: propose, submit, suggest

puzzled *see* bewildered, confused

quality

CHARACTERISTIC: aspect, attribute, characteristic, essence, feature, mark, nature, peculiarity, property, trait

VALUE: calibre, class, condition, grade, merit, rank, state, value, worth

quantity

amount, extent, number, size, strength, sum, total, volume, weight

quarrel

noun argument, clash, conflict, controversy, difference of opinion, disagreement, dispute, fight, row, squabble

verb argue, bicker, clash, differ, disagree, dispute, fall out, fight, row, squabble

queen

empress, maharani, monarch, princess, rani, sovereign; *see also* **king**, **ruler**

queer

bizarre, curious, extraordinary, funny, mysterious, puzzling, strange, unusual, weird; *see also* **peculiar**

quick

FAST: brisk, fast, headlong, hurried, rapid, rushed, speedy, sudden, swift; *see also* **brief**, **prompt**

INTELLIGENT: bright, clever, intelligent, perceptive, quick-witted, sharp, smart

quiet

NOT LOUD: hushed, silent, subdued

CALM: calm, placid, restrained, serene, untroubled

PEACEFUL: calm, peaceful, restful, still, tranquil

GENTLE: docile, gentle, mild

NOT BUSY: isolated, lonely, remote, secluded, sheltered

quite

fairly, moderately, rather, somewhat; *see also* **absolutely**, **very**

raise

LIFT: elevate, heave, hoist, lift

BREED: breed, cultivate, grow, produce, propagate

INCREASE: boost, enhance, heighten, increase, intensify, promote, reinforce, strengthen

CREATE: arouse, cause, create, develop, engender, give rise to, instigate, occasion, provoke, start

SUGGEST: pose, present, suggest

rank

caste, class, degree, grade, level, position, quality, status

rapid *see* brief, prompt, quick

rare

exceptional, few, infrequent, scarce, sparse, sporadic, uncommon, unusual

rarely

exceptionally, hardly ever, infrequently, little, seldom

ready

WILLING: agreeable, disposed, eager, happy, glad, inclined, keen, prepared, willing

HAVING BEEN PREPARED: all set, arranged, completed, cooked, finished, fixed, organized, prepared, primed, waiting

AVAILABLE: accessible, available, convenient, near, on call, on tap, present, to hand

PROMPT: immediate, prompt, quick, rapid, speedy, swift, unhesitating

real

actual, authentic, bona fide, genuine, honest, sincere, tangible, true, veritable; *see also* pure

realize

comprehend, gather, grasp, learn, perceive, recognize, see, sense, spot, understand

reason

CAUSE: aim, cause, end, incentive, intention, motive, object, objective, purpose

EXCUSE: argument, excuse, explanation, grounds, justification, rationale

SENSE: common sense, intellect, intelligence, judgement, logic, mind, sanity, sense, wisdom

receive

accept, acquire, collect, get, obtain, pick up, suffer, sustain, undergo

reckless

daring, foolhardy, harebrained, ill-advised, imprudent, irresponsible, rash; *see also* mad

recommend

advise, advocate, commend, counsel, endorse, praise, suggest, urge, vouch for

recover

get better, heal, improve, mend, pick up, rally, recuperate

reduce

alleviate, cut, cut down, decrease, diminish, lessen, lower, moderate, shorten, weaken

reduction

LESSENING: alleviation, cut, cutback, decline, decrease, diminution, drop, easing, moderation, shortening

LOWERING OF COST: discount, rebate, refund

refuge

asylum, harbour, haven, hideout, sanctuary, shelter

refuse

noun garbage, junk, litter, rubbish, trash, waste

verb decline, deny, reject, repudiate, spurn, withhold

regard

LOOK AT: consider, eye, look at, observe, scrutinize, see, view, watch

THINK: believe, consider, deem, imagine, judge, suppose, think, treat

region

area, country, district, locality, neighbour-hood, place, surroundings, territory

regret

noun bitterness, disappointment, grief, remorse, repentance, shame, sorrow

verb deplore, grieve over, lament, mourn, repent

regular

NORMAL: consistent, daily, everyday, fixed, habitual, normal, ordinary, prevailing, routine, standard; *see also* **traditional, usual**

RHYTHMIC: constant, even, rhythmic, steady, uniform

regularly

consistently, habitually, normally, on a regular basis, routinely, time after time, typically, usually

reject

verb decline, deny, disallow, discard, refuse, repudiate, scrap, spurn
noun cast-off, discard, failure, second

rejoice

celebrate, cheer, delight, glory, revel, triumph

related

affiliated, akin to, allied, associated, connected, kindred, linked

relaxed

calm, carefree, casual, composed, cool, easy-going, laid-back (*informal*), nonchalant, placid

reliable

dependable, faithful, honest, responsible, safe, solid, sound, staunch, sure, trustworthy

reluctant

averse, disinclined, grudging, hesitant, loath, unenthusiastic, unwilling

remain

continue, endure, last, linger, persist, stay, survive, wait

remark

verb comment, declare, mention, observe, say, state
noun comment, mention, observation, opinion, reflection, statement, thought, utterance, word

remarkable

extraordinary, incredible, notable, noteworthy, striking, surprising, unbelievable; *see also* **amazing, unusual**

remedy

answer, antidote, cure, medicine, panacea, solution, treatment

remember

commemorate, recall, recollect, reminisce, think back

remove

delete, detach, eliminate, erase, extract, take away, take off, take out

repair

darn, fix, heal, mend, overhaul, patch up, rectify, renovate, restore

reply

noun acknowledgement, answer, reaction, rejoinder, response, retort
verb acknowledge, answer, react, rejoin, respond, retort

request

verb apply for, ask, ask for, beg, desire, entreat, pray, seek, solicit, want
noun appeal, application, call, demand, desire, entreaty, petition, prayer, want, wish

require

NEED: lack, necessitate, need
COMMAND: command, compel, demand, direct, force, insist, make, oblige, order, request

rescue

free, liberate, ransom, recover, salvage, save

resemblance

image, likeness, sameness, similarity; *see also* **copy**

resemble
look like, parallel, take after; *see also* copy

resign
abdicate, leave, quit, stand down, step down

resist
combat, counteract, defy, fight, fight back, oppose, repel, stand up to, withstand

respect
verb admire, appreciate, esteem, honour, pay homage to, revere, venerate

noun admiration, appreciation, esteem, homage, honour, regard, reverence, veneration

rest
noun WHAT REMAINS: balance, excess, extra, leftovers, others, remainder, remains, remnants, residue, surplus

noun RELAXATION: break, breather (*informal*), lull, pause, relaxation, standstill, stop; *see also* sleep

verb PAUSE: break, discontinue, halt, pause, relax, take a break, take five (*informal*); *see also* sleep, stop

verb POSITION: lay, lean, lie, perch, prop, remain, settle, sit, stand, stay

result
consequence, effect, fruit, outcome, reaction, upshot

retire
leave, quit, resign

return
verb COME BACK: come back, reappear, recur
verb GIVE BACK: give back, hand back, refund, restore, send back
noun homecoming, reappearance, recurrence

reveal
announce, betray, disclose, display, divulge, expose, leak, manifest, proclaim; *see also* show

rich
WEALTHY: affluent, in the money (*informal*), loaded (*informal*), opulent (*formal*), prosperous, wealthy, well-heeled (*informal*), well-off, well-to-do

EXPENSIVE: costly, expensive, gorgeous, lavish, luxurious, palatial, priceless, splendid, sumptuous

HAVING A LOT OF CREAM, ETC: creamy, fatty, heavy, spicy, sweet, sugary

FERTILE: fertile, lush, productive

ridiculous
absurd, daft, foolish, idiotic, ludicrous, lunatic, preposterous, senseless, silly; *see also* mad

right
adjective ACCURATE: accurate, correct, exact, precise, spot-on (*informal*), true

adjective APPROPRIATE: appropriate, deserved, fair, fitting, honourable, just, lawful, moral, proper, suitable

noun POWER: authority, business, claim, freedom, liberty, licence, permission, power, prerogative, privilege

noun WHAT IS MORAL: good, goodness, honour, justice, lawfulness, morality, righteousness, virtue

riot
commotion, disorder, disturbance, insurrection, lawlessness, protest, revolt, uproar

risk
noun chance, danger, gamble, hazard, peril, possibility, speculation, uncertainty, venture

verb chance, dare, endanger, gamble, hazard, imperil, jeopardize, speculate, venture

rival
adversary, antagonist, challenger, competitor, opponent

road

alley, boulevard, cul-de-sac, highway, lane, motorway, path, street, track, way

rob

burgle, embezzle, hijack, mug, rustle, steal

robber

bandit, burglar, embezzler, hijacker, mugger, pickpocket, pirate, rustler, thief

robbery

break-in, burglary, embezzlement, hijack, mugging, piracy, stealing, theft

room

APARTMENT: apartment, chamber (*formal*), compartment, cubicle, office
SPACE: area, capacity, elbow-room, leeway, margin, play, range, space
OPPORTUNITY: chance, occasion, opportunity, scope

rot

corrode, corrupt, decay, decompose, deteriorate, disintegrate, fester, go bad, putrefy, spoil

rough

NOT SMOOTH: bristly, broken, coarse, hairy, irregular, jagged, ragged, rugged, uneven
HARSH: brusque, brutal, coarse, harsh, nasty, unceremonious, unfeeling, unkind; *see also* **rude**
HOARSE: grating, gruff, harsh, hoarse, husky, rasping, raucous
APPROXIMATE: approximate, ballpark (*informal*), estimated, general, imprecise, inexact, loose, round, vague

round

CURVED: ball-shaped, circular, curved, cylindrical, disc-shaped, globular, ring-shaped, spherical
APPROXIMATE: *see* **rough**

row

column, file, line, queue, series, string, tier

rubbish

NONSENSE: drivel, gibberish, gobbledegook, twaddle; *see also* **nonsense**
TRASH: debris, flotsam and jetsam, garbage, junk, litter, refuse, waste

rude

NOT POLITE: cheeky, discourteous, disrespectful, ill-mannered, impolite, impudent, insolent, insulting
OBSCENE: blue, coarse, crude, obscene, vulgar

ruin

noun DESTRUCTION: collapse, defeat, destruction, devastation, downfall, failure, fall, overthrow, undoing, wreck
noun FINANCIAL COLLAPSE: bankruptcy, collapse, crash, failure, fall, insolvency
verb DESTROY: destroy, devastate, mangle, mar, spoil, waste, wreck
verb CAUSE TO COLLAPSE FINANCIALLY: bankrupt, impoverish

rule

noun LAW: decree, law, policy, regulation
noun PRINCIPLE: axiom, canon, criterion, guideline, law, maxim, principle, standard, tenet
noun CONTROL: administration, authority, command, control, direction, government, jurisdiction, leadership, reign
noun HABIT: convention, custom, habit, practice, routine, way, wont (*literary*)
verb GOVERN: administer, command, control, direct, dominate, govern, manage, oversee, reign; *see also* **run**
verb DECIDE: adjudicate, decide, decree, determine, judge, pronounce

ruler

commander, controller, governor, leader, monarch, president, sovereign; *see also* **king, queen**

run

verb GO QUICKLY: bolt, charge, dash, gallop, hurry, race, rush, speed, sprint, tear

verb FLOW: flow, gush, pour, spill, spout, spread, stream, trickle

verb CONTROL: administer, conduct, control, co-ordinate, direct, lead, manage, operate, oversee, supervise; *see also* **rule**

noun DASH: dash, gallop, jog, race, ride, sprint, spurt

noun TRIP: drive, excursion, jaunt, journey, outing, trip

run away

abscond, beat it (*informal*), bolt, clear off (*informal*), elope, escape, flee, scram (*informal*)

rush

verb charge, dash, gallop (*informal*), hare, hotfoot it (*informal*), hurry, race, stampede (*informal*), tear; *see also* **run**

noun bolt, gallop (*informal*), hurry, race, sprint, stampede

ruthless

callous, cold-blooded, heartless, merciless, pitiless; *see also* **cruel**

sad

UNHAPPY: dejected, depressed, despondent, disconsolate, downhearted, gloomy, glum, heartbroken, unhappy, upset; *see also* **miserable**, **sorry**

DISTRESSING: depressing, distressing, heart-breaking, heart-rending, painful, poignant, touching, tragic, upsetting

REGRETTABLE: regrettable, tragic, unfortunate

DULL: dismal, dreary, dull, gloomy

sadden

depress, dismay, distress, grieve, upset

sadness

distress, grief, heartache, sorrow, unhappiness; *see also* **misery**

safe

UNHARMED: alive and well, OK, out of harm's way, safe and sound, secure, undamaged, unharmed, unhurt, uninjured, unscathed

HARMLESS: harmless, innocuous, non-poisonous, non-toxic, sure, tame, wholesome

FREE FROM HARM: immune, impregnable, invulnerable, protected, secure

RELIABLE: dependable, foolproof, proven, reliable, tried, trustworthy, unfailing

safety

immunity, protection, refuge, sanctuary, security, shelter

salary

earnings, income, pay, remuneration, stipend (*of member of clergy*), wages

satisfactory   *see* acceptable

satisfy

GIVE WHAT IS WANTED: appease, atone, compensate, placate, please, reassure, reimburse

BE ENOUGH: answer, fill, fulfil, meet, suffice, suit

CONVINCE: assure, convince, persuade

save

RESCUE: free, liberate, redeem, recover, rescue, salvage

PROTECT: guard, preserve, protect, safeguard, shelter, shield

NOT WASTE: conserve, cut back on, economize on, husband, reclaim, recover, recycle

GATHER, KEEP: collect, gather, hoard, keep, put aside, put by, reserve, store

say

add, announce, comment, express, mention, remark, speak, state, swear, tell; *see also* **answer**, **assert**, **suggest**

scare

alarm, dismay, frighten, intimidate, panic, petrify, startle, terrify, unnerve, worry

scatter

break up, disintegrate, disperse, disseminate, sow, spread, sprinkle, strew

scene

PLACE: area, environment, locality, location, place, setting, site, situation
SIGHT: landscape, sight, view, vision

scent

aroma, bouquet, fragrance, odour, perfume, savour, smell, whiff

scold

censure, chide, give someone a piece of one's mind, lecture, rebuke, reprimand, reproach, reprove, tell off, tick off

scolding

a piece of one's mind, lecture, rebuke, reprimand, talking-to, telling-off, ticking-off, tongue-lashing

scorn

verb deride, despise, disdain, dismiss, disparage, laugh at, look down on, sneer at, spurn
noun contempt, derision, disdain, disparagement, sarcasm, scornfulness, sneers

scream

verb cry, cry out, howl, roar, screech, shriek, squeal, wail, yell, yowl
noun cry, howl, roar, screech, shriek, squeal, wail, yell, yowl

search

verb explore, forage, hunt, inquire, investigate, look, probe, pry, rummage, scour
noun exploration, hunt, inquiry, investigation, pursuit, quest, research

secret

HIDDEN: clandestine, concealed, covert, disguised, hidden, hush-hush (*informal*), stealthy, undercover
MYSTERIOUS: arcane, cryptic, enigmatic, esoteric, mysterious, mystic, obscure, occult

secretly

clandestinely, furtively, in confidence, in private, in secret, on the quiet, stealthily, surreptitiously

secure

adjective SAFE: impregnable, immovable, invulnerable, protected, safe, safe and sound, sheltered, unassailable
adjective FIXED: fastened, firm, fixed, stable, steady, tight
verb FASTEN: bolt, chain, fasten, fix, lock, moor, nail, tie, tie up
verb GET: acquire, gain, get, get hold of, obtain, procure

see

HAVE IN SIGHT: catch sight of, discern, glimpse, make out, notice, picture, set eyes on, spot, visualize, witness; *see also* look
UNDERSTAND: appreciate, comprehend, discover, fathom, get (*informal*), grasp, make out, perceive, understand
MAKE SURE: ensure, guarantee, make sure

seem

appear, look

seize

arrest, capture, catch, clutch, confiscate, grab, grasp, grip, nab (*informal*), snatch

seldom

infrequently, hardly ever, now and again, now and then, occasionally, rarely, scarcely

select

choose, opt for, pick, prefer, single out

selection

anthology, assortment, choice, collection, medley, miscellany, range, variety

selfish

egocentric, egotistical, greedy, mean, miserly, self-centred, self-serving

send

broadcast, convey, dispatch, emit, fling, forward, hurl, propel, radiate, transmit

separate

verb disconnect, diverge, divide, divorce, isolate, part, sever, split up

adjective detached, disconnected, discrete, distinct, divided, independent, individual, isolated, single

several

assorted, different, discrete, distinct, many, some, sundry, various

severe

STRICT: fierce, hard, harsh, rigorous, stern, strict, stringent, tough; *see also* cruel

SERIOUS: acute, bad, extreme, grave, great, intense

SAID OF WEATHER, ETC: bad, bitter, extreme, fierce, harsh, inclement

shade

verb cover, darken, dim, obscure, overshadow, screen, shelter

noun SHELTER: cloud, cover, darkness, dimness, gloom, screen, shadow, shelter

noun COLOUR: colour, hue, tinge, tint, tone

noun SLIGHT AMOUNT: dash, degree, hint, shadow, suggestion, suspicion, trace, vestige

shadow

noun DARKNESS: cloud, darkness, dimness, gloom, obscurity, shade

noun SADNESS: gloom, sadness

noun SLIGHT AMOUNT: hint, suggestion, suspicion, trace, vestige

shake

MOVE ABOUT: quiver, rattle, rock, shiver, shudder, tremble, vibrate, wag, wave, wobble

DISTURB: disturb, frighten, rattle, rouse, shock, undermine, unnerve, unsettle, upset; *see also* worry

share

verb allot, distribute, divide up, give out, parcel out, split

noun allowance, contribution, due, portion, quota, ration

shelter

noun accommodation, asylum, cover, protection, refuge, sanctuary, shade

verb accommodate, cover, guard, hide, protect, put up, shade, shield

shine

verb flash, glare, gleam, glimmer, glisten, glitter, glow, shimmer, sparkle, twinkle

noun glare, gleam, glitter, gloss, glow, lustre, polish, sheen, shimmer, sparkle

shock

verb appal, disgust, dismay, distress, horrify, nauseate, offend, outrage, scandalize, shake; *see also* astonish

noun SOMETHING THAT SHOCKS: blow, bolt from the blue, bombshell, thunderbolt

noun STATE OF SHOCK: consternation, dismay, distress, disgust, dismay, horror, outrage, surprise, turn, upset; *see also* astonishment

noun IMPACT: bang, blow, bump, collision, concussion, impact, jar, jolt, knock

shocked

appalled, disgusted, dismayed, horrified, offended, outraged, revolted, shaken; *see also* astonished

shocking

appalling, atrocious, disgraceful, disgusting, dreadful, outrageous, revolting, scandalous, terrible

short

NOT LONG: concise, condensed, limited, low, momentary, reduced, succinct; *see also* **brief**, **small**

NOT MUCH, NOT ENOUGH: deficient, inadequate, insufficient, lacking, limited, reduced, scant, scarce, sparse

shout

verb bellow, call, cheer, cry, exclaim, roar, scream, shriek, yell

noun bellow, call, cheer, cry, exclamation, roar, scream, shriek, yell

show

verb DISPLAY: demonstrate, disclose, display, exhibit, manifest, present, register, reveal

verb PROVE: attest, demonstrate, exemplify, explain, illustrate, indicate, prove, reveal

noun PERFORMANCE: circus, exhibition, extravaganza, display, performance, play, presentation, spectacle

noun APPEARANCE: affectation, appearance, demonstration, display, pretence, semblance

noun FLAMBOYANCE: dash, flamboyance, ostentation, pageantry, panache, pizzazz, razzle-dazzle

shrink

contract, decrease, diminish, dwindle, lessen, shorten, shrivel, wither

shy

bashful, coy, diffident, reserved, retiring, self-effacing, timid

sick

NOT WELL: ill, indisposed (*formal*), nauseous, off-colour, out of sorts, poorly, queasy, under the weather, unwell

NOT LIKING: bored, displeased, fed up, tired, weary

side

edge, face, flank, surface

sign

INDICATION: clue, evidence, hint, indication, manifestation, mark, pointer, proof, symptom, trace; *see also* **warning**

SYMBOL: badge, coat of arms, crest, emblem, insignia, logo, mark, motif, symbol, trademark

silly

NOT WISE: absurd, foolish, idiotic, ludicrous, pointless, preposterous, ridiculous, senseless, stupid, unwise; *see also* **mad**

NOT BEHAVING SENSIBLY: childish, immature, puerile, scatterbrained

similar

alike, analogous, comparable, corresponding, equivalent, like, resembling, same, uniform

similarity

agreement, closeness, correspondence, equivalence, likeness, resemblance, sameness, uniformity; *see also* **copy**

simple

EASY: easy, elementary, idiot-proof, straightforward, uncomplicated, understandable, user-friendly

PLAIN: ordinary, plain, unadorned, unalloyed, unembellished, unpretentious

NOT SOPHISTICATED: childlike, credulous, feeble-minded, green, guileless, half-witted, innocent, naïve, unsophisticated

single

ONLY: individual, lone, one, only, separate, sole, solitary, unique

NOT MARRIED: unattached, unmarried

site

location, place, position, setting, situation, spot

situation

PLACE: context, environment, location, place, position, site, surroundings
CIRCUMSTANCES: ball-game (*informal*), circumstances, plight, position, predicament, scenario, state of affairs

size

amount, area, dimensions, extent, magnitude, measurements, quantity, volume

skilful

accomplished, adept, deft, expert, masterly, polished, practised, proficient, skilled

slack

NOT TIGHT: baggy, limp, loose, sagging
CARELESS: careless, lax, lazy, negligent, permissive, remiss, sloppy

sleep

noun forty winks (*informal*), nap, siesta, snooze
verb doze, have forty winks (*informal*), snooze, take a nap

sleepy

drowsy, dull, heavy, lethargic, sluggish, soporific

slender *see* slim

slide

glide, skate, slip, slither

slight

faint, flimsy, limited, meagre, poor, remote, slim, small, superficial

slim

NOT FAT: delicate, lean, slender, svelte, thin, trim
NOT LARGE: faint, limited, poor, remote, slight, thin; *see also* **small**

slope

noun gradient, inclination, incline, slant, tilt
verb fall away, incline, lean, slant, tilt

slow

adjective NOT FAST: gradual, leisurely, long-drawn-out, prolonged, protracted, slow-moving, sluggish, time-consuming, unhurried
adjective NOT ON TIME: behind, delayed, late, unpunctual
adjective NOT QUICK-WITTED: dense, dim, dull, dumb, obtuse, stupid, thick (*informal*)
verb brake, check, curb, delay, detain, handicap, hold up, retard

small

diminutive, dwarf, little, mini, miniature, narrow, petite, pigmy, pocket-size; *see also* **short, slight, tiny, young**

smell

aroma, odour, scent, whiff
PLEASANT SMELL: aroma, bouquet, fragrance, perfume, scent
BAD SMELL: B.O., body odour, niff (*slang*), pong (*slang*), reek, stench, stink

sob

bawl, cry, howl, weep

solemn

ceremonious, dignified, formal, grave, majestic, serious, sober, stately

song

anthem, ballad, carol, chorus, folk-song, hymn, lullaby, number (*informal*), psalm, shanty

sorrow

anguish, distress, grief, heartache, misery, pain, sadness, suffering, unhappiness, woe (*literary*)

sorry

APOLOGETIC: apologetic, ashamed, conscience-stricken, contrite, penitent, regretful, remorseful, repentant, shamefaced, sorrowful; *see also* sad
NOT GOOD: deplorable, dismal, distressing, pathetic, pitiful, poor, rotten, wretched
COMPASSIONATE: compassionate, moved, sympathetic

sort

brand, breed, category, class, genre, kind, race, species, type, variety

spacious

big, broad, large, roomy, sizable, wide

spare

additional, emergency, extra, fresh, more, new, reserve, supplementary, surplus

speech

address, communication, conversation, dialogue, discourse, lecture, talk

speed

acceleration, haste, hurry, momentum, pace, quickness, rapidity, tempo, velocity

splendid

EXCELLENT: brilliant, excellent, fantastic, great, marvellous, superb, wonderful
IMPRESSIVE: gorgeous, grand, imposing, impressive, lavish, luxurious, magnificent, ornate, sumptuous; *see also* beautiful

split

verb SHARE: allocate, allot, apportion, distribute, halve, parcel out, partition, share, share out
verb BREAK: break, burst, crack, cut, part, rip, slash, snap, tear
verb SEPARATE: branch, disband, divorce, fork, part, separate
noun BREAK: break, burst, crack, cut, fissure, gap, opening, rip, slash, tear
noun PARTING: break-up, divorce, estrangement, schism, separation

spoil

RUIN: damage, harm, impair, injure, mar, ruin, waste, wreck
PAMPER: coddle, cosset, indulge, mollycoddle, pamper

spread

verb MAKE OR BECOME LARGER: broaden, fan out, extend, multiply, mushroom, proliferate, stretch, swell, widen; *see also* increase
verb GIVE OUT OR GO OUT: broadcast, circulate, diffuse, disseminate, distribute, publicize, radiate, scatter, strew, transmit
noun expansion, extension, growth, increase, proliferation, rise

stand

TOLERATE: abide, accept, bear, brook, endure, put up with, stomach, tolerate, withstand
GET UP: arise, get up, rise

start

verb BEGIN: begin, commence, kick off, set out
verb SET GOING: activate, initiate, instigate, launch, open, pioneer
verb SET UP: establish, found, institute, set up
noun BEGINNING: beginning, birth, commencement, dawn, kick-off, onset, outset
noun ESTABLISHING: foundation, inauguration, initiation, launch, opening

state

verb announce, declare, report, say, specify
noun COUNTRY: country, kingdom, land, nation, republic, territory
noun CONDITION: circumstances, condition, position, shape, situation

stationary

motionless, standing, static, still, stock-still, unmoving

stay

continue, last, remain, stop, wait

steady

CONTINUOUS: constant, continuous, non-stop, persistent, relentless, unbroken, uninterrupted

RELIABLE: consistent, dependable, faithful, firm, reliable, sensible, steadfast

CALM: calm, equable, imperturbable, level-headed, placid, staid

NOT MOVING: firm, fixed, immovable, stable

REGULAR: even, regular, rhythmic, uniform

steal

nick (*informal*), pilfer, pinch (*informal*), poach, rip off (*informal*), shoplift, swipe (*informal*)

stern

authoritarian, hard, harsh, inflexible, rigid, rigorous, severe, steely, strict, unsmiling

sticky

LIKE GLUE: adhesive, gluey, glutinous, gooey, self-adhesive, syrupy, tacky, viscous

DIFFICULT: awkward, delicate, difficult, embarrassing, thorny, tricky

stiff

HARD: brittle, firm, hard, rigid, solid

STRONG: fierce, formidable, heavy, powerful, stout, strong, stubborn, tough, vigorous

TOO FORMAL: awkward, forced, formal, laboured, pompous, stilted, wooden

still

PEACEFUL: calm, peaceful, quiet, silent, tranquil, undisturbed

NOT MOVING: motionless, stationary

stop

verb NOT CONTINUE: break, call it a day, cease, come to an end, conclude, desist, finish, halt, pack it in (*informal*); *see also* rest

verb PUT A STOP TO: bar, block, end, hinder, obstruct, prevent, put an end to, staunch, suspend, terminate

noun HALT: break, cessation, close, conclusion, discontinuation, finish, halt, interruption, pause, stoppage; *see also* rest

store

noun SHOP: boutique, chain store, corner shop, department store, hypermarket, shop, supermarket, warehouse

noun HOARD: cache, fund, hoard, lot, quantity, reserve, stock, stockpile, supply, wealth

verb hoard, hold, keep, lay aside, reserve, save, stockpile

storm

BAD WEATHER: blizzard, cyclone, gale, hurricane, sandstorm, squall, tempest, tornado, whirlwind

COMMOTION: clamour, commotion, furore, outburst, outcry, row, rumpus, turmoil

story

TALE: account, anecdote, bedtime story, history, narrative, novel, saga, tale; *see also* myth

LIE: falsehood, fib (*informal*), lie, tale, untruth

straight

DIRECT: direct, flat, horizontal, level, perpendicular, square, upright, vertical

FRANK: candid, frank, honest, open

strange

bizarre, curious, eccentric, extraordinary, funny, odd, peculiar, queer, remarkable, weird; *see also* unusual

UNFAMILIAR: alien, foreign, novel, unfamiliar

stranger

alien, foreigner, guest, incomer, newcomer, visitor

street

alley, alleyway, avenue, boulevard, crescent, drive, lane, path, road, way

strength

POWER, FORCE: energy, force, intensity, power, stamina, vehemence, vigour

MENTAL POWER: fibre, firmness, fortitude, resolution, resolve, spirit; *see also* **bravery**

COMPARATIVE AMOUNT CONTAINED: concentration, potency

ASSET: advantage, asset, backbone, mainstay, virtue

strike

verb HIT: bang into, collide with, hit, tap, thump, wallop, whack

verb ATTACK: afflict, assail, assault, attack, invade, raid

verb STOP WORK: down tools, mutiny, walk out, work to rule

noun ATTACK: assault, attack, invasion, raid

noun REFUSAL TO WORK: mutiny, sit-in, stoppage, walk-out, work-to-rule

striking

arresting, conspicuous, impressive, memorable, notable, noteworthy, noticeable, outstanding, remarkable, surprising

strong

POWERFUL: athletic, brawny, burly, muscular, powerful, strapping, sturdy, well-built

ACTING WITH FORCE OR INTENSITY: determined, fierce, firm, forceful, intense, keen, robust, staunch, steadfast; *see also* **severe**, **violent**

CONVINCING: clear, clear-cut, cogent, compelling, convincing, persuasive, well-founded

stubborn *see* obstinate

stupid

NOT SENSIBLE: absurd, cock-eyed (*informal*), crazy, daft (*informal*), foolish, idiotic, ludicrous, lunatic, mad, senseless; *see also* **reckless**, **silly**

NOT ALERT: dazed, dopey, groggy, thick-headed

style

MANNER: appearance, design, fashion, form, manner, method, mode, pattern, trend, way; *see also* **habit**, **sort**

STYLISHNESS: chic, elegance, flamboyance, grace, luxury, pizzazz, polish, refinement, sophistication

sudden

abrupt, hasty, prompt, quick, rapid, snap, swift, unexpected, unforeseen

suffer

bear, endure, put up with, stand, stomach, tolerate

sufficient *see* enough

suggest

advise, advocate, allege, claim, hint, imply, indicate, insinuate, propose, recommend

suggestion

INDICATION, SLIGHT AMOUNT: breath, hint, indication, suspicion, trace, whisper

PROPOSAL: innuendo, insinuation, motion, plan, proposal, proposition, recommendation

suitable

applicable, appropriate, apt, due, fitting, opportune, proper, relevant, right, seemly

supply

contribute, equip, fill, furnish, give, grant, produce, provide

support

noun HELP: agreement, aid, approval, assistance, backing, encouragement, help, patronage, sponsorship

noun HELPER: assistant, backbone, champion, helper, mainstay, pillar, supporter

verb APPROVE OF: advocate, approve of, champion, defend, encourage, endorse, second

verb GIVE HELP TO: aid, assist, back, finance, help, promote, rally round, sponsor, subsidize

supporter

adherent, advocate, champion, disciple, follower, henchman, member, patron, seconder, sponsor; *see also* fan

suppose

assume, believe, expect, guess, hypothesize, imagine, infer, judge, presume, think

supreme

chief, foremost, greatest, head, highest, leading, paramount, pre-eminent, principal, top

sure

FEELING CERTAIN: certain, confident, convinced, persuaded, positive, satisfied
CERTAIN TO HAPPEN: bound, certain, definite, dependable, effective, foolproof, guaranteed, infallible, sure-fire, trustworthy
SAFE: safe, secure

surprise

noun STATE OF BEING SURPRISED: amazement, astonishment, shock, wonder, wonderment
noun SOMETHING THAT SURPRISES: bolt from the blue, bombshell, shock
verb amaze, astonish, astound, disconcert, flabbergast, shake, shock, stagger, startle, stun
adjective unexpected, unforeseen

surprising

amazing, astonishing, astounding, extraordinary, remarkable, startling, unexpected, unforeseen

surrender

verb capitulate, give in, resign, submit, yield
noun capitulation, submission

suspicious

FEELING SUSPICION: chary, distrustful, doubtful, dubious, sceptical, uneasy, wary
CAUSING SUSPICION: dodgy (*informal*), doubtful, dubious, fishy (*informal*), peculiar, queer, questionable, shady, suspect

swearing

abuse, bad language, blasphemy, curses, expletives, foul language, profanity

sweet

appealing, attractive, charming, cute, dear, delightful, lovely, nice, pretty; *see also* kind

swift   *see* brief, prompt, quick

sympathy

compassion, empathy, feeling, fellow-feeling, pity, understanding

symptom

evidence, indication, manifestation, mark, sign, syndrome, token

take

REMOVE: abduct, appropriate, eliminate, pinch (*informal*), pocket, steal, subtract
CAPTURE: arrest, capture, catch, seize
GET: accept, acquire, choose, obtain, pick, receive, select, win
GET HOLD OF: grasp, grip, hold, seize
CARRY: bring, carry, cart, convey, ferry, haul, move, remove, transport
LEAD: accompany, bring, conduct, escort, fetch, guide, lead, usher
TOLERATE: abide, bear, brook, cope with, endure, put up with, stand, stomach, tolerate, withstand
NEED: call for, demand, necessitate, need, require
HOLD: accommodate, have room for, hold, seat

tale

STORY: account, anecdote, fairy tale, history, reminiscence, saga, short story; *see also* myth
LIE: falsehood, fib (*informal*), lie, story, traveller's tale, untruth

talk

verb CONVERSE: chat, chatter, communicate, confer, converse, gossip, natter (*informal*), negotiate, parley, speak

verb GIVE OUT INFORMATION: blab (*informal*), blow the gaff (*informal*), grass (*slang*), inform, let the cat out of the bag

noun LECTURE: harangue, lecture, lesson, sermon, speech, seminar, tutorial

noun DISCUSSION: chat, consultation, conversation, dialogue, discussion, meeting, natter (*informal*), negotiation

noun GOSSIP: gossip, hearsay, rumour, tittle-tattle (*informal*)

tall

big, giant, gigantic, high, lanky (*informal*), lofty, soaring, towering

target

GOAL: aim, ambition, end, goal, intention, object, objective, purpose

THING AIMED FOR IN SPORT: bull's-eye, butt, hole, jack, mark, pin

VICTIM: butt, object, prey, quarry, scapegoat, victim

taste

FLAVOUR: flavour, savour, tang

LIKING: appetite, desire, fancy, fondness, inclination, liking, partiality, penchant, preference, relish

ELEGANCE: culture, discernment, discrimination, elegance, judgement, polish, refinement, style

SMALL AMOUNT: bit, bite, drop, morsel, mouthful, nibble, nip, sip, spoonful, swallow

tasty

appetizing, delicious, luscious, mouthwatering, savoury, scrumptious (*informal*)

teach

coach, demonstrate, drill, educate, guide, instruct, school, show, train, tutor

teacher

coach, guru, instructor, lecturer, mentor, professor, schoolteacher, trainer, tutor

team

corps, crew, force, gang, group, party, side, squad, troop, unit

tell

INFORM: acquaint, apprise, communicate, disclose, explain, inform, mention, notify, report, reveal; *see also* **announce**, **describe**, **say**

ORDER: command, demand, direct, enjoin, instruct, order

temporary

NOT PERMANENT: acting, interim, makeshift, provisional, reserve, stop-gap, substitute

NOT LONG-LASTING: ephemeral, passing, transient, transitory

tender

GENTLE: affectionate, compassionate, delicate, gentle, sensitive, sympathetic; *see also* **kind**

SOFT: breakable, delicate, fragile, frail, soft

PAINFUL: bruised, inflamed, irritated, painful, sore

tense

FEELING TENSION: anxious, apprehensive, edgy, fidgety, jittery, jumpy, nervous, stressed, uneasy, uptight; *see also* **worried**

CAUSING TENSION: anxious, exciting, nerve-wracking, stressful, worrying

terrible

abysmal, appalling, atrocious, awful, dire, dreadful, frightful, harrowing, severe, shocking; *see also* **horrible**

terrific

EXCELLENT: awesome, breathtaking, brilliant, fabulous, fantastic, great, magnificent, marvellous, phenomenal, sensational; *see also* **amazing**, **splendid**

LARGE, GREAT *see* **huge**, **intense**

terrified
afraid, alarmed, daunted, fearful, frightened, horrified, intimidated, panic-stricken, petrified, scared

terror
alarm, consternation, dread, fear, fright, horror, panic, shock

thanks
acknowledgement, appreciation, gratitude, recognition

thick
DENSE: abundant, deep, dense, impenetrable, luxuriant
FULL: brimming, bristling, covered, crawling, crowded, full, packed, swarming, teeming
CONDENSED: concentrated, condensed, solid, soupy

thief
bandit, burglar, embezzler, hijacker, mugger, pickpocket, pirate, robber, rustler, shoplifter

thin
NOT FAT: bony, emaciated, gaunt, lean, skeletal, slender, slim, spindly
SAID OF MATERIAL: delicate, diaphanous, fine, flimsy, light, see-through, sheer, transparent
NOT MANY: rare, scant, scarce, scattered, sparse
NOT MUCH: meagre, poor, slim, small

thing
OBJECT: apparatus, artefact, article, device, gadget, implement, instrument, item, object
FEATURE: aspect, feature, facet, factor, point
FEELING: dislike, fetish, fixation, mania, obsession, phobia, preoccupation, problem

think
BELIEVE: be under the impression, conceive, conclude, consider, envisage, expect, hold, maintain, reason, reckon; *see also* accept, **believe, guess, suppose**
PONDER: brood, consider, deliberate, meditate, mull over, muse, ponder, reflect, wonder

thorough
CAREFUL: careful, complete, comprehensive, detailed, exhaustive, full, in-depth, intensive, meticulous, painstaking
UTTER: absolute, complete, out-and-out, perfect, unmitigated, utter

thoroughly *see* completely

thrive
blossom, boom, flourish, grow, increase, prosper, succeed

throw
bowl, fling, hurl, lob, pitch, propel, sling, toss

tidy
adjective clean, neat, ordered, orderly, organized, smart, systematic
verb arrange, clean, clear, neaten, order, organize, smarten, systematize

tie
attach, bind, fasten, join, knot, moor, rope, secure, tether, truss

tight
close, close-fitting, constricted, cramped, narrow, sealed, secure, stretched, taut

tiny
minuscule, minute; *see also* small

tolerate
accept, bear, endure, permit, put up with, stand, stomach, suffer, turn a blind eye to, withstand; *see also* allow

top
apex, cap, crest, crown, head, high point, peak, pinnacle, summit, zenith

topic

issue, matter, question, subject, theme

total

adjective ENTIRE: all, complete, comprehensive, entire, full, sweeping, thorough, undivided, whole

adjective PERFECT: absolute, complete, downright, out-and-out, perfect, sheer, thorough, thoroughgoing, unmitigated, utter

noun aggregate, amount, entirety, lot, mass, sum, totality, whole

verb ADD: add up, calculate, count, tally, tot up

verb EQUAL: add up to, amount to, come to, equal, reach

totally *see* absolutely

trace

SIGN: evidence, fingerprint, footprint, hint, indication, mark, record, sign

SMALL AMOUNT: bit, dash, drop, hint, iota, shadow, spot, suggestion

trade

COMMERCE: barter, business, buying and selling, commerce, dealing, traffic

JOB: business, calling, employment, job, occupation, profession

traditional

customary, established, routine, standard, time-honoured

tranquil

calm, gentle, peaceful, restful, serene, still, undisturbed

transmit

broadcast, communicate, pass on, radio, relay, send, spread

travel

go, hitch-hike, journey, roam, sail, tour, trek, voyage, wander

tremble

quiver, shake, shiver, shudder, vibrate, wobble

tremendous

WONDERFUL: excellent, fantastic, great, incredible, sensational, super (*informal*), superb, terrific, wonderful

BIG, HEAVY: colossal, huge, immense, massive, terrific

trick

noun dodge (*informal*), hoax, ploy, practical joke, prank, ruse, sleight of hand, subterfuge; *see also* deception

verb bamboozle, cheat, con (*informal*), defraud, dupe, fool, pull a fast one (*informal*), swindle; *see also* deceive

trip

noun cruise, excursion, expedition, journey, outing, run, voyage

verb fall, slip, stumble

trouble

verb DISTRESS: bother, concern, distress, disturb, harass, inconvenience, perturb, pester, plague; *see also* annoy, worry

verb TAKE THE TROUBLE: bother, exert oneself

noun PROBLEM: bother, defect, difficulty, distress, inconvenience, irritation, nuisance, predicament, problem, spot; *see also* complaint, danger, worry

noun DISTURBANCE: bother, commotion, disturbance, riot, strife, unrest, upheaval

noun EFFORT: bother, care, effort, exertion, inconvenience, pains

noun ILLNESS: ailment, complaint, illness

true

DEVOTED: dedicated, devoted, faithful, loyal, sincere, staunch, unswerving

REAL: actual, correct, factual, faithful, honest, perfect, proper, real, truthful, valid; *see also* accurate, genuine

trust

verb RELY ON: bank on, confide in, count on, depend on, rely on, swear by

verb THINK: assume, believe, expect, hope, imagine, presume, suppose, surmise, think

noun assurance, belief, confidence, conviction, credence, faith, reliance, responsibility, safekeeping

try

verb ATTEMPT: attempt, endeavour, seek, strive, struggle, undertake, venture

verb ANNOY: annoy, irk, irritate, plague

noun attempt, bash (*informal*), crack (*informal*), endeavour, effort, go, shot, stab

turn

verb GO ROUND: go round, pivot, revolve, roll, rotate, spin, swivel, twirl, twist, whirl

verb BECOME OR MAKE: become, go, make, metamorphose, mutate, transform

noun cycle, revolution, rotation, spin, twist

type

brand, breed, category, class, genre, kind, sort, species, variety

ugly

disagreeable, hideous, misshapen, nasty, objectionable, repulsive, unattractive, unprepossessing, unsightly; *see also* **horrible**

uncommon

infrequent, rare, scarce; *see also* **unusual**

unconscious

NOT AWAKE: comatose, out, out cold, out for the count, senseless, stunned

UNTHINKING: automatic, blind, inadvertent, instinctive, involuntary, reflex, subconscious

UNAWARE: oblivious, unaware, unwitting

understand

COMPREHEND: appreciate, comprehend, cotton on (*informal*), fathom, gather, get the picture, grasp, realize, recognize, see; *see also* **believe, conclude**

SYMPATHIZE: commiserate, empathize, sympathize

unfriendly

aloof, antagonistic, chilly, cold, cool, distant, hostile, stand-offish, unsociable, unwelcoming

unhappiness

the blues (*informal*), dejection, depression, despondency, melancholy, misery, sadness, sorrow

unhappy

SAD *see* **sad**

INAPPROPRIATE: ill-advised, ill-chosen, ill-timed, inappropriate, injudicious, tactless, unfortunate, unsuitable

unite

amalgamate, band together, coalesce, combine, join, join forces, link, merge, pool, unify

unkind

callous, inconsiderate, insensitive, mean, nasty, spiteful, thoughtless, uncaring, unfeeling, unsympathetic; *see also* **cruel, unfriendly**

unknown

anonymous, incognito, nameless, uncharted, unexplored, unfamiliar, unidentified, unnamed; *see also* **hidden, secret**

unnatural

ABNORMAL: abnormal, anomalous, bizarre, extraordinary, freak, outlandish, queer, strange, supernatural, weird; *see also* **peculiar, unusual**

NOT GENUINE: contrived, feigned, forced, insincere, laboured, phoney, self-conscious, stilted, strained, studied

unpleasant

annoying, disagreeable, distasteful, horrible, nasty, objectionable, obnoxious, offensive, painful, repulsive

unsatisfactory

defective, imperfect, inadequate, second-rate, shoddy, substandard, third-rate; *see also* **poor**

unusual

bizarre, extraordinary, odd, out of the ordinary, rare, remarkable, strange, uncommon, unconventional; *see also* **peculiar**

urge

verb advise, advocate, beg, counsel, entreat, exhort, implore, incite, plead, recommend; *see also* **persuade**, **warn**

noun compulsion, desire, drive, impulse, inclination, itch, longing, wish, yearning

use

employ, exercise, handle, manipulate, operate, work

useful

handy; *see also* **profitable**

use up

consume, expend, exhaust, spend, swallow, waste

usual *see* **common**, **habitual**, **normal**

usually

as a rule, by and large, commonly, generally, generally speaking, mainly, mostly, normally, on the whole, ordinarily

vacant

abandoned, disused, empty, free, to let, unoccupied

vague

NOT CLEAR IN OUTLINE: blurred, dim, fuzzy, hazy, indistinct, misty, obscure, unclear

NOT CLEAR IN DETAIL: evasive, ill-defined, imprecise, indefinite, inexact, loose, undefined, unspecified, woolly

vain

PROUD: arrogant, big-headed, boastful, conceited, haughty, high and mighty, proud, self-important, stuck-up (*informal*)

USELESS: abortive, fruitless, futile, pointless, unproductive, useless

valuable

EXPENSIVE: costly, dear, esteemed, expensive, precious, prized, treasured

USEFUL: beneficial, handy, helpful, invaluable, productive, profitable, useful, worthwhile

value

noun COST: cost, price, worth

noun BENEFIT: advantage, benefit, good, help, importance, merit, profit, use, usefulness, utility

verb ASSESS THE VALUE OF: appraise, assess, compute, estimate, evaluate, rate

verb CONSIDER VALUABLE: appreciate, cherish, esteem, hold dear, prize, regard, respect, treasure

vanity

affectation, airs, big-headedness, conceit, conceitedness, egotism, pretension, pride

variety

RANGE: array, assortment, collection, medley, miscellany, mixture, multiplicity, range

SORT: brand, breed, category, class, kind, race, sort, species, strain, type

various

assorted, disparate, distinct, diverse, heterogeneous, miscellaneous, several, sundry, varied, varying; *see also* **different**

vast

colossal, enormous, extensive, great, huge, immense, limitless, massive, prodigious

verdict

assessment, conclusion, decision, finding, judgement, opinion, sentence

very

awfully, deeply, dreadfully, exceedingly, extremely, greatly, highly, immensely, severely, terribly; *see also* **absolutely, quite**

vicious

brutal, malicious, mean, nasty, savage, slanderous, spiteful, venomous, vindictive, wicked; *see also* **cruel, unkind**

victim

butt, casualty, dupe, fall guy (*informal*), scapegoat, target, sucker (*informal*), sufferer

victory

conquest, prize, success, triumph, win

view

noun OPINION: attitude, conviction, estimation, feeling, impression, judgement, opinion, perspective, sentiment; *see also* **belief**
noun SIGHT: glimpse, look, outlook, panorama, prospect, scene, sight, vision, vista
verb WATCH: contemplate, examine, inspect, observe, scan, survey, watch, witness
verb CONSIDER: consider, deem, judge, regard

violent

SAID OF A PERSON, TEMPER, ETC: brutal, furious, intemperate, savage, tempestuous, uncontrollable, vicious, wild; *see also* **cruel**
SAID OF A STORM, ETC: destructive, devastating, intense, raging, severe, strong

vivid

bright, clear, colourful, dramatic, expressive, graphic, lifelike, realistic, striking

voyage

crossing, cruise, journey, passage, sail, trip

want

call for, covet, crave, desire, fancy, hanker after, hunger for, long for, wish, yearn for; *see also* **need**

warn

advise, alert, caution, counsel, forewarn, inform, notify, prophesy, tip off (*informal*)

warning

admonition, caution, notification, omen, portent, prophecy, tip-off (*informal*), wake-up call

wary

alert, apprehensive, careful, cautious, chary, circumspect, suspicious, vigilant, watchful

way

PATH: access, alley, approach, channel, passage, path, route, track, trail; *see also* **road**
METHOD: fashion, means, method, mode, procedure, scheme, system, technique
HABIT: custom, fashion, habit, idiosyncrasy, manner, practice, routine, style

weak

NOT PHYSICALLY STRONG: delicate, exhausted, feeble, flimsy, fragile, frail, infirm, puny
NOT MENTALLY STRONG: cowardly, indecisive, ineffectual, insipid, irresolute, spineless, timid, timorous, weak-kneed
NOT FORCEFUL ENOUGH: ineffective, ineffectual, toothless
INCAPABLE: impotent, incapable, powerless
NOT STRONG IN TASTE, ETC: dilute, diluted, tasteless, thin, watery, wishy-washy
NOT LOUD: faint, imperceptible, muffled, quiet, slight, soft
NOT STRONGLY PROTECTED: defenceless, exposed, helpless, open, unprotected, vulnerable
NOT CONVINCING: flimsy, hollow, inconclusive, invalid, lame, unconvincing, untenable
LACKING: deficient, inadequate, lacking, unsatisfactory, wanting

wealth

PROSPERITY: affluence, fortune, luxury, opulence (*formal*), prosperity, riches, substance

POSSESSIONS: assets, estate, fortune, funds, goods, money, possessions, property, worldly goods

PLENTY: abundance, cornucopia, plenty, profusion, store

weary

EXHAUSTED: all in, dead beat (*informal*), dog-tired, drained, exhausted, sleepy, tired, whacked (*informal*), worn out

BORED: bored, browned off (*informal*), fed up, sick and tired, tired

weep

cry, howl, lament, sob

welcome

verb accept, embrace, greet, hail, meet, receive

noun greeting, hospitality, reception, red carpet

adjective acceptable, agreeable, appreciated, delightful, desirable, enjoyable, gratifying, pleasant, pleasing, refreshing

wet

NOT DRY: clammy, damp, dank, drenched, dripping, humid, moist, soaking, sodden, soggy

BOGGY: boggy, marshy, muddy, waterlogged

RAINING: damp, drizzly, pouring, pouring wet, rainy, showery

whole

entire, full, intact, total, unabbreviated, unabridged, uncut, undivided, unedited; *see also* complete

wholly

absolutely, altogether, categorically, completely, entirely, perfectly, positively, thoroughly, totally, utterly

wicked

depraved, dissolute, dreadful, evil, heinous, immoral, iniquitous, scandalous, shameful, sinful; *see also* cruel

wild

UNCONTROLLED: boisterous, chaotic, frantic, furious, riotous, rowdy, uncontrollable, uncontrolled, unruly, uproarious; *see also* excited, mad, violent

NOT TAME: feral, ferocious, fierce, savage, undomesticated, untamed

UNCIVILIZED: barbarian, barbaric, savage, uncivilized

ANGRY: angry, fizzing, fuming, furious, incensed, infuriated, irate, mad (*informal*), outraged

STORMY: blustery, stormy, rough, windy

willing

agreeable, amenable, content, disposed, game (*informal*), happy, inclined, pleased, prepared, ready

win

verb CONQUER: conquer, overcome, prevail, succeed, triumph

verb GET: accomplish, achieve, attain, come away with, earn, gain, get, obtain, secure, take

noun conquest, success, triumph, victory

wisdom

common sense, enlightenment, foresight, intelligence, insight, intuition, prudence, sense, understanding; *see also* knowledge

wise

clever, discerning, enlightened, judicious, learned, perceptive, prudent, sensible, well-advised; *see also* intelligent

wish

verb aim, crave, desire, dream, hanker, hope, hunger, long, want, yearn

noun aim, aspiration, desire, dream, hankering, hope, hunger, inclination, urge, yearning

withdraw

back out, drop out, leave, quit, retreat

wonder

noun AMAZEMENT: amazement, astonishment, awe, fascination, surprise

noun MARVEL: curiosity, marvel, miracle, phenomenon, prodigy, rarity, sight, spectacle

verb THINK: ask oneself, inquire, meditate, ponder, puzzle, query, question, reflect, speculate, think

verb BE AMAZED: marvel

wonderful

brilliant, fabulous, fantastic, great, magnificent, marvellous, sensational, splendid, stunning, stupendous; *see also* amazing, excellent, incredible

worried

anxious; *see also* frightened, nervous

work

noun JOB: business, calling, employment, job, livelihood, occupation, profession, task, trade

noun EFFORT: drudgery, effort, elbow grease, exertion, graft, grind, labour, slog (*informal*), toil

noun SOMETHING DONE: achievement, doing, handiwork, undertaking

verb FUNCTION: function, go, move, operate, run

verb RUN: control, drive, handle, manage, manipulate, manoeuvre, operate, run, use

verb LABOUR: beaver away, labour, slog (*informal*), sweat, toil

verb CAUSE: accomplish, achieve, arrange, bring about, bring off, cause, contrive, manage, perform, pull off

worry

noun anxiety, apprehension, concern, disquiet, foreboding, misgiving, nervousness; *see also* fear

verb ALARM: alarm, bother, concern, dismay, disturb, faze, trouble; *see also* frighten

verb THINK IN A WORRIED WAY: agonize, fret, struggle, wrestle

worrying

alarming, disquieting, disturbing, frightening

worsen

MAKE WORSE: aggravate, exacerbate, heighten, increase, intensify

BECOME WORSE: decay, decline, degenerate, deteriorate, sink

worship

verb adore, exalt, glorify, honour, idolize, praise, venerate; *see also* love

noun adoration, glorification, honour, praise, veneration; *see also* love

worth

merit, price, quality, use, value

worthless

deplorable, good-for-nothing, hopeless, miserable, paltry, pathetic, pitiful, poor, useless

wound

noun INJURY: bruise, cut, gash, graze, hurt, injury, laceration, lesion, scar

noun DISTRESS: anguish, distress, grief, heartbreak, hurt, insult, offence, pain, shock

verb INJURE: bruise, cut, gash, graze, hit, hurt, injure, lacerate, pierce, scar, slash

verb DISTRESS: distress, grieve, hurt, insult, offend, pain, shock, upset

wreck

noun destruction, devastation, mess, ruin, ruination, shipwreck, write-off *verb* break, destroy, devastate, ruin, shatter, smash, spoil, write off

yield

verb GIVE: bear, bring in, earn, generate, give, pay, produce, provide, supply

verb GIVE IN: admit defeat, capitulate, cave in, comply, concede, give in, give way, submit, surrender, throw in the towel

noun crop, earnings, harvest, income, output, proceeds, produce, product, profit, returns

young

baby, infant, juvenile, little, small

youth

YOUNG AGE: adolescence, boyhood, childhood, girlhood, schooldays, teens

YOUNG MAN: boy, teenager, youngster

DO IT YOURSELF

A Using the synonym lists, replace the words in italics with a single word that has the same meaning.

> *Example:*
>
> We *went on foot* to the cinema.
> We **walked** to the cinema.

Hint

Look in the synonym lists of the words that are in italics.

1. Can't you see my mother is in *great pain*?

2. Are you going to *go* there *by car*?

3. I think I need a *short sleep*.

4. We're having a *party to celebrate moving into our new house* next Saturday.

5. The car was *very dirty*.

6. There were *marks left by people's feet* all over the garden.

7. It started to rain and by the time we got home we were *very wet*.

8. She hit the *centre of the target* with every arrow.

9. Unfortunately we had to leave before the *end of the show*.

10. When the bomb went off, everyone *ran away*.

11. When the bomb went off, everyone ran away in *great fear*.

12. My sister *likes* strawberries *very much*.

13. The police examined the doors and windows for *marks left by people's fingers*.

14. It's not polite to *eat* your food *quickly and noisily* like that.

15. What a *very unpleasant* person she is!

16. My boss is extremely *careful about details*.

17. We need more soap powder, so I bought *a large but cheaper* packet.

18. He built a *hut joined to the wall* at the bottom of the garden.

B Using the thesaurus, rewrite the following pairs of sentences replacing the words in italics with different synonyms.

> *Example:*
>
> We had a *nice* day at the zoo.
> We had an ***enjoyable*** day at the zoo.
>
> What a *nice* man her father is!
> What a ***charming*** man her father is!

There may, of course, be more than one possible appropriate synonym.

H i n t

It may sometimes be necessary to use the cross-references to find possible synonyms.

> We had an ***enjoyable/pleasant/lovely*** day at the zoo.
> What a ***charming/pleasant/friendly/likeable*** man her father is!

1. Why don't you *ask* Mary to the party?
   After the earthquake, the government *asked* for international aid.

2. That was a *lovely* meal!
   That's a *lovely* hat!

3. The *next* day we went back into town.
   The television was on in the *next* room.

4. The concert was *very* successful.
   She was *very* upset at his personal remarks.

5. The concert was a *big* success.
   The house is surrounded by a *big* garden.

6. He was in *severe* pain.
   A good teacher knows when to be lenient and when to be *severe*.

7. A *small* child was looking at us intently.
   There's only a *small* chance of success, you realize.

8. I earned far more in my *old* job than I do now.
   An *old* woman was sitting begging at the corner of the street.

9. Please write *clearly* in black ink.
   She was *clearly* very upset.

10. I *imagine* she'll be along later.
    Try to *imagine* what the finished house will look like.

11. Have you had an *answer* to your letter?
    Have you found the *answer* to your problem?

12. *Rich* food doesn't agree with me.
    She hopes her daughters will find *rich* husbands.

13. There's a *funny* smell in the house.
    My brother keeps all the children amused with his *funny* stories.

14. What a *splendid* idea!
    She rents a *splendid* apartment in a fashionable part of the city.

15. It's not my *business* to look after her.
    I set up this *business* four years ago.

16. Her mother was *furious* when she heard the news.
    A *furious* battle then began.

17. We'll need to find some *strong* arguments to back our case.
    A *strong* wind was blowing from the east.

18. I can remember when I was a *poor* student with hardly enough money to buy food.
    Thanks to the team's *poor* performance last week, we're certainly not going to come top of the League this year.

19. It's a *difficult* climb to the top of that hill.
    We get some really *difficult* people to deal with at the shop.

20. Is this a *good* time for me to have a talk with you?
    Mrs Chen is very *good* to her grandchildren.

21. Sheila was really *mad* when the bus didn't stop for her.
    Their proposal is completely *mad*, you know.

22. It was a *calm* summer's evening.
    We need someone who will remain *calm* under pressure.

23. I only had time to give your report a *quick* read before the meeting.
    I'm sorry to rush you but we need a *quick* reply to our offer.

24. Digging the garden is *hard* work.
    That's a *hard* question to answer.

25. No matter what happened, I would never *abandon* my children.
    Due to unforeseen circumstances, the company has had to *abandon* its plans for expansion.

C From the options in brackets, choose the correct synonym for the words in italics in the following sentences.

1. The story is that he *bumped off* his wife.
    (pushed, murdered, hated)

2. We need to keep everything *above-board*.
    (high, pleasant, legal)

3. This plan does have a few *shortcomings*.
    (advantages, defects, opponents)

4. I think we've been *double-crossed*!
    (helped, hindered, cheated)

5. She's extremely *big-headed*.
    (vain, important, obstinate)

6. I saw a terrible *pile-up* on the road on the way here.
    (accident, heap, building)

7. Mrs Grant was *dumbfounded* when she heard the news.
    (quiet, happy, astonished)

8. We live a very *humdrum* life these days.
    (boring, exciting, unusual)

9. As the saying goes, my *get-up-and-go* seems to have got up and gone. (wealth, energy, youth)

10. She is just being *pig-headed*.
    (cruel, obstinate, silly)

11. I just love visiting *far-flung* corners of the earth.
    (distant, unusual, interesting)

12. Outside, she heard a *blood-curdling* scream.
    (loud, frightening, strange)

13. I was feeling slightly *under the weather* yesterday.
    (ill, cold, wet)

14. It was a *heart-rending* tale that the old woman told.
    (frightening, amusing, sad)

15. My sister was *over the moon* when she learned she had got second prize in the poetry competition.
    (disappointed, delighted, surprised)

D With the help of the lists of synonyms, fill in the blank spaces in the following sentences to complete the synonyms for the words in brackets.

> *Example:*
>
> He's just being _____-*headed.* (obstinate)
> He's just being ***pig-headed.***

1. Suddenly there was an _____-*piercing* shriek. (loud)

2. She was _____-*broken* when she didn't get the job at the local radio station. (sad)

3. I do wish someone would write a really _____-*friendly* guide to computer programming. (simple)

4. I was sitting watching one of those *run-of-the-*_____ gardening programmes on television last night when the phone rang. (ordinary)

5. The boys had a _____-*raising* journey over the mountains. (frightening)

6. It was _____-*breaking* to see the children begging in the streets. (sad)

7. When the bomb went off, there was a _____-*stricken* rush to get out of the stadium. (frightened)

8. There are a few _____-*chilling* moments in the film. (frightening)

9. They put forward some _____-*baked* scheme involving raising money by collecting old envelopes. (impractical)

10. Being found out like that left me rather _____-*faced.* (embarrassed)

2 ▶ Hyponyms

While a synonym is a word that means *the same* as another word, a **hyponym** /ˈhaɪpənɪm/ is a word that denotes a *type* or *kind* of something. For example, ***dog***, ***cat***, ***monkey*** and ***snake*** are hyponyms of ***animal*** (that is, they are words for different *kinds of animal*), and ***boxer***, ***bulldog***, ***poodle***, ***spaniel*** and ***greyhound*** are hyponyms of ***dog*** (they are the names of different *types of dog*).

How to use the lists of hyponyms

▶ Words in the lists that are *informal* or *literary* have been labelled as such. American terms are labelled *US*.

▶ Note that words that are labelled *dated* are themselves no longer in common use, whereas words that are labelled *old* refer to things that are no longer in use.

▶ This unit contains some lists of parts of things, such as motor vehicles, and some of these lists also include words that are related to that particular topic, such as computing. Such words are not actually hyponyms, since they do not denote *types* or *kinds* of things, but for convenience they have nevertheless been included here.

aircraft

aeroplane (*US* airplane), airliner, airship, autogiro/autogyro, biplane, balloon, bomber, fighter, fighter-bomber, flying machine (*dated*), glider, gunship, hang-glider, helicopter, hot-air balloon, jet, jumbo jet, microlight, monoplane, plane, seaplane, stealth bomber, stealth fighter, swing-wing, triplane, VTOL, Zeppelin

spacecraft

flying saucer, lunar module, rocket, satellite, spacecraft, space platform, space probe, spaceship, space shuttle, space station, UFO, unidentified flying object

animals

amphibian, biped, crustacean, dinosaur, invertebrate, mammal, marsupial, mollusc, primate, reptile, quadruped, rodent, vertebrate

aardvark, abominable snowman, alligator, anteater, antelope, ape, armadillo, ass, axolotl, badger, baboon, bandicoot, bat, bear, beaver, bison, buffalo, bull, camel, caribou, cat, chameleon, cheetah, chimp (*informal*)/chimpanzee, chinchilla, chipmunk, cougar, cow, coyote, crab, crocodile, deer, dog, dolphin, donkey, dromedary, duck-billed platypus, elephant, ferret, field mouse, fox, frog, gazelle, gerbil, gibbon, giraffe, gnu, goat, gopher, gorilla, guinea pig, hamster, hare, hedgehog, hippo/hippopotamus, horse, hyena, iguana, jackal, jaguar, kangaroo, koala, lemming, lemur, leopard, lion, lizard, llama, lobster, mandrill, marmoset, marmot, mink, mole, mongoose, monkey, moose, mule, muskrat, newt, ocelot, opossum, orang-utan, otter, ox, panda, panther, pig, polar bear, porcupine, porpoise, prawn, puma, rabbit, raccoon, rat, reindeer, rhino/rhinoceros, salamander, scorpion, seal, sea lion, sheep, shrew, shrimp, skunk, sloth, slug, snail, snake, spider, squirrel, stoat, tadpole, terrapin, tiger, toad, tortoise, turtle, vole, wallaby, walrus, water buffalo, weasel, whale, wildebeest, wolf, wombat, worm, yak, yeti, zebra

cats

Abyssinian, angora, Burmese, longhair, Manx, Persian, shorthair, Rex, Siamese, tabby, tortoiseshell

dogs

Afghan hound, Alsatian, basenji, basset-hound, beagle, border collie, borzoi, boxer, bulldog, bull mastiff, bull terrier, chihuahua, chow, cocker spaniel, collie, corgi, dachshund, Dalmatian, Doberman pinscher, foxhound, fox terrier, German shepherd, golden retriever, Great Dane, greyhound, husky, Irish wolfhound, Jack Russell, King Charles spaniel, Labrador, lhasa apso, lurcher, mastiff, Newfoundland, Old English sheepdog, Pekingese, pit bull terrier, pointer, poodle, pug, retriever, Rottweiler, saluki, samoyed, schnauzer, setter, Shetland sheepdog, shih tzu, spaniel, springer spaniel, St Bernard, terrier, West Highland terrier, whippet, wolfhound, Yorkshire terrier

snakes

adder, anaconda, asp, boa, boa constrictor, bushmaster, cobra, grass snake, king cobra, krait, mamba, pit viper, puff adder, python, rattlesnake, sidewinder, taipan, tree snake, viper, water moccasin

arts and crafts

batik, calligraphy, carpentry, carving, ceramics, collage, crochet, drawing, dyeing, embroidery, engraving, etching, flower arranging/ikebana, knitting, macramé, marquetry, metalwork, needlework, oil painting, origami, painting, patchwork, photography, pottery, printing, pyrography, sculpture, sketching, spinning, tapestry, watercolour, weaving, woodcarving

birds

bird of prey, game bird, songbird, waterfowl

albatross, auk, babbler, barbet, bird of paradise, bittern, blackbird, bluebird, bowerbird, budgie (*informal*)/budgerigar, bulbul, bunting, buzzard, canary, cassowary, chickadee, chicken, cockatiel, cockatoo, condor, coot, cormorant, crane, crow, cuckoo, dodo, dove, duck, eagle, egret, emu, falcon, finch, flamingo, flycatcher, gannet, goose, grebe, grouse, guineafowl, gull, hawk, hen, heron, hoopoe, hornbill, hummingbird, ibis, jay, kingfisher, kite, kiwi, kookaburra, lark, lovebird, lyrebird, macaw, magpie, martin, mockingbird, moorhen, mynah, nightingale, oriole, ostrich, owl, parrot, parakeet, partridge, peacock, pelican, penguin, petrel, pheasant, pigeon, pipit, plover, quail, rail, raven, robin, sandpiper, seagull, shrike, skylark, snipe, sparrow, spoonbill, starling, stork, swallow, swan, swift, tern, thrush, tit, toucan, treecreeper, turkey, vulture, wagtail, warbler, waxbill, weaver, whip-poor-will, whydah, woodpecker, wren

boats and ships

aircraft carrier, ark, barge, battleship, cabin cruiser, canal boat, canoe, catamaran, clipper (*old*), cruiser, destroyer, dhow, dinghy, dredger, felucca, ferry/ferryboat, fishing boat, freighter, frigate, galleon, galley, gondola, gunboat, houseboat, hovercraft, hydrofoil, kayak, ketch, landing-craft, launch, lifeboat, liner, longboat, longship (*old*), man-of-war/man-o'-war (*old*), minesweeper, motorboat, oil tanker, packet-boat/packet-ship, paddle-steamer, puffer, punt, raft, rowing-boat, sampan, schooner, sloop (*old*), smack, speedboat, steamboat, steamer/steamship, sub (*informal*)/ submarine, supertanker, tanker, torpedo boat, trawler, trimaran, trireme (*old*), tug/tugboat, U-boat, warship, yacht

body

parts of the body

Achilles' tendon, Adam's apple, ankle, anus, aorta, arm, artery, back, backbone, beard, bone, bottom, breast, bronchial tube, brow, buttocks, calf, capillary, cartilage, cheek, chest, diaphragm, duodenum, ear, elbow, eye, eyeball, eyebrow, eyelash, eyelid, finger, fingernail, foot, forehead, foreskin, genitals, gland, groin, gullet, gum, hair, hand, hard palate, head, intestine, iris, kidney, knee, kneecap, knuckle, larynx, leg, ligament, lip, liver, lung, mouth, moustache, muscle, neck, nose, nostril, oesophagus, palate, pelvis, penis, pharynx, pubic hair, pupil, rib, scrotum, shin, shoulder, skin, skull, soft palate, spinal column/spine, spleen, stomach, taste bud, temple, tendon, testicle, thigh, throat, toe, toenail, tongue, tooth, trunk, uterus, uvula, vagina, vein, vertebrae, vulva, windpipe, womb, wrist

bones

anklebone, anvil, backbone, breastbone, carpal, cheekbone, clavicle, coccyx, collarbone, cranium, femur, fibula, funny bone (*informal*), hammer, hipbone, humerus, ilium, ischium, jawbone, kneecap, leg bone, mandible, maxilla, metacarpal, metatarsal, patella, pelvis, pubic bone, pubis, radius, rib, scapula, shoulder blade, skull, spine, sternum, stirrup, tarsal, thighbone, tibia, ulna, vertebra, wristbone

books

hardback, paperback, softback album, almanac, annual, anthology, atlas, catalogue, concordance, cookery book/ cookbook, diary, dictionary, encyclopaedia, gazetteer, grammar book, guidebook, handbook, hymnbook, manual, notebook, omnibus, photograph album, picture book, recipe book, scrapbook, stamp album, textbook, telephone book/telephone directory, thesaurus, vocabulary book, yearbook

buildings

parts of a building
See also rooms

alcove, attic, back door, balcony, baluster, banister, battlement, ceiling, cellar, chimney, cupboard, dado, dome, door, doorstep, double glazing, downpipe, drainpipe, eaves, elevator (especially *US*), escalator, fireplace, floor, front door, granny flat, gutter, hall, hallway, landing, lift, mantelpiece, porch, roof, room, side door, skirting-board, spire, stair, staircase, steeple, tower, turret, verandah, wall, window, window sill

types of building
abbey, bank, barn, barracks, beach-hut, block of flats, boat-house, bungalow, bus station, cabin, café, castle, cathedral, chalet, chateau, church, cinema, condominium (*US*)/condo (*US informal*), convent, cottage, crematorium, factory, farmhouse, filling station, fire station, flat, fort, fortress, garage, greenhouse, gymnasium, hospital, hotel, house, hut, igloo, leisure centre, library, lighthouse, log cabin, manse, mansion, mill, minaret, monastery, mosque, museum, office, office block, pagoda, palace, parsonage, penthouse, petrol station, police station, power station, prefab (*informal*), prison, pub (*informal*)/public house, railway station, ranch-house, rectory, restaurant, school, semi (*informal*), shed, shop, skyscraper, stable, studio, summerhouse, supermarket, surgery, synagogue, temple, tent, tepee, theatre, tower block, vicarage, villa, warehouse, wigwam, windmill, yurt

clothing

anorak, bathing costume, bathrobe, bedsocks, belt, bikini, blazer, blouse, body stocking, bonnet, bow tie, boxer shorts, bra/brassière, braces, briefs, caftan/kaftan, cagoul/cagoule, camisole, cap, cape, cardigan, chador, cheongsam, cloak, coat, cords, corset, cravat, culottes, cummerbund, denims, dhoti, dinner jacket, drainpipes (*informal*)/drainpipe trousers, dress, dressing-gown, duffel coat, dungarees, earmuffs, flannels, frock (*dated*), glove, greatcoat, hankie (*informal*)/handkerchief, hat, headscarf, hot pants, housecoat, jacket, jeans, jerkin, jersey, jodhpurs, jumper, kilt, kimono, knickerbockers, knickers, leggings, leg-warmers, leotard, Levis®, mac (*informal*)/mackintosh, mini, miniskirt, mitten, monokini, negligee, nightie (*informal*)/nightdress, overalls, overcoat, pantaloons, pants, panties, pantyhose (*US*), parka, petticoat, plus-fours, polo-neck, poncho, pullover, pyjamas, raincoat, safari jacket, sari, sarong, scarf, shawl, shell suit, shift, shirt, shorts, slacks, slip, smock, sock, stocking, stole, suit, string vest, suspender belt, suspenders, sweater, swimming costume, swimming trunks, swimsuit, tail-coat, tie, tights, tracksuit, trench coat, trews, trousers, trouser suit, T-shirt/tee-shirt, turtle-neck, tuxedo (*US*), twin-set, underpants, veil, vest, V-neck, waistcoat, windcheater, yashmak, Y-fronts®

footwear

ballet shoe, boot, bootee, brogue, clog, flip-flop (*informal*), football boot, galoshes, gumboot, gym shoe, moccasin, plimsoll, pump, rugby boot, sandal, sandshoe, shoe, slingback, slipper, sneaker, snowshoe, stiletto, tennis shoe, thong (*informal*), trainer, wellington/welly (*informal*)/wellington boot

hats

balaclava, baseball cap, bearskin, beret, biretta, boater, bonnet, bowler/bowler hat, busby, cap, crown, deerstalker, derby (*US*), fez, glengarry, helmet, kepi, mitre, mortar-board, panama, pith helmet, skullcap, sombrero, sou'wester, stetson, straw hat, sunhat, tammy (*informal*)/tam-o'-shanter, ten-gallon hat, topper (*informal*)/ top hat, topi/topee, toque, trilby, turban, yarmulka

colours

black, blue, brown, green, grey, orange, pink, purple, red, white, yellow

blacks
charcoal, ebony, jet

blues
cobalt blue, indigo, navy blue, peacock blue, petrol blue, royal blue, sky blue

browns
auburn, bay, bronze, chestnut, chocolate, cinnamon, copper, fawn, khaki, mahogany, ochre, rust, sepia, tan, taupe

greens
aquamarine, avocado, bottle-green, chartreuse, eau de nile, emerald, jade, sage, turquoise

greys
silver, slate

oranges
apricot, coral, tangerine

pinks
peach, rose, salmon pink

purples
lavender, lilac, mauve, plum, violet

reds
burgundy, cerise, cherry, crimson, magenta, maroon, ruby, scarlet, vermilion

yellows and creams
amber, beige, canary yellow, cream, gold, lemon yellow, magnolia, saffron

whites
milk-white, snow-white

computer terminology

access, applet, ASCII, attachment, backup, bit, boot, byte, CD, CD-ROM, central processing unit, character, chip, compact disk, computer game, computer graphics, CPU, crash, cursor, database, default, desktop, directory, disk, disk drive, dot-matrix printer, earcon, electronic mail, e-mail, file, floppy disk, folder, format, function, graphic user interface, GUI, hacker, hard disk, hardware, icon, interface, Internet, joystick, keyboard, kilobyte, laptop, laser printer, macro, mainframe, megabyte, memory, menu, microcomputer, modem, monitor, mouse, mouse mat, network, palmtop, PC, peripheral, personal computer, pixel, printer, program, RAM, random access memory, read-only memory, ROM, save, screen, scroll, silicon chip, software, sound card, spam, spellchecker, template, terminal, time out, toggle, toolbar, VDU, virtual reality, virus, visual display unit, web page, window, wizard, word-processor, World Wide Web, worm, WYSIWYG

containers

bags and cases
attaché case, backpack, bag, briefcase, carrier bag, Gladstone bag, handbag, haversack, holdall, kitbag, knapsack, overnight bag, pocket, portfolio, portmanteau, pouch, purse, quiver, rucksack, sack, satchel, shoulder bag, suitcase, trunk, valise, wallet

barrels
barrel, cask, drum, keg

baskets
basket, hamper, pannier, punnet

bottles and jars
bottle, carafe, decanter, demijohn, flagon, flask, gravy boat, jamjar/jampot, jar, jug, milk bottle, milk jug, pitcher, Thermos® flask, wine bottle

bowls and dishes

basin, beaker, bowl, cauldron, coffee pot, dish, pot, ramekin, sugar bowl, teapot, tub, tureen, urn, vase, vat

boxes

biscuit tin, box, cake tin, can, canister, carton, case, casket, chest, cool-box, crate, hatbox, jewellery box, matchbox, pencil case, shoebox, strongbox, suggestion box, tea-caddy, tea-chest, tin, toolbox

cups and glasses

beaker, beer mug, coffee cup, cup, glass, mug, schooner, sherry glass, tankard, teacup, tumbler, wineglass

other containers

bin, bucket, dustbin, kettle, pail, pan, safe, saucepan, tank, trough, tube, waste-paper basket, water tank

cooking: ways of cooking food

bake, barbecue, boil (*hard-boiled*, *soft-boiled*), braise, broil, casserole, coddle, deep-fry, fry, grill, microwave, poach, pot-roast, roast, sauté, scramble, simmer, steam, stew, stir-fry, toast

cosmetics

blusher, cleanser, eyebrow pencil, eyeliner, eye shadow, face cream, face mask, face pack, foundation, lip gloss, lipstick, mascara, moisturizer, nail polish/nail varnish, powder, rouge, toner

dances

ballet, ballroom dancing, folk dance, war dance

belly-dance, bolero, bossa nova, break-dancing, can-can, cerok, cha-cha/cha-cha-cha, Charleston, conga, disco, fandango, flamenco, foxtrot, Highland fling, jig, jive, lambada, limbo, macarena, mambo, mazurka, merengue, military two-step, minuet, morris-dance, paso doble, Paul Jones, polka, quadrille, quickstep, reel, rock'n'roll, rumba, salsa, samba, strathspey, sword dance, tango, tap, twist, waltz

diseases and disorders

AIDS, Alzheimer's disease, anaemia/anemia, angina, anorexia nervosa, anthrax, arthritis, asbestosis, asthma, athlete's foot, autism, beriberi, blindness, botulism, bronchitis, brucellosis, bubonic plague, bulimia, cancer, cerebral palsy, chickenpox, cholera, cirrhosis, coeliac disease, cold, consumption (*dated*), croup, cystic fibrosis, deafness, dengue fever, diabetes, diphtheria, dropsy (*dated*), dysentery, emphysema, encephalitis, enteritis, flu (*informal*), gangrene, German measles, glandular fever, glaucoma, gonorrhoea, green monkey disease, haemophilia, herpes, hepatitis, hydrophobia, impetigo, influenza, Legionnaires' disease, leprosy, leukaemia, lockjaw, malaria, ME, measles, meningitis, motor neurone disease, MS, multiple sclerosis, mumps, muscular dystrophy, osteoporosis, paralysis, Parkinson's disease, peritonitis, pneumonia, polio/poliomyelitis, rabies, rheumatic fever, rheumatism, rickets, ringworm, river blindness, rubella, scabies, scarlet fever, schizophrenia, scurvy, septicaemia, shingles, silicosis, sleeping sickness, smallpox, syphilis, tapeworm, TB, tetanus, thrombosis, thrush, tinnitus, tuberculosis, typhoid, typhus, vertigo, whooping cough, yellow fever

drinks

alcoholic drink, long drink, soft drink

barley water, cappuccino, chocolate, cocoa, coffee, cream, cream soda, expresso/espresso, fruit juice, ginger beer, green tea, herbal tea, lemonade, milk, mineral water, orangeade, root beer (*US*), skimmed milk, soda water, squash, tea, tonic water, water

alcoholic drinks

absinthe, advocaat, ale, beer, bourbon, brandy, Calvados, champagne, cider, claret, Cognac, crème de menthe, daiquiri, eggnog, gin, gin and tonic, home brew, lager, mead, ouzo, perry, piña colada, plonk (*informal*), port, punch, retsina, rum, rye whisky, sake, sangria, schnapps, shandy, sherry, stout, tequila, toddy, vermouth, vodka, wine, whisky/whiskey

fairies and other supernatural beings

angel, archangel, brownie, centaur, cherub, elf, demon, devil, dwarf, faun, fox fairy, genie, gnome, goblin, guardian angel, houri, imp, jinn, leprechaun, mermaid, merman, nymph, pixie, satyr, seraph, sprite, sylph, troll

abominable snowman, bigfoot, Loch Ness monster, phoenix, sasquatch, unicorn, werewolf, yeti

family

aunt, brother, child, cousin, dad (*informal*), daddy (*informal*), father, grandad/granddad (*informal*), grandchild, granddaughter, grandfather, grandma (*informal*), grandmother, grandpa (*informal*), grandson, granny (*informal*), half-brother, half-sister, husband, mom (*US informal*), mommy (*US informal*), mother, mum (*informal*), mummy (*informal*), nephew, niece, parent, pop (*US informal*), sis (*informal*), sister, stepbrother, stepdaughter, stepfather, stepmother, stepsister, stepson, uncle, wife

fish and other water creatures

anchovy, angelfish, anglerfish, barbel, barracuda, bass, bream, brill, carp, catfish, cichlid, cod, coelacanth, conger eel, dab, dogfish, dory, Dover sole, eel, flatfish, flounder, flying fish, four-eyed fish, goby, goldfish, gourami, grouper, guppy, gurnard, haddock, hake, halibut, herring, John Dory, koi, lamprey, lungfish, mackerel, marlin, minnow, monkfish, moonfish, moray eel, mud skipper, mullet, neon tetra, oarfish, opah, perch, pike, pilchard, piranha, plaice, porgy, pufferfish, ray, roach, salmon, sardine, sea horse, sea wolf, shark, Siamese fighting fish, snapper, sole, stickleback, stingray, stonefish, sturgeon, sunfish, swordfish, tarpon, trout, tuna, turbot, whiting, wolf-fish, wrasse

shellfish, etc

abalone, barnacle, clam, cockle, conch, coral, cowrie/cowry, crab, crawfish, crayfish, crustacean, cuttlefish, dolphin, jellyfish, king prawn, limpet, lobster, mollusc, mussel, octopus, oyster, plankton, porpoise, Portuguese man-of-war, prawn, scallop, scampi, sea anemone, sea urchin, shellfish, shrimp, sponge, squid, whale, whelk

flowers and flowering plants

alyssum, anemone, antirrhinum, aster, azalea, begonia, bluebell, broom, buddleia, busy Lizzie, buttercup, cactus, calendula, camellia, candytuft, carnation, Christmas cactus, chrysanthemum, clematis, clover, coleus, cornflower, crocus, cyclamen, daffodil, dahlia, daisy, dandelion, delphinium, forget-me-not, foxglove, freesia, fuchsia, gentian, geranium, gladiolus, gorse, heather, hollyhock, honeysuckle, hosta, hyacinth, hydrangea, iris, jasmine, laurel, lavender, lily, lily-of-the-valley, lobelia, lupin, mallow, marigold, mimosa, narcissus, nasturtium, orchid, pansy, passion flower, peony, petunia, phlox, pink, poinsettia, polyanthus, poppy, potentilla, primrose, primula, rhododendron, rose, saxifrage, snapdragon, snowdrop, stock, sunflower, sweet pea, sweet william, thistle, tulip, viola, violet, wallflower, water lily

food

See also fruit, vegetables, spices and herbs, meats and sausages *and* plants

biscuits, bread and cakes

baguette, biscuit, bread, cake, chocolate biscuit, croissant, crumpet, Danish pastry, digestive biscuit, doughnut, éclair, flapjack, fruitcake, gateau, gingerbread, hot cross bun, macaroon, Madeira cake, muffin, oatcake, pancake, pitta bread, potato scone, roll, scone, shortbread, tea biscuit

pasta

cannelloni, lasagne, macaroni, macaroni cheese, noodle, pasta, ravioli, spaghetti, spaghetti bolognese

pies and tarts

flan, pie, quiche, tart

puddings

apple crumble, banoffi pie/banoffee pie, cheesecake, Christmas pudding, crêpes Suzette, custard, dumpling, Eve's pudding, fool, fruit cocktail, fruit salad, ice cream, jelly, lemon meringue pie, mousse, pavlova, profiteroles, queen of puddings, rhubarb crumble, rice pudding, semolina, soufflé, sundae, trifle, zabaglione

soups

broth, chowder, clear soup, consommé, gazpacho, minestrone, mulligatawny, Scotch broth, soup, vichyssoise

stews

casserole, chilli con carne, goulash, hotpot, Irish stew, kedgeree, moussaka, ragout, ratatouille, stew

sugars

brown sugar, caster sugar/castor sugar, demerara sugar, granulated sugar, icing sugar, sugar

other food words

batter, blue cheese, boiled egg, brown rice, burger, butter, caramel, cauliflower cheese, cereal, chips, chop suey, chow mein, chutney, coleslaw, corn flakes, cottage pie, couscous, croquette, crouton, curry, cutlet, dressing, dumpling, fondue, French fries (chiefly *US*), fricassee, fritter, fromage frais, fudge, gravy, haggis, honey, hotdog, jam, jelly, kedgeree, ketchup, maple syrup, margarine/marge (*informal*), marmalade, mayonnaise, molasses, muesli, olive oil, omelette, paella, pastry, pasty, pickle, pilau rice, pizza, poached egg, porridge, potato crisp (*US* potato chip), preserve, rarebit, risotto, sago, salad, salad dressing, samosa, sandwich, sauce, scrambled egg, shepherd's pie, stock, stuffing, suet, sunflower oil, sweet-and-sour, syrup, tandoori, terrine, toffee, tofu, treacle, vegetable oil, vindaloo, vinegar, vol-au-vent, wild rice, yogurt

fruit

apple, apricot, banana, bergamot, blackberry, blackcurrant, blueberry, breadfruit, clementine, crab apple, cranberry, currant, damson, date, durian, fig, gooseberry, gourd, grape, grapefruit, greengage, guava, jackfruit, kiwi fruit, kumquat/cumquat, lemon, lime, loganberry, loquat, lychee, mandarin, mango, mangosteen, melon, nectarine, olive, orange, pear, persimmon, plantain, plum, pomegranate, pumpkin, quince, raisin, rambutan, raspberry, redcurrant, rhubarb, rosehip, satsuma, sloe, star fruit, strawberry, sultana, ugli fruit, watermelon

nuts

almond, brazil/Brazil nut, cashew, chestnut, coconut, hazelnut, macadamia, monkey nut (*informal*)/peanut, pecan, pistachio, walnut

games

board game, card game

bagatelle, battleships, billiards, blind man's buff, bowling, charades, consequences, craps (*US*), darts, dice, dominoes, forfeits, hangman, hide and seek, I-spy, jigsaw/jigsaw puzzle, musical chairs, noughts and crosses, pass the parcel, ping-pong (*informal*), pin the tail on the donkey, pool, postman's knock, roulette, sardines, shove ha'penny, skittles, snooker, solitaire, statues, table-tennis, ten-pin bowling, tiddlywinks

board games
chess, Chinese chequers, Cluedo®, draughts (*US* checkers), ludo, Monopoly®, Scrabble®, snakes and ladders, Trivial Pursuit®

card games
baccarat, beggar-my-neighbour, bezique, blackjack, brag, bridge, canasta, cheat, chemin de fer, cribbage, donkey, gin rummy, happy families, old maid, pairs, patience (*US* solitaire), Pelmanism, piquet, poker, pontoon, rummy, snap, solo whist, stud poker, whist

gemstones

agate, amber, amethyst, aquamarine, beryl, bloodstone, cairngorm, coral, cornelian, cubic zirconia, diamond, emerald, garnet, jade, jasper, jet, lapis lazuli, marcasite, moonstone, mother-of-pearl, onyx, opal, pearl, quartz, rhinestone, ruby, sapphire, tiger's eye, topaz, tourmaline, turquoise, zircon

household equipment and furniture

See also kitchen equipment and utensils
alarm clock, answering machine, barbecue, bath, bidet, boiler, bookends, breadbin, breadboard, bucket, candle, candlestick, card table, carpet-sweeper, cassette-player, central heating, clock, coffee table, cooker, desk, dishwasher, drawer, dressing-table, dustbin, duvet, extractor fan, fan, fan heater, fan oven, fire extinguisher, freezer, fridge, hat-stand, iron, ironing board, juice extractor, lamp, lampshade, light, light bulb, mattress, microwave/microwave oven, mirror, mobile phone, mop, nest of tables, ornament, oven, pail, picture, pillow, planter, plant pot, radiator, radio, record player, refrigerator, sandwich maker, sink, smoke alarm, spice rack, standard lamp, table, telephone, television/TV/TV set, toaster, toast-rack, trolley, tumble-drier, vacuum cleaner, vase, video, washbasin, washing machine, waste-paper basket, water tank, wine rack

beds
bed, camp bed, cot, cradle, double bed, four-poster bed, single bed, twin beds, water-bed

carpets and soft furnishings
carpet, curtain, cushion, rug

chairs
armchair, bed-chair, bed-settee, chair, chaise longue, couch, deck-chair, divan, easy-chair, footrest/footstool, high-chair, lounger, pouffe, rocking-chair, seat, settee, sofa, stool

cupboards
bathroom cabinet, bedside cabinet, bookcase, bureau, chest of drawers, commode, cupboard, filing cabinet, sideboard, tallboy, vanity unit, wall unit, wardrobe

dishes
ashtray, basin, beaker, beer mug, bowl, butter dish, cafetière, cake plate, cake-stand, coffee cup, coffee pot, cup, dinner plate, glass, gravy boat, jar, jug, milk jug, mug, pepper pot, percolator, plate, pot, pudding plate, saltcellar, saucer, schooner, sherry glass, side plate, soup plate, sugar bowl, tankard, teacup, tumbler, tureen, wineglass

washing equipment and toiletries
aftershave, bathmat, facecloth, hairdrier, razor, shaver, shower, shower cap, soap, sponge, talc/talcum powder, toothbrush, toothpaste, towel

insects and similar creatures

caterpillar, chrysalis, cocoon, grub, larva, nymph, pupa

ant, aphid, bedbug, bee, beetle, blackfly, bluebottle, bug, bumblebee, butterfly, cicada, clothes moth, cockroach, cranefly, cricket, damselfly, dragonfly, dung beetle, earwig, firefly, flea, fly, glowworm, gnat, grasshopper, greenfly, honey bee, hornet, horsefly, lacewing, ladybird, locust, louse, mayfly, mealworm, midge, mosquito, moth, nit, praying mantis, roach (*US*), scarab, silkworm, stick insect, termite, tick, tsetse fly, wasp, water beetle, weevil, whitefly, woodworm

insect-like creatures

centipede, leech, millipede, mite, scorpion, spider, tarantula, tick, woodlouse, worm

jewellery

anklet, bangle, beads, bracelet, brooch, cameo, chain, charm bracelet, choker, cufflink, earring, engagement ring, hatpin, locket, necklace, necklet, nose-ring, pendant, ring, signet-ring, string of pearls, stud, tiara, tie-clip, tiepin, tietack, watch, wedding ring, wristwatch

kitchen equipment and utensils

biscuit tin, blender, bottle-opener, bread knife, breadmaker, butter knife, cake fork, cake knife, cake tin, can-opener, carving knife, casserole, cheese knife, chopping-board, chopsticks, cleaver, coffee grinder, coffee percolator, colander, corkscrew, dessert spoon, draining spoon, egg-timer, fish knife, fish slice, fork, frying-pan, garlic press, grater, grill pan, kettle, knife, ladle, liquidizer, measuring jug, measuring spoon, mincer, mixing bowl, mortar and pestle, nutcracker, peppermill, pot, pan, potato-masher, potato-peeler, pressure cooker, ramekin, rolling-pin, saucepan, scales, scissors, sieve, skewer, skillet, slow cooker, soup spoon, spatula, spoon, steak knife, sugar tongs, tablespoon, teaspoon, tea strainer, terrine, tin-opener, tongs, whisk, wok, wooden spoon

materials

asphalt, Bakelite®, bitumen, brick, cardboard, cast iron, celluloid®, cellulose, cement, china, chipboard, clay, concrete, crêpe paper, earthenware, fibreglass, glass, hardboard, leather, marble, metal, paper, paper-mâché/papier-mâché, parchment, Perspex®, plaster, plasterboard, plastic, plywood, polythene, porcelain, PVC, rubber, sand, sandstone, sheepskin, silicone, slate, stainless steel, steel, stone, tarmac, Teflon®, terracotta, thatch, tile, timber, vinyl, wood

fabrics

calico, canvas, cashmere, cheesecloth, chiffon, cloth, cotton, crêpe, damask, denim, felt, flannel, gauze, gingham, hessian, horsehair, lace, linen, mohair, muslin, nylon, polyester, rayon, silk, suede, taffeta, towelling, tweed, velvet, viscose, wool

meats and sausages

bacon, beef, beefburger, black pudding, brains, burger, chicken, chipolata, chop, corned beef, cutlet, duck, escalope, faggot, fillet, frankfurter, gammon, goose, grouse, haggis, ham, hamburger, hare, heart, hotdog, kebab, kidney, lamb, liver, meatball, meat loaf, mince, mortadella, mutton, offal, oxtail, partridge, pastrami, pâté, pâté de foie gras, pheasant, pigeon, pork, quail, rabbit, rissole, salami, sausage, sirloin, spare rib, steak, sweetbread, T-bone steak, tongue, tripe, turkey, venison, white pudding

fish

anchovy, catfish, caviar, clam, cod, cod roe, crab, crawfish, crayfish, eel, fish and chips, fishcake, fish-finger, gurnard, haddock, hake, halibut, herring, king prawn, kipper, lobster, mackerel, monkfish, mullet, pilchard, plaice, prawn, prawn cocktail, salmon, sardine, scampi, shark, shellfish, sole, squid, taramasalata, trout, turbot, tuna, whiting

medical disciplines and therapeutic techniques

See also sciences

acupressure, acupuncture, Alexander technique, anatomy, aromatherapy, bacteriology, cardiology, chemotherapy, chiropractic, dentistry, dermatology, dietetics, embryology, faith healing, genetics, geriatrics, gynaecology, haematology, herbalism, homeopathy, hypnotherapy, immunology, medicine, microbiology, neurology, obstetrics, occupational therapy, oncology, ophthalmology, optometry, orthodontics, orthopaedics, osteopathy, pathology, pharmacy, pharmacology, physiology, physiotherapy, psychiatry, psychodrama, psychology, psychotherapy, radiology, radiotherapy, reflexology, reiki, shiatsu, speech therapy, toxicology

metals

aluminium (*US* aluminum), brass, bronze, chromium, copper, gold, iron, lead, magnesium, manganese, mercury, nickel, platinum, silver, stainless steel, steel, tin, tungsten, zinc

musical instruments

brass, keyboard, percussion, strings, woodwind

instruments with strings

acoustic guitar, balalaika, banjo, bass guitar, bouzouki, cello, double bass, electric guitar, erh hu, fiddle (*informal*), guitar, harp, lute, lyre, mandolin, sitar, tamboura/tambura, ukulele, viola, violin, violoncello, zither

instruments you blow

bagpipes, bassoon, bugle, clarinet, cor anglais (*US* English horn), didgeridoo, euphonium, fife, flügelhorn, flute, French horn, harmonica, horn, kazoo, mouth organ, oboe, ocarina, panpipes, penny whistle, piccolo, recorder, saxophone, sousaphone, tin whistle, trombone, trumpet, tuba

instruments you hit or shake

bass drum, bell, bongo drums/bongos, castanets, cymbal, drum, glockenspiel, hi-hat/high-hat, kettledrum, maracas, marimba, snare drum, steel drum, tabla, tambourine, timpani/tympani, tom-tom, triangle, xylophone

instruments with keyboards or buttons

accordion, concertina, grand piano, harmonium, harpsichord, melodeon, organ, piano, piano accordion, spinet, synthesizer

musicians

accordionist, bassoonist, bugler, cellist, clarinettist, drummer, fiddler (*informal*), flautist, guitarist, harpist, oboist, organist, pianist, piper, saxophonist, timpanist/tympanist, trombonist, trumpeter, violinist, violist, xylophonist

accompanist, busker, conductor, instrumentalist, leader of the orchestra, singer, soloist, vocalist

musical groups

band, duet, duo, group, quartet, quintet, octet, orchestra, septet, sextet, trio

planets

[*Note that the planets are listed in their order from the sun outwards.*]

Mercury, Venus, Earth, Mars, Jupiter, Saturn, Uranus, Neptune, Pluto

plants

See also flowers and flowering plants, trees and shrubs *and* vegetables

alga, annual, biennial, bonsai, bush, cane, cereal, climber, creeper, cultivar, herbaceous, deciduous plant, dicotyledon, evergreen, fern, flower, fungus, grass, hedge, houseplant, hybrid, lawn, lichen, mildew, monocotyledon, moss, mushroom, perennial, pondweed, pot plant, rush, sapling, seaweed, sedge, seedling, shrub, succulent, toadstool, tree, vegetable, vine, weed, wild flower

cereals

barley, corn, maize, millet, oats, rice, rye, sorghum, sweetcorn, wheat

some other plants

bamboo, flax, hemp, ivy, mistletoe, nettle, pampas grass, papyrus, tree fern, yeast

parts of plants

anther, bark, bough (*literary*), branch, bud, bulb, calyx, carpel, corm, corolla, flower, inflorescence, leaf, ovary, ovule, panicle, pedicel, petal, pistil, raceme, root, sepal, shoot, spadix, spike, stalk, stamen, stem, stigma, style, trunk, twig, umbel

ranks

[*Note: In this section the ranks are listed in order of seniority rather than alphabetically.*]

army ranks

private, lance corporal, corporal, sergeant, staff sergeant, warrant officer, sergeant-major, second lieutenant, lieutenant, captain, major, lieutenant colonel, colonel, brigadier, major-general, lieutenant-general, general, field marshal

navy ranks

ordinary seaman, able seaman, leading seaman, petty officer, chief petty officer, fleet chief petty officer, sub-lieutenant, lieutenant, lieutenant-commander, commander, captain, commodore, rear admiral, vice admiral, admiral, admiral of the fleet

air force ranks

aircraft(s)man/aircraft(s)woman, leading aircraft(s)man/-woman, senior aircraft(s)man/-woman, corporal, sergeant, chief technician, flight sergeant, warrant officer, pilot officer, flying officer, flight lieutenant, squadron leader, wing commander, group captain, air commodore, air vice marshal, air marshal, air chief marshal, marshal of the Royal Air Force

police ranks

constable, sergeant, inspector, chief inspector, superintendent, chief superintendent, assistant chief constable, deputy chief constable, chief constable

rooms

rooms in a house

attic, basement, bathroom, bedroom, bedsit (*informal*), box-room, cellar, cloakroom, conservatory, den (*esp US*), dining-room, drawing-room, dressing-room, hall, hallway, kitchen, kitchenette, larder, lavatory, library, living-room, loft, lounge, nursery, pantry, playroom, porch, scullery, shower-room, sitting-room, study, sun lounge, toilet, vestibule, wine celler

other rooms

anteroom, changing-room, classroom, cubicle, dormitory, foyer, gym/gymnasium, laboratory, music room, office, sickbay, storeroom, studio, vestry, waiting-room, ward, workshop

sciences

See also medical disciplines and therapeutic techniques

acoustics, aerodynamics, agricultural science, anthropology, archaeology, astronomy, astrophysics, biology, botany, chemistry, civil engineering, climatology, computer science, cosmology, cybernetics, dynamics, ecology, economics, electrical engineering, electronics, engineering, entomology, environmental science, food science, geography, geology, geophysics, hydraulics, information technology, linguistics, marine biology, mathematics, mechanical engineering, mechanics, mineralogy, nuclear physics, oceanography, optics, ornithology, palaeontology, particle physics, physics, robotics, sociology, space technology, spectroscopy, technology, thermodynamics, veterinary science, zoology

shapes

circle, cone, crescent, cube, cuboid, cylinder, diamond, ellipse, hemisphere, kite, oblong, oval, parallelogram, polygon, polyhedron, prism, pyramid, quadrant, quadrilateral, rectangle, rhombus, segment, semicircle, sphere, square, trapezium, triangle

polygons

pentagon (= *polygon with 5 sides*), hexagon (6 sides), heptagon (7 sides), octagon (8 sides), nonagon (9 sides), decagon (10 sides), hendecagon (11 sides), dodecagon (12 sides)

polyhedrons

tetrahedron (= *polyhedron with 4 faces*), pentahedron (5 faces), hexahedron (6 faces), octahedron (8 faces), decahedron (10 faces), dodecahedron (12 faces)

triangles

equilateral triangle (= *triangle with three equal sides*), isosceles triangle (= *triangle with no two sides equal*), right-angled triangle, scalene triangle (= *triangle with no two sides equal*)

shops and services

baker/bakery, bank, barber, beautician/beauty parlour/beauty salon/beauty therapist, betting shop/bookmaker, bookshop, butcher, chemist, clothes shop, confectioner, cook shop, dairy, delicatessen, DIY store, draper, drugstore (*US*), estate agent, fish-and-chip shop, fishmonger/fish-shop, florist/flower shop, furniture store, garden centre, greengrocer, grocer, haberdasher, hairdresser, hardware shop, health-food shop, ironmonger, jeweller, licensed grocer, milliner, newsagent (*US* newsdealer), off-licence, optician, outfitter, pawnbroker, pharmacy, post office, record shop, saddler, shoe shop, stationer, sweet shop, tailor, take-away, tobacconist, tool shop, toy shop, travel agent

boutique, cash-and-carry, chain store, corner shop, department store, emporium (*dated*), hypermarket, shopping centre, shopping mall, supermarket

spices and herbs

angelica, anise, allspice, basil, bay leaves, borage, caper, caraway, cardamom, cayenne/cayenne pepper, chamomile/camomile, chervil, chilli pepper, chives, cinnamon, clove, comfrey, coriander, cumin, curry powder, dill, fennel, fenugreek, garlic, ginger, lemon balm, lovage, mace, marjoram, mint, mustard, nutmeg, oregano, paprika, parsley, pepper, rosemary, saffron, sage, savory, sesame, sorrel, tarragon, thyme, turmeric, vanilla

sports and athletic activities

aerobics, aikido, American football, angling, archery, association football, athletics, Australian rules football/rules (*informal*), badminton, baseball, basketball, bobsleigh, bowling, bowls, boxing, canoeing, clay-pigeon shooting, cricket, croquet, cross-country running, curling, cycling, decathlon, discus, diving, drag-racing, dressage, equestrianism, eventing, fencing, five-pin bowling, football, fox-hunting, gliding, go-karting, golf, greyhound-racing, gymnastics, handball, hang-gliding, heptathlon, high jump, hockey (*US* field hockey), horse-racing, hurdling, ice hockey, ice skating, javelin, jogging, judo, jujitsu, karate, keep-fit, kendo, lacrosse, lawn tennis, long jump, marathon, martial arts, moto-cross, motor cycling, motor racing, mountaineering, netball, orienteering, pentathlon, pole vault, polo, pot-holing, putting, rackets, rallying, real tennis, relay race, roller-skating, rowing, rugby league, rugby union, sailing, shinty, shooting, shotput, show-jumping, skateboarding, skiing, skin-diving, sky-diving, snowboarding, soccer, softball, speed-skating, speedway, squash, stock-car racing, sumo, surfing, swimming, table-tennis, tae kwon do, tennis, ten-pin bowling, three-day event, throwing the hammer, tobogganing, tossing the caber, trampolining, triple jump, tug of war, volleyball, walking, water polo, water skiing, weightlifting, wrestling, yachting

tools

adze, auger, awl, bow saw, brace and bit, bradawl, brush, chisel, circular saw, clamp, cold chisel, crowbar, drill, file, fretsaw, gimlet, hacksaw, hammer, hod, jack, jigsaw, knife, lathe, mallet, paintbrush, penknife, pick, pickaxe, pincers, plane, pliers, plumbline, punch, rasp, paint-roller, sander, sandpaper, saw, scissors, screwdriver, sledgehammer, soldering iron, spanner, spirit level, spray-gun, staple-gun, stapler, vice, wrench

drawing instruments
compasses, crayon, dividers, eraser, felt-tip/felt-tip pen, pen, pencil, protractor, rubber, ruler, set-square, T-square

garden and agricultural tools
axe, barrow, chainsaw, cultivator, dibber, fork, harrow, hatchet, hedge-trimmer, hoe, lawnmower, pitchfork, plough, pruning knife, rake, riddle, scythe, secateurs, shears, shovel, sickle, spade, trowel, wheelbarrow

medical instruments
forceps, lancet, needle, scalpel, splints, stethoscope, tweezers

transport and vehicles

See also aircraft *and* boats and ships

bicycles and *similar vehicles*
bicycle/bike (*informal*), cycle, moped, motorbike/motorcycle, motor scooter, penny-farthing (*old*), rickshaw, scooter, sidecar, tandem, tricycle/trike (*informal*), trishaw

buses and trams:
bus, charabanc, coach, double-decker, minibus, omnibus (*dated*), people mover, single-decker, stagecoach (*old*), tram, tramcar, trolleybus

cars
bubble-car, car, convertible, coupé, estate car, hatchback, jeep, limo (*informal*)/limousine, patrol car, people carrier, snowmobile, sports car, station wagon, taxi

lorries and vans
ambulance, articulated lorry, camper/camper van, dustcart, furniture van, juggernaut, lorry, pantechnicon, pickup/pickup truck (*US*), truck (*US*), van

military vehicles
armoured car, jeep, personnel carrier, tank

railways
carriage, engine, funicular railway/funicular, locomotive, metro, monorail, railway (*US* railroad), sleeper, subway, train, truck, tube, underground

sledges
bobsleigh, sled, sledge, sleigh, toboggan, troika

work vehicles
bulldozer, caterpillar tractor, combine harvester, crane, fire engine, fork-lift truck, roadroller, snowplough, tanker, tractor

other forms of transport
cable-car, caravan, ferry, litter, sedan-chair (*old*), ski-lift

trees and shrubs

conifer, cycad, deciduous tree, evergreen, hardwood, softwood

acacia, apple, apricot, ash, avocado, balsa, banyan, baobab, beech, birch, bo tree/ bodhi tree, box, breadfruit, carob, cedar, cherry, chestnut, coconut, cypress, date palm, deodar, durian, ebony, elder, elm, eucalyptus, fig, fir, gingko, grapefruit, gum tree, hawthorn, hazel, hickory, holly, jackfruit, juniper, kauri, laburnum, larch, lemon, lilac, lime, locust tree, magnolia, mahogany, mango, mangosteen, mangrove, maple, monkey puzzle, mountain ash, oak, palm, peach, pear, persimmon, pine, pipal, plane, plum, poplar, privet, redwood, rowan, rubber, sequoia, spruce, sycamore, tamarind, teak, traveller's tree, walnut, willow, yew, ylang-ylang, yucca

vegetables

brassica, leaf vegetable, root vegetable

aduki bean/adzuki bean, artichoke, asparagus, aubergine, bean, bean sprout, beetroot, broad bean, broccoli, Brussels sprout, butter bean, cabbage, capsicum, carrot, cassava, cauliflower, celeriac, celery, chickpea, chicory, chilli/chilli pepper, Chinese leaves, chives, courgette, cress, cucumber, eggplant (*US*), endive, fennel, French bean, garlic, green bean, horseradish, kale, kidney bean, leek, lentil, lettuce, mange-tout, marrow, mung bean, mushroom, okra, onion, pak choi, parsnip, pea, pepper, petits pois, potato, pumpkin, radish, runner bean, shallot, soya bean, spinach, spring onion, sugar beet, swede, sweetcorn, sweet potato, tomato, turnip, watercress, yam, zucchini (*US*)

vehicles

parts of vehicles

ABS, accelerator (*US* gas pedal), airbag, air-conditioning, anti-lock braking system, anti-roll bar, ashtray, axle, battery, bodywork, bonnet (*US* hood), boot (*US* trunk), brake, brake light, brake pad, bumper (*US* fender), catalytic converter, central locking, chassis, clutch, courtesy light, crankshaft, dashboard, dimmer, disc brake, door, door-lock, engine, exhaust pipe, fog lamp, fuel gauge, gearbox, gear change/gear lever/gear stick/(*US*) gear shift, glove compartment, headlight, headrest, heater, horn, hubcap, ignition, ignition key, indicator, instrument panel, mirror, number plate (*US* license plate), petrol tank (*US* gas tank), rear light, rearview mirror, roof-rack, reversing light (*US* backup light), seat, seatbelt, shock absorber, sidelight, silencer (*US* muffler), speedometer, steering wheel, sunroof, tyre (*US* tire), wheel, window, windscreen (*US* windshield), windscreen-wiper, wing, wing mirror

weapons

axes and clubs

axe, battleaxe, club, hatchet, knobkerrie, shillelagh, tomahawk, truncheon

bombs

atom bomb, ballistic missile, bomb, bullet, cluster bomb, depth-charge, grapeshot, grenade, guided missile, hand-grenade, H-bomb, hydrogen bomb, incendiary bomb, landmine, mine, Molotov cocktail, napalm bomb, petrol bomb, shrapnel, time-bomb, torpedo

guns

airgun, air rifle, automatic, bazooka, blunderbuss (*old*), Bren gun, cannon, field gun, gun, howitzer, kalashnikov, machine-gun, mortar, musket (*old*), petard (*old*), pistol, revolver, rifle, shotgun, sten gun, sub-machine gun, tommy-gun

knives and swords

bayonet, Bowie knife, broadsword, claymore, cutlass, dagger, dirk, epee, flick-knife, foil, knife, kris, kukri, machete, penknife, rapier, scimitar, skean dhu, stiletto, sword

spears and arrows

arrow, assegai, bolt, bow and arrow, crossbow, halberd (*old*), harpoon, lance, longbow, pike, spear

other weapons

blowpipe, boomerang, catapult, flame-thrower, poison gas, sling

weather

mist and fog

cloud, fog, heat haze, mist, sea mist, smog

rain and storms

cloudburst, deluge, downpour, drizzle, lightning, raindrop, shower, tempest, thunder, thunderstorm, tropical storm

snow and ice

black ice, blizzard, frost, hail, hoar frost, ice, icicle, slush, sleet, snow, snowfall, snowflake, snowstorm

sun and hot weather

dog days (*literary*), drought, dry spell, heatwave, Indian summer, scorcher (*informal*), sun, sunshine

winds

anticyclone, breeze, cyclone, dust devil, easterly, east wind, gale, hurricane, monsoon, northerly, north wind, sea breeze, southerly, south wind, squall, tornado, typhoon, trade wind, twister (*US*), water spout (*US*), westerly, west wind, whirlwind, wind, zephyr (*literary*)

other weather words

cold front, dew, rainbow, sandstorm, thaw, warm front

writing materials and instruments

ballpoint pen/ballpoint, Bic®, Biro®, blotter, blotting paper, carbon paper, chalk, correction fluid, crayon, envelope, eraser, felt-tip/felt-tip pen, ink, notebook, notelet, notepad, notepaper, paper, pen, pencil, pencil sharpener, postcard, rubber, window envelope, writing paper

zodiac

air signs, earth signs, fire signs, water signs

[*The signs of the zodiac are listed in order of their occurrence, beginning in January.*]

Aquarius (the Water-carrier), Pisces (the Fish), Aries (the Ram), Taurus (the Bull), Gemini (the Twins), Cancer (the Crab), Leo (the Lion), Virgo (the Virgin), Libra (the Scales), Scorpio (the Scorpion), Sagittarius (the Archer), Capricorn (the Goat)

DO IT YOURSELF

A Choose the correct word from those given in brackets to complete the following sentences.

1. A *salmon* is a type of _____ . (bird, fish, flower)

2. A *parsnip* is a kind of _____ . (fruit, tree, vegetable)

3. A *monsoon* is a kind of _____ . (wind, aeroplane, boat)

4. A *lance* is a _____ . (rank in the army, weapon, tool)

5. A *balaclava* is a _____ . (musical instrument, bone, hat)

6. A *chateau* is a kind of _____ . (bag, cake, building)

7. An *iris* is a kind of _____ . (bird, flower, cake)

8. A *barrow* is a kind of _____ . (garden tool, bird, animal)

9. A *bear* is a kind of _____ . (garden tool, bird, animal)

10. A *downpour* is a period of _____ weather. (hot, wet, rainy)

11. *Dividers* are a tool for _____ with. (cutting, drawing, sawing)

12. A *mussel* is _____ . (a part of the body, a part of a plant, a shellfish)

13. A *trowel* is a _____ . (vehicle, tool, fish)

14. A *chrysanthemum* is a kind of _____ . (insect, flower, musical instrument)

15. An *axle* is _____ . (a tool, an animal, a part of a vehicle)

16. A *hubcap* is _____ . (a hat, part of a vehicle, a weapon)

17. *Rum* is the name of a _____ . (dance, drink, shoe)

18. A *porch* is _____ . (a tree, part of a computer, part of a building)

19. A *pointer* is a _____ . (dog, snake, fish)

20. A *femur* is a _____ . (dance, bone, animal)

21. A *lemur* is a _____ . (dance, bone, animal)

22. A *moccasin* is a _____ . (spice, shoe, bottle)

23. A *water moccasin* is a _____ . (plant, fish, snake)

24. A *flask* is a type of _____ . (bag, box, bottle)

25. A *foxtrot* is a _____ . (dance, bone, animal)

B Choose the correct word from those given in brackets to complete the following sentences.

1. I need a new *table*. Do you know where there's a good _____ shop? (tool, furniture)

2. I want to buy a *goldfish*. Do you know where there's a good _____ shop? (fish, pet)

3. I must buy some *scones*. Where's the nearest _____ ? (bakery, pharmacy)

4. I need some *money*. Where's the nearest _____ ? (cash-and-carry, bank)

5. We need more *sugar*. Pop along to the _____ for me, will you? (grocer's, greengrocer's)

6. I bought some lovely *flowers* at the _____ on the way home. (bank, florist)

7. I can't eat this. It has *pecans* in it and I'm allergic to _____ . (cereals, nuts)

8. Lots of people keep *birds* as pets. My mother has a _____ (budgerigar, didgeridoo, cockatoo)

C Choose the correct colour (black, blue, brown, green, red, purple, etc) to complete the following sentences.

1. *Indigo* is a variety of _____ .

2. *Ebony* is a variety of _____ .

3. *Vermilion* is a variety of _____ .

4. *Lilac* is a variety of _____ .

5. *Crimson* is a variety of _____ .

6. *Fawn* is a variety of _____ .

7. *Tan* is a variety of _____ .

8. *Lavender* is a variety of _____ .

9. *Maroon* is a variety of _____ .

10. *Auburn* is a variety of _____ .

3 ▷ **Antonyms**

Antonyms are words that are opposite in meaning.

How to use the lists of antonyms

▶ When a word has more than one meaning or belongs to more than one part of speech, the antonyms for each meaning or part of speech are given separately, following the same system as for the synonym lists in Unit 1.

In addition, the # symbol is used in this unit to indicate a change in meaning within a list of synonyms. For example in the entry for the verb **stop** the synonym list reads *begin, commence (formal), start # carry on, continue, go on, persevere, persist*. This means that in one way the opposite of **to stop** is **to begin**, **to commence** or **to start**, while in another way the opposite of **to stop** is **to carry on**, **to continue**, etc. Similarly, at **night** we have *day # morning*, which means that in one sense the opposite of **night** is *day* while in another sense the opposite of **night** is *morning*.

▶ *Formal, informal, slang* and *literary* words have been labelled as such in the lists of antonyms. American words have been labelled *US*.

▶ The lists in this unit should be used in conjunction with the synonym lists in Unit 1. To avoid needless duplication, not all possible antonyms have been included in the entries and further antonyms may be found by referring to the lists of synonyms. For example, given **mad** as one of the antonyms of **sane**, cross-referring to the list of synonyms for **mad** in Unit 1 will produce a longer list of possible antonyms for **sane**: *crazy, daft, deranged, foolish, …*

▶ As with synonyms, it may occasionally be necessary to refer to a dictionary in order to ascertain the exact grammar and usage of the antonyms listed.

abandon

LEAVE: remain with, stay with, maintain, keep, support

GIVE UP: continue, keep on, persist, persevere

abandoned

DESERTED: inhabited, in use, occupied

WICKED: decent, modest, respectable, restrained, seemly

abbreviate

amplify, expand, extend, increase, lengthen

ability

inability, inadequacy, incompetence, ineptitude

able

helpless, incapable, incompetent, impotent, unable

abnormal

average, common, normal, routine, typical, usual

abolish

continue, keep, retain # create, found, initiate, start

abominable

delightful, desirable, nice, pleasant

about

exactly, precisely

above

below, under, underneath

abrupt

QUICK: gradual, leisurely, slow

RUDE: civil, courteous, polite, well-mannered

absence

appearance, attendance, existence, presence

absent

at home, at work, here, in attendance, present, there

absent-minded

alert, attentive, aware, careful, concentrating, mindful, on the ball (*informal*)

absolute

conditional, limited, partial, slight

abstract

actual, concrete, practical, real

absurd

logical, plausible, rational, reasonable, sensible, wise

abundance

dearth, deficiency, lack, scarcity

abundant

lacking, rare, scarce, sparse

accelerate

CAUSE TO GO FASTER: delay, hamper, hinder, impede, retard, slow, slow down

GO FASTER: brake, slow, slow down

accept

TAKE: decline, refuse, reject, spurn, turn down

AGREE: deny, disagree, dispute, dissent, reject, quibble

TOLERATE: appeal, complain about, object, oppose, protest, take exception

acceptable

intolerable, unacceptable, unsatisfactory, unwelcome

acceptance

TAKING: refusal, rejection

AGREEMENT: denial, disagreement, dispute, dissent, rejection, quibble

TOLERATING: complaint, exception, objection, opposition, protest

accidental

deliberate, intentional, planned

acclaim

verb condemn, criticize, disapprove, disparage, scorn

noun condemnation, criticism, disapproval, disparagement, scorn

accuracy

approximation, impreciseness, imprecision, inaccuracy, vagueness

accurate

approximate, imprecise, inaccurate, incorrect, inexact, rough, vague

achieve fail, fall short of, miss

acknowledge

AGREE: deny

PAY ATTENTION TO: cold-shoulder, disown, ignore, snub

acquire

forfeit, give away, lose, relinquish, sell

acquit

condemn, convict, sentence

active

FUNCTIONING: dormant, inactive, inert, passive

DOING MANY THINGS: idle, lazy, lethargic

COMMITTED: armchair, uncommitted

IN GRAMMAR: passive

actual

apparent, imaginary, possible, theoretical

acute

SERIOUS: mild, minor, slight

SUDDEN: chronic

add

deduct, delete, remove, subtract, take away

addition

deletion, removal, subtraction

additional

fewer, less

adequate

inadequate, insufficient, unacceptable, unsatisfactory

adjacent

distant, far-away, remote, separate

adjourn

convene, start # continue, go on

admirable

contemptible, deplorable, despicable, pathetic, poor, wicked, worthless

admiration

contempt, disdain, dislike, hatred, scorn

admire

despise, disdain, dislike, hate, look down on, scorn, sneer at

admit

CONFESS: deny, reject

LET IN: bar, exclude, keep out, shut out

ALLOW: disallow, prevent, prohibit

adore

abhor, detest, dislike, hate, loathe

adult

noun child, infant, juvenile (*formal*), youngster

adjective immature, juvenile (*formal*), small, young

advance

verb GO FORWARD: retire, retreat, withdraw

verb MAKE PROGRESS: delay, hamper, hinder, hold back, impede, retard

noun FORWARD MOVEMENT: retreat, withdrawal

noun PROGRESS: decay, decline, deterioration, fall, worsening

advantage

disadvantage, drawback, flaw, problem, snag, weakness

adverse
advantageous, beneficial, favourable, helpful

adversity
good fortune, prosperity, success

affection
antipathy, coldness, dislike, hatred, loathing

affectionate
cold, distant, undemonstrative, unfriendly

affirm
deny, reject

affirmative
negative

afraid
bold, brave, confident, courageous, unafraid

after
before

afterwards
before, beforehand

against
for

aggravate
ANNOY: appease, calm, mollify, pacify, placate, soothe
WORSEN: alleviate, improve, moderate, reduce, relieve

aggressive
calm, docile, gentle, meek, peaceful, placid, submissive

agile
awkward, clumsy, lumbering, stiff

agree
BE IN AGREEMENT: conflict, contradict, differ, disagree, dissent, diverge
BE WILLING: decline, refuse

agreeable
PLEASANT: disagreeable, nasty, objectionable, repulsive, unfriendly, unpleasant
WILLING: disinclined, loath, reluctant, unenthusiastic, unwilling

agreement
HARMONY: argument, conflict, disagreement, dissent, friction, strife
CONSISTENCY: clash, disagreement, discrepancy, inconsistency
WILLINGNESS: disinclination, refusal, reluctance, unwillingness

ahead
behind

aid
verb hamper, handicap, hinder, hold back, hold up, impede, obstruct, slow
noun handicap, hindrance, impediment, obstacle, obstruction

alarm
calm, reassure, relax, quieten, soothe

alert
absent-minded, asleep, inactive, inattentive, unwary

alike
different, dissimilar, unalike, unlike

alive
LIVING: dead, lifeless # extinct
LIVELY: dull, inactive, lethargic, sluggish

all
determiner: no # a few, part of, some
pronoun: none, nothing # some
adverb: partly, partially, slightly, to some extent

allow
PERMIT: ban, bar, disallow, forbid, prevent, veto, withhold
AGREE: deny, disagree, reject

ally
adversary, antagonist, enemy, foe (*literary*), opponent

alone
accompanied, chaperoned, escorted, together

alter
fix, keep, maintain, retain

always
never # occasionally, sometimes

amateur
professional

amazed
blasé, calm, indifferent, unimpressed

ambiguous
clear, definite, unambiguous

amiable
disagreeable, hostile, nasty, rude, unfriendly, unpleasant, unsociable

ample
inadequate, insufficient, lacking, meagre, scant, scarce

amusing
boring, dull, serious, solemn, tedious

anarchy
law and order, order, system

ancestor
descendant, offspring

ancient
contemporary, current, modern, new, present-day, up-to-date; *see also* old

angel
demon, devil, evil spirit, fiend

anger
noun appeasement, calmness, forbearance, forgiveness, propitiation
verb appease, calm, pacify, please, propitiate, soothe

angry
calm, content, happy, patient, pleased

annoy
appease, calm, gratify, pacify, please, soothe

annoyed
glad, happy, pleased

annoying
agreeable, delightful, gratifying, pleasant, pleasing, welcome

answer
noun REPLY: inquiry, query, question
noun SOLUTION: dilemma, predicament, problem, puzzle
verb ask, enquire/inquire, query

antique
contemporary, modern, new, present-day, up-to-date; *see also* old

anxiety
calmness, composure, confidence, coolness, equanimity, serenity

anxious
calm, carefree, composed, confident, cool, placid, unafraid, untroubled

apart
connected, joined, together, united

appear
disappear, leave, go, vanish

appease
aggravate, anger, annoy, infuriate, irritate

applaud
censure, condemn, criticize, disapprove of, disparage, scorn

applause
censure, condemnation, criticism, disapproval, disparagement, scorn

appoint
dismiss, fire, sack (*informal*) # reject

apprentice
expert, master

appropriate
ill-timed, improper, inapplicable, inappropriate, irrelevant, unsuitable, untimely

approve
censure, condemn, criticize, disapprove, disparage, scorn

approximately
absolutely, exactly, precisely

arrest
verb free, liberate, release, set free
noun liberation, release

arrival
departure

arrive
depart, leave

arrogant
deferential, humble, meek, modest, self-effacing, unassuming # obsequious, sycophantic

artificial
authentic, genuine, natural, real

ascend
climb down, descend, go down

ascent
descent

ashamed
defiant, glad, impenitent, proud, unabashed, unashamed, unrepentant

ask
answer, reply, respond

asleep
awake

assemble
GATHER: disperse, scatter, separate
BUILD: disassemble, dismantle, take to pieces

assert
deny, rebut, refute

asset
disadvantage, drawback, liability

assist
hamper, hinder, hold back, impede, prevent, stop, thwart

assistance
hindrance, impediment, obstacle, resistance

attach
detach, unfasten, untie

attack
noun defence, resistance # retreat, withdrawal
verb defend, repulse, resist # retreat, withdraw

attention
carelessness, disregard, inattention

attract
disgust, nauseate, repel, repulse

attractive
disagreeable, horrible, repulsive, unappealing, unattractive, uninviting, unpleasant

avoidable
inevitable, unavoidable

awful
agreeable, good, great, nice, pleasant

awake
asleep

awkward
CLUMSY: careful, elegant, graceful
INCONVENIENT: convenient, opportune, suitable, timely
NOT CO-OPERATIVE: amenable, co-operative, easy-going, helpful, pleasant, undemanding, willing
NOT RELAXED: at ease, comfortable, relaxed

back
front

backwards
forwards, onwards

bad
UNPLEASANT: enjoyable, good, nice, pleasant
UNSATISFACTORY: adequate, competent, good, perfect, satisfactory, skilful
HARMFUL: beneficial, good, harmless
EVIL: good, honest, honourable, virtuous
NAUGHTY: good, obedient, well-behaved
MOULDY: fresh
SEVERE: mild, slight
ILL, SICK: good, well

badly
NOT WELL: adequately, competently, satisfactorily, well
VERY: a bit, a little, slightly

ban
verb allow, approve, authorize, permit
noun approval, authorization, dispensation, permission

barbaric
civilized, cultured, enlightened, sophisticated; *see also* cruel

barren
fertile, fruitful, productive, rich

base
apex, peak, summit, tip, top

bashful
confident, forward, self-assured, self-confident

bearable
insufferable, insupportable, intolerable, unbearable

beautiful
disagreeable, hideous, repulsive, ugly, unattractive

before
after

beforehand
afterwards

begin
cease (*formal*), end, finish, quit, stop

beginning
end, finale, finish

behave
misbehave

behind
preposition ahead of, before, in front of
adverb ahead, forward, in front

belief
agnosticism, atheism, disbelief, doubt, scepticism

believable
amazing, beyond belief, fantastic, inconceivable, incredible, unbelievable

believe
agnostic, atheist, disbelieve, distrust, doubt, mistrust, question

believer
doubter, doubting Thomas, sceptic, unbeliever

below
: *adverb* above, on top
preposition above, on top of

beneath *see* below

beneficial
: detrimental, harmful, unhelpful, useless

benefit
: damage, detriment, disadvantage, harm

best
: worst

better
: inferior, worse

big
: LARGE: little, small
OLD: little, small, young
IMPORTANT: humble, insignificant, minor, unimportant

bitter
: SOUR: sweet
UNHAPPY: contented, happy, pleased, satisfied
COLD: balmy, hot, mild, warm

blame
: *verb* approve, commend, praise, vindicate
noun approval, commendation, praise, vindication

bless
: blame, condemn, curse, scorn

blessing
: BENEFIT: disadvantage, drawback
APPROVAL: blame, condemnation, curse, scorn

blossom
: fade, wither

blunt
: NOT SHARP: keen, pointed, sharp
RUDE: diplomatic, polite, sensitive, tactful

boastful
: humble, modest, quiet, self-effacing, unassuming

bold
: bashful, cautious, diffident, faint-hearted, shy, timid, timorous

boring
: eventful, exciting, imaginative, inspiring, interesting, lively, stimulating

borrow
: give, lend

bottom
: top; *see also* base

bow (of ship)
: stern

brave
: cowardly, faint-hearted, spineless, timid, timorous

bravery
: cowardice, faint-heartedness, fear, spinelessness, timidity

break
: DAMAGE: mend, repair
DISOBEY: keep, maintain, obey, observe

brief
: LASTING A SHORT TIME: lengthy, long, protracted
SPEAKING A SHORT TIME: long-winded, tedious, verbose

bright
: SHINING: dark, dim, dull, tarnished
CLEVER: dim, dull, stupid, thick (*informal*)
CHEERFUL: depressed, depressing, gloomy, glum, sad

brilliant
: EXCELLENT: average, poor, undistinguished
BRIGHT: dim, dull
CLEVER *see* bright

bring
> remove, take

broad
> LARGE: cramped, narrow, restricted
> NOT EXACT: exact, precise

brutal
> gentle, humane, kind, kindly, merciful

build
> demolish, destroy, knock down, raze

bury
> dig up, exhume (*formal*), unearth

busy
> free, idle, inactive, unoccupied

buy
> sell

calm
> *adjective* NOT WORRIED: anxious, disturbed, flustered, nervous, troubled, worked up, worried
> *adjective* NOT EXCITED: elated, enthusiastic, excited, thrilled
> *adjective* NOT STORMY: blustery, stormy, wild, windy
> *adjective* SAID OF THE SEA: choppy, rough
> *verb* agitate, disturb, frighten, worry

capability
> inability, incapability, incompetence, inefficiency

capable
> incapable, incompetent, inefficient, unable, unfit, unsuited

captivity
> freedom, liberty

capture
> *verb* free, liberate, release, rescue, set free
> *noun* liberation, release, rescue

care
> carelessness, inattention, negligence, shoddiness, slackness, sloppiness

careful
> WORKING WITH CARE: careless, inattentive, slipshod, sloppy
> BEING CAUTIOUS: reckless, unwary

careless
> NOT WORKING WITH CARE: accurate, careful, meticulous, painstaking
> NOT CAUTIOUS: cautious, wary

catch
> NOT DROP: drop, miss
> TAKE HOLD OF: free, release, set free

cause
> consequence, effect, result

cautious
> careless, heedless, impetuous, imprudent, incautious, reckless

cease
> begin, commence (*formal*), start # continue, go on, keep going

central
> distant, marginal, outlying, out-of-the-way, peripheral

centre
> border, edge, outside, perimeter, periphery
> CENTRE OF TOWN: outskirts, suburbs

certain
> HAVING NO DOUBTS: doubtful, hesitant, uncertain, unsure
> CAUSING NO DOUBTS: inconclusive, uncertain, unconvincing, unlikely, unreliable

chance
> *noun* certainty # plan
> *adjective* deliberate, intentional, planned

change

keep, preserve, retain

chaos

order, organization, system

charming

repulsive, ugly, unattractive, unfriendly, uninviting, unpleasant

cheap

costly, dear, expensive

cheer

verb SHOUT HOORAY: boo, jeer
verb MAKE CHEERFUL: depress, discourage, dishearten, sadden
noun boo, catcall, jeer

cheerful

HAPPY: dejected, depressed, gloomy, moody, sad
CAUSING HAPPINESS: depressing, gloomy, sad

chief

junior, least, minor, unimportant

child

adult, grown-up (*informal*)

childhood

adulthood, manhood, maturity, old age, womanhood

childish

adult, mature, sensible

civilized

barbaric, barbarous, primitive, savage, uncivilized

clean

adjective dirty, filthy, impure, polluted, tarnished
verb dirty, pollute, soil, stain, tarnish

clear

DEFINITE: ambiguous, confused, confusing, fuzzy, inexplicit, muddled, vague

CERTAIN: uncertain, unconvinced, unsure
ABLE TO BE SEEN THROUGH: cloudy, opaque, translucent
BRIGHT: cloudy, dull, foggy, misty, overcast

clever

foolish, senseless, stupid, thick (*informal*), unwise

climb

descend, go down

close

adjective distant, far, faraway, far-flung
verb SHUT: open
verb END: begin, commence (*formal*), start
noun beginning, commencement (*formal*), opening, start

closed

open, unfastened, unlocked

cloudy

bright, clear, cloudless, sunny

clumsy

deft, elegant, graceful, masterly, nimble

coarse

ROUGH: fine, smooth
NOT POLITE: polished, polite, refined, sophisticated

cold

NOT WARM: boiling (*informal*), hot, roasting (*informal*), warm
NOT SYMPATHETIC: enthusiastic, friendly, responsive, sympathetic, warm, welcoming

collect

disperse, distribute, scatter, spread

combine

divide, separate, split, split up # isolate, segregate

come

depart, go, go away, leave

comic
sad, serious, solemn, tragic

command
obey

common
EVERYDAY: infrequent, out of the ordinary, rare, uncommon, unconventional, unfamiliar, unusual
INFERIOR: refined, superior
SHARED: personal, private, unique

compassion
cruelty, hard-heartedness, indifference, inhumanity, ruthlessness

complete
incomplete, partial

complex
easy, elementary, simple, straightforward

complicate
simplify

complicated *see* complex

compliment
noun blame, criticism, insult
verb blame, criticize, insult, slate (*informal*)

compulsory
discretionary, optional, voluntary

concave
convex

conceal
disclose, display, reveal, show, uncover

conceited
humble, modest, self-effacing, unassuming

concentrated
SAID OF LIQUID: dilute, diluted, watered down
SAID OF ACTIONS: random, sporadic

concise
lengthy, long, unabridged, uncut, wordy

concrete
abstract, theoretical, vague

condemn
BLAME: approve, commend, praise
DECLARE GUILTY: absolve, acquit, exonerate, reprieve, vindicate

confident
afraid, anxious, diffident, doubtful, nervous, timid, uncertain, worried

confirm
deny, rebut, refute

conflict
verb agree, be in harmony, harmonize
noun agreement, friendship, harmony, peace

confused
NOT CLEAR: clear, definite
IN DISORDER: neat, orderly, organized, tidy

confusion
NOT BEING CLEAR: clarity, explicitness, precision, unambiguousness
NOT BEING TIDY: order, organization, system, tidiness

connect
detach, disconnect

constant
intermittent, irregular, occasional, sporadic

constructive
destructive, negative, unhelpful

contempt
admiration, regard

content, contented
bitter, discontented, displeased, dissatisfied, unhappy, unwilling

continual
continuous, unbroken, uninterrupted

continuous
broken, continual, discontinuous, intermittent, irregular, repeated, sporadic

contract
dilate, enlarge, expand, grow, increase, spread, widen

contradict
agree, concur, confirm, correspond, corroborate, square with

contrast
likeness, similarity # monotony, sameness

convex
concave

convict
absolve, acquit, exonerate, reprieve, vindicate

cool
NOT WARM: balmy, hot, warm
NOT FRIENDLY: affectionate, friendly, sympathetic, warm, welcoming
NOT ENTHUSIASTIC: ardent, enthusiastic, excited, keen, lively, warm
CALM: excited, flustered, nervous, worried

correct
inaccurate, incorrect, inexact, mistaken, wrong

country
town

courage
cowardice, faint-heartedness, fear, spinelessness, timidity

courageous
afraid, faint-hearted, spineless, timid, timorous

courteous
brusque, churlish, discourteous, impolite, insolent, rude, uncivil

cover
disclose, expose, reveal, uncover, unearth, unveil

coward
hero

cowardice
bravery, courage, daring, heroism, valour (*formal*)

cowardly
brave, courageous, daring, heroic

cramped
large, roomy, spacious

crazy
plausible, rational, reasonable, sane, sensible, wise

create
destroy

creditor
debtor

criticize
commend, extol, praise, support

cruel
compassionate, gentle, kind, humane, merciful

cruelty
compassion, kindness, mercy

cunning
guileless, honest, open # ingenuous, innocent, naïve

curse
verb bless
noun blessing

damage
fix, mend, repair

danger
safety, security

dangerous
harmless, innocuous, safe, secure

daring
adjective afraid, cautious, cowardly, spineless, timid
noun caution, cowardice, fear, spinelessness, timidity

dark
bright, light, shining

darkness
brightness, daylight, light

dawn
dusk, sunset

day
night

dead
alive, living

deadly
harmless, innocuous, non-poisonous, non-toxic, safe

defeat
victory

dear
COSTLY: cheap, inexpensive
LOVED: disliked, hated, hateful, unloved

death
birth # life

debtor
creditor

decline
verb NOT ACCEPT: accept, acquiesce, agree

verb DECREASE: develop, expand, increase, intensify, multiply, rise, spread # improve, rally, recover
noun expansion, extension, increase, intensification, rise, spread # improvement, recovery

decrease
verb expand, extend, increase, intensify, multiply, rise, spread
noun expansion, extension, increase, intensification, rise, spread

deep
HAVING A LOT OF WATER: shallow
GOING DOWN FAR: high
THOROUGH: hasty, passing, shallow, superficial
STRONG: mild, slight

defend
accuse, attack

deficit
excess, surfeit, surplus # sufficiency

delete
add, insert # keep, retain

deliberate *see* intentional

delicate
POWERFUL: brawny, healthy, not powerful, robust, rough, strong
HARD-WEARING: coarse, not hard-wearing, strong, tough

delicious
horrible, unappetizing, unpalatable, unpleasant

delighted
disappointed, dismayed, displeased, sad, sorry, unhappy

delightful
disagreeable, horrible, repulsive, ugly, unattractive, unfriendly, unpleasant

demand
supply

deny
SAY NO: accept, admit, agree, allow
NOT GIVE: afford, allow, give, permit

depart
appear, arrive, come, come back, reach, return # stay

departure
appearance, arrival, coming, return

depressed
bright, cheerful, happy

depth
HEIGHT: shallowness # height
THOROUGHNESS: hastiness, perfunctoriness, shallowness, superficiality

descendant
ancestor, forebear, forefather (*literary*)

descend
ascend, go up, rise

descent
ascent

desert
remain, stand by, stay, support # enlist, join

despair
cheerfulness, happiness, hope, resilience

despise
admire, appreciate, esteem, like, love, prize, revere

destroy
build, create # keep, maintain, preserve

destructive
beneficial, constructive, helpful, useful

devil
angel

die
live, survive

differ
AGREE: disagree, concur
BE DIFFERENT: correspond, match, tally

different
NOT ALIKE: alike, identical, same, similar, uniform
NOT NORMAL: conventional, normal, ordinary, run-of-the-mill, usual

difficult
NOT EASY: easy, simple, straightforward
NOT CO-OPERATIVE: co-operative, easy-going, manageable, undemanding

difficulty
ease

dilute
concentrated

diminish
boost, enhance, increase, raise, strengthen

dirty
NOT CLEAN: clean, pure, spotless, sterile, uncontaminated
OBSCENE: clean, decent, pure

disagreeable
agreeable, amiable, charming, enjoyable, friendly, nice, pleasant

disappear
appear, arrive, emerge, show up, turn up

disappoint
delight, please, satisfy

disaster
SOMETHING DISASTROUS: success, triumph
SOMETHING UNWANTED: blessing, godsend

disciple
guide, guru, master, teacher

discourage
buoy up, cheer, comfort, encourage, hearten, inspire, reassure, rouse, spur

disgrace
honour, respect

dislike
noun attachment, fondness, like, liking, love
verb adore, be fond of, enjoy, favour, like, love

dismal
DULL: bright, cheerful, happy, joyful
POOR: commendable, excellent, good, outstanding, satisfactory, splendid

dismiss
PUT OUT OF EMPLOYMENT: appoint, employ, engage # keep on, retain
ACCEPT: accept, admit, agree, allow

disorder
neatness, order, organization, system, tidiness

disperse
accumulate, assemble, collect, congregate, gather, group

display
camouflage, conceal, cover, hide, mask, obscure, screen

dissatisfied
content, contented, happy, pleased, satisfied

dissuade
persuade

distant
NOT FAR: close, near
NOT FRIENDLY: approachable, close, cordial, friendly, warm, welcoming

divide
amalgamate, join, merge, unify, unite

doubtful
FEELING NO DOUBT: certain, confident, definite, satisfied, sure
CAUSING NO DOUBT: agreed, assured, certain, decided, definite, fixed, settled

dress
undress

drunk
sober

dry
adjective NOT WET: damp, humid, moist, soaking, wet
adjective BORING: interesting, lively, stimulating
adjective SAID OF WINE: sweet
verb dampen, moisten, soak, wet

dull
NOT LIGHT: bright, sunny
NOT INTERESTING: exciting, interesting, stimulating
NOT INTELLIGENT: alert, bright, brilliant, clever, intelligent, sharp, smart
NOT SHARP: sharp

dusk
dawn, daybreak, sunrise

dwarf
noun giant
adjective enormous, huge, giant

eager
apathetic, bored, indifferent, lukewarm, reluctant, unenthusiastic

early
late # on time, punctual

easy
complex, complicated, demanding, difficult, hard, puzzling

ebb
flow

economical
extravagant, uneconomical, wasteful

edge
centre, core, heart, middle

effect
cause

elder
younger

elegant
SAID OF BEHAVIOUR, ETC: awkward, clumsy, inelegant, ungainly
SAID OF CLOTHES, ETC: unfashionable, unsophisticated

emigrant
immigrant

emigrate
immigrate

emphasize
gloss over, play down, understate

employ
dismiss, sack (*informal*)

employee
employer

employer
employee

empty
adjective crammed, crowded, filled, full, loaded, stuffed
verb cram, crowd, fill, load, stuff

encourage
depress, discourage, dishearten, dismay

end
noun beginning, birth, commencement (*formal*), onset, outset, start
verb begin, commence (*formal*), start

enemy
ally, comrade, friend

enjoy
abhor, detest, dislike, hate, loathe

enjoyable
boring, disagreeable, unpleasant

enormous
insignificant, minute, tiny; *see also* big

enough
inadequate, insufficient, lacking, short

enthusiastic
apathetic, bored, cool, indifferent, listless, unenthusiastic

entrance
exit, way out

envious *see* jealous

essential
inessential, optional, unimportant, unnecessary

even
SAID OF NUMBERS: odd, uneven
EQUAL: asymmetrical, disparate, disproportionate, one-sided, unequal

evening
morning

evil
noun goodness, righteousness, virtue
adjective good, honourable, righteous, virtuous

exact
ballpark (*informal*), broad, fuzzy, imprecise, inaccurate, inexact, vague

excellent
bad, dismal, inadequate, inferior, poor, second-rate, unsatisfactory

excess

dearth, deficiency, lack, moderation, shortage, shortfall

excited

apathetic, blasé, bored, calm, cool, unenthusiastic, unimpressed

exciting

boring, dreary, dull, tedious, unexciting

exclude

admit, allow in, include, let in

exclusion

inclusion

exhale

breathe in, inhale

exit

entrance, way in

expand

abbreviate, abridge, compress, contract, shorten, shrink

expected

startling, sudden, unexpected, unforeseen, unplanned

expensive

cheap, cut-price, inexpensive, low-cost

expert

apprentice, learner, novice

export

import

extend

contract, curtail, cut, lessen, reduce, shorten

exterior

interior, inside

external

internal, inside

extraordinary

commonplace, everyday, normal, ordinary, run-of-the-mill, usual

extravagant

careful, economical, thrifty # mean, miserly

fail

pass, prosper, succeed, triumph

failure

pass, success, triumph

fair

JUST: biased, prejudiced, unfair, unjust
LIGHT-HAIRED: brunette, dark

fall

verb escalate, increase, intensify, mount, proliferate, rise, soar
noun escalation, increase, intensification, proliferation, rise, upsurge

false

NOT TRUE OR GENUINE: accurate, authentic, correct, genuine, honest, real, true, valid
NOT FAITHFUL: faithful, honest, loyal, reliable, trustworthy

familiar

foreign, new, strange, unaccustomed, unfamiliar, unusual

famine

abundance, plenty # excess, glut, surfeit

famous

obscure, unheard of, unknown, unrecognised, unsung

fancy

plain, simple, unadorned

far

close, near, nearby

fascinating

boring, dreary, dry, tedious, uninspiring, uninteresting

fast

adjective gradually, leisurely, plodding, ponderous, slow, unhurried

adverb gradually, leisurely, ponderously, slowly, unhurriedly

fasten

detach, loosen, undo, unfasten, untie

fat

lean, slender, slim, thin

fear

bravery, confidence, courage, heroism

fearless

afraid, faint-hearted, frightened, spineless, timid, timorous

feeble

NOT STRONG: powerful, robust, strong, sturdy

LACKING FORCE: concentrated, formidable, intense, potent, strong

NOT GOOD: adequate, excellent, good, satisfactory

NOT CONVINCING: compelling, convincing, persuasive

female

male; *see also* feminine

feminine

manly, masculine; *see also* female

fertile

arid, barren, desert, infertile

few

countless, innumerable, lots of, many, numerous

fierce

calm, friendly, gentle, kind, mild

fill

clear, drain, empty, unload

final

first, initial, introductory, opening

find

lose, mislay, misplace

fine

coarse, rough, thick

finish

noun begin, commence (*formal*), start

verb begin, commencement (*formal*), start

finite

boundless, endless, infinite, unending, unlimited

firm

SOLID: flabby, floppy, soft, spongy

STABLE: rocky, unstable, unsteady, wobbly

DEFINITE: hesitant, uncertain, undecided

first

final, last, latest

fit

HEALTHY: unfit, unhealthy, weak

SUITABLE: incapable, incompetent, unfit, unworthy

flexible

hard, inflexible, rigid, stiff

float

sink

flow

ebb

follow

lead

follower

commander, leader, master, ringleader

folly

common sense, good sense, prudence, sense, wisdom

foolish
clever, prudent, smart, sensible, wise

foolishness *see* folly

forbid
agree to, allow, approve, consent to, permit

foreign
indigenous, local, native, resident

foreigner
local, native, resident

forget
remember

forgive
blame, censure, punish

former
latter # current, present

fortunate
regrettable, unfortunate, unlucky

forwards
backwards

found
lost

free
verb arrest, capture, confine, enslave, imprison, restrain, restrict, tie up
adjective NOT ATTACHED OR RESTRICTED: attached, tied, unconfined
adjective NOT IN USE: busy, in use, occupied

freedom
captivity, confinement, imprisonment, restraint, restriction, slavery

freeze
defrost, melt, thaw, unfreeze

fresh
mouldy, old, stale

friend
antagonist, enemy, foe (*literary*), opponent

friendly
antagonistic, cold, cool, hostile, unfriendly, unsociable, unwelcoming

friendship
antagonism, enmity, hatred, hostility

frighten
calm, quieten, reassure, relax

frightened
bold, brave, calm, composed, cool, courageous, unperturbed, untroubled

frown
smile

front
back, rear

full
COMPLETE: fragmentary, incomplete, limited, partial, superficial
LEAVING NO ROOM: empty

funny
sad, serious, solemn, tragic

future
past # present

gain
verb lose
noun debt, deficit, loss

gather
disperse, distribute, scatter, spread

gay
CHEERFUL: dismal, gloomy, grave, sad, sombre
HOMOSEXUAL: heterosexual, straight (*informal*)

general
limited, particular, special, specific, unique

generous
WILLING TO GIVE: mean, miserly, selfish, stingy (*informal*), tight-fisted (*informal*)
LARGE: meagre, paltry, small

gentle
brutal, cruel, harsh, pitiless, rough, ruthless, severe, stern

genuine
NOT IMITATION: artificial, bogus, counterfeit, fake, false, imitation, phoney, sham
SINCERE: hypocritical, insincere, two-faced

get
give, lose

get off
board, embark, get on, mount

get on
BOARD: alight, disembark, dismount, get off
AGREE: disagree, fight, quarrel

get up
lie down, sit down

giant
noun dwarf, midget
adjective diminutive, dwarf, midget, tiny

give
get, receive, take, withhold # hold on to, keep, retain

glad
annoyed, angry, miserable, sad, unhappy

gloomy
SAD: bright, cheerful, happy, joyful
DARK: bright, light

go
arrive, come # remain, stay

good
WELL DONE, ADEQUATE, SKILLED: amateurish, bad, inadequate, incompetent, inefficient, inexpert, poor, second-rate, unsatisfactory
PLEASANT: bad, disagreeable, unpleasant
FAVOURABLE, USEFUL: bad, inappropriate, inauspicious, inconvenient, inopportune, useless
MORALLY GOOD: bad, disobedient, evil, immoral, mischievous, naughty, wicked
KIND: inconsiderate, unkind
ACCURATE: inaccurate, incorrect, imprecise
NOURISHING: bad, harmful, poisonous

goodbye
hello

gradual
abrupt, immediate, steep, sudden

grateful
unappreciative, ungrateful

gratitude
ingratitude

great
IMPORTANT: insignificant, minor, unimportant, unknown
ENJOYABLE: bad, disagreeable, unpleasant
SKILFUL: amateurish, bad, incompetent, poor, slipshod, sloppy
LARGE: slight, small, tiny

greatest
least

grief
elation, happiness, joy, jubilation, pleasure, satisfaction

grow
abate, contract, decline, decrease, dwindle, shrink, subside

guilty
innocent

habitual

casual, infrequent, occasional, rare

handsome

plain, repulsive, ugly, unattractive

happy

PLEASED: annoyed, angry, discontented
NOT SAD: dismal, gloomy, miserable, sad, solemn, unhappy
WILLING: disinclined, unwilling

hard

DIFFICULT: easy, simple, straightforward
SOLID: flabby, flexible, liquid, pliable, soft, spongy
STERN: kind, lenient, mild, soft

hardworking

idle, indolent, lazy, work-shy

harmful

harmless, innocuous, non-poisonous, non-toxic

harmless

dangerous, destructive, harmful, lethal, noxious, poisonous, toxic

harmony

conflict, discord, dissension, dissent, strife

harsh

SEVERE: gentle, kind, lenient, mild, soft, sympathetic, tender
ROUGH: gentle, smooth, soft

hasty

careful, considered, deliberate, leisurely, slow, unhurried

hate

noun HATING: affection, fondness, liking, love
noun SOMETHING HATED: cup of tea (*informal*), like, love
verb adore, approve of, cherish, esteem, enjoy, like, love, relish

hatred *see* hate

health

illness, sickness

healthy

ill, poorly, sick, sickly, unhealthy, unwell

heaven

hell, torment, torture

heavy

light

hell

bliss, heaven, paradise

height

depth

help

noun hindrance
verb hamper, hinder, impede, retard, slow down # counter, obstruct, oppose

hero

coward

heroism

cowardice

hide

COVER: display, exhibit, expose, reveal, show, uncover
KEEP SECRET: announce, divulge, proclaim, reveal

high

low # deep

hinder

advance, aid, assist, boost, foster, further, help, promote

hit

miss

honest
crooked (*informal*), devious, dishonest, lying, unscrupulous, untruthful

honour
verb blame, censure, criticize, denigrate, disparage, impugn, malign, revile, vilify
noun PRAISE: blame, censure, criticism, denigration, disparagement, vilification
noun DECENCY: disgrace, dishonesty, dishonour, treachery

hope
despair, pessimism

horizontal
erect, vertical

horrible
agreeable, attractive, lovely, nice, pleasant

hostile
enthusiastic, favourable, friendly, warm, welcoming

hot
cold, cool, freezing, mild

huge
insignificant, microscopic, minuscule, minute, tiny; *see also* big

humble
arrogant, big-headed, pretentious, proud, self-important, vain

humorous
grave, serious, solemn

hurry
verb GO QUICKLY: dawdle, loiter, slow down
verb MAKE QUICKER: delay, hinder, hold back, retard, slow down
noun leisureliness

hypocrisy
sincerity

identical
different, dissimilar, unalike

idle
active, busy, energetic, hardworking, industrious

ignorant
aware, knowledgeable, learned, sophisticated, wise

ignorance
awareness, knowledge, sophistication, wisdom

ill
healthy, well

illegal
authorized, lawful, legal, permitted

illness
health, well-being

imaginary
actual, concrete, factual, real, tangible

imitation
authentic, genuine, real

immense *see* huge

immigrant
emigrant

immigrate
emigrate

immune
liable, susceptible

impatient
long-suffering, patient, self-controlled, tolerant, uncomplaining

impolite
courteous, polite, respectful, well-mannered

import
export

important
SIGNIFICANT: insignificant, minor, negligible, petty, trivial, unimportant
FAMOUS: minor, unknown

impossible
achievable, conceivable, feasible, possible, reasonable, workable

impressive
commonplace, dull, mediocre, run-of-the-mill, unimpressive, unremarkable

improbable
believable, convincing, likely, plausible, probable

improve
aggravate, decline, degenerate, deteriorate, exacerbate, worsen

improvement
decline, degeneration, deterioration, worsening

include
eliminate, exclude, keep out, leave out, weed out

inclusion
elimination, exclusion

increase
verb decrease, diminish, drop, fall, lessen, reduce, shrink, subside
noun decrease, drop, fall, reduction

incredible
believable, credible, likely, plausible, possible

inferior
OF POOR QUALITY: better, choice, excellent, first-rate, high-grade, superior
OF LESSER RANK: higher, senior, superior

infinite
finite, limited

inhale
breathe out, exhale

initial
closing, final, last

inner
outer

innocence
LACK OF GUILT: guilt
LACK OF EXPERIENCE: experience, sophistication, wisdom

innocent
NOT GUILTY: guilty
NOT EXPERIENCED: experienced, sophisticated, wise, worldly-wise

insane
rational, sane

inside
exterior, outside

insignificant
enormous, great, important, large, major, significant

insufficient
adequate, ample, enough, plenty, sufficient
excess, excessive, too much

intelligence
foolishness, ignorance, stupidity

intelligent
dull, dim, foolish, ignorant, stupid

intense
mild, moderate, slight, weak

intentional
accidental, chance, inadvertent, unforeseen, unintended, unplanned

interesting
boring, dreary, dry, dull, monotonous, tedious, uninteresting

interior
exterior, outside

internal
external, outside

intricate
easy, plain, simple, straightforward

inward
outward

irritable
calm, gentle, mild, patient

irritating
agreeable, congenial, delightful, pleasant, pleasing, welcome

jealous
content, contented, satisfied

join
detach, disconnect, divide, part, separate, sever, untie

joy
depression, despair, grief, sadness, sorrow, unhappiness

joyful
depressed, despondent, dismal, gloomy, miserable, sad, unhappy

junior
senior

just
undeserved, unfair, unjust

justice
injustice, unfairness

keen
EAGER: apathetic, half-hearted, lazy, lukewarm, unenthusiastic
SHARP: blunt, dull

keep
give away, lose

kind
brutal, callous, cruel, harsh, heartless, hurtful, severe, unkind

knowledge
ignorance

lack
abundance, plenty, profusion, sufficiency # glut, excess

large
little, small; *see also* **huge**

last
first, initial

lasting
brief, impermanent, momentary, short-lived, temporary, transient

late
early # on time, punctual

latter
former

lavish
meagre, mean, miserly, sparing

lazy
conscientious, diligent, energetic, hard-working, industrious, keen

lead
follow

lean
fat, obese, overweight, stout, tubby (*informal*)

least
greatest, most

leave
arrive, come, return # remain, stay

left
right

legal
illegal, unauthorized, unlawful

lend
borrow

lengthen
cut, decrease, shorten

lenient
harsh, severe, stern, strict, tough

level
NOT SLOPING: slanting, sloping, steep
SMOOTH: bumpy, rough, uneven
EQUAL: unequal

liability
advantage, asset, benefit, blessing, boon

liable
free, exempt, immune, resistant

lie
truth

life
death

light
adjective BRIGHT: dark, dingy, dull, gloomy, unlit
adjective NOT HEAVY: heavy
adjective NOT SERIOUS: heavy, serious, solemn
noun darkness, dullness, gloom

like
verb abhor, detest, dislike, hate, loathe
adjective dissimilar, unalike, unlike

likely
implausible, improbable, incredible, unbelievable, unlikely

liking
abhorrence, dislike, hate, hatred, loathing

liquid
noun gas, solid
adjective gaseous, solid

little
adjective big, bulky, huge, immense, large, vast
pronoun a lot, much

live
adjective dead
verb die

lively
boring, dreary, dull, listless, quiet

loathe *see* hate

local
distant, foreign

loiter
hasten, hurry, rush # depart, go on, leave, move on

long
abbreviated, abridged, concise, short

look after
neglect

loose
NOT TIGHT: clinging, close-fitting, tight
NOT SECURE: fastened, fixed, secure, tight

loosen
tighten

lose
FAIL: succeed, win
NO LONGER HAVE: acquire, find, gain, make

loss
> OPPOSITE OF GETTING: gain, profit
> DEFEAT: victory, win

lost
> found

loud
> SAID OF SOUNDS: hushed, low, muted, quiet, soft, subdued
> SAID OF COLOURS: dull, muted, soft, subdued

love
> *noun* abhorrence, hate, hatred, loathing
> *verb* abhor, detest, hate, loathe

lovely
> disagreeable, hideous, nasty, repulsive, ugly, unpleasant

low
> NOT HIGH: high, tall, towering
> QUIET: blaring, booming, loud

lower
> *adjective* higher, senior, upper
> *verb* enhance, increase, intensify, raise, rise

loyal
> disloyal, treacherous, unfaithful

luxury
> hardship, penury, poverty

mad
> INSANE: rational, sane, sensible
> ANGRY: delighted, overjoyed, pleased, thrilled
> KEEN: unenthusiastic, uninterested

magnificent
> humble, lowly, modest, poor

majority
> fewest, minority

main
> lesser, minor, secondary, subordinate

male
> female; *see also* masculine

manage
> NOT SUCCEED: fail
> RUN WELL: mismanage

many
> few, some

masculine
> feminine, womanly; *see also* male

master
> MALE OWNER, TEACHER, ETC: mistress
> OWNER: servant, slave
> EXPERT: apprentice, learner, novice
> LEADER: follower

mature
> childish, immature, puerile

maximum
> minimum

maybe
> certainly, definitely

mean
> SELFISH: big-hearted, generous, ungrudging, unselfish
> NASTY: kind, sympathetic

melt
> freeze, harden, solidify

mend
> break, damage

merciful
> cruel, hard-hearted, merciless, pitiless, severe, unforgiving

merciless
> compassionate, forgiving, generous, gracious, lenient, merciful; *see also* cruel

mercy
> cruelty, heartlessness, severity

middle
border, edge, end, outside, perimeter, periphery

midget *see* dwarf

mild
GENTLE: fierce, harsh, intense, severe, stern, strict, tough
SAID OF CLIMATE: cold, harsh, severe

minimum
maximum

minor
important, major, paramount, principal, significant

minority
majority, most, preponderance

mischievous
good, well-behaved

miser
spendthrift

miserable
UNHAPPY: cheerful, contented, delighted, happy, pleased
NOT GOOD: commendable, excellent, good, outstanding, satisfactory
NOT MUCH: generous, lavish, liberal, sumptuous

misery
comfort, contentment, happiness, luxury, pleasure

miss
NOT HIT: hit, strike
NOT FIND: find
NOT CATCH: catch

mistress
FEMALE OWNER, TEACHER, ETC: master
OWNER: servant, slave

modern
ancient, antiquated, antique, dated, old, old-fashioned, outdated, outmoded, out of date

modest
NOT PROUD: arrogant, conceited, proud, vain
NOT LAVISH: lavish, luxurious, sumptuous

monotony
change, diversity, variation, variety

more
less

morning
afternoon # evening # night

most
least

mourn
celebrate, rejoice

movable
fixed, immovable

much
little

multiple
single, sole, solitary

multiply
IN MATHEMATICS: divide
INCREASE: cut down, decrease, reduce

narrow
broad, wide

nasty
agreeable, amiable, charming, delightful, kind, lovely, pleasant

native
adjective alien, immigrant, foreign
noun alien, foreigner, immigrant, stranger

natural
NORMAL: abnormal, atypical, odd, peculiar, uncommon, unnatural, unusual
NOT ARTIFICIAL: artificial, man-made, manufactured, synthetic
SINCERE OR HONEST: affected, contrived, feigned, forced, insincere, stilted, strained

near
distant, far, faraway, remote

neat
disorderly, jumbled, messy, muddled, untidy

necessary
avoidable, gratuitous, needless, preventable, superfluous, uncalled-for, unnecessary

negative
NOT POSITIVE: positive
USEFUL: constructive, helpful, useful

neglect
verb care for, look after
noun care

negligent
careful, conscientious, meticulous, painstaking, scrupulous, thorough

nervous
bold, calm, composed, confident, laid-back (*informal*), relaxed

never
always, forever # occasionally, sometimes

new
NOT OLD: old, old-fashioned, outdated, outmoded, out of date
UNFAMILIAR: familiar, established, normal, routine, standard, traditional
OWNED FOR THE FIRST TIME: second-hand, used

nice
disagreeable, horrible, horrid, nasty, unfriendly, unkind, unpleasant

night
day # morning

noble
dishonourable, ignoble, selfish, wicked

noise
calm, hush, peace, quiet, silence, stillness, tranquillity

noisy
calm, hushed, peaceful, quiet, silent, still, tranquil

none
all, every

nonsense
sense, wisdom

normal
USUAL: abnormal, atypical, irregular, odd, peculiar, uncommon, unconventional, unusual
SANE: eccentric, mad, odd, peculiar, weird

normally
rarely, seldom

notable
FAMOUS: obscure, unknown
NOTICEABLE: commonplace, inconspicuous, ordinary, unimpressive, unremarkable, usual

novice
master, past master, veteran

numerous
few, rare, scarce, sparse

obedient
contrary, disobedient, rebellious, wilful

obey

disobey, refuse, resist # command, order

obscure

NOT FAMOUS: celebrated, famous, renowned, well-known
NOT CLEAR: clear, definite, distinct, obvious, well-defined

obstinate

acquiescent, agreeable, amenable, biddable, easy-going, helpful, obliging, willing

obvious

concealed, faint, hazy, hidden, indistinct, obscure, unclear, vague

occasionally

frequently, often, regularly # always

occupied

empty, free, unoccupied, vacant

odd

NOT NORMAL *see* peculiar
NOT EVEN: even

offend

appease, mollify, pacify, placate, please

often

occasionally, now and again, now and then, rarely, seldom # never

old

NOT OF TODAY: avant-garde, contemporary, fashionable, modern, new, present-day, up-to-date; *see also* ancient, antique
NOT YOUNG: little, small, young

old age

adolescence, boyhood, childhood, girlhood, infancy, youth

old-fashioned

fashionable, modern, up-to-date

opaque

clear, see-through, transparent

open

adjective NOT SHUT: closed, covered, fastened, locked, sealed, shut
adjective NOT PROTECTED OR HIDDEN: concealed, covered, protected, sheltered
adjective ACCESSIBLE: inaccessible, restricted, unapproachable, unavailable, unreceptive
adjective FRANK: deceitful, devious, evasive, secretive, shifty (*informal*)
adjective CLEARLY SEEN: clandestine, covert, hidden, secret, stealthy, surreptitious
verb BEGIN: close, end, finish
verb UNSEAL: block, cover, fasten, lock, seal

oppose

advocate, back, champion, support

optimist

pessimist

optional

compulsory, essential, mandatory, necessary, obligatory, required

oral

written # aural

order

noun anarchy, chaos, confusion, disorder, muddle
verb obey

ordinary

abnormal, atypical, exceptional, out of the ordinary, special, unusual

outer

central, inner

outlaw

allow, legalize, permit

outside

inside

outskirts
centre, middle

outstanding
average, mediocre, ordinary, poor, undistinguished, unexceptional, unremarkable

outward
inner, inward

over
below, under

pain
comfort, ease, pleasure, relief

pardon
verb avenge, condemn, punish, sentence
noun condemnation, punishment, revenge, sentence, vengeance

part
whole

partial
complete, entire, total, whole

particular
general

pass
fail

passing
lasting, permanent

passive
IN GRAMMAR: active
NOT FORCEFUL: active, aggressive, assertive, dynamic, energetic, forceful, vigorous

past
future # present

patient
bad-tempered, impatient, irascible, irritable, quick-tempered

pause
continue, go on, keep going

peace
ABSENCE OF WAR: fighting, strife, war
QUIETNESS: commotion, disorder, hurly-burly, noise, turmoil, uproar

peaceful
QUIET: disorderly, noisy, stormy, uproarious, violent, wild
NOT WARLIKE: aggressive, violent, warlike, wild

peculiar
common, conventional, familiar, normal, ordinary, typical, usual

perfect
faulty, flawed, imperfect, imprecise, inaccurate, inadequate, inexact, poor

perhaps
certainly, definitely

perish
last, live, survive

permanent
INTENDED TO LAST: impermanent, makeshift, temporary
LASTING FOREVER: ephemeral, passing, transient

permit
ban, bar, disallow, forbid, prohibit

persuade
dissuade

pessimist
optimist

pitiless
compassionate, kind, merciful

pity

cruelty, harshness, heartlessness, inhumanity, ruthlessness, severity

plain

NOT ELABORATE: decorated, elaborate, fancy, ornate, pretty

NOT CLEAR: ambiguous, confusing, cryptic, puzzling, unclear, vague

pleasant

disagreeable, nasty, obnoxious, unfriendly, unpleasant

please

anger, annoy, displease, irritate

pleased

annoyed, angry, displeased

plentiful

lacking, missing # rare, scanty, scarce, sparse

plenty

adjective few, rare, scarce
noun lack, rarity, scarcity

plural

singular

polite

blunt, brusque, discourteous, impolite, rude

poor

NOT RICH: affluent, loaded (*informal*), prosperous, rich, wealthy, well-off

NOT GOOD: adequate, commendable, excellent, good, satisfactory

NOT FERTILE: fertile

positive

NOT NEGATIVE: negative

CERTAIN: uncertain, unsure

poverty

affluence, comfort, luxury, riches, wealth

powerful

STRONG: feeble, puny, weak

IMPORTANT: minor, petty, unimportant

CONVINCING: feeble, flimsy, implausible, unconvincing, weak

practice

principle, theory

praise

noun blame, condemnation, derision, rebuke, scorn, telling-off

verb blame, chide, condemn, deride, rebuke, scold, scorn, tell off

precious

cheap, worthless

precise

ambiguous, imprecise, inaccurate, incorrect, inexact, inexplicit, vague

predecessor

successor

presence

absence

preserve

destroy

present

adjective absent
noun future # past

pretty

disagreeable, plain, ugly, unattractive, unprepossessing

prevent

allow, authorize, permit

priceless

cheap, worthless

pride

humility, modesty # disgrace, dishonour, shame

principal
junior, lesser, minor, subsidiary

private
open, public

probable
implausible, improbable, unlikely

professional
amateur

profit
loss

profitable
fruitless, futile, ineffectual, pointless, unproductive, unprofitable, useless, vain

progress
verb decline, deteriorate
noun decline, deterioration

prohibit
allow, authorize, permit

prompt
delayed, leisurely, slow, tardy, unhurried

prosper
collapse, fail

prosperity
destitution, hardship, penury, poverty

prosperous
destitute, hard up (*informal*), impoverished, poor, poverty-stricken

proud
CONCEITED: humble, modest, self-effacing, unassuming
PLEASED: ashamed, humbled

prove
disprove

public
personal, private

pull
push, shove

punish
forgive, pardon # reward

punishment
forgiveness, mercy, pardon # reward

pupil
instructor, master, teacher; *see also* apprentice, disciple

pure
CLEAN, UNMIXED: adulterated, contaminated, impure, mixed, polluted, soiled, tainted
INNOCENT: bad, evil, impure, naughty, obscene, wicked

purify
adulterate, contaminate, defile, dirty, pollute

push
drag, haul, pull

queer
conventional, familiar, natural, normal, ordinary, orthodox, unremarkable, usual

question
noun answer, reply, response
verb ASK A QUESTION: answer, reply, respond
verb DOUBT: accept, swallow, wear

quick
FAST: leisurely, slow
BRIEF: long-drawn-out, prolonged
INTELLIGENT: dim, dull, slow, stupid, thick (*informal*)

quiet
noun clamour, commotion, hubbub, noise, pandemonium, uproar
adjective NOT NOISY: boisterous, lively, loud, noisy, riotous, uproarious
adjective NOT SAYING MUCH: chatty (*informal*), talkative

raise
    LIFT: drop, lower
    INCREASE: decrease, diminish, lessen, lower, minimize, moderate

rapid *see* quick

rare
    average, common, commonplace, everyday, regular, routine, run-of-the-mill, usual

rarely
    frequently, often, usually

raw
    cooked, finished, prepared

ready
    WILLING: disinclined, unwilling
    PREPARED: unfinished, unprepared, unready

real
    fake, false, fictitious, imaginary, phoney (*informal*), sham, unreal

receive
    GET: award, give, hand over
    SAID OF A RADIO, ETC: broadcast, transmit

recent
    ancient, distant, old; *see also* modern

reckless
    careful, cautious, prudent, sensible, wary, wise

reduce
    amplify, enlarge, expand, extend, heighten, increase, intensify, raise

reduction
    amplification, enlargement, expansion, extension, increase, intensification, rise

refuse
    accept, agree, comply, grant

regular
    NORMAL: abnormal, anomalous, atypical, exceptional, irregular, unorthodox, unusual
    SYMMETRICAL: asymmetrical, irregular
    AT EQUAL INTERVALS: intermittent, irregular, occasional, sporadic, spasmodic

reject
    accept # choose, opt for, pick, select

rejoice
    grieve, lament, mourn

relaxed
    anxious, apprehensive, nervous, on edge, tense, uneasy, worried

release
    arrest, capture, catch, seize # hold, hold on to, keep, keep hold of

reliable
    irresponsible, unpredictable, unreliable, untrustworthy

reluctant
    eager, enthusiastic, keen, willing

remain
    depart, go, leave

remarkable
    average, common, commonplace, ordinary, run-of-the-mill, surprising, unbelievable, unusual

remember
    forget

remove
    leave # replace

renowned
    obscure, unknown

repel
attract

reply
noun enquiry/inquiry, query, question
verb ask, enquire/inquire, query, question

rescue
verb capture, imprison
noun capture, imprisonment

resemblance
contrast, difference, dissimilarity

resemble
contrast, differ from

resist
attack, invade, raid # give in, yield

respect
verb deride, despise, disdain, scorn, sneer at
noun contempt, derision, disrespect, scorn

rest
noun NOT WORKING: activity, work
noun NON-MOVEMENT: motion, movement
verb continue, keep going, move, work

result
cause, origin, source

retard
accelerate, boost, improve, promote, speed up

retreat
advance, attack, charge

return
verb COME BACK: depart, go away, leave
verb GIVE BACK: borrow, take
noun departure

reveal
cover, cover up, conceal, hide, mask, veil

reward
verb punish
noun punishment

rich
WEALTHY: destitute, hard up (*informal*), impoverished, penniless, poor, poverty-stricken
EXPENSIVE: cheap, shabby
FERTILE: barren
SAID OF FOOD: low-fat, plain, simple

riches
destitution, penury, poverty

right
adjective NOT LEFT: left
adjective CORRECT: erroneous, false, inaccurate, incorrect, inexact, mistaken, wrong
adjective GOOD, MORAL: bad, dishonest, inappropriate, sinful, unfair, unjust, unlawful, wrong
noun evil, sin, wickedness, wrong, wrong-doing

rigid
bendable, bendy (*informal*), flexible, pliable

rise
decrease, drop, fall; *see also* increase

rough
NOT SMOOTH: smooth
SAID OF THE SEA: calm
HARSH: gentle, mild, refined
HOARSE: pleasant, sweet
APPROXIMATE: exact, precise

round
CURVED: flat, square, straight
APPROXIMATE: exact, precise

rude
NOT POLITE: courteous, polite, well-mannered
NOT REFINED: polished, refined, sophisticated

rural

urban

rush

dawdle, loiter, take one's time

sad

NOT HAPPY: cheerful, glad, happy, joyful, merry

DISTRESSING: glad, happy, joyful # fortunate, lucky

safe

HARMLESS: dangerous, harmful, hazardous, noxious, poisonous, toxic

FREE FROM HARM: exposed, insecure, precarious, unprotected, vulnerable

RELIABLE: unproven, unsafe, untried, untrustworthy

safety

danger, harm, injury, peril, risk, trouble

same

contrasting, different, variable, varying

sane

crazy, eccentric, foolish, insane, mad

satisfactory

inadequate, mediocre, poor, unacceptable, unsatisfactory

satisfied

disappointed, discontented, dissatisfied, unhappy

save

spend, squander, waste

savoury

sweet

scarce

abundant, ample, common, copious, plentiful, ten a penny

scarcity

abundance, enough, plenty, profusion, sufficiency, wealth

scare *see* frighten

scatter

accumulate, assemble, collect, gather, unite

scold

commend, compliment, praise

scorn

verb acclaim, admire, applaud, approve, honour, praise

noun acclaim, admiration, applause, approval, honour, praise

secret

barefaced, blatant, flagrant, open, overt, public, undisguised

secure

insecure, unprotected, vulnerable

seize

free, let go, release

seldom

frequently, generally, often, usually

selfish

considerate, generous, kind, magnanimous, selfless, unselfish

sell

buy, purchase

send

get, receive

senior

junior

sense

bunkum (*informal*), nonsense, rubbish, twaddle

senseless
  sensible, wise

sensible
  foolhardy, foolish, senseless, silly, stupid, unwise

separate
  verb amalgamate, blend, combine, integrate, join, link, merge, unite
  adjective combined, together, united

serious
  SEVERE, IMPORTANT: mild, slight, trivial, unimportant
  NOT SMILING: happy, laughing, smiling
  NOT JOKING: facetious, frivolous, funny

severe
  NOT GENTLE: easy-going, gentle, lenient, mild
  SERIOUS: mild, slight

shallow
  deep

sharp
  WITH CUTTING EDGE: blunt, dull
  IN MUSIC: flat, natural

short
  NOT TALL OR LONG: long, tall
  SHORTENED: complete, entire, full, unabridged
  LASTING A SHORT TIME: lengthy, long, long-drawn-out, protracted

shortage
  abundance, plenty, sufficiency # excess, glut, too much

shorten
  add to, increase, lengthen

shout
  mutter, whisper

show
  cloak, conceal, cover, cover up, disguise, hide

shrink
  expand, increase

shut
  open

sick
  ILL: healthy, well
  NOT LIKING: content, fond, happy, pleased

silence
  clamour, clatter, commotion, noise, racket, uproar

silent
  loud, noisy

silly
  mature, responsible, sensible, wise

similar
  contrasting, different, unalike, unlike

similarity
  contrast, difference, dissimilarity

simple
  EASY: complex, complicated, convoluted, difficult, elaborate, involved
  PLAIN: elaborate, fancy, ornate
  NOT SOPHISTICATED: sophisticated, worldly, worldly-wise

simplify
  complicate

sincerity
  hypocrisy, insincerity

single
  ONE ONLY: many, multiple, several, various
  NOT MARRIED: married

singular
  plural

sink
  float, swim # come up, rise

skilful
awkward, clumsy, inexpert, unskilful

slack
taut, tight

slender *see* slim

slight
NOT EXTENSIVE: extensive, great, widespread
NOT LARGE *see* slim

slim
NOT FAT: fat, plump, stout, tubby (*informal*)
NOT LARGE: considerable, good, great, serious, significant, strong

slow
adjective NOT FAST: fast, hasty, hurried, quick, rushed
adjective NOT ON TIME: on time, punctual
adjective NOT QUICK-WITTED: bright, quick, smart
verb accelerate, hasten, hurry, promote, speed up

small
NOT BIG: big, large, sizable, spacious; *see also* tiny
YOUNG: adult, big, grown-up (*informal*), old

smart
CLEVER: dim, dull, foolish, stupid, thick (*informal*)
SAID OF CLOTHES: dull, faded, shabby, thread-bare, worn

smile
frown, scowl

smooth
jagged, rough, serrated

sober
drunk, intoxicated

soft
NOT HARD: hard, rigid, solid, tough
GENTLE, NOT LOUD: deafening, ear-piercing, harsh, loud, noisy
EASY-GOING: hard, strict, tough

solemn
carefree, frivolous, light-hearted, jolly, joyful, playful

solid
adjective NOT HOLLOW: hollow
adjective NOT HARD: flexible, soft, spongy, springy; *see also* hard, rigid
adjective NOT FLUID: fluid, gaseous, liquid
noun NOT FLUID: fluid, gas, liquid

solidify
liquefy, melt, soften, thaw

soon
eventually, sometime # late

sooner
later

sorrow
happiness, joy, pleasure

sorry
APOLOGETIC: glad, happy, unapologetic, unashamed, unrepentant
NOT GOOD: excellent, good, satisfactory
FEELING COMPASSION: unsympathetic

sour
NOT SWEET: sweet
NOT CONTENT: content, contented, good-natured, happy, pleasant

spacious
confined, cramped, narrow, small, tiny

sparing
extravagant, generous, lavish, liberal, prodigal, wasteful

sparse
abundant, dense, numerous, plentiful, thick

special
average, everyday, general, ordinary, plain, routine, run-of-the-mill, unexceptional, unremarkable

spendthrift
miser

splendid
EXCELLENT: bad, feeble, mediocre, poor, unsatisfactory; *see also* special
EXPENSIVE: cheap, dilapidated, poor, rundown, shabby, worn

split
combine, join, link, merge, unite

spread
close up, come together, concentrate

stale
fresh

start
verb cease (*formal*), close, end, finish, stop
noun cessation (*formal*), close, end, finish, stop

stationary
mobile, moving

stay
depart, go, leave, quit

steady
CONTINUOUS: broken, discontinuous, irregular, occasional, sporadic, spasmodic
NOT MOVING: shaky, unsteady, wobbly
CALM: agitated, jumpy (*informal*), nervous
RELIABLE: unreliable, untrustworthy, wavering

steep
gentle, gradual # level

stern
adjective easy-going, gentle, lenient, mild
noun bow (*of ship*)

stiff
HARD *see* **hard, rigid**
NOT AGILE: agile, supple
STRONG: feeble, weak
TOO FORMAL: casual, easy-going, informal, relaxed

stop
verb begin, commence (*formal*), start # carry on, continue, go on, persevere, persist
noun start; *see also* **end**

stout
lean, slender, slim, thin

straight
WITHOUT CURVES: bent, circular, crooked, curved, winding, zigzag
FRANK: crooked (*informal*), devious, dishonest, evasive, insincere
HONEST: bent (*slang*), crooked (*informal*), dishonest

straightforward *see* **simple**

strange
common, familiar, normal; *see also* **peculiar**

stranger
local, native

strength
PHYSICAL POWER: feebleness, fragility, puniness, weakness
FORCE OR INTENSITY: faintness, feebleness, weakness # gentleness, mildness
ABILITY TO DO SOMETHING: impotence, powerlessness, weakness
ABILITY TO CONVINCE: feebleness, weakness
GOOD POINT: drawback, failing, shortcoming, weakness

strengthen
weaken

strong
POWERFUL: anaemic, delicate, feeble, fragile, puny, weak
WITH FORCE OR INTENSITY: faint, feeble, weak # gentle, mild
ABLE TO DO SOMETHING: impotent, powerless
CONVINCING: feeble, unconvincing, weak
GREAT: insignificant, slight, slim, small

stupid
NOT SENSIBLE: prudent, sensible, well-advised, wise
NOT ALERT: alert, awake
NOT CLEVER: brilliant, clever, intelligent, smart

subtract
add

succeed
fail

success
disaster, failure, wash-out (*informal*)

successor
predecessor

sudden
QUICK: gentle, gradual, slow, unhurried
NOT EXPECTED *see* surprising

suitable
inappropriate, unsuitable

summit
base, bottom, foot

superior
inferior

supply
demand

support
verb BACK: oppose
verb AGREE WITH: contradict
noun hostility, opposition

sure
CERTAIN: doubtful, problematic, questionable, uncertain, unsure
SAFE: hazardous, insecure, risky, unsafe

surplus
deficiency, deficit, shortage, shortfall

surprising
anticipated, awaited, expected, foreseeable, predicted

survive
die, perish

susceptible
immune, resistant

suspicion
trust

sweet
PLEASANT: disagreeable, nasty, repulsive, ugly, unattractive, unpleasant
SWEET-TASTING: bitter, savoury, sour

swift
leisurely, lingering, long-drawn-out, prolonged, slow

take
give # leave, reject # put back, replace

talkative
quiet, silent, subdued, taciturn, tongue-tied, withdrawn

tall
short, small

tame
DOMESTICATED: feral, undomesticated, wild
NOT FIERCE: ferocious, fierce
NOT EXCITING: exciting, lively, stimulating

tasty
bland, tasteless, unappetizing

taut
loose, slack

teach
learn

teacher
pupil, student; *see also* master

temporary
permanent # lasting, long-lasting, long-term

tender
GENTLE: cruel, hard-hearted, harsh, tough, unfeeling, unkind, unsympathetic
SOFT: chewy, hard, tough

tense
adjective calm, laid-back (*informal*), relaxed
verb relax

terrible
brilliant, excellent, marvellous, splendid, terrific, wonderful

terrific
EXCELLENT: abysmal, appalling, dreadful, pathetic, poor, terrible
HUGE: gentle, little, mild, slight, small

thaw
freeze

theory
practice

thick
NOT THIN: narrow, slender, slim, thin
COMMON, DENSE: rare, scarce, sparse, uncommon

thin
NOT FAT: fat, plump, stout, tubby (*informal*)
NOT THICK: thick
SPARSE: abundant, plentiful, swarming, teeming # dense, impenetrable, thick

thorough
CAREFUL: casual, cursory, hasty, hurried, perfunctory, superficial
UTTER: slight

thrift
extravagance, waste

thrive
decline, fail, wither

tidy
untidy

tie
unfasten, untie

tight
SAID OF CLOTHES: baggy (*informal*), loose
SAID OF A ROPE, ETC: slack

tighten
loosen, slacken

timid
adventurous, bold, brave, confident, daring, intrepid

tiny
colossal, enormous, huge, immense, massive, tremendous

top
base, bottom, foot

total
fragmentary, incomplete, partial

tough
NOT GENTLE: gentle, kind, lenient, tender
NOT TENDER TO EAT: tender

town
country

tragic
amusing, comic, comical, funny, happy

tranquil

NOT WORRIED: agitated, disturbed, placid, troubled, worried
PEACEFUL: noisy

transmit

receive

transparent

cloudy, opaque

treacherous

dependable, devoted, faithful, loyal, reliable, staunch, steadfast

true

DEVOTED: disloyal, faithless, false, unfaithful, untrustworthy
REAL, ACCURATE: false, inaccurate, inauthentic, incorrect, inexact, invalid

trust

verb distrust, doubt, mistrust, question, suspect
noun distrust, doubt, mistrust, scepticism, suspicion

truth

deceit, falsehood, lie

ugly

appealing, attractive, beautiful, good-looking, gorgeous, handsome, pretty

unbearable

bearable, tolerable

unconscious

NOT AWAKE: awake, conscious
UNAWARE, UNTHINKING: calculated, conscious, deliberate, intentional

under

over

understand

misunderstand

uneven

SAID OF NUMBERS: even
NOT FLAT: flat, level, smooth

unfit

NOT STRONG AND HEALTHY: fit, healthy, strong
NOT SUITABLE: capable, competent, fit, suitable, worthy

unfriendly

affectionate, amiable, friendly, warm, welcoming

unhappiness

cheerfulness, happiness, joy, pleasure

unhappy

SAD: cheerful, happy, joyful
INAPPROPRIATE: appropriate, fortunate, judicious, tactful, well-chosen, well-timed

uninteresting

absorbing, exciting, interesting, stimulating

unite

divide, separate, sever, split

unkind

caring, considerate, friendly, humane, kind, sensitive, sympathetic, thoughtful; *see also* cruel

unknown

celebrated, famous, well-known

unlikely

NOT PROBABLE: likely, probable
NOT BELIEVABLE: believable, plausible, reasonable

unnatural

natural, normal, ordinary, typical, unexceptional, unremarkable

unnecessary

essential, indispensable, necessary, vital

unpleasant

charming, enjoyable, nice, pleasant, pleasing, welcome

untidy

neat, tidy

unusual

common, conventional, natural, normal, typical, unexceptional, unremarkable

upper

lower

urban

rural

usual

abnormal, atypical, exceptional, remarkable, uncommon, unconventional, unnatural

usually

occasionally, rarely, seldom

vacant

in use, occupied

vague

clear, definite, explicit, precise, unambiguous

vain

PROUD: humble, modest, unassuming
USELESS: fruitful, productive, successful, useful, worthwhile

valuable

EXPENSIVE: cheap, worthless
USEFUL: fruitless, pointless, unproductive, useless

vanish

appear # remain, stay

vanity

humility, modesty

variety

monotony, sameness, uniformity

vast

small, tiny

vertical

flat, horizontal

veteran

beginner, novice

vice

morality, virtue

vicious

SAID OF A PERSON: considerate, gentle, kind, kindly
SAID OF AN ANIMAL: docile, tame

victory

defeat

violent

calm, docile, gentle, mild, placid

virtue

evil, vice, wickedness

vivid

FULL OF DETAIL: boring, dull, lifeless
BRIGHT: dull, muted, subdued

voluntary

compulsory, necessary, obligatory, required

wane

increase, wax (*literary*)

war

peace

warm

FAIRLY HOT: chilly, cold, cool
FRIENDLY: chilly, cold, cool, distant, unfriendly, unwelcoming

wary

trustful, trusting, unwary

wasteful

careful, economical, thrifty

wax

abate, decrease, wane (*literary*)

weak

NOT PHYSICALLY STRONG: athletic, brawny, powerful, robust, strong, tough
NOT MENTALLY STRONG: determined, firm, resolute, steadfast, strong, strong-minded
NOT SEVERE: acute, extreme, severe, vehement, violent
NOT FORCEFUL: effective, formidable, strong, zealous
NOT STRONG IN TASTE, ETC: concentrated, hot, pungent, strong
NOT LOUD: loud
NOT STRONGLY PROTECTED: impregnable, invulnerable, protected, well-protected
NOT CONVINCING: convincing, persuasive, powerful, strong, telling

weaken

strengthen

weakness

PHYSICAL WEAKNESS: brawniness, robustness, strength, toughness
MENTAL WEAKNESS: determination, firmness, resolution, steadfastness, strength, strong-mindedness
MILDNESS: acuteness, severity, vehemence, violence
LACK OF FORCE: effectiveness, force, strength, zeal
WEAKNESS IN TASTE, ETC: pungency, strength
QUIETNESS: loudness
UNPROTECTEDNESS: impregnability, invulnerability
INABILITY TO CONVINCE: persuasiveness, strength

wealth

PROSPERITY: destitution, penury, poverty
PLENTY: lack, scarcity, sparseness

wealthy

destitute, hard up (*informal*), impoverished, poor, poverty-stricken

welcome

verb SAY HELLO TO: ignore, snub
verb BE PLEASED ABOUT: regret
noun rejection
adjective annoying, displeasing, irritating, undesirable, unpleasant, unwelcome

well

adjective ill, indisposed, off-colour, poorly, sick, unwell
adverb badly, poorly

well-known

unknown

wet

NOT DRY: dry
RAINING: dry, fine, sunny

whisper

shout, yell

whole

part

wholly

in part, partially, partly

wicked

decent, good, honourable, kind, noble, virtuous

wide

narrow

wild

UNRULY, MAD: calm, controlled, gentle, peaceful
NOT TAME: domestic, domesticated, farm, pet, tame
UNCIVILIZED: civilized
ANGRY: calm, pleased
STORMY: balmy, calm, windless

willing
averse, disinclined, loath, unenthusiastic, unwilling

win
verb lose
noun defeat

wisdom
folly, foolishness, imprudence, stupidity

wise
foolish, imprudent, stupid, unwise

wither
bloom, blossom, flourish

within
preposition beyond
adverb outside

wonderful
bad, boring, dismal, mediocre, pathetic, poor, second-rate, unimpressive

worried *see* anxious

worry
noun calmness, composure # reassurance
verb calm, reassure, soothe

worse
better

worsen
get better, improve

worst
best

worthless
OF NO VALUE: precious, valuable
NOT GOOD OR USEFUL: good, excellent, profitable, satisfactory, worthwhile
NOT MORALLY GOOD: good, hardworking, honest, respectable, worthy

wrong
accurate, correct, just, proper, right, suitable

young
aged, elderly, old

youth
YOUNG AGE: adulthood, old age
YOUNG PERSON: adult, old age pensioner, senior citizen

DO IT YOURSELF

A Many words in English form antonyms by adding prefixes such as *a-, ab-, dis-, il-, im-, in-, ir-, mis-* and *un-*. Using the antonym lists in this unit, find the antonyms for the following words.

ability	expected	pleasant
able	expensive	polite
accurate	fortunate	possible
adequate	friendly	regular
agree	honest	reliable
appear	natural	sane
avoidable	necessary	typical
behave	normal	understand
courteous	patient	welcome

B Replace the words in italics in the following sentences by their opposites.

Hint

Note that there may be more than one possible correct answer.

1. a *sharp* knife
2. the *bow* of a ship
3. *dilute* orange juice
4. *stale* bread
5. furniture of *superior* quality
6. an *amateur* football team
7. *shallow* water
8. a *dull* story
9. at the *entrance*
10. their *ancestors*
11. My hands are *clean*.
12. I *hate* cabbage.
13. *Knowledge* can be a dangerous thing.
14. She looked down at the little boy with a *smile*.
15. She's the *junior* partner in the firm.

C Complete the following sentences by filling in the blank space with an antonym of the word in italics.

> *Example:*
>
> The project wasn't a *failure*. In fact, it was a great _____.
> The project wasn't a failure. In fact, it was a great *success*.

1. I wasn't *angry* at what she said. In fact, I was quite _____.

2. I don't *agree* with you. In fact, I totally _____ with you.

3. I'm not a *pessimist*. In fact, I'm really quite an _____.

4. There has been no *increase* in crimes of violence over the past twelve months. In fact , there has been a slight _____.

5. 'Athletics' may look like a *plural* noun, but in fact it is _____.

6. I took over a failing company from my *predecessor*, but I intend to hand over a highly successful company to my _____.

7. He is always looking for the *maximum* profit with the _____ of risk.

8. Our *imports* are other countries' _____.

9. I didn't say I would meet you *before* the concert, I said I would meet you _____ it.

10. She refuses to *admit* that she was his accomplice. In fact, she totally _____ ever having met him.

11. *Drunk* or _____, he's a brilliant musician.

12. Somehow they always manage to turn *defeat* into _____.

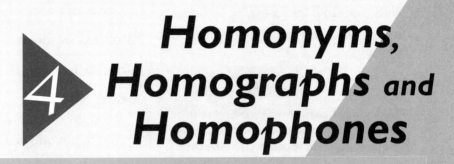

Homonyms, Homographs and Homophones

4

Homonyms are words that are alike both in sound and spelling, e.g. the **bark** of a tree and the **bark** of a dog. **Homographs** are words that have the same spelling but are pronounced differently, such as a **lead** /led/ *pipe* and a *dog's* **lead** /li:d/. **Homophones** are words that have the same pronunciation but are spelt differently, such as a *sandy* **beach** and a **beech** *tree*.

In the following lists of common homonyms, homographs and homophones, the words are distinguished by short phrases, sentences or definitions, and where necessary also by stress marks or phonetics.

How to use the lists

▶ In the lists, homonyms, homographs and homophones are grouped together, e.g. **bough** /baʊ/, **bow** /baʊ/ and **bow** /boʊ/ or **so** /soʊ/, **sew** /soʊ/, **sow** /soʊ/ and **sow** /saʊ/.

▶ Where the stress patterns of words have to be distinguished by means of a stress mark, the stress mark precedes the stressed syllable. For example, **'convict** is stressed on the syllable **con-**, whereas **con'vict** is stressed on the syllable **-vict**.

advocate

An advocate /ˈædvəkət/ is a lawyer who pleads cases in a law-court.

I advocate /ˈædvəkeɪt/ accepting the proposal.

Did You Know ?

There are many pairs of words in English that differ in the pronunciation of their endings in the same way as *an advocate* and *to advocate*. In such cases, if a word that ends in *-ate* is a noun or an adjective, the *-ate* ending is pronounced /-ət/, e.g. *estimate* /ˈestɪmət/, *moderate* /ˈmɒdərət/. On the other hand, if the word is a verb, the *-ate* ending is pronounced /-eɪt/, e.g. /ˈestɪmeɪt/, /ˈmɒdəreɪt/.

Among the other words of this type are: *affiliate, animate, approximate, aspirate, associate, delegate, deliberate, designate, elaborate, graduate, initiate, intimate, precipitate, separate* and *subordinate*.

---

abuse *see* use

aid, aide, AIDS

After the disaster, the government appealed for international aid. / Peppermint aids digestion.

The president called a meeting of his aides (= *advisers*).

AIDS is a terrible disease.

air, heir

We breathe the air around us.

He is the heir /ɛə/ to the throne.

aisle, isle

An aisle /aɪl/ is a passageway in a church or a supermarket.

The Isle /aɪl/ of Man is an island off the coast of England.

alight

The children were playing with matches and set the house alight.

Passengers for Redcar should alight (= *get out of the train*) at Darlington and catch the Saltburn train.

allowed *see* aloud

alms *see* arms

aloud, allowed

Read the passage aloud.

You're not allowed to come in here.

altar, alter

An altar is a sort of table in a church.

To alter something is to change it.

arc, ark

An arc is a curved line. / The ball arced through the air.

The ark is, according to the story in the Bible, the boat that Noah built to save all the animals and his family from being drowned in a flood.

arms, alms

The sailor had tattoos on both his arms.

the nuclear arms race

Alms is money given to the poor.

ascent, assent

The ascent of a mountain is the process of climbing it.

You give your assent to something when you agree to it.

assent *see* ascent

ate, eight

Who ate all the chocolate?

Sheila has eight brothers.

aural, oral

Aural /ˈɔːrəl/ means 'relating to the sense of hearing'.

Oral /ˈɔːrəl/ means 'relating to the mouth or to speaking'.

bail, bale

Bail is money given as security for the release of a prisoner. / If you get arrested, I'll come and bail you out.

A bail is a little piece of wood that forms part of the wickets in cricket.

A bale is a tight bundle of something. / a bale of cotton / This machine bales the hay as it is cut.

You bale out or bail out a boat if it has water in it.

You bale out or bail out of an aeroplane if you jump out of it.

baited *see* bated

bale *see* bail

ball, bawl

The boys accidentally kicked the ball through a window.

Who's your partner for the end-of-term ball? / a ball-gown

My mother bawled at me for being late for dinner. / The baby let out a loud bawl.

band, banned

Put an elastic band round the papers to keep them together.

My brother plays in a dance band.

He was banned from driving for five years.

bank

There were some boys fishing on the river bank.

You should put your money in the bank./ a piggy-bank / Who do you bank with?

banned *see* band

bare, bear

bare feet / with one's bare hands / the bare minimum / As part of the ceremony, he had to bare his right arm.

Such disappointments are hard to bear. /

Will the ice bear our weight, do you think?

a polar bear / a grizzly bear

bark

the bark of a tree

the bark of a dog / A dog barks.

base, bass

the base of a tree / an army base / On what do you base your conclusions?

I can sing the tenor or the bass /beɪs/ part. / A double-bass looks like a very large violin. / a bass guitar

A bass /bas/ is a type of fish.

bat

A flying fox is a type of bat.

a cricket bat / a baseball bat / Which team is going to bat first?

bated, baited

They watched with bated breath to see what would happen.

a baited hook for fishing with / They baited their hooks with mealworms.

baton, batten

A conductor's baton is a short stick./ A policeman's baton is a sort of club./ The runners in a relay race pass a baton from one to another.

A batten is a long piece of wood used to fasten or strengthen something. / You batten down the hatches on a ship.

bawl *see* ball

bay

A bay is a wide bend in the coastline.

a bay tree / bay leaves

A bay is part of a building: a loading bay.

Bay is a reddish-brown colour. / A bay is a horse of that colour.

Certain types of dog are said to bay rather than bark.

be, bee

When I grow up, I'm going to **be** an actor.

Is that a **bee** or a wasp?

beach, beech

a sandy **beach**

a **beech** tree

bean, been

peas and **beans**

Where on earth have you **been**?

bear *see* bare

beat, beet

the **beat** of a drum / **Beat** the eggs and mix in the flour. /We **beat** our rivals four–nil in Saturday's match.

Sugar **beet** is a root vegetable from which sugar is obtained.

bee *see* be

beech *see* beach

been *see* bean

beer, bier

Beer is an alcoholic drink.

A **bier** is a flat stand on which a coffin is placed or a dead bodied carried.

beet *see* beat

bell, belle

the **bell** on a bicycle / a door**bell**

She was the most beautiful girl at the dance, the **belle** of the ball.

berry, bury, beret

Ivy **berries** are red.

Every time you give it a bone, our dog goes out into the garden and **buries** it.

Berets /'bereɪz, 'beriz/ are round flat caps.

berth, birth

I've booked a **berth** on the overnight ferry. / The ship is due to **berth** at two o'clock this afternoon. / We'd been advised to stay away from her, so we gave her a wide **berth**.

I was present at the **birth** of both my daughters.

bier *see* beer

bight *see* bite

bill

We've run up a huge telephone **bill** this month. / The telephone company **bills** me every three months.

A bird's **bill** is its beak.

birth *see* berth

bit

a **bit** of cake

Your dog just **bit** me.

A **bit** is part of a horse's bridle.

In computing, there are usually eight **bits** in a byte.

bite, byte, bight

I do hope your dog doesn't **bite**. / a flea **bite**

In computing, a **byte** is a unit of computer memory.

A **bight** is an inward curve in a coastline. / the Great Australian **Bight**

blew, blue

The wind **blew** furiously all through the night.

a **blue** carpet

block, bloc

a **block** of wood / a **block** of flats / a road **block** / a mental **block** / The path was **blocked** by a fallen tree.

A **bloc** is a group of countries united by a common interest or ideology / the Communist **bloc**

blond, blonde

He is blond. / He has blond hair. / She is blonde. / She has blonde (*or* blond) hair./ He was seen around town with a glamorous blonde.

blow

They attempted to blow up the bridge. / Blow your nose.

Her death was a terrible blow to her family.

blue *see* blew

boar, bore

A boar is a male pig, or a wild pig.

I think politics is such a bore! / I can't think of anything that would bore me more.

You'll need a special drill to bore a hole in that wall. / The bore is the diameter of a rifle barrel. / a small-bore rifle

Surprisingly, he bore me no ill-will.

board, bored

a wooden board /an ironing-board / the board of directors of a company / The pirates boarded the ship. / Everyone intending to sail with the ship should get on board at once. / Board and lodgings means a room in someone's house with meals provided. / When I was at university, I boarded with a really nice old lady.

I'm bored. I've got nothing to do.

I've bored holes in that shelf to hold my screwdrivers.

boil

A boil is a sore swelling on your skin.

Boil the eggs for three minute. / boiled eggs / Bring the water to the boil.

bolt

I'll need to put a bolt on that door so that we can keep it closed. / The framework of the greenhouse was held together by nuts and bolts.

The horses have all gone. They've bolted (= *run away*). / She knew she had to get out so she made a sudden bolt (= *rush*) for the door.

bore *see* boar

bored *see* board

born, borne

I was born in 1949. / She was born of an Irish father and a Welsh mother. / Her suspicion was born of (= *caused by*) fear.

She has already borne six children and doesn't want any more. / He has borne his troubles with great courage. / The following points should be borne in mind. / His assertion is not borne out by the facts. / I found myself borne along by the crowd. / The cost will be borne by the taxpayer.

bough, bow

the bough /baʊ/ of a tree

The bow /baʊ/+ of a ship is its front end.

Don't forget to bow /baʊ/+ when the Queen passes. / The little boy made a beautiful bow.

She tied a bow /boʊ/ in the ribbon.

An archer shoots arrows with a bow /boʊ/.

bowl

a bowl of fruit

In some games, you must bowl a ball rather than throw it. / A bowl is one of the large balls used in sports such as ten-pin bowling and bowls.

box

a box of matches

You're a good boxer. Where did you learn to box?

boxer

A boxer is a person who takes part in boxing matches.

A boxer is a breed of dog.

boy, buoy

boys and girls

There was a buoy marking the position of the wrecked ship. / I was buoyed up (= *elated*) by my success. (*Note: In American English,* buoy *is pronounced* /'buːi/*.*)

brake, break

The car's brakes failed. / a hand-brake

Did you break the vase?

breach, breech

There was a breach (= *a break or gap*) in the fortifications and the soldiers poured through it into the fort. / The invaders had breached the city walls. / The money had caused a breach between the sisters (= *they were no longer friendly*). / a breach of promise (= *a failure to do what you have promised*) / a breach of the peace (= *a fight in a public place*) / You are in breach of Clause 2 of the contract. / They have breached the agreement.

The breech of a gun is the back part of it, where you load it.

Breeches /'brɪtʃɪz/ are trousers, especially of a kind that are drawn in at the knee, such as riding breeches.

bread, bred

bread and cakes

Have pandas ever bred in a zoo before?

break *see* brake

bred *see* bread

breech, breeches *see* breach

bridal, bridle

a bride's bridal gown

a horse's bridle / She bridled at (= *reacted angrily to*) the criticism.

brooch, broach

A brooch /broʊtʃ/ is a piece of jewellery that you pin to your clothing. / a diamond brooch

To broach a subject is to introduce it, or to begin to talk about it. / To broach a barrel of beer, etc, is to open it.

buries *see* berries

buy, by, bye

We're going to buy a new car.

I was bitten by a dog when I was a child. / We'll go by bus. / Your bag's over there by the door.

Bye. I'll see you tomorrow.

In cricket, a bye is a run scored without the batsman touching the ball.

byte *see* bite

cache *see* cash

calf

a cow and her calf

Your calf is the fleshy part at the back of your leg.

can

a can of beer / an oil-can / a tin can / I worked all summer in a factory where they can peas.

Can you help me, please?

cape

The ship sailed round the Cape of Good Hope.

Instead of a coat, she was wearing a long cape.

cannon, canon

A cannon is a large gun. / He came rushing along the corridor and cannoned (= *bumped*) into me.

A canon is a member of the clergy.

A canon is a set of recognized rules or principles, or a set of books recognized as authoritative in a particular subject, etc.

canvas, canvass

Canvas is a type of fabric.

To canvass people in an election is to ask for their support or to ask how they intend to vote.

carrot, carat

potatoes, carrots and turnips

an 18-carat gold ring

case

a packing-case / a suitcase / a glass case full of porcelain ornaments

Six more cases of food-poisoning have been reported. / The prosecution intend to sum up their case tomorrow. / In that case, I'll come back tomorrow.

cash, cache

Cash is money, especially coins and notes. / He's just trying to cash in on his fame (= *get money because of it*).

A cache of something is a secret store of it

cast, caste

the cast of a play / She was cast in the role of the wicked stepmother.

The witch cast a spell on the villagers. / When my brother broke his leg, he had to have a plaster cast on it for six weeks. / The curtains are grey, with a bluish cast (= *a tinge or slight appearance of blue*). / She has a cast (= *a slight squint*) in one eye.

In India, castes are different social classes. / the Hindu caste system.

caster, castor

caster or castor sugar

Casters or castors are small wheels on an armchair, etc.

ceiling, sealing

the ceiling of a room

Sealing the letter carefully, she placed it in her bag.

cell, sell

a prison cell

I've decided to sell my car.

cent *see* sent

cereal, serial

Wheat is a cereal.

a television serial

cheap, cheep

a cheap car / If you buy three packets, you get them cheap.

Baby birds go cheep.

check, cheque

I'll check and see if they have arrived yet. / a security check at an airport

Here's a cheque for $500. (*Note: In American English, a cheque is a* check.)

chord *see* cord

cite, site, sight

Could you cite a single example in history of a benevolent dictator?

That's the site of the new parliament building.

It was an amazing sight to see.

clause, claws

A clause is part of a sentence.

a cat's claws

close

Close /klouz/ that door, please.

How close /klous/ do you think we are to the border?

clutch

a clutch of eggs in a nest

You use the clutch pedal in a car when you change gear.

She continued to clutch her baby in her arms.

coarse, course

a coarse fabric / a coarse remark

a four-course dinner / Of course I'll help you. / The river follows a winding course through the town. / a golf course / Tears coursed (= *ran*) down his cheeks.

colon

A colon is a punctuation mark, (:).

The colon is part of the intestine.

compliment, complement

May I compliment /ˈkɒmplɪment/ you on your good taste? / pay someone a compliment /ˈkɒmplɪmənt/.

Good wine complements /ˈkɒmplɪments/ good food. / Good wine is a complement /ˈkɒmplɪmənt/ to good food. / In the sentence 'The sky is blue', 'blue' is a complement. / The full complement for this ship is five officers and one hundred and twenty sailors.

Did You Know ?

There are other words ending in *-ment* that show similar pronunciation patterns to those of *compliment* and *complement*. In such cases, the final syllable of the nouns is pronounced /-mənt/ and the final syllable of the verbs is pronounced /-ment/.

Among the words of this type are: *document, experiment, fragment, implement, ornament, regiment, segment* and *supplement*.

complimentary, complementary

A complimentary remark is one that makes a compliment. / A complimentary ticket is one that is given to you free.

Things that are complementary go well together or work well together, each supplying something that the other one lacks.

content

I am quite content /kənˈtent/ with what I have.

Empty out the contents /ˈkɒntents/ of the can into a bowl.

contrary

ˈContrary to what I had expected, there was a large turn-out at the meeting.

I have never met such a contrary /kənˈtreəri/ child. She never does what you ask her to do.

converse

The ˈconverse of something is its opposite.

To conˈverse with someone is to talk to them.

convict

A ˈconvict is a person who has been conˈvicted of committing a crime.

Did You Know ?

There are many words in English that have the same pronunciation patterns as *converse* and *convict*, with the noun or adjective being stressed on the first syllable and the verb on the second syllable. For example,

How many children are ˈabsent today? / To avoid trouble, I decided to abˈsent myself from the meeting.

An ˈaddict is a person who is adˈdicted to something, such as drugs or alcohol.

'Truth' and 'beauty' are ˈabstract nouns. / This is an ˈabstract of the planners' report. / These are the main points that one could abˈstract from this report.

An ˈexport is something that is exˈported from a country. An ˈimport is something that is imˈported into a country.

Among the many words of this type are: *accent, compact, compound, conduct,* conflict, consort, contest, contract, contrast, convert, decoy, extract, incline, indent, permit, produce, progress, project, prospect, protest, record, recoil, refill, refit, reject, remake, remit, reprint, retread, survey, suspect and torment.

Other similar words, such as **present** and **refuse**, are dealt with as separate entries in this unit.

cord, chord

The spinal cord is your backbone. / The vocal cords in your throat are what allow you to make sounds. / cord trousers / The cord of an electrical appliance is the wire that connects it to the electricity supply.

A chord in music is a number of notes played together.

corn

Corn is a cereal such as wheat or maize.

A corn is a hard painful lump of skin on your foot.

corporal

Corporal punishment is punishment inflicted on a person's body, e.g. a whipping.

A corporal is a soldier lower in rank than a sergeant.

council, counsel

a town council / the Marriage Guidance Council / the Language Research Council

the counsel for the defence in a court of law / I would counsel you to be very cautious about this proposal.

councillor, counsellor

A councillor is a member of a council such as a town council.

A counsellor is someone who gives advice, even if they are a member of or are working for a council. / a marriage guidance counsellor

count

A count is a member of the nobility of some countries.

Count to ten before you open your eyes. / Count yourself lucky to be alive.

counter

A counter is a sort of table in a shop.

A counter is someone or something that counts.

The government tried in vain to counter (= *fight*) the false reports of an impending food crisis.

course *see* coarse

cricket

Cricket is a game played by two teams with a bat and a ball.

A cricket is an insect that resembles a grasshopper.

crow

Crows are large black birds.

The rooster always crows at daybreak.

cue *see* queue

curb, kerb

We'll have to curb her enthusiasm a bit./ We'll have to put a curb on her enthusiasm.

The kerb is the edge of the pavement in a street. (*Note: In American English, a 'kerb' is a curb.*)

currant, current

currants and raisins / blackcurrants

the currents and tides in the sea / electric current flowing through a wire

current trends in literature / current affairs

cycle

A cycle is a bicycle. / I always cycle to work.

A cycle is a repeated series of events. / the life-cycle of the butterfly

cygnet, signet

A cygnet /ˈsɪgnət/ is a young swan.

A signet ring is one with letters or some other design carved on it.

date

Dates are a type of fruit that grow on palm trees.

What date is it today? / Don't forget to date and sign the letter. / I've got a new girlfriend and we're going on our first date tonight. / We haven't been dating long.

dear, deer

Fruit is very dear at this time of the year. / She is a very dear friend of mine.

Deer are animals with horns.

defect

A ˈdefect is a fault or flaw.

Three generals suddenly deˈfected to (= *joined*) the enemy.

dependent, dependant

My children are still financially dependent on me.

Your dependants are members of your family who depend on you financially.

desert, dessert

a sandy desert /ˈdezət/

Several soldiers have deˈserted. (= *left without permission*). / I would never desert my family.

Dessert /dɪˈzɜːt/ is pudding.

One of these days he'll get his just deˈserts (= *punishment for something bad he has done*).

dew, due

There were little beads of dew on the grass.

Payment is due within seven days.

die, dye

I was so ill, I thought I was going to die.

What colour are you going to dye your skirt? / a vegetable dye

Die is a more formal word for a dice. / The die is cast, there's no turning back now.

disc, disk

A disc is a round flat object. / A disc is one of the layers of cartilage between the bones in the spine. (*Note: The normal US spelling of disc is* disk. Disk *is also the normal spelling in computing:* a compact disk / a floppy disk.)

discreet, discrete

Above all, I expect my personal assistant to be discreet (= *careful to keep secrets and not to say anything that might cause trouble or embarrassment.*)

These algae were once classified together but are now regarded as discrete (= *separate*) species.

disk *see* disc

doe, dough

A doe is a female deer. (*see also* does)

Dough /doʊ/ is a mixture of flour, water, etc used to make bread and cakes. / 'Dough' is also a slang word for money.

does, dose, doze

Does /doʊz/ are female deer.

Does /dʌz/ your mother know you are here?

A dose /doʊz/ of medicine is the amount you are given to take at one time. / He's got a bad dose of flu. / He dosed himself with cough medicine.

A doze is a brief light sleep. / He dozed off during the lecture.

dough *see* doe

down

She ran down the stairs.

Down is soft hair or soft feathers.

doze *see* does

draft, draught

I've submitted a draft (= *a rough preliminary version*) of my paper to the committee for its comments. / I must sit down and draft an outline of the book. / A draft of money is an order for its payment by a bank. / a bank draft / In America, the draft is the process of conscripting young men into the armed forces. / He considered various ways of avoiding being drafted into the army.

There's a terrible draught (= *current of air*) in this room. / He took a long draught (= *drink*) of ale. / The draught of a ship is the minimum depth of water in which it will float. (*Note: In American English, 'draught' is spelt* draft.)

Draughts is a game played on a board of black and white squares. (*Note: In American English, 'draughts' is called* checkers.)

duck

ducks and geese

He was so tall, he had to duck as he went through the door.

dual, duel

He has dual nationality, and has both a British and French passport. / A dual carriageway is a road divided in two by a narrow strip of grass or some other central barrier.

He had no option but to fight a duel. / Duelling was banned by the king.

due *see* dew

duel *see* dual

dye *see* die

dying, dyeing

Those flowers are dying.

What colour are you dyeing your skirt?

ear

an ear of corn

The ball hit the boy on the ear. / My sister has a good ear for music.

egg

a hen's egg / a boiled egg

To egg someone on is to encourage them to do something.

eight *see* ate

elicit, illicit

To elicit /ɪˈlɪsɪt/ information from someone is to force them or persuade them to give it to you.

Illicit /ɪˈlɪsɪt/ means 'unlawful': illicit relations with an under-age girl

ensure, insure

Please ensure that your seat belt is fastened before the plane takes off.

We insured the painting for $10,000.

entrance

the ˈentrance to the castle

The little girl was enˈtranced by the performing elephants.

even

even numbers and odd numbers / Try to keep the room at an even temperature. / A last-minute goal unexpectedly evened the score.

I didn't even stop for lunch today. / My hands were dirty, but hers were even dirtier.

ewe *see* you

excuse

An excuse /ɪkˈskjuːs/ is an explanation you give for your behaviour in the hope that someone will excuse /ɪkˈskjuːz/ it.

eye, I

Your eye is what you see things with.

I don't know what to do with myself today.

fair, fare

fair hair / Is that a fair assessment of the situation?

A fair is a large market, or a collection of stalls and amusements that travel from place to place.

Your fare is the money you pay to travel on a bus, aeroplane, etc.

fan

a football fan / fan mail

an electric fan / She fanned herself with a newspaper to keep cool.

fare *see* fair

fast

a fast car / How fast can you run?

To fast is to stop eating for a time, for religious or medical reasons. / a 24-hour fast

feet, feat

Your feet are the parts of your body you walk on.

To sail round the world alone is an amazing feat.

fell

I tripped and fell over in the street.

We'll have to get a tree surgeon to fell (= *cut down*) that old tree.

felt

I felt such a fool when I fell over.

Felt is a woollen fabric. / a felt hat

fiancé, fiancée

A girl's fiancé is the man she is engaged to; a man's fiancée is the girl he is engaged to.

file

A file is a steel tool used to rub wood or metal smooth or to shape it. / He filed the end of the stick into a point.

a file of papers / File that letter under 'nutcases'.

The path was so narrow, they had to walk in single file (= *one behind the other*).

find, fined

I can't find my glasses!

He was fined £500 for dangerous driving.

fine

fine weather / fine clothes / That suits me fine.

a £500 fine / The judge said he would fine him rather than send him to prison.

fined *see* find

fir, fur

a fir tree

an animal's fur

firm

firm ground / a firm commitment / Can we firm up this proposal?

A business firm is a company.

fit

How soon will I be fit again, doctor? / I don't think this coat fits me.

A fit is a sudden attack of illness, laughter, etc. / an epileptic fit / a fit of coughing

flag

The Swiss flag is red with a white cross on it.

After running for several miles, he began to flag (= *become tired and slow down*).

flare, flair

A flare is sudden flash of light or a sudden flame. / He struck a match and it flared in the darkness. / The ship's crew sent up flares (= *devices that produce a strong blaze of light*) to show the lifeboat their position. / Fighting has flared up again between rival gangs. / I could see his nostrils flare

(= *grow wider*). / The legs of the trousers **flared** (= *widened*) towards the bottom.

A **flair** for something is a natural talent for it.

flea, flee

A **flea** is a small insect.

When the volcano erupted, the people in the nearby towns had to **flee** for their lives.

floe *see* flow

flour, flower

You use **flour** to make bread and cakes.

Tulips and daffodils are popular garden **flowers**.

flow, floe

a **flow** of air / the **flow** of ideas in a meeting / The rivers **flow** very quickly down the mountains.

A **floe** is a sheet of floating ice.

flower *see* flour

flush

To **flush** is to go red in the face, e.g. from embarrassment. / To **flush** a toilet is to make water go through it to clean it after use.

Make sure that the window is **flush** with the wall (= *level with it, not sticking out or sunk in deeper than it*).

fool, full

You think I'm a **fool** /fuːl/, don't you? / You can't **fool** me, you know.

Is the cup half-**full** /fʊl/ or half-empty?

for *see* four

forbear, forebear

I shall for'**bear** (= *refrain*) from making any criticism.

Your '**forebears** or '**forbears** are your ancestors.

fore *see* four

forebear *see* forbear

forge

To **forge** someone's signature is to copy it onto a cheque or a letter, etc, and pretend that it is genuine. / A blacksmith's **forge** is where he makes horseshoes, etc.

Despite all the problems, we're **forging** ahead with the project.

foul, fowl

a **foul** smell / **foul** language / This weather is really **fouling** up my plans for the garden. / The team lost after their goal-keeper was sent off for committing a very bad **foul**. / He was sent off for repeated **fouling**.

'**Fowl**' is a formal word for certain types of large bird. / Ducks, geese and swans are water**fowl**. / Hens, turkeys, etc are farmyard **fowl**.

found

I **found** a £5 note lying on the pavement.

The school was **founded** in the tenth century.

four, for, fore

Two and two makes **four**.

What's that switch **for**?

The explosion occurred in the **fore** part of the ship. / an animal's **forelegs**

fowl *see* foul

full *see* fool

fur *see* fir

gait *see* gate

gambol, gamble

Lambs **gambol** in the fields.

People **gamble** with cards.

gate, gait

a garden gate

He walks with a curious gait (= *way of walking*).

gild *see* guild

gilt *see* guilt

gorilla *see* guerrilla

grate *see* great

grave

a grave mistake / The situation is very grave.

The body had been buried in a shallow grave.

graze

Sheep and cattle graze (= *eat grass*) in the fields.

I grazed my hand on that rough wall. / That's a nasty graze. Let's put some antiseptic on it.

grease, Greece

Grease /griːs/ is an oily or fatty substance.

To grease /griːz/ something is to put grease on it.

Greece is a country in Europe.

great, grate

There are a great many things to be done. / Wasn't that a great film!

A grate is the metal framework that holds burning coal or wood in place in a fireplace.

Shall I grate some cheese over the spaghetti bolognese? / Her whining voice really grates on me (= *annoys me*).

grill, grille

A grill is a device for cooking food. / Grill the meat for five minutes.

A grille or grill is a screen of bars or wires, for example one separating staff and customers at a bank.

groan, grown

He gave a loud groan. / He groaned as he tried to get up.

Haven't those plants grown quickly!

ground

ground almonds / She ground the peppercorns to powder.

The plane broke up when it hit the ground. / a football ground / What grounds have you for thinking she's a thief?

guild, gild

A guild /gɪld/ is an association of people, for example people who work in a particular trade or craft.

To gild something is to cover it with gold.

guilt, gilt

Don't you feel any guilt about what you have done to her? / Her guilt was proved beyond doubt.

Gilt is gold material used for gilding picture frames, ornaments, etc.

guerrilla, gorilla

A guerrilla (*or* guerilla) /gəˈrɪlə/ is a member of an independent fighting force. / guerrilla warfare.

A gorilla is a type of large ape.

hail, hale

Hail is small balls of ice that fall like rain. / a hailstone / It was hailing heavily this morning.

We're late. Let's hail a taxi. / The place you hail from is your native town or region.

I've been off work for a few days with flu, but I'm feeling hale and hearty again now.

hair, hare

Go and comb your hair. / You need a haircut.

A hare is an animal that resembles a rabbit. / She hared off down the road as fast as she could.

hale *see* hail

hall, haul

Come in and hang your coat up in the **hall**. / a town **hall**

The fishermen were **hauling** in their nets. / When I say 'now', give a **haul** on that rope.

hangar, hanger

A **hangar** is a large shed where aircraft are kept.

You hang clothes on a **hanger**. / a coat-**hanger**

hare *see* hair

hatch

When do think the eggs will **hatch**? / Those two seem to be **hatching** some cunning plan.

A **hatch** is a door-like opening in a wall, floor or ceiling, or the cover of such an opening.

haul *see* hall

heal, heel

That cut won't take long to **heal**.

Your **heel** is the back part of your foot.

hear, here

Can everyone **hear** me?

Is everyone **here**?

heard, herd

Have you **heard** the news?

a **herd** of cattle

heel *see* heal

herd *see* heard

here *see* hear

heroine, heroin

A **heroine** is a female hero.

Heroin is a drug.

heir *see* air

hide

An animal's **hide** is its skin. / The purse is made of cow**hide**.

Quick, somebody's coming! Where can we **hide**?

higher, hire

Put the sweets on a **higher** shelf so that the children can't reach it.

Boats for **hire**. / We **hired** bikes and cycled round the island.

him, hymn

I don't know where John is. I haven't seen **him** today.

A **hymn** /hɪm/ is a religious song sung, for example, in church.

hind

The dog was standing on its **hind** /haɪnd/ legs.

A **hind** /haɪnd/ is a female deer.

hire *see* higher

hoard, horde

a **hoard** of gold / When the rumours of food shortages started, people began to **hoard** food in case supplies ran out.

a **horde** of insects / a **horde** of tourists

hold

Hold that rope for me, will you? / Keep a tight **hold** on that string.

The ship's **hold** was full of boxes.

hole, whole

There's a **hole** in your jersey.

You haven't eaten the **whole** cake, have you?

hour, our

There are sixty minutes in an **hour**.

This is **our** house.

hymn *see* him

I *see* eye

idle, idol

That boy is bone **idle** (= *very lazy*). / I drew the picture during an **idle** moment (= *a moment when I had nothing else to do*). / The machines were lying **idle** (= *were not in use*). / The boys were **idling** on a street corner.

They worshipped a golden **idol** (= *a statue of a god*). / What happened to the pop stars who were the **idols** of our teenage years?

incense

There was 'incense burning on the altar.

She was in'censed (= *very angry*) when she found out that she'd been cheated.

insure *see* ensure

invalid

I may have a slight cold but that hardly makes me an 'invalid, does it? / He was 'invalided out of the army suffering from stress.

That's an in'valid argument. / I was just about to get on the plane when I found that my visa was in'valid.

isle *see* aisle

it's, its

It's means 'it is'.

Its means 'of it'.

jam, jamb

marmalade and **jam**

a traffic **jam** / Just **jam** all your clothes into one suitcase if you can.

A door **jamb** /dʒam/ or window **jamb** is the post forming the side of the doorway or window frame.

jar

a **jar** of jam

There was a slight **jar** as the car braked. / Rap music really **jars** on my nerves.

kerb *see* curb

key, quay

the front-door **key** / the **key** to solving a problem / This is a **key** point in my argument. / I pressed the wrong **key** and my computer crashed. / **Key** in your password. / This piece is written in the **key** of A minor.

The ship was tied up at the **quay** /kiː/.

kid

A **kid** is a young goat. / That's my **kid** brother.

Don't **kid** yourself that you've got any chance of winning the prize.

kind

a **kind** man

What **kind** of animal is an oryx?

knead *see* need

knew, new

I **knew** I was right.

a **new** car

knight, night

a **knight** in shining armour / He was **knighted** by the Queen.

night and day

knit, nit

My mother is going to **knit** me a cardigan for my birthday. / After you have broken your leg, the bones take some time to **knit** again.

A **nit** is an insect or insect egg found in hair. / A foolish person can be called a **nit**.

knot, not

Tie a **knot** in the string. / The string had been tightly **knotted**.

I'm **not** going to the party, and that's final.

know, no

Do you **know** the answer?

No, I don't.

knows, nose, noes

Nobody **knows** where he is now.

You've got a spot on your **nose**.

I've checked the votes and we have 16 yesses and 13 **noes**.

lair, layer

The bear returned to its **lair** (= *den, home*).

Put alternate **layers** of pasta, meat and cheese sauce into the dish. / The ground was covered with a thin **layer** of snow.

lain, lane

The book had **lain** undiscovered in the library for centuries.

A **lane** is a narrow road.

launch

A **launch** is a large motorboat.

The ship was **launched** last year.

lay

She **lay** down on the bed.

Lay the picture on the table so that we can look at it.

A **lay** person is someone who is not a professional or who has no expertise or training in a subject. / a **lay** preacher

lead, led

Dogs must be kept on a **lead** /liːd/ in the park.

Who is going to **lead** /liːd/ the expedition?

She **led** the children to safety.

Lead /led/ is a metal.

leak, leek

A **leak** is an escape of liquid or gas. / Water is **leaking** out of the tank somehow.

A **leek** is a vegetable.

lean

Lean meat has little or no fat in it.

He was **leaning** on a lamppost at the corner of the street.

leave

When does the next train **leave**?

Our son is home on **leave** from the army.

led *see* lead

leek *see* leak

left

left and right

I must have **left** my umbrella on the bus.

lessen, lesson

Is there anything you can do to **lessen** the pain?

a maths **lesson**

let

House to **let** (= *that can be rented*).

Let me help you with that.

lie

Lie down and go to sleep.

Don't **lie** to me – tell me the truth. / Don't tell **lies**.

light

I can carry the suitcase, it's quite **light**. / a **light** meal / **light**-blue cushions

Switch the **light** on, will you. / sun**light** / **Light** a fire if you feel cold.

lightning, lightening

thunder and **lightning** / A flash of **lightning** momentarily lit the landscape.

Find ways of **lightening** your work load. / The sky was **lightening** in the east.

like

Do you **like** chocolate? / **likes** and dislikes

She looks just **like** me.

live

Her brother and his wife **live** /lɪv/ next door to me.

a **live** /laɪv/ bird / **live** ammunition / The concert will be broadcast **live**.

loan, lone

I got a **loan** of $1000 from my father.

A **lone** figure was waiting at the door.

long

a **long** piece of string / a **long** road

I **long** to be able to retire.

madam, madame

Madam /'madəm/ is used as a polite form of address to a lady, for example by shop assistants or waiters.

Madame /'madəm/ or /mə'dɑːm/ is the French equivalent of Mrs. It is often shortened to Mme.

made, maid

Look at the mess you've **made**!

A **maid** is a female servant.

mail, male

Letters and parcels are delivered by the Royal **Mail**. / e-**mail** / air**mail**

Mail was a sort of armour made of metal rings or plates.

A **male** goose is called a gander.

main, mane

The **main** reason I have come is to see you.

A horse's **mane** is the hair that covers its neck. / a lion's **mane**

march

March is the third month of the year.

The soldiers **marched** along the street. / It had been a long **march**.

maroon

Maroon is a dark red colour.

The sailors found themselves **marooned** on a desert island.

marshal, martial

A field **marshal** is a high-ranking army officer. / **Marshal** your facts before you start to speak.

Martial means 'relating to war, soldiers or military matters' / a court-**martial**

mat, matt

There was a brightly coloured **mat** on the floor. / a mouse **mat** for a computer

Matt or **mat** means 'having a non-glossy surface' / **matt** paint / Would you like the photos with a **matt** or glossy finish?

match

a football **match** / The wallpaper **matches** the curtains. He was no **match** for his opponent.

He took out a box of **matches** and tried to light a fire.

matt *see* mat

may

May is the fifth month of the year.

I **may** be at the meeting, but I **may** not be.

mean

What does 'laudable' **mean**?

That was a **mean** trick! / Don't be **mean**. Lend me $5.

The **mean** of a set of numbers is their average.

I'd like to come to your house but I've no **means** of getting there.

meat, meet, mete

meat and potatoes

I'll **meet** you outside the cinema.

To **mete** out punishment is to impose it on wrongdoers.

medal, meddle

Soldiers get medals for bravery.

Don't meddle in other people's affairs.

meet *see* meat

metal, mettle

A metal is a substance such as gold, silver, steel or iron.

Mettle is your strength of character. / You are 'on your mettle' when you are ready to act with courage.

mete *see* meat

metre, meter

A metre is a unit of length equal to 100 centimetres.

Metre is also the rhythm of poetry.

A meter is a measuring device. / an electricity meter / a parking meter

(*Note: In American English, the spelling* meter *is used for all these words.*)

mettle *see* metal

might, mite

I might be able to help you.

The barbarians were unable to withstand the might of the Roman army.

A mite is a small creature like a spider.

mine

Is that your pen or mine?

a coal mine /a gold mine / People have been mining for gold here for over a century.

miner, minor

a coal miner

a minor accident

minute

There are sixty seconds in a minute /ˈmɪnɪt/.

The police found a minute /maɪˈnjuːt/ trace of blood on his shoes.

miss

This is Miss Wang.

Did I miss the target? / three hits and two misses

missed, mist

You completely missed the target. / Sorry I'm late. I missed the bus.

We couldn't see anything because of the mist.

misuse *see* use

mite *see* might

mole

A mole is an animal that lives underground.

A mole is a dark spot on your skin.

mood

She's in a bad mood today.

The verb 'goes' is in the indicative mood.

morning, mourning

morning and night

The whole country is in mourning following the death of the president.

mould

There's some blue mould on this cheese.

Pour the plaster into the mould and let it set. / You can mould the dough into interesting shapes before you bake it.

muscle, mussel

A muscle /ˈmʌsl/ is a part of your body.

A mussel is a kind of shellfish.

naught *see* nought

naval, navel

Naval means 'relating to a navy or to ships'.

Your navel is the shallow hole in the front of your abdomen.

need, knead

I **need** a new pair of shoes.

When making bread, you must **knead** the dough.

net, nett

a fishing-**net** / **net** curtains

What is the **net** (*or* **nett**) weight of the parcel? (= *the weight of the contents without the packaging*)

new *see* knew

night *see* knight

nit *see* knit

no *see* know

noes *see* knows

none, nun

None of them had seen anything suspicious.

A **nun** is a religious woman who lives in a convent.

nose *see* knows

not *see* knot

nought, naught

A **nought** is a zero.

If a plan comes to **naught**, it fails or is thwarted. / To set something at **naught** is to show contempt for it or disregard it.

(*Note: In American English the spelling* **naught** *is used for 'zero'.*)

novel

That's a **novel** idea. What made you think of that?

I'm reading a **novel** by Conan Doyle.

nun *see* none

oar, or, ore

You can't row a boat with only one **oar**.

Tea **or** coffee?

iron **ore**

oral *see* aural

ore *see* oar

object

There's a strange **object** /ˈɒbdʒɪkt/ in the front garden. / The **object** of this exercise is to practise irregular verbs.

I **object** /əbˈdʒekt/ to what he is saying about my wife.

one, won

I've only got **one** sister, not two.

Who **won** the prize?

our *see* hour

pad

Put a **pad** of cotton wool on the wound. / a **pad** of paper / a note**pad**

I could hear the **pad** of the cat's paws on the garage roof. / There's someone **pad**ding about upstairs.

paddle

A **paddle** is a sort of oar for rowing a canoe. / Don't **paddle** your boat too far from the shore.

I want to **paddle** (= *walk with bare feet*) in the sea. / Are you coming for a **paddle**?

page

Turn in your books to **page** 127.

A **page** is a boy who works in a hotel or club. / a **page**boy at a wedding

pail, pale

a **pail** of water

a **pale**-blue shirt

pain, pane
> aches and pains
>
> a pane of glass

pair, pare, pear
> a pair of gloves / They paired up for the dance.
>
> Pare the rind off the cheese with a sharp knife.
>
> apples and pears

pale *see* pail

pane *see* pain

pare *see* pair

passed, past
> I've passed my driving test at last! / He passed the ball to the striker.
>
> I just saw her driving past the house a moment ago. / Forget about the past and concentrate on what you will do in the future. / We talked about our past successes and failures.

pastel, pastille
> Pastel colours are pale colours. / Pastels are chalks or crayons used by artists.
>
> A pastille /ˈpastɪl/ is a type of sweet, especially a medicated one.

pause, paws
> There was a sudden pause in the conversation. / Let's pause there for a moment.
>
> a cat's paws

peace, piece
> war and peace
>
> a piece of cake / The police tried to piece together the evidence.

peal, peel
> When bells peal, they ring loudly. / He could hear peals of laughter coming from the other room.

orange peel / Would you like to peel the potatoes for me?

pear *see* pair

pedal, peddle
> the pedals of a bicycle / I pedalled as fast as I could.
>
> To peddle goods is to take them from place to place to sell. / She was suspected of peddling drugs. (*Note: A person who peddles goods is a* pedlar.)

peel *see* peal

peep
> I peeped out of the window to see who was at the door. / Take a peep and see who's there.
>
> The baby birds were peeping in the nest.

peer *see* pier

pen
> a felt-tip pen / a ballpoint pen / I've just penned this little poem.
>
> The sheep were safely in their pen for the night. / The sheep need to be penned every night to protect them from wolves.

pick
> You can pick whichever prize you want. / Take your pick of the prizes.
>
> A pick is a long-handled tool with a metal head with pointed ends, used for breaking up hard ground, etc.

pidgin *see* pigeon

piece *see* peace

pigeon, pidgin
> A pigeon /ˈpɪdʒən/ is a type of bird.
>
> A pidgin is a language that has developed from two or more other languages, originally as a means of communication between speakers of different languages, for example in ports, etc. / Pidgin English

pier, peer

The boats were tied up at the pier.

She peered at me over her glasses.

A peer is a member of the nobility.

plain, plane

a plain brown envelope / It's quite plain to me that they've made a mistake. / It's cooler in the mountains than down on the plain. / You describe a task as plain sailing if it is something that is easily done.

I'm going by plane rather than by boat.

A plane is a tool with a metal blade, used to make wood smooth. / I'll need to plane half a centimetre off the bottom of that door.

In geometry, a plane is a flat surface. / To plane is to glide through the air or to move smoothly over water.

A plane is also a kind of tree.

please, pleas

Could you please stop doing that!

They ignored the woman's pleas for help.

poach

To poach an egg is to boil it without its shell.

To poach animals or fish is to hunt and kill them illegally.

pole, poll

The horse was tied to a pole.

It's cold at the North Pole.

A poll is an election or vote. / an opinion poll / The Conservative candidate polled more than half the votes cast.

pool, pull

a pool /puːl/ of water

Pool is a game like snooker and billiards.

When I say 'Now!', pull /pʊl/ this rope.

pore, pour, poor

Sweat comes out through the pores in your skin.

Pour me a cup of coffee, will you.

I wish we had more money. I hate being poor /pɔː, pʊə/.

port

When does the ship get into port?

Port is a type of wine.

On a ship, port means 'left' and starboard means 'right'.

post

Tie the tree to a post to stop it being blown down by the wind. / a fence post

Your cheque is in the post. / I'll post the cheque to you.

My son has got a new post in the psychology department at the university. / Soldiers sometimes get posted abroad.

practice, practise

Practice is a noun, practise is a verb: you practise because you need practice. (*Note: In American English,* practice *is the spelling for both the noun and the verb.*)

pray/prays, prey/preys, praise

Pray that God will forgive you. / She prays every morning.

The eagle's prey is rabbits and other animals. / An eagle preys on rabbits and other animals.

His courage earned him great praise.

present

past, 'present and future / At 'present our policy seems to be working. / I myself was 'present at the meeting.

a Christmas 'present / a birthday 'present

The prizes will be pre'sented by the headmaster's wife.

prey *see* pray

principal, principle

the principal speaker at a meeting / the principal of a college or university

I refuse to betray my principles. / I refuse to go on principle. / In principle it is a simple process, but in practice it often goes wrong.

prize, prise

My mother won first prize in a painting competition. / I prize your friendship very highly.

Prise (*or prize*) open the box (= *force it open*) with a knife.

proceed

To pro'ceed is to begin or continue with some course of action.

'Proceeds are profits from an event or activity.

(*See also* page 187)

programme, program

a television programme / a theatre programme / How shall we programme the evening's events?

a computer program / Program your computer to do a virus check whenever it is rebooted.

(*Note: In American English, the spelling program is normal in all these senses.*)

prune

A prune is a dried plum.

Prune the roses (= *cut off their stems*) at the end of the year.

pull *see* pool

punch

A punch is a blow with one's fist. / She punched him hard and ran off.

A punch is a tool for making holes in things. / Punch holes in the cardboard.

Punch is an alcoholic drink.

pupil

Your pupil is the dark central part of your eye.

a school pupil

quay *see* key

queue, cue

There was a long queue outside the theatre. / We had to queue for hours for a bus.

A cue is a long thin stick used to hit the balls in snooker and billiards.

An actor's cue is the words or gestures of another actor that tell the first actor when to come on stage, speak, move, etc. / Cue the clowns.

race

the human race / a race of cattle

the 400-metres race / Who won the race? / I'll race you to the corner of the street.

racket, racquet

There must be something wrong with the car, the engine's making a terrible racket. / He's been involved in a drugs racket (= *illegally dealing in drugs*).

a tennis racket/racquet

rain, rein, reign

rain and snow / Do you think it will rain?

a horse's reins / You need to rein in (= *restrain*) your enthusiasm a bit.

All this happened during the reign of Queen Victoria. / How long did Victoria reign?

raise, rays, raze

She tried to raise her head from the pillow./ We're having a cycle run to raise money for charity / The landlord has raised the rent on our flat again.

the rays of the sun

The building was razed to the ground (= *completely destroyed*).

rap/rapped, wrap/wrapped, rapt

rap music / There was a rap at the door. / Someone rapped at the door.

Wrap the parcel carefully. / They wrapped the ornaments carefully.

They listened to the speaker with rapt attention (= *very attentively*).

rash

a rash decision / It was a bit rash of you to lend them all that money.

Those spots are turning into a nasty rash.

rays, raze *see* raise

read, reed, red

Read /riːd/ me a story.

A reed /riːd/ is a grass-like plant that grows in lakes and rivers.

I've already read /red/ you two stories.

a red car

real, reel

Is that a real camera? / Theft from cars is a real problem.

a reel of thread / a reel of film / When he felt a tug on his fishing-line, he began to reel in the fish / Loud music makes my head reel. / A reel is a type of Scottish or Irish dance.

rear

We found ourselves at the rear of the parade. / a car's rear tyre

The horse reared up on its hind legs. / I'm going to buy a house in the country and rear chickens.

red, reed *see* read

reel *see* real

refuse

I refuse /rɪˈfjuːz/ to answer that question.

Refuse /ˈrefjuːs/ is rubbish, e.g. from houses. / a refuse dump / refuse collection

rest, wrest

Where is the rest of the money?

You should stop for a rest every hour. / I'll rest here for a moment.

He tried to wrest the gun (= *take it by force*) from the man's hand.

retch *see* wretch

review, revue

A review of a book, play or film is a report that describes it and judges it, indicating its good and bad points. / The play was reviewed in the Straits Times.

A revue is a form of theatrical entertainment consisting of a series of amusing acts.

riddle

A riddle is a sort of word-puzzle.

A riddle is a garden tool rather like a large sieve for separating stones and earth. / Riddle the soil to get rid of the stones.

right, rite, write

right and left / the right answer / The government should take action to right this wrong. / It could easily be put right. / What right have you to say that?

She's made a study of ancient Greek marriage rites. / funeral rites

Write down exactly what I say.

ring, wring

a diamond ring / a three-ring circus. / The children were sitting in a ring listening to a story.

Ring me when you get home. / OK, I'll give you a ring when I get back.

Wring the water out of the skirt before hanging it up to dry. / She just stood there, wringing her hands in despair.

rite *see* right

road, rode, rowed

There's a big hole in the middle of the road.

We **rode** all the way there on our bikes.

He **rowed** the boat across the lake.

rock

If the baby cries, **rock** it in its cradle. / **rock** music / **rock** 'n' roll

The children were climbing over the **rocks** on the seashore.

roe *see* row

roll, role

a **roll** of paper / a bread **roll** / The pencil **rolled** off the table.

What **role** do you have in the play? / He played a leading **role** in the workers' protest.

root, route

the **root** of a tree / the **root** of the problem

The parade will follow the same **route** /ruːt/ as last year.

(*Note: In American English,* **route** *may also be pronounced* /raʊt/. *See also* page 189.)

rose *see* rows

rote *see* wrote

rouse *see* rows

route *see* root

row, roe

a **row** /roʊ/ of houses in a street

How far could you **row** /roʊ/ this boat?

I got a terrible **row** /raʊ/ for being late home. / My mother and father are always **rowing** about something.

Cod **roe** /roʊ/ is cods' eggs.

rows, rose, rouse

rows /roʊz/ of seats in a theatre

A **rose** is a flower.

The sun **rose** yesterday and no doubt it will rise again tomorrow.

We had several **rows** /raʊz/ about it before we came to an agreement.

He was fast asleep, and it was difficult to **rouse** him.

rowed *see* road

rung, wrung

She was standing on the top **rung** of the ladder.

I've **rung** you three times but you never answer the phone.

Once she had **wrung** the water out of the clothes, she hung them out to dry in the sunshine.

rush

I can't stay long, I'm in a terrible **rush**. / She **rushed** into the room and **rushed** out again.

Rushes are grass-like plants that grow in water.

rye, wry

Rye is a cereal like wheat or oats.

He gave a **wry** smile.

sail, sale

I don't like flying. I prefer to **sail**. / We could go for a **sail** this afternoon. / The wind was blowing the ship's **sails**.

House for **sale**. / I bought these shoes in a **sale**.

saw

I **saw** a friend of yours yesterday.

This **saw** isn't very sharp, it won't cut through this wood. / **Saw** the plank to the correct length.

scale

Most fish are covered in scales.

Scales are used to weigh things.

The plans are not to scale (= *not showing all the parts in their correct relative sizes*). / A scale model has all its parts in their correct relative sizes. / How would you rate her performance on a scale of one to five (= *giving a score between one and five*)?

How long would it take you to scale (= *climb*) that cliff?

scene, seen

What happens in the first scene of the play? / She made a terrible scene in the restaurant when the waiter dropped her soup. / Pop music just isn't my scene.

I've never seen anything like that before.

scent *see* sent

school

a primary school / a grammar school / a schoolteacher / I've schooled myself to notice and remember what goes on round about me.

A group of porpoises or whales is called a school.

sea/seas, see/sees, seize

Look at the waves on the sea. / seas and oceans

Can you see anything? / Every time she sees a dog, she screams.

The generals attempted to oust the president and seize power.

seal

A seal is an animal with flippers that lives in the sea.

Seal the envelope carefully before posting it. / Check the jar before opening it to make sure that the seal has not been broken

sealing *see* ceiling

seam, seem

Sew a seam on the dress.

You don't seem very pleased to see me.

second

There are sixty seconds /ˈsekəndz/ in a minute. / I'll be with you in a second.

The horse I backed came second /ˈsekənd/ in the race. / I second that proposal.

He's been seconded /sɪˈkɒndɪd/ temporarily to another department (= *sent to work in that department*).

see *see* sea

seem *see* seam

seen *see* scene

seize *see* sea

sell *see* cell

sent, scent, cent

I sent the letter by airmail.

the scent of a flower

dollars and cents

serial *see* cereal

sew *see* so

shoe, shoo

boots and shoes / a horseshoe / The horse needs shoed.

'Shoo! Go away!' she said to the dog. / She shooed the children out of the room.

side, sighed

There was scratch along the side of the car.

She sighed deeply.

sight, site *see* cite

signet *see* cygnet

size

What size of shoe do you take?

Size is a type of glue.

skate

a roller-skate / ice-skates / There was so much ice, you could almost skate along the pavement.

A skate is a type of fish.

slight, sleight

There's a slight dent in this tray.

The magician was famous for his sleight /slaɪt/ of hand (= *skill in doing tricks*).

smack

If you misbehave again, you'll get a smack. / I'll smack you.

The government's policy smacks of (= *gives the impression of*) desperation. / There's a smack of treachery here.

smelt

I thought I smelt smoke.

To smelt ore is to melt it in a hot furnace to get the metal out of it.

so, sew, sow

I'm so glad you came!

I'll need to sew /soʊ/ a button on this shirt.

Sow /soʊ/ the seed in early May.

A sow /saʊ/ is a female pig.

soar, sore

They watched the eagle soar into the air.

a sore finger

sole, soul

Are you the sole (= *only*) owner of this property?

A sole is a type of fish.

When we die, do our souls go to heaven? / The poor soul, what happened to her?

some, sum

I have some money with me.

I have a large sum of money in the bank. / To sum up, I'd just like to thank everyone for their support.

son, sun

sons and daughters

the sun and the moon

soot, suit

Some soot /sʊt/ has fallen out of the chimney

a suit /suːt/ of clothes / Those clothes really suit you.

sore *see* soar

soul *see* sole

sound

Sssh! Don't make a sound! / When you get to the gate, sound your horn and we'll let you in.

Here we are at last, safe and sound. / That is very sound advice, and I would follow it if I were you.

The ship sailed up the narrow sound between the islands.

sow *see* so

spell

How do you spell 'embarrass'?

The witch put a spell on the children.

We've had a lovely spell of warm weather recently.

spoke

I spoke to John about your plan and he's willing to try it.

The spoke of a wheel is a rod joining the centre of the wheel to its rim.

spray

The bride was carrying a **spray** of pink and white flowers.

A sudden **spray** of water came out of the hosepipe. / In hot weather you need to **spray** the flowers regularly.

squash

There were ten people **squashed** into the car. / **Squash** is a game like tennis or badminton. / Orange **squash** or lemonade?

A **squash** is a type of large vegetable with a hard skin and soft flesh.

stable

Horses are kept in a **stable**.

The doctors say she is very ill but in a **stable** condition.

stair, stare

I tripped on the top **stair** and nearly fell all the way down again.

It's rude to **stare** at people.

stake *see* steak

stalk

the **stalk** of a flower

The hunters had to **stalk** the wounded animal for miles.

stationary, stationery

A **stationary** vehicle is one that isn't moving.

Stationery is writing-paper, envelopes, etc.

steak, stake

a T-bone **steak** / a **steak** pie

Tie the tree to a **stake** to avoid it being blown down by the wind. / **Stake** all the new trees carefully.

There's a lot of money at **stake** in this project, so it had better succeed. / I'm sure that was the man I saw robbing the bank. I'd **stake** my life on it.

steal, steel

Children should be taught that it is wrong to **steal**.

iron and **steel**

stern

The **stern** of a ship is the back of the ship.

Our teacher looks very **stern**, but he's really very kind.

stick

He threw a **stick** for his dog to fetch.

Stick the pages together with glue.

stile *see* style

stole

Who **stole** the money?

She was wearing a silk **stole** over her ball-gown.

story, storey

a fairy **story** / a detective **story**

a three-**storey** building (*Note: In American English,* **storey** *is usually spelt* **story**.)

straight, strait

a **straight** line / Go **straight** home. / The runners are in the final **straight** (= *the straight part of a race track*).

The **Strait** of Gibraltar is the narrow channel of water between Spain and North Africa. / the **Strait** of Malacca / You say that somebody is in dire **straits** when they are in serious trouble, especially because of a lack of money.

strain

Strain the soup through a sieve. / I think I've **strained** a muscle in my leg. / The **strain** of teaching nowadays is more than I could face.

The virus seems to have developed a new, more virulent **strain** (= *variety*).

strait *see* straight

sty, stye

Pigs are kept in a **sty**.

A **sty** or **stye** is a painful swelling on your eyelid.

style, stile

I'm not keen on modern **styles** of clothes.

The farmer had built a **stile** (= *a set of steps*) so that people could get over the fence.

suit *see* soot

suite, sweet

a **suite** of furniture / a three-piece **suite**

Sugar is **sweet**. / For the **sweet** course of the meal, I chose apple tart.

sum *see* some

sun *see* son

Sunday, sundae

Sunday is the first day of the week.

We all had chocolate **sundae** /'sʌndeɪ/ for dessert.

swallow

Swallow what you have in your mouth before you take another bite. / He drank the whole glassful in one **swallow**.

A **swallow** is a small bird with a forked tail.

swat, swot

You **swat** flies.

You **swot** (= *study*) for exams. / He's a bit of a **swot** – always reading books.

sweet *see* suite

swot *see* swat

tail, tale

The dog wagged its **tail**.

The old man had an interesting **tale** to tell.

tap

the cold-water **tap**

He felt a **tap** on his shoulder. / Did somebody **tap** me on the shoulder?

taught, taut

I **taught** French for two years and then I decided I didn't want to be teacher.

Keep the rope **taut**. Don't let it go slack.

tea, tee, T

Coffee or **tea**?

A golfer balances his ball on a **tee**.

a **T**-shirt/**tee**-shirt

tear, tier

There's **tear** /tɛə/ in this shirt. / Be careful not to **tear** your coat on that nail.

A **tear** /tɪə/ ran down her cheek.

A **tier** /tɪə/ is a layer or level. / a three-**tier** wedding cake

tee *see* tea

there, their, they're

There's someone at the door. / **There's** no-one **there**.

Have they taken all **their** bags with them?

They're going to France next week.

threw, through

The boy **threw** a stone at the dog.

The stone went **through** a window.

throes *see* throws

throne, thrown

The king sits on a **throne**.

You shouldn't have **thrown** a stone at that cat.

throws, throes

Anybody who **throws** a stone at an animal deserves to be punished.

The country is in the **throes** of a major crisis.

through *see* **threw**

tick, tic

the **tick** of a clock / Clocks and watches **tick**.

Put a **tick** beside each correct answer. / **Tick** the boxes wherever appropriate.

A **tick** is a small insect-like creature.

A **tic** is a sudden contraction of the muscles of the face.

tide, tied

Tides are the movement of the sea up and down the shore. / high **tide** / low **tide**

He **tied** a knot in the string.

till

Just wait **till** we get home.

The shopkeeper put the money in the **till**.

tip

the **tip** of an arrow

He gave the waitress a **tip** when he paid the bill. / I always **tip** (= *give the staff money for their service*) in restaurants.

Be careful or that vase will **tip** over.

I'll give you a useful **tip** – never lend a friend money. / The police said that someone had **tipped** them off about the robbery (= *told them it was going to happen*).

tire, tyre

I **tire** easily these days. I must be getting old. / I don't want to **tire** you out.

the **tyres** on a car (*Note: In American English, tyre is spelt tire.*)

to *see* **too**

toe, tow

the **toe** on your foot

The car won't start; we'll need to **tow** it to a garage.

told, tolled

I **told** you not to do that.

They **tolled** (= *rang*) the bell slowly as the funeral procession went by.

ton, tonne

A **ton** /tʌn/ equals 2240 pounds in the United Kingdom and 2000 pounds in the United States.

A **tonne** /tʌn/ or 'metric **ton**' equals 1000 kilograms.

too, two, to

Is that music **too** loud?

She's has **two** cats and a dog.

Do you want **to** come with us? / I went **to** Japan last year.

tow *see* **toe**

troop, troupe

a **troop** of soldiers / The teacher was followed by a **troop** of children. / **Troops** of tourists visit the shrine every day. / A country's **troops** are its soldiers. / We **trooped** into the hall to see what was going on.

a **troupe** /truːp/ of actors / a dancing **troupe**

T-shirt *see* **tea**

two *see* **too**

use

I didn't **use** /juːz/ all the paint. There's still some left.

Can you find a **use** /juːs/ for this pot?

> *drug **abuse** /ə'bjuːs/*
>
> *Don't **misuse** /mɪs'juːz/ your time.*
>
> *The machine had been subjected to a lot of **misuse** /mɪs'juːs/.*

utter

She looked at me in utter disbelief.

She didn't utter a word.

vain, vein, vane

We tried to reach her but in vain. / She's extremely vain, full of her own importance.

Blood flows through your veins.

the vanes of a propeller

veil, vale

Her face was hidden by a veil.

Vale is an old or literary word for a valley, sometimes used in place-names.

vain *see* vein

vale *see* veil

vane *see* vein

vice

A vice is a tool that is fastened to a work-bench and is used for holding things firmly while they are being sawn, filed, etc.

Vice is wicked behaviour.

wage

£4 an hour is hardly a reasonable wage.

The Romans waged war against the barbarians.

waist, waste

How much do you measure round the waist?

I was brought up not to waste money. / This is just a waste of time.

wait, weight

I had to wait half an hour for a bus. / I had a long wait too.

You're eating too many cakes. You've put on weight (= *become heavier*) since I last saw you.

waive *see* wave

waste *see* waist

wave, waive

A huge wave overturned the boat. / sound waves / A wave of hysteria swept through the crowd. / She gave a wave as she got into the plane. / Wave bye-bye to Daddy. / The crowd were cheering and waving flags.

He has agreed to waive (= *not ask for*) his normal fee and work for nothing.

way, weigh

There must be a way of doing this more quickly.

How much do you weigh?

weak, week

I felt very weak when I had the flu. / That was a pretty weak excuse.

There are seven days in a week.

weather, whether

Hasn't the weather been terrible lately! / We shall no doubt weather the storm.

I don't know whether I should go with him or not.

week *see* weak

weigh *see* way

weight *see* wait

well

You sang that very well.

They have to go to the well every day to fetch water.

wet, whet

a wet day / I'm soaking wet / Water splashed up from the gutter and wet my dress.

A holiday in France served to whet my appetite for travel (= *made me keen to travel*). / To whet an axe or a knife is to sharpen it.

whether *see* weather

which, witch

Which car is yours?

The witch cast a spell on the prince and turned him into a frog.

whine *see* wine

whit *see* wit

whole *see* hole

wind

The wind /wɪnd/ was blowing through the trees.

Wind /waɪnd/ the rope round your body before starting to climb down.

wine, whine

a glass of wine

the whine of a motor / The dog sat at the door and whined.

witch *see* which

won *see* one

wood, would

The box was made of some kind of dark-brown wood. / There's a pine wood near our house where you can see all kinds of birds.

I would help you if I could.

wound

The knife had made a nasty wound /wuːnd/ in his leg.

He took the key and wound /waʊnd/ up the clock. / She wound a hankie round her cut finger.

wrap, wrapped *see* rap

wrest *see* rest

wretch, retch

Why would anyone want to help a wretch like me?

To retch is to try to be sick but without actually vomiting.

wring *see* ring

write *see* right

wrote, rote

I wrote to you last week

To learn something by rote is to learn it by memorizing it without necessarily understanding it. / rote learning

wrung *see* rung

wry *see* rye

yard

Three feet equal one yard.

The lorries were parked in the yard at the back of the house. / a farmyard

yew *see* you

yoke, yolk

The oxen were kept together by a yoke (= *a sort of wooden collar*). / They were yoked together. / Scotland struggled to free itself from the yoke (= *control, oppression*) of England.

Egg yolk is yellow.

you, ewe, yew

Where are you going?

A ewe is a female sheep.

a yew tree

your, you're

Is that your house?

You're not going out dressed like that.

DO IT YOURSELF

A Select the appropriate word from each of the pairs in brackets to complete the sentences correctly.

1. There were (*hordes, hoards*) of people in town this afternoon.

2. My son has just been elected to the town (*council, counsel*).

3. Is it wrong to (*steel, steal*) food when your family is starving?

4. Looking after pigs is a real (*boar, bore*).

5. A bucket is the same thing as a (*pail, pale*).

6. My daughter decided to (*die, dye*) her hair red.

7. I bought a bottle of perfume for my wife. It cost me 23 dollars and 50 (*scents, cents*).

8. Of (*course, coarse*) I'll come and help you start your car.

9. There's no need to (*altar, alter*) your plans on my account.

10. I've got a terrible (*pane, pain*) in my stomach, doctor.

11. Passengers should not alight until the train is (*stationery, stationary*).

12. Can you smell gas? There must be a (*leek, leak*) somewhere.

13. The driver had to (*brake, break*) sharply when a little girl ran out in front of his car.

14. I bought this boat cheap in the end-of-season (*sail, sale*).

15. The children were feeding buns to the (*bears, bares*) at the zoo.

16. The prisoners were locked up in tiny (*sells, cells*).

17. The crowd (*raised, razed*) a cheer as the procession drove (*passed, past*).

18. I was (*born, borne*) 50 years ago today. I was the eighth child that my mother had (*born, borne*).

19. The band consisted of a drummer, pianist, saxophonist and a (*base, bass*) guitarist.

20. The (*principal, principle*) benefit of this method is its simplicity.

21. I love wandering down country (*lanes, lains*) on warm summer evenings.

22. A man was killed this afternoon when several (*bales, bails*) of hay fell off a lorry onto his car.

B Using the lists of homonyms, find a suitable word to answer the following riddles.

> *Example:*
>
> What do trees and dogs have in common?
> Their b____k.
> The answer is, of course, their **bark**.

1. What would be a rather wet place to keep money in?
   A river b____k.

2. What might fish use to weigh things?
   Sc____s.

3. What do people and cereals have in common?
   They both have e____s.

4. Why does a female deer always stand on her back legs?
   Because they're her h____d legs.

5. Why are there calendars hanging from that tree?
   Because it's a d____e palm.

6. What do you call a dark furry spot on your arm?
   A m____e.

7. Why was the body buried in the wrong cemetery?
   It was a gr____e mistake.

8. Why did the girl make a ringing sound at the dance?
   Because she was the b____e of the ball!

9. What do you get when you boil cars and sugar together?
   A traffic j____m.

10. What sort of dog is forever getting into fights?
    A b____r.

11. Why did the doctor decide to remove all the patient's spots?
    It was a r____h decision.

12. What stretches and makes beautiful music?
    An elastic b____d.

Words that Are
Often Confused
or Misused

5

How to use the lists

As in Unit 4, where the stress patterns of words have to be distinguished by means of a stress mark, the stress mark precedes the stressed syllable. For example, 'convict is stressed on the syllable con-, whereas con'vict is stressed on the syllable -vict.

abuse, misuse

Both these words refer to the 'wrong use' of something.

Abuse is most often used to refer to something being used for the wrong purposes: *drug abuse / abuse of power*. Misuse may also denote the use of something for the wrong purposes: *He was accused of misusing party funds.*

When what is meant is the use of something in an *incorrect* way, misuse is the right word to use: *Your washing-machine has clearly been subjected to a lot of misuse. It's hardly surprising it has broken down.*

Abuse also denotes cruel or unkind treatment, as in *child abuse*, and rude or unkind words, as in *He got a lot of abuse from his neighbours when he started burning rubbish in his front garden.*

accept, except

If you accept /ək'sept/ something, you receive it gladly or you agree to it: *Please accept this gift. / They've accepted our proposal.*

Except /ɪk'sept/ means 'not including': *I answered all the questions except the last one.*

Except can also be used as a verb, meaning to exclude, leave out or make an exception of someone or something: *Some folk are terribly lazy, present company excepted, of course.*

access, excess

You have access /'akses/ to something when you are able to see it or use it: *We'll need to have access to all your files.* You also access information on a computer.

An access of something is a sudden fit of it: *In an access of generosity, he offered to pay for lunch.*

An excess /'ekses/ of something is too much of it: *Most people have an excess of fat in their diet.* Excesses are outrageous actions: *The government deplores the excesses of some of its supporters.*

accord, account

If you do something of your own accord, you do it without being told to do it or forced to do it. If you do something on your own account, you do it for your own benefit.

addition, edition

An addition to something is something added it: *We're expecting an addition to the family (= another child) in September.* Addition is also the process of adding up: *Your addition is wrong.*

An edition of a book or newspaper is a set of copies of it that are printed at one time: *The first edition had a few errors which we corrected in the second edition.*

adverse, averse

Adverse /'advɜːs/ circumstances, conditions, or criticism are unfavourable ones: *He coped amazingly well in adverse circumstances. / I'm immune to adverse criticism. I just do what I think is best.*

If you are averse /ə'vɜːs/ to something, you object to it: *I'm not averse to a small whisky at bedtime.*

advice, advise

Advice /əd'vaɪs/ is a noun, advise /əd'vaɪz/ is a verb: you advise someone, or you give them advice.

affect, effect

You are affected /ə'fektɪd/ by something if it changes things for you, or makes you change in some way: *Nobody over 40 will be affected by the new legislation. / Working at a computer all day is beginning to affect my eyesight. / Her plight has affected me deeply.*

Affect also means 'to pretend': *She affected not to recognize him when he came in.*

The **effect** /ɪˈfekt/ of something is its result or consequence, or the impression it makes: *What effect will the new legislation have on those under 40? / Her pleas had no effect on her captors.* To **effect** something is to make it happen: *The alterations to the traffic flow will be effected as soon as possible. / She tried to effect a reconciliation between her parents.*

afflict, inflict

Afflict means 'to cause pain or distress to someone': *Exam nerves afflict most students at some time or another.*

Inflict means 'to cause something bad or unpleasant to happen to someone': *They inflicted heavy casualties on the enemy.*

Notice that you **inflict** some*thing* on some*one* but you **afflict** some*one* with some*thing*.

alibi, alias

An **alibi** /ˈaləbaɪ/ is a form of defence against a criminal charge, the defence being that the accused person was somewhere else when the crime was committed: *I can prove I didn't steal the jewels. I have an alibi for that night.* ('Alibi' is a Latin word meaning 'somewhere else'.)

An **alias** /ˈeɪlɪəs/ is a false name that a person uses to hide their real identity: *She wrote the book under an alias.* ('Alias' is a Latin word meaning 'otherwise'.)

allay, alley, ally

To **allay** /əˈleɪ/ somebody's fear, hunger, etc is to make it less: *This new piece of information allayed her suspicions.*

An **alley** /ˈali/ is a narrow street. It is also a place where you can go bowling: *a bowling-alley.*

An **ally** /ˈalaɪ/ is a friend, especially a political one: *Britain and France were allies during the war. / Italy allied herself to Germany.*

allude, elude

To **allude** /əˈluːd/ to something is to refer to it indirectly without mentioning it specifically: *I was alluding to her recent Broadway success.*

Something **eludes** /ɪˈluːdz/ you when it escapes you: *His name eludes me* (= I can't remember it). */ The perpetrators of the hoax have so far eluded detection.*

allusion, delusion, illusion

You make an **allusion** /əˈluːʒən/ to something when you allude to it: *You find plenty of allusions to contemporary politics in his plays.*

A **delusion** /dɪˈluːʒən/ is a false belief that arises in a person's mind, often as a result of mental unbalance: *You begin to suffer from the delusion that everyone is against you.*

An **illusion** /ɪˈluːʒən/ is a wrong impression, often a visual one, that is caused by something outside a person's mind: *You can use mirrors to create an illusion of space. / I have no illusions about the house – I know it's in need of a great deal of repair.*

ally *see* allay

ambiguous, ambivalent

An **ambiguous** statement is one that can have more than one meaning.

If you are **ambivalent** /amˈbɪvələnt/ about something, you have mixed feelings or emotions about it: *I'm rather ambivalent about Scottish independence.*

amiable, amicable

Both these adjectives mean 'friendly'.

Amiable /ˈeɪmɪəbəl/ is chiefly used about people: *an amiable companion / an amiable smile.* When used of other things, it means 'pleasant', 'not causing offence': *We had an amiable chat. / He made a few amiable remarks and then left the meeting.*

Amicable /ˈamɪkəbəl/ means 'done in a friendly way', and is used mainly about dealings or relationships between people: *I'm sure we can come to some amicable arrangement about payments. / They lived together amicably for years but never married.*

among *see* between

amoral, immoral

Amoral /eɪˈmɒrəl/ means 'not concerned about matters of right and wrong'.

Immoral /ɪˈmɒrəl/ means 'wicked', 'morally wrong'.

angel, angle

An angel /ˈeɪndʒəl/ is a heavenly being who comes as a messenger from God.

An angle /ˈaŋgəl/ is a corner formed by two lines or surfaces: *How many angles has an octagon got?*

An angle on something is an opinion or viewpoint or aspect: *The Times had a different angle on the matter. / Let's try to look at this from a different angle.*

artist, artiste

An ˈartist paints pictures, makes sculptures, etc. You are also an artist at something if you are good at it: *She's an artist at making birthday cakes.*

An artiste /ɑːˈtiːst/ is a theatrical or circus performer. This kind of performer can also be called an artist: *a tightrope artiste/artist.*

auspicious, propitious

Both these words mean 'favourable to future success', but they are not quite synonymous.

Circumstances are auspicious when they give you hope of success in the future (e.g. because something about them is considered a good omen, whether or not it will itself lead directly to success), whereas circumstances that are propitious should lead to success (e.g. because they provide favourable conditions for whatever is being undertaken): *With so few people turning out, it was not an auspicious opening for her new play. / With a high rate of inflation, the government did not think it was a propitious time to call an election.*

(*Note:* In phrases such as *on this auspicious occasion* {often used in speeches when no idea of future success is intended}, auspicious simply means 'important'.)

authoritarian, authoritative

Authoriˈtarian means 'demanding obedience from others': *an authoritarian government.*

Auˈthoritative means 'having authority', 'able to be trusted because of the knowledge, status or expertise of the person making it': *an authoritative opinion.*

averse *see* adverse

baleful *see* baneful

ballet, ballot

Ballet /ˈbaleɪ/ is a form of dance.

A ballot /ˈbalət/ is a secret vote taken to elect somebody or to decide something: *There will have to be a ballot of all union members. / We shall be balloting our members on this issue.*

baneful, baleful

Baneful means 'harmful': *There was a discussion on whether television has a baneful effect on children's behaviour.*

Baleful may also mean 'harmful', but is more commonly used to mean 'threatening harm' rather than 'causing harm'. It may also mean 'sad' or 'dismal': *a baleful look.*

barbarian, barbaric, barbarous

A bar'barian is a person who belongs to a relatively uncivilized society. A rough or uncultured person may be called a barbarian.

The adjective barbaric means 'relating to or typical of barbarians': *barbaric tribes*.

Bar'baric may also mean 'typical of a barbarian' in a good sense, but is more usually used to convey a notion of cruelty: *Many people consider fox-hunting barbaric*.

'Barbarous also means 'cruel': *barbarous crimes against humanity*.

Barbarous language is ungrammatical or not idiomatic.

The nouns bar'barity and 'barbarism both mean 'cruelty'. Barbarism also means 'the state of being a barbarian', and 'an example of ungrammatical language'.

bath, bathe

To bath /bɑːθ/ somebody is to wash them in a bath or a bathtub.

To bathe /beɪð/ a wound or an injured part of the body is to wash it gently: *His injured hand was bathed and bandaged*.

You bathe when you go for a swim. (*Note:* This use of the word is only found in British English.)

If you are very hot, you may be bathed /beɪð/ in sweat.

(*Note:* In American English, you bathe when you take a bath, and you bathe someone when you wash them in a bath.)

behalf, part

On behalf of means 'for or as a representative of someone', and on the part of means 'by or of someone': *I am writing on behalf of the local women's art group. / This was surely an error on the part of the treasurer*.

between, among

Things are shared out between two people or groups but among three or more people or groups. An exception to this is when the exact number of people or groups is stated, when it is correct to use either among or between: *The cakes were shared out between/ among all six children*.

When the reference is to discussions, agreements, shared knowledge, physical position, etc, between is quite correctly used to relate three or more people, groups or things: *There have been all-night discussions between representatives of the government, the revolutionaries and the bishops who are acting as mediators. / Laos lies between Myanmar, Thailand, Cambodia, Vietnam and China*.

biennial, biannual

Bi'ennial means 'happening or coming once every two years', while bi'annual means 'happening or coming twice a year'.

billion

In British English, a billion is a million millions, in American English it is a thousand millions. Similarly, a trillion is a million million millions in British, but a thousand thousand millions in American English.

The situation is further confused by the fact that in scientific and financial contexts, many speakers of British English follow the American usage.

blatant *see* flagrant

boil *see* broil

broil, boil

To broil food is to cook by direct heat, especially on a grill.

To boil food is to cook it in hot water.

censor, censure, census

A **censor** is an official who checks books, films, etc before they are released to the public, and who can order parts of them to be deleted, or even forbid their publication or release altogether: *a film censor / Parts of the film had been censored.*

Censure /ˈsenʃə/ is disapproving criticism: *He met with a lot of censure for not taking a firmer stand against corruption. / She was censured for her part in the deception.*

A **census** /ˈsensəs/ is an official survey of the population of a country, etc in order to find out how many people there are and to gather information about them.

childish, childlike

Childish means 'like a child in a bad sense': *stupid childish behaviour.*

Childlike means 'like a child in a good sense': *childlike innocence.*

choose, chose

Choose /tʃuːz/ is the present tense of the verb, **chose** /tʃəʊz/ is the past tense: *Choose a suitable partner. / The donor chose to remain anonymous.*

clothes, cloths

Clothes /kləʊðz/ are items of clothing: *What clothes shall I put on today?*

Cloths /klɒθs/ is the plural of cloth: *Are there any cleaning cloths in the kitchen cupboard?*

college, collage

A **college** /ˈkɒlɪdʒ/ is an educational institution, such as a high school or a university.

A **collage** /kɒˈlɑːʒ/ is a picture made by sticking small pieces of cloth, etc onto something to make a picture.

comma, coma

A **comma** /ˈkɒmə/ is the punctuation mark (,).

A **coma** /ˈkəʊmə/ is a prolonged state of unconsciousness.

complacent, complaisant

Complacent /kəmˈpleɪsənt/ people are too easily satisfied with themselves or their achievements: *Don't be complacent – always try to improve!*

A **complaisant** /kəmˈpleɪzənt/ person likes to keep other people happy and is inclined to always agree to whatever they want: *a complaisant wife.*

comprise

There is often confusion about how to use this verb correctly. An object that is made up of several parts **comprises** its separate parts, and the separate parts **comprise** the whole object: *Great Britain comprises Scotland, England and Wales. / The countries that comprise Great Britain are Scotland, England and Wales.*

It is quite common to hear people say that something **is comprised of** its separate parts. This was once incorrect, but is now quite acceptable in everyday language, although some people still frown on it.

confident, confidant, confidante

Confident /ˈkɒnfɪdənt/ means 'self-assured' or 'quite convinced about something': *a confident, outgoing person / I'm quite confident that we shall succeed.*

A (male) **confidant** /ˈkɒnfɪdant/ or (female) **confidante** is a person you tell your secrets to: *His younger sister was his chief confidante.*

continual, continuous

Continual means 'happening again and again'. **Continuous** means 'going on without a break, without stopping'. **Continual** noise comes in repeated bursts with periods of silence in between, whereas **continuous** noise never stops.

corps, corpse

A **corps** /kɔː/ is a group of people engaged together on particular projects or duties: *the diplomatic corps / a cadet corps*. (The plural is **corps** /kɔːz/).

A **corpse** /kɔːps/ is a dead body.

critic, critique

A **'critic** is a person who criticizes someone or something: *a newspaper's theatre critic / This policy does have its critics, but most people agree with it.*

A **critique** /krɪ'tiːk/ is a detailed analysis and assessment of something, such as the work of a writer.

cynic *see* sceptic

definite, definitive

'Definite means 'clear' or 'certain': *I'll need a definite answer by tomorrow.*

De'finitive means 'final, complete, settling a matter once and for all': *He has written what I think must be the definitive book on who murdered President Kennedy* (= a book that gives the final answer to the question, that says all that there is to say about it).

delusion *see* allusion

deny *see* refute

deprecate, depreciate

To **deprecate** /'deprəkeɪt/ something is to disapprove of it or to express disapproval of it: *I deprecate your going but I won't stop you.*

To **depreciate** /dɪ'priːʃieɪt/ is to fall in value or become less: *The value of a car depreciates even more rapidly if it isn't looked after.* To **depreciate** something also means 'to talk about it as if it has little value or importance': *I feel this report depreciates the contribution our*

department has made to the project. / *You shouldn't depreciate your achievements. You've done a lot.*

(*Note:* Although the derived forms **depreciating**, **depreciatory** and **self-depreciation** do exist, they are nowadays commonly replaced by derived forms of **deprecate – deprecating**, **deprecatory** and **self-deprecation**: *He made deprecating comments about his skill as a pianist* {= comments that depreciated his skill}).

derisive, derisory

Derisive /dɪ'raɪsɪv/ means 'mocking, laughing at something': *derisive laughter.*

Derisory /dɪ'raɪsəri/ means 'ridiculous, deserving to be laughed at': *The union said that the pay rise on offer was derisory and completely unacceptable.*

device, devise

A **device** /dɪ'vaɪs/ is a tool used to perform a task or a means of doing something: *a device for removing cherry stones.*

Devise /dɪ'vaɪz/ is a verb: *She devised a means of attaching her mobile phone to her handbag.*

disability, inability

A **disability** is a physical or mental handicap such as blindness or lameness.

Inability is the state of being unable to do something: *I don't understand your apparent total inability to follow simple instructions.*

discomfort, discomfit

Discomfort is a noun meaning 'a slight pain' or 'a lack of comfort': *Take painkillers if you experience any discomfort over the next few days. / Sleeping on the floor won't bother me. I can put up with a bit of discomfort.*

Discomfit is a verb meaning 'to embarrass or disconcert': *He became very quiet, evidently discomfited at being criticized so publicly.*

disinterested

Disinterested usually means 'not showing any bias', 'not influenced by one's own feelings, desires or selfish motives': *We need to get the opinion of a disinterested party.* It can, however, also mean 'having no interest in something'.

distinct, distinctive

Something that is distinct is very clearly seen, heard, smelled, etc: *There was a distinct smell of whisky on his breath.*

Something that is distinctive is something that is characteristic of one person or thing, something that clearly distinguishes one person or thing from others: *Whisky has a very distinctive smell.*

edition *see* addition

effect *see* affect

eligible, illegible

Eligible /ˈelɪdʒɪbəl/ means 'suitable or qualified for something': *You are eligible for a pension at the age of sixty-five.*

Illegible /ɪˈledʒɪbəl/ means 'not legible', 'not readable': *illegible handwriting.*

elude *see* allude

eminent, imminent

An eminent person is somebody who is distinguished or important: *an eminent surgeon.*

An imminent event is one that is about to happen: *their imminent departure for the United States.*

emission, omission

An emission of something is a release or discharge of it: *an emission of radioactive gas from the power station.*

The omission of something is the act or mistake of leaving it out: *He was offended by the omission of his name from the guest list.*

enquire, enquiry, inquire, inquiry

The verb can be spelt enquire or inquire with no distinction of meaning.

For the noun also, many people make no distinction between the two spellings.

However, for some speakers of English, an enquiry is a single, simple question, whereas inquiry is used for an investigation: *the enquiry desk in a shop / a government inquiry into the measles epidemic.*

envelop, envelope

To enˈvelop something is to surround and cover it: *The mountain was enveloped in mist.*

An ˈenvelope is a sealed cover for a letter.

envisage, visualize

Both envisage and visualize mean 'to form a mental picture of something': *Try to visualize/envisage what the house will look like when it is completed.*

Envisage has a further meaning, 'to foresee or expect something': *I don't envisage any difficulties.*

equable, equitable

An ˈequable person is calm, cheerful and not easily upset. An equable climate is one that is never extremely cold nor extremely hot.

An ˈequitable arrangement between people is one that is fair to everyone.

especially, specially

Especially means 'particularly': *It's lonely here, especially in the winter.*

Specially means 'specifically and solely': *I made this dessert specially for you because I know you like it.*

except *see* accept

excess *see* access

exercise, exorcize

People exercise, or take exercise, to get fit and healthy.

To exorcize a ghost or a demon is to get rid of it by prayer or other means.

farther, further

Farther is used only with reference to distance: *The summit was farther away than we had thought.*

Further is used with reference to distance: *I can't go any further.* It is also used in the sense of 'additional': *Further instructions will be sent tomorrow.*

Further is also a verb meaning 'to help or advance something': *This unexpected publicity could further our chances of success.*

fatal, fateful

Fatal means' causing death or disaster': *a fatal accident / a fatal mistake.*

Fateful means 'of great importance', 'having important consequences': *I still remember that fateful day when I decided to quit my job and emigrate to Australia.*

fewer, less

Fewer should be used when what is being referred to is a number of individual people or things: *There were fewer than twenty people at the meeting.*

Less should be use when referring to amounts or quantities: *I take less sugar in my coffee than I used to. / The whole computer package cost less than $900.*

fictional, fictitious

A ˈfictional character, place or event is one that appears in a story, play, etc, but that has no existence in the real world: *Tazenda is a fictional country created for the film 'The Queen of Tazenda'.*

Something that is ficˈtitious has no basis in reality, and may be invented in order to deceive people: *He gave the police a fictitious address.*

final, finale

Final means 'last': *in the final stages of the project.* A final is the deciding match of a competition: *a cup final.*

The finale /fɪˈnɑːli/ of a show, etc is the grand final scene or event: *Everyone appears on stage for the finale.*

flagrant, blatant, fragrant

Flagrant /ˈfleɪgrənt/ misbehaviour is behaviour that is very obviously outrageous or wicked: *flagrant immorality.*

Blatant /ˈbleɪtənt/ means 'quite clear or obvious': *That was a blatant lie.*

Fragrant /ˈfreɪgrənt/ means 'sweet-smelling': *fragrant herbs.*

flammable, inflammable, non-flammable, non-inflammable

Flammable and inflammable both mean 'readily burning or catching fire': *highly flammable substances / inflammable fabrics.* Their antonyms are non-flammable and non-inflammable.

flaunt, flout

To flaunt something is to show it off: *She went around the office flaunting her engagement ring.*

To flout the law, a rule or a convention is to break it.

fortunate, fortuitous

Fortunate means 'lucky, timely, convenient, etc': *It was fortunate that you came along just at that moment.*

Fortuitous means 'accidental, happening by chance': *It was quite fortuitous that I was there at all.*

fragrant *see* flagrant

further *see* farther

goal, gaol

A goal /goʊl/ is what you score or defend in football and other games: *We'll try Dave in goal. / a goalkeeper.*

A goal is also an aim or purpose: *My goal is to be a millionaire by the time I'm thirty.*

A gaol /dʒeɪl/ is a prison, a jail: *He had to spend a night in gaol. / She was gaoled for her part in the robbery.*

gourmand, gourmet

A gourmand /ˈɡʊəmənd/ is a greedy person.

A gourmet /ˈɡʊəmeɪ/ is a person who is an expert on good food.

hanged, hung

Hung is the usual past tense and past participle of the verb hang: *I hung my coat on a peg. / Coloured lanterns had been hung from the ceiling.*

Hanged is used when you are referring to someone dying or being killed by hanging: *He was in such despair that he hanged himself. / People were hanged for stealing in the old days.*

historic, historical

Historic means 'famous or important in history': *the site of a historic battle.*

Historical means 'having actually happened or existed at some time in history': *Is the Battle of Glasgow a historical event, or is it just a legend?* Historical also means 'relating to history': *historical studies.*

human, humane

A human is a person: *Computers can't do everything that humans can.* Human is also an adjective meaning 'relating to people': *human beings / To make mistakes is only human.*

Humane /hjuːˈmeɪn/ means 'kind, not cruel': *This is the most humane method of slaughtering cattle.*

hung *see* hanged

illegible *see* eligible

illusion *see* allusion

immoral *see* amoral

immunity, impunity

Immunity is freedom from something or resistance to it: *One vaccination will give you immunity to tetanus for ten years. / Foreign diplomats have diplomatic immunity, which means they cannot be prosecuted for crimes they commit.*

Impunity means 'freedom from punishment or from unpleasant consequences': *You cannot expect to repeatedly break the drink-driving law with impunity. You'll get caught eventually.*

imply *see* infer

impractical, impracticable

An impractical person lacks manual skills or common sense. An impractical idea or plan is one that is not sensible or realistic.

An impracticable plan or proposal is one that cannot be carried out because there are too many difficulties: *It's an attractive scheme, but quite impracticable.*

impunity *see* immunity

inability *see* disability

infer, imply

To infer something is to form an opinion based on what you already know: *From the look on her face, I inferred that she was not entirely happy.*

To imply something is to hint at it without actually saying it: *Are you implying that I was lying?*

(*Note:* **Infer** is often used in the same sense as **imply:** *Are you inferring I'm a liar?* This use of the word is often condemned, but has in fact been common in English for over 400 years and is found in the works of some of the best English writers.)

inflammable *see* flammable

inflict *see* afflict

ingenious, ingenuous

Ingenious means 'very clever, especially in a surprising or original way': *a new and ingenious method of preparing skin grafts.*

Ingenuous means 'innocent', 'childlike', 'trusting', 'lacking suspicion', 'open and frank'. The notion is usually one of being naïve or too trusting: *ingenuous young girls.*

inhuman, inhumane

Both in'human and inhu'mane mean 'cruel'. Inhuman is stronger in meaning than inhumane, meaning not just 'cruel or unkind' but 'cruel to a degree almost unbelievable of a human being': *Their treatment of their prisoners was not just inhumane but absolutely inhuman.*

Inhuman also means simply 'not human'.

inquire, inquiry *see* enquire

intense, intensive

Intense means 'strong': *I had a sudden feeling of intense anger.*

Intensive means 'concentrated, thorough': *They made an intensive search for the missing girl.*

laid, lain

Laid is the past tense and past participle of **lay**: *He went to sleep as soon as he laid his head on the pillow. / Have you laid the table?*

Lain is the past participle of **lie**: *The letter had lain unopened on the doormat for a whole week.*

lay, lie

You lay something somewhere when you put it there: *Ask the guests to lay their coats on the bed.*

To lay the table is to set out the mats, cutlery, etc required for people to eat a meal.

Lay is also the past tense of the verb **lie**: *I lay down and went to sleep. / The letter lay unopened on the doormat. / I wondered what difficulties lay ahead.*

Lie means 'to rest in a horizontal position' or 'to be situated somewhere': *I'll go and lie down on the sofa. / The village lies just beyond the next range of hills. / I know where the blame for this lies.*

To lie also means 'to say something that is untrue. The past tense and past participle of this verb lie are lied: *He lied about his age.*

less *see* fewer

loose, lose

Loose /luːs/ is an adjective: *I'd better tighten this loose screw.*

Lose /luːz/ is a verb: *Don't lose your train ticket.*

luxurious, luxuriant

A luxurious flat is one that is expensive and that has a lot of expensive things in it.

Luxuriant means 'abundant, growing vigorously': *the luxuriant growth of plants in a warm, wet climate.*

masterful, masterly

Masterful means 'showing power or determination': *She likes a man to be masterful.*

Masterly means 'showing great skill': *It was a masterly display of swordsmanship.*

militate, mitigate

Circumstances **militate** against something when they make it difficult or impossible: *Pressure on hospitals to free up beds militates against patients receiving the ideal amount of care before being discharged.*

Circumstances **mitigate** something when they make it less bad: *Her sentence was changed from the death penalty to life imprisonment because the cruelty she had suffered from her husband was seen as a mitigating circumstance.*

misuse *see* abuse

mitigate *see* militate

momentary, momentous

A **momentary** happening lasts only a moment: *a momentary lapse of memory.*

A **momentous** happening is an important event that makes history: *momentous scientific discoveries.*

moral, morale

The 'moral of a story is a principle of behaviour that you learn from it.

Morals are principles of good behaviour by which people try to live. **Moral** is also an adjective meaning 'relating to principles of right and wrong behaviour': *moral standards.*

Your **morale** /məˈrɑːl/ is your state of confidence: *The team's morale is high.*

motive, motif

A person's **motive** /ˈməʊtɪv/ for doing something is what makes them do it: *Which of the suspects had the most convincing motive for murder?*

A **motif** /məʊˈtiːf/ is a pattern or design, such as a manufacturer's logo on clothing, etc. A **motif** can also be a recurring theme in a piece of music.

mystic, mystique

Mystic and **mystical** mean 'mysterious' or 'miraculous', especially in a spiritual or religious way: *mystic rites / a mystic light.*

A **mystic** is a person who attempts to get a knowledge of truth and a direct vision of God through prayer, meditation, etc.

The **mystique** /mɪˈstiːk/ associated with an activity is the specialist knowledge and expertise that make it seem difficult to master: *There's really no mystique about Chinese cuisine; it's quite straightforward.*

non-flammable, non-inflammable
see flammable

oblivious

Oblivious originally meant 'having forgotten something, no longer aware of it'. This meaning is rare now, and **oblivious** usually simply means 'not aware': *He was completely oblivious to (or of) the trouble he was causing.*

Oblivious does not, however, mean 'unaffected by something'. The word for this is **impervious**: *He was completely impervious to criticism.*

observance, observation

To observe a law or a tradition is to keep to it or obey it. The noun relating to this sense of the verb is ob'servance: *I insist on strict observance of all the rules and regulations.*

'Observe' can also mean 'to watch somebody or something' or 'to make a remark about something'. The noun relating to these senses of the verb is obser'vation: *After the accident, she was kept under observation overnight in hospital before being sent home the next day. / He made a few observations about the state of the roads.*

official, officious

An official is someone who holds a position of authority in an organization: *I spoke to an official sitting at the desk.* Something that is official is backed by authority: *This is an official order.*

An officious person is somebody who is self-important and too inclined to use their position of authority to give other people orders, especially unnecessary ones.

omission *see* emission

paramount, tantamount

'Paramount means 'supreme, greater than any other: *a paramount chief / Education is of paramount importance in a developing country.*

'Tantamount to means 'equivalent to, having the same effect as': *His actions were considered tantamount to treason.*

part *see* behalf

partly, partially

Partly means 'in parts': *The sculpture was partly of wood and partly of stone.*

Partially means 'not to a state of completion': *The house was only partially built when I last saw it.*

personnel, personal

The personnel /pɜːsə'nel/ of a company, etc is its staff: *Airline personnel have to be very carefully selected. / the personnel manager.*

Personal /'pɜːsənəl/ means 'relating to or concerning an individual person': *personal possessions / My relationship with Judy is a purely personal matter. / Will the princess make a personal appearance at the concert? / I thought your remarks were a bit personal (= rudely commenting on some aspect of a person's character, appearance, etc).*

practical, practicable, pragmatic

Practical means 'concerned with action as distinct from theory': *Put your ideas to practical use.*

A practical person has plenty of common sense or is good at manual tasks. Practical also means 'efficient, sensible, useful, etc': *I know a spade is a very practical present, but I'd have preferred to get something a little more exciting. / There must be a more practical way of doing this.*

A practicable plan is one that can be carried out successfully.

To be prag'matic about something is to decide to follow whatever course of action is possible or most sensible in the circumstances you find yourself in, even if it is not what you would choose to do from preference or in theory.

precede, proceed

To precede something or somebody is to come before it or them: *Migraine is often preceded by visual disturbances. / She preceded me onto the stage. / You will find some useful emergency numbers on the preceding page.*

To proceed is to start some activity, or to continue with it: *The doctor proceeded to examine her. / Please proceed with your work.*

(*See also* page 163)

prescribe, proscribe

A doctor prescribes medicine to a patient. The laws of a country prescribe the penalties for various crimes.

To proscribe something is to ban it or forbid it: *Certain activities are proscribed by law.*

proceed *see* precede

pronunciation, pronouncement

The way a word is pronounced is its pro'nunciation (*Note*: not spelt 'pronounciation'): *What is the correct pronunciation of 'ricochet'?*

A pro'nouncement is an official statement about something: *In spite of government pronouncements to the contrary, everyone thinks there is going to be an election in May.*

prophecy, prophesy

Prophecy /'prɒfɪsi/ is a noun, prophesy /'prɒfɪsaɪ/ is a verb.

proof, prove

Proof is a noun, prove /pruːv/ is a verb: *Have you any proof that she's lying? / Her fingerprints on the vase proved that she was the thief.*

propitious *see* auspicious

proscribe *see* prescribe

prove *see* proof

purposefully, purposely

Purposefully means 'with some aim or purpose' or 'showing that one has some aim or purpose in mind': *She was walking purposefully towards me, obviously about to ask me for a favour.*

Purposely means 'deliberately, on purpose, for a particular reason': *I purposely left my keys here on the table because I didn't want to forget them. So why did you move them?*

raise, rise

To raise something is to lift it or make it higher: *He raised his hand and waved. / We've decided to raise your salary. / Don't raise your voice.*

Rise is an irregular intransitive verb meaning 'to go upwards or higher': *New buildings were rising up everywhere. / He has risen fast in his career.*

(*Note*: Rise and raise are used in British and American English respectively as nouns meaning 'an increase in salary': *They've promised me a rise/raise next year.*)

refute, deny

To refute something is strictly speaking not just to deny it but to show that it is incorrect. However, increasingly nowadays refute is used in the sense of 'denying something strongly' rather than proving it wrong. This unfortunately means that refute is now ambiguous: if you say that someone refuted an accusation, it is not clear whether you mean they proved it wrong or simply that they strongly denied it. To avoid ambiguity, it is best to use another verb such as rebut, which does unambiguously mean 'prove an accusation, etc to be false or unfounded'.

regretful, regrettable

Regretful means 'sad' or 'feeling regret'.

Regrettable means 'unfortunate' or 'causing regret': *It's regrettable that you won't be at the meeting.*

replace *see* substitute

respectful, respective, respectively

Respectful words or gestures express respect: *He made a respectful bow. / Speak more respectfully in future.*

The respective jobs, possessions, etc of the people in a group are those specific to each one of them: *They returned to their respective tasks.*

Respectively refers back to named individuals in the order in which they are mentioned: *George and Michael were aged 10 and 8 respectively* (i.e. George was 10 and Michael was 8).

rout, route

To **rout** /raʊt/ the enemy in battle is to defeat them decisively and send them in headlong retreat: *The invaders were routed. / The defeat turned into a rout.*

Your **route** /ruːt/ somewhere is the way by which you arrive there: *My route took me through several pretty villages. / The procession has been routed along the High Street and through George Square.*

sceptic, cynic, septic

A **sceptic** /ˈskeptɪk/ is a person who doubts something that other people believe, or who does not support something that others are enthusiastic about: *Most people accept this theory, but there are still a few sceptics. / Euro-sceptics are British politicians who do not think that it is in British interests for the European Union to have more power over the United Kingdom.* (*Note:* In American English, the spelling is **skeptic**.) The associated adjective is **sceptical**.

A **cynic** /ˈsɪnɪk/ is a person who has a poor opinion of people and their motives, and who thinks the worst about everything: *He's a complete cynic. He thinks politicians are only interested in power and money rather than making the world a better place.*

The related adjective is **cynical**, which can refer both to a person's opinions or to their own behaviour: *He has a very cynical attitude to politicians. / He showed a cynical disregard for the truth.*

A cut or wound goes **septic** /ˈseptɪk/ when it becomes infected.

sensual, sensuous

Sensual means 'relating to or appealing to bodily desires, especially sexuality and sexual desire': *a sensual and voluptuous woman / sensual lips / Some people give in too easily to their sensual desires.*

Things that are **sensuous** appeal more to the mind than to bodily desires, and to a person's senses and perceptions rather than to their intellect: for example, things such as a beautiful sunset, soft fabrics, colours, reflections in water and beautiful music may give you a **sensuous** thrill.

septic *see* sceptic

so, therefore

So and **therefore** both mean 'for that reason'. It is becoming increasingly common in everyday speech for these two words to be used together where strictly speaking one or the other would be sufficient: *We don't have enough so therefore we're going to have to borrow some.* This is acceptable in colloquial speech, but it should be avoided in formal speech and writing: use so, **therefore**, **and so** or **and therefore**.

specially *see* especially

substitute, replace

Substitute does not mean exactly the same as **replace**. If A is put in the place of B, then A **replaces** B or is **substituted** for B, and B is **replaced by/with** A. It is not correct to say that A is 'substituted by' B.

suit, suite

A **suit** /suːt/ of clothes, a **suite** /swiːt/ of furniture. A **three-piece suite** usually consists of two armchairs and a sofa.

tantamount *see* paramount

tenor, tenure

The **tenor** /ˈtenə/ of something is its general course or character: *Nothing disturbed the even tenor of their lives. / That was the tenor of her remarks.*

A **tenor** is also a male singer with a voice higher than that of a bass: *We have too few tenors. / Can you sing tenor?*

Tenure /ˈtenjə/ of a job or of property is that fact or situation of holding the job or possessing the property. **Tenure** in a teaching post, e.g. at a university, is the security of having a long-term contract for it.

thrash, thresh

To **thrash** somebody is to beat them hard, usually as a punishment, or to defeat them thoroughly: *He was often thrashed as a child. / We thrashed the other team seven – nil.*

To **thresh** corn is to separate the seeds from the stalks by beating them.

People **thresh** about or **thrash** about, for example while lying down, when they toss about with violent movements of the arms and legs.

trillion *see* billion

unique

Strictly speaking, something that is **unique** is the only one of its kind. It is therefore wrong to speak of something as being 'fairly unique' or 'slightly unique' – either it is unique or it isn't. If you mean that something is not very common, then it is better to say that it is 'quite rare', 'fairly uncommon', 'rather unusual', 'scarce', etc.

urban, urbane

'**Urban** means 'relating to the city': *urban scenery / an urban railway.*

Ur'**bane** describes a person or their manner, and means 'sophisticated', 'elegant', 'refined'.

visualize *see* envisage

DO IT YOURSELF

A Select the correct word from the pairs in brackets to complete the following sentences.

1. We're all here (*accept, except*) John.

2. These are particularly (*flagrant, fragrant*) roses.

3. His lack of experience was not the only thing that (*militated, mitigated*) against him being chosen for the job.

4. I don't drink much, but I'm not (*adverse, averse*) to an occasional glass of sherry.

5. Alcohol (*effects, affects*) the functioning of the brain.

6. How long are you going to leave these dirty clothes (*laying, lying*) there?

7. My mother is very ill, but she's in the hands of an (*imminent, eminent*) doctor, so we are hopeful she will make a full recovery.

8. I bought a new watch today to (*substitute, replace*) the one I lost last week.

9. You won't be (*eligible, illegible*) to join the club until you're twenty-one.

10. After a (*momentous, momentary*) hesitation, she decide to go with them.

11. The hens have (*lain, laid*) more than a dozen eggs today.

12. The boats in the round-the-world race have all been (*affected, effected*) by (*adverse, averse*) weather conditions.

13. Scientific progress often comes via (*fortunate, fortuitous*) discovery rather than deliberate experimentation.

14. The trouble with doctors is that when they (*prescribe, proscribe*) drugs, their writing is often (*eligible, illegible*).

15. After the flooding there was an (*imminent, eminent*) danger of an outbreak of cholera.

16. In spite of her weakness, she tried to (*rise, raise*) from the bed to answer the telephone.

17. It is (*specially, especially*) nice to be here because it gives me the opportunity to meet so many old friends.

18. Saying that is (*paramount, tantamount*) to calling him a liar.

B The words in italics in the following sentences are either not quite the correct words or are not correctly spelt. Using the information given in this unit, replace them with the correct words correctly spelt.

1. The pole was sticking out at a 90-degree *angel* to the wall.

2. One of my front teeth is *lose*.

3. The police said they knew of no *motif* for the killing.

4. Britain and America were *alleys* during the war.

5. I've thrown out my old armchairs and bought a new three-piece *suit*.

6. If you are interested in working for this company, please apply in writing to the *personal* manager.

7. The union held a *ballet* to elect a new president.

8. She popped the cheque into the *envelop* and carefully sealed it.

9. I intend to go to art *collage* when I leave school.

10. I have no *allusions* about him – I know he can't be trusted.

11. Her father is an *imminent* surgeon.

12. The garden was full of *flagrant* flowers.

6 ▶ Prefixes, Suffixes and Combining Forms

Affixes and Combining Forms

Suffixes and Stems

▶ A **suffix** is a 'word-ending', a word-building element that is added to a word either to provide grammatical information, such as tense or number, or to form a different word altogether:

walks, walked, walking, books, singer, laughable, addition, careful, careless, slowly, slowness, foolish, absurdity, warmth.

▶ The word that a suffix is added to is called the **stem** of the new word:

walks, **walk**ed, **walk**ing, **book**s, **sing**er, **laugh**able, **addit**ion, **care**ful, **care**less, **slow**ly, **slow**ness, **fool**ish, **absurd**ity, **warm**th.

Did You Know ?

A **stem** is very often a complete English word, but it may not be. For example, in the following words the stems are themselves English words:

warmth, **six**th, **grow**th; **odd**ity, **acid**ity; **eat**able, **read**able, **wash**able.

In these words, however, the stems are not words:

length, **dep**th; **abil**ity, **san**ity, **van**ity; **applic**able, **negoti**able, **separ**able, **toler**able.

And in some cases, the stems undergo minor adjustments in spelling when a suffix is added to them:

eight → **eigh**th, *nine* → **nin**th, *true* → **tru**th;
active → **activ**ity, *dense* → **dens**ity, *pure* → **pur**ity;
cure → **cur**able, *note* → **not**able, *vary* → **vari**able;
industry → **industri**al.

Inflection and Derivation

▶ When a suffix is added to a stem simply to provide grammatical information, the process is called **inflection**. For example, in *he walks* and *he walked*, the suffixes indicate different tenses of the verb, and in *books, shoes, dogs*, etc the *-s* suffix indicates that the nouns are plural.

▶ When, on the other hand, new words are formed by means of suffixes, the process is known as **derivation**. For example, when *-less, -ful, -ly* and *-ness* are added to stems, the words that are created are completely different words from the stems they are based on: *careless* and *careful* are not forms of the word *care* (*care* is a noun, whilst *careless* and *careful* are adjectives), and *carelessly* and *carelessness* are not forms of the word *careless* (*careless* is an adjective, *carelessly* is an adverb and *carelessness* is a noun).

Did You Know ?

Notice that suffixation is not the only type of inflection found in English. For example, while the past tense of **walk** is **walked**, the past tense of **sing** is **sang** and the past tense of **write** is **wrote**. Similarly, while the plural of **book** is **books**, the plural of **foot** is **feet** and the plural of **mouse** is **mice**. This is inflection, involving not suffixes but **vowel change**.

Prefixes

A **prefix** is a word-forming element that is attached to the beginning of a stem to form a new word: *dis**loyal, **in**accurate, **mis**understand, **re**load* and **un**common.*

Did You Know ?

Prefixes and suffixes are together known as **affixes**.

Stems and Roots

▶ The **stem** of a word is what remains when you take away the last affix to have been added in the formation of that word:

industry is the stem of *industrial (industry + -al)*

industrial is the stem of *industrialize (industrial + -ize)*

industrialize is the stem of *industrialization (industrialize + -ation)*

nation is the stem of *national (nation + -al)*

national is the stem of *nationalist (national + -ist)*

nationalist is the stem of *nationalistic (nationalist + -ic)*

respect is the stem of *disrespect (dis- + respect)*

disrespect is the stem of *disrespectful (disrespect + -ful)*

disrespectful is the stem of *disrespectfully (disrespectful + -ly)*

▶ The **root** of a word is what remains when all the affixes have been removed from it:

industry is the root of *industrialize* and *industrialization*

nation is the root of *nationalist* and *nationalistic*

respect is the root of *disrespectful* and *disrespectfully*

Compound Words

Some words are made simply by joining two or more roots together, without any affixes at all:

black + bird   → blackbird
class + room   → classroom
sun   + shine   → sunshine
son   + in + law → son-in-law.

Words formed in this way are called **compounds**.

Combining Forms

Most compounds are formed from roots that are themselves English words. However, there is one common type of compound that is formed by combining roots that are not English words but word-forming elements known as **combining forms**, e.g. *geo-, bio-, hydro-, astro-, micro-, -graphy, -logy, -lysis*, etc:

> *geology, geometry, geography, biography, biology;*
> *astrology, astronomy, astronaut, cosmonaut;*
> *hydrology, hydrolysis, electrolysis;*
> *microscope, microphone, telephone, telescope*

and so on. Many English combining forms are derived from the classical languages Latin and Greek. For this reason, words such as *biography, astrology, electrolysis, telescope*, etc are known as **neoclassical compounds**, that is, modern compounds created using word-building elements taken from the classical languages.

Did You Know ?

Like affixes, combining forms can be attached to existing words to make new words:

astro- + *physics* → *astrophysics*
hydro- + *electricity* → *hydroelectricity*
micro- + *processor* → *microprocessor*

For this reason, combining forms are often classed as affixes. There is, nevertheless, an important difference between the two.

An **affix** must *always* be attached to a stem. You cannot make a word simply by joining two affixes together. (There are no words such as 'unly' or 'misness', for example.)

Combining forms, on the other hand, can not only be added to stems to form new words, as in *astrophysics* and *microprocessor*, but can also combine with each other to form words, as in *astrology* and *microscope*. Affixes cannot do this.

Combining forms can also be combined with affixes, as in *hydrant, hydrous, thermal*, etc.

The Latin and Greek roots that underline some English affixes and combining forms are also found in English words that come directly from Latin and Greek words. For example, *biannual* (= happening twice every year) is formed by adding the prefix *bi-* to the word *annual*, while *biennial* (= happening once every two years) comes directly from Latin *biennium* 'a period of two years'.

Similarly while *centimetre* (= one hundredth of a metre) is created by adding the combining form *centi-* to the word *metre*, *centenary* (= a hundredth anniversary) comes directly from Latin *centenarius* 'of a hundred'.

Further examples of this are included in the lists on the following pages.

Prefixes

Prefix	Meaning	Examples
a-, an-	not	*amoral* = not concerned with morality; *atypical* = not typical; *anarchy* = an absence of law and order; *anechoic* = without an echo; *anhydrous* = not containing water; *anonymous* = without the person's name being known
ante-	before	*antenatal* = before birth (i.e. relating to pregnancy); *ante-room* = a room that serves as a waiting-room for a larger and more important room
anti-	1 against	*antifreeze* = a chemical that prevents water freezing; *anti-British* = hostile to Britain (Also in *antagonist* = someone who is against you or hostile to you)
	2 the opposite of	*anticlimax* = a disappointing ending when something exciting had been expected; *anticlockwise* = in a direction opposite to clockwise (Also in *Antarctic* = the part of the earth opposite the Arctic)
arch-	chief	*archbishop*; *archenemy* = one's main enemy; *archangel* /ˈɑːkeɪndʒəl/ = a chief angel
be-	(various meanings)	*befriend* = to become the friend of; *belittle* = to treat as unimportant; *bejewelled* = covered in jewels
bi-	two, twice	*biannual* = happening twice a year; *biennial* = happening once every two years; *bicycle* = a two-wheeled vehicle; *bigamy* = being married to two people at the same time; *bilingual* = speaking two languages; *bisect* = to cut into two parts
circum-	around	*circumference* = the line forming a circle; *circumnavigate* = to sail around (the world); *circumpolar* = around the North or South Pole (Also in *circulate* = to pass around or spread around)
co-	together with; working with another	*co-author* = one of two or more people who have written a book together; *co-existence* = existing together; *co-pilot* = an assistant pilot; *co-operate* = to work with someone; *co-worker*

Prefix	Meaning	Examples
col-, com-, con,- cor-	*Col-, com-, con-* and **cor-** (as in **collaborate**, **compassion**, **construct** and **correspond**) are usually treated as English prefixes, meaning 'with' or 'together'. Strictly speaking, though, they are not English prefixes at all, but Latin prefixes. Words like **collaborate**, **compassion**, **construct** and **correspond** are not formed in English by adding **col-**, **com-**, **con-** and **cor-** to *laborate*, *passion*, *struct* and *respond*, but are directly derived from the Latin words *collaborare* 'to work together', *compassio* 'suffering with someone', *construere* 'to pile together' and *correspondere* 'to reply to one another'. Similar examples are **companion**, from Latin *companio* 'a person you share your bread (Latin *panis*) with', and **convene**, from Latin *convenire* 'to assemble', 'to come together'.	
contra-	against; opposite	*contraceptive* = preventing conception; *contradict* = to assert the opposite of something that has been said; *contravene* = to break a law, etc
counter-	against; opposite	*counterattack* = an attack made in response to an enemy's attack; *counteract* = to act against something; *counter-intelligence* = actions taken against another country's spies; *countermand* = to give a command that cancels a previous command
cross-	across; between	*cross-country running*; *cross-border* = passing across a border or involving those on both sides of a border
cyber-	computer technology	*cybercafé* = a café where customers can pay to use computers and get access to the Internet; *cyberspace* = the space around us considered as the environment in which computer communication takes place
de-	1 reversing or undoing a process	*defrost* = to thaw out something that has been frozen; *devaluation* = the lowering in value of a country's currency
	2 removing someone or something	*decaffeinated* = having had the caffeine removed; *decontaminate* = to remove contamination from
demi-	half	*demisemiquaver* = half of a semiquaver (in music)
di-	two	*diphthong* = a speech sound consisting of two vowel sounds forming a single syllable; *disyllabic* = consisting of two syllables
dis-	1 the opposite of	*disconnect* = to undo a connection; *disbelieve* = not to believe; *distrust* = not to trust; *disloyal* = not loyal; *dishonest* = not honest
	2 the reversal of	*disinfect* = to remove infection from

Prefix	Meaning	Examples
down-	at or to a lower level	*downgrade* = to reduce to a lower level; *downstairs*
e-	electronic	*e-mail; e-commerce* = business done over the Internet
em-, en-	to cause someone or something to be ___ or to be in ___	*embitter* = to make someone bitter; *endanger* = to cause someone to be in danger; *enlarge* = to make something larger; *enrich* = to make something richer
ex- (1)	former	*ex-president; ex-wife*
ex- (2)	In words derived from Latin, **ex-** often has the sense of 'out', 'out of' or 'outwards': *except* = not including; *exclude* = to keep out; *exhale* = to breathe out; *exit* = a way out; *expand* = to spread out; *extend* = to make or become larger or longer.	
extra-	outside	*extracurricular* = outside the normal curriculum; *extramarital* = outside marriage; *extraordinary* = beyond what is normal
fore-	1 front; the front part of	*foreleg; forearm; forename* = a person's first name
	2 before; in advance	*forewarn* = to warn in advance
in- (1), il- im-, ir-	not	*illegal; illegible; immoderate; immoral; inconsiderate; indefinite; inedible; irrelevant; irreligious* (Also **ig-** in *ignoble*)
in- (2)	in, into	*income; inland; inmate* = someone living in a prison or other institution
in- (3)	In words derived from Latin, **in-** often has the meaning 'in' or 'within': *include* = to count as part of something; *inhale* = to breathe in; *inject* = to force in by means of a syringe, etc.	
infra-	below	*infrared* = radiation with a wavelength below that of red light
inter-	between	*interactive* = allowing a two-way flow of information between a computer and a user; *inter-school* = between schools; *international* = between nations

Prefix	Meaning	Examples
intra-	within	*intradepartmental* = within a department; *intravenous* = within a vein
mal-	bad, badly	*maltreat* = to treat badly; *malfunction* = faulty functioning
maxi-	large	*maxiskirt* = a very long skirt
mid-	middle	*midsummer* = the middle of the summer; *midday*; *midnight*
mini-	small; very small	*minicomputer*; *miniskirt* = a very short skirt
mis-	1 bad, badly; wrong, wrongly	*misfortune* = bad luck; *misspell*; *mistreat*; *misunderstand*; *misuse*
	2 lack of ; the opposite of	*mistrust*
non-	not; the opposite of	*non-violent*; *non-smoker* = someone who does not smoke; *non-event* = something disappointing; *nonsense* = something that does not make sense
out-	1 longer than; better than; beyond	*outlive* = to live longer than; *outdo* = to do better than; *outgrow* = to grow too big or too old for
	2 out; outside	*outhouse* = a small extra building attached to or belonging to a house or farm; *outlaw* = a criminal who has placed outside the protection of the law; *outcast* = someone who has been excluded from society
over-	1 too much	*overpopulated* = having too many people living there; *overwork* = too much work; *overload* = an excess load
	2 over, across	*overseas* = across the sea; *overcoat* = a coat worn over other clothes
post-	after	*postwar* = after a war, especially World War II; *postgraduate* = an advanced student who has completed a first degree at university; *postpone* = to put off to a later time
pre-	before	*prefix*; *pre-arranged* = arranged in advance; *pre-cooked* = cooked in advance; *preview* = an advance showing of something; *prehistoric* = dating from a time before historical records
		(Also in many words derived directly from Latin in which there is an idea of 'before in time, place,

Prefix	Meaning	Examples
		preference, importance, etc', e.g. *precede* = to go before; *precursor* = someone or something that comes before another; *predecessor* = someone who comes before another; and also *predict, prefect, prefer, prepare, preposition* and *previous*)
pro-	1 in favour of	*pro-British* = favouring or supporting Britain
	2 in place of	*proconsul* = a deputy consul
quasi-	1 partly	*quasi-stellar* = in some ways like a star
	2 false, falsely	*quasi-scientific* = appearing to be scientific but not actually so
re-	again	*re-appear; rewrite; reread; replay; reload; relive* (Also in *resume* = to start again)
semi-	half, partially	*semicircle; semibreve* = a note equal to half a breve in music; *semiliterate* = only able to read and write a little; *semifinal* = the stage in a contest before the final; *semicolon* = a punctuation mark indicating a break in a sentence that is (in some ways) half as strong as that marked by a colon
step-	by remarriage	*stepfather* = a man who is not one's father but who is married to one's mother; *stepmother; step-parent; stepson; stepdaughter; stepsister* = a girl who is the daughter of one's step-parent; *stepbrother*
sub-	under; below	*substandard* = below the required or expected standard; *submarine* = a ship that travels under water (Also in *submerge* = to go below the surface of water, *subscribe* = originally 'to sign at the bottom of a document')
super-	1 above	*superstructure* = something built on something else; *supersonic* = above the speed of sound (Also in *superficial* = not going below the surface of something)
	2 greater or better than others	*superman* = a very strong man; *superglue* = very strong glue; *supertanker* = a very large oil-tanker; *supermarket* = a large shop

Prefix	Meaning	Examples
sym-, syn-, syl-	Like **col-/ com-/ con-/ cor-**, **sym-**, **syn-** and **syl-** are often treated as English prefixes, meaning 'with' or 'together', but are strictly speaking not English prefixes but Greek prefixes. Words like **sympathy** and **synonym** are not formed in English by adding **sym-** and **syn-** to **pathy** and **onym**, but are directly derived from the Greek words *sympatheia* 'shared feeling' and *synonymos* 'having the same name or the same meaning'. **Syn-** is, however, sometimes used in English to form new technical words in science and medicine.	
trans-	across	*trans-Atlantic* = across the Atlantic Ocean; *transcontinental* = across a continent (Also in many words directly derived from Latin in which there is a notion of 'across' or 'through', e.g. *transmit, transparent* and *transport;* also in words in which there is a notion of 'change', e.g. *transfer, transform and translate*)
tri-	three	*trioxide* = a chemical containing three atoms of oxygen; *trilingual* = speaking three languages (Also in many words containing the idea of 'three', e.g. *triangle, tricycle, trinity, triple,* and *tripod*)
ultra-	1 beyond	*ultraviolet* = denoting radiation with a wavelength less than that of violet light; *ultrasonic* = above the upper limit of human hearing
	2 very; extremely	*ultra-conservative; ultramodern*
un-	1 not	*uncomfortable; uncommon; unhappy; unkind; unnecessary; unscientific; unwelcome*
	2 the reversal of	*undo; undress; unfasten; untie; unveil; unwind*
under-	1 below	*underclothes* = clothes worn under other clothes, next to the skin; *undermanager* = a deputy manager
	2 too little; less than normal	*undercooked* = not sufficiently cooked; *undervalue* = to place too little value on
up-	at or to a higher level	*upgrade* = to raise to a higher level; *upstairs*
vice-	deputy	*vice-president*

Suffixes

Suffix	Meaning	Examples
-able	forming adjectives meaning 'able to be ___ed'	*eatable* = able to be eaten; *washable* = able to be washed; *bearable; readable; unforgivable* (Also *laughable* = that deserves to be laughed at; *reliable* = able to be relied on)
		Nouns formed from adjectives ending in *-able* end in *-ability*: *suitable* → *suitability*; *readable* → *readability*.
-acy	forming nouns from some adjectives ending in *-ate*	*accurate* → *accuracy*; *celibate* → *celibacy*; *literate* → *literacy*
-ade	forming nouns meaning 'a drink'	*lemonade; orangeade*
-age	forming nouns meaning:	
	1 an action or its result	*breakage; drainage; shrinkage*
	2 the cost of something	*postage*
	3 a set of something	*baggage; luggage* (= *cases that are 'lugged' or carried*)
	4 the amount of something	*mileage*
	5 a state or rank	*peerage*
-aholic	forming nouns and adjectives with the meaning 'addict' or 'addicted'	*workaholic* = someone who works long hours because they feel unable to stop working

Suffix	Meaning	Examples
-al	1 forming adjectives meaning 'relating to ___'	*coastal; national; political; seasonal; tidal; functional* = serving a particular function; *legal* = relating to the law
	2 forming nouns meaning 'an action or its result'	*approval; arrival; proposal; referral; refusal*
-an	forming adjectives and nouns meaning 'relating to ___, or someone or something that relates to ___'	*American; Italian; suburban* = relating to the suburbs of a town *comedian; historian* = someone who studies history
-ance, -ancy	forming nouns meaning: 1 an action or its result	*appearance; performance; utterance*
	2 a state or condition described by an adjective ending in *-ant*	*arrogant* → *arrogance; brilliance; pregnancy; relevance/relevancy*
-ant	1 forming adjectives meaning 'in a state or condition of ___'	*arrogant; brilliant; pregnant; relevant* (Also in *observant* = good at noticing things)
	2 forming nouns meaning 'someone or something that does something'	*assistant; defendant* = the accused person in a criminal trial; *dependant* = someone who depends on another person, especially for financial support; *accountant; disinfectant; inhabitant; servant*
-ar	1 forming nouns meaning 'someone who ___s'	*beggar* = someone who begs; *liar* = someone who tells lies
	2 forming adjectives meaning 'relating to ___'	*muscular* = relating to a muscle or the muscles; *stellar* = relating to a star or stars
-ard	forming nouns meaning 'a person with a stated quality or habit', or 'someone related to something'	*drunkard; Spaniard* = a person from Spain

Suffix	Meaning	Examples
-arian	forming adjectives and nouns meaning 'connected with ___' or 'someone who is connected with ___'	*humanitarian* = concerned with the welfare of humanity; *vegetarian* = someone who eats fruit and vegetables but no meat
-ary (1)	forming adjectives meaning 'related to ___'	*budgetary* = relating to a budget; *planetary* = relating to the planets (Also in the noun *dictionary*)
-ary (2)	forming nouns with the meaning 'someone who has a particular relationship to something'	*functionary* = someone with an official function; *beneficiary* = someone who benefits from something left to them in a will; *dignitary* = a person of high rank or status
-ate	1 forming adjectives meaning 'showing a particular quality'	*affectionate; passionate* (Also in *literate* = able to read and write, *numerate* = able to count)
	2 forming verbs meaning 'to cause to become ___'	*activate; alienate; motivate* (Also in *liberate* = to cause to be free)
	3 forming nouns meaning 'a group of people'	*electorate* = people who vote in an election; *inspectorate* = inspectors
	4 forming nouns meaning 'a degree or status'	*doctorate* = the university degree of Doctor of ___; *caliphate* = the rank of caliph
	5 forming nouns meaning 'the territory ruled by a ___'	*emirate*
	6 forming nouns meaning 'a chemical salt'	*carbonate; phosphate*
-ation	used to form nouns from verbs	*combine* → *combination; deprive* → *deprivation; examination; exploration; formation; imagination; simplify* → *simplification; application; unification*

Suffix	Meaning	Examples
-ative	used to form adjectives meaning 'tending to do or show something'	*argumentative* = tending to argue a lot; *imaginative* = showing a lot of imagination; *talkative* = tending to talk a lot
-cy	used to form nouns meaning:	
	1 a state or condition	*bankruptcy*
	2 a rank or status	*baronetcy* = the rank or status of baronet; *captaincy*
-dom	used to form nouns meaning:	
	1 the rank of ___, or the territory rule by a ___	*dukedom; kingdom; serfdom*
	2 people who share some characteristic	*officialdom* = officials
	3 a state or condition	*freedom; wisdom*
-ed (1), -d	used to form past tenses and past participles	*asked; baked; begged; cried; dived; kicked; lived; moved; waited*
-ed (2), -d	used to form descriptive adjectives	*bearded; crested; spotted; bad-tempered; black-headed; long-legged; red-haired; wide-eyed*
-ee	used to form nouns meaning 'someone who does something or has something done to them'	*absentee* = someone who is absent; *employee* = someone who is employed; *escapee* = someone who has escaped; *refugee; trainee*
-eer	used to form nouns meaning 'someone who does something'	*auctioneer* = someone who runs an auction; *mountaineer* = someone who climbs mountains
-en (1), -n	used to form past participles	*blown; broken; eaten; given; hidden; known; seen; stolen; written*
-en (2), -n	used to form verbs meaning 'to become ___ or to cause to be ___'	*broaden; darken; lengthen; ripen; strengthen; widen*
-en (3)	used to form adjectives meaning: 'like or made of ___'	*brazen* = originally 'of or like brass'; *golden*; *leaden* = grey or heavy like lead; *wooden; woollen*

Suffix	Meaning	Examples
-en (4)	used to form the plurals of some nouns	*brethren* = brothers; *oxen; children*
-ence, -ency	used to form nouns meaning:	
	1 an action or its result	*emergence; existence; occurrence; reference*
	2 a state or condition described by an adjective or noun ending in -*ent*	*dependency; difference; efficiency; presidency*
-ent	1 forming adjectives that describe states or conditions	*apparent* = appearing to be something; *dependent* = depending on someone or something; *different* = differing from someone or something else
	2 forming adjective and nouns meaning 'doing something, or someone who does something'	*resident; student; superintendent*
-er (1), -r	1 used to form nouns meaning 'someone or something that ___s'	*buyer; dancer; reader; runner; screwdriver; singer; smoker; writer*
	2 used to form nouns meaning 'someone who comes from ___'	*Londoner; villager*
	3 used to form descriptive compounds	*three-wheeler* = a vehicle with three wheels; *four-pounder* = something that weighs four pounds
-er (2), -r	used to form comparative adjectives and adverbs	*bigger; blacker; drier; faster; older; slower*
-ery	used to form nouns meaning:	
	1 a state, condition or action	*bravery; slavery; snobbery* = being snobbish; *trickery*
	2 a collection of ___	*greenery* = green leaves, etc; *machinery*
	3 a place where someone is or something is done	*bakery; brewery; nunnery* = a convent; *oil-refinery*

Suffix	Meaning	Examples
-ese	used to form nouns and adjectives meaning: 1 nationality 2 language	*Chinese; Japanese* *Chinese; Japanese; journalese* = the language used by journalists
-esque	used to form adjectives meaning 'like ___'	*Kafkaesque* = in the style of the writer Franz Kafka
-ess	used to form nouns denoting females	*lioness* = a female lion; *waitress; actress* (*Note:* It is becoming less and less usual to use the **-ess** ending when referring to women. A woman shepherd should nowadays always be referred to as a **shepherd**, not as a **shepherdess**. **Authoress** and **poetess** have both dropped out of use, and although **actress** is still in use, many actresses prefer to be called **actors**. While **manageress** might be used to refer to a woman who manages a shop, in other situations both men and women are **managers**.)
-est	forming superlative adjectives and adverbs	*biggest; blackest; driest; fastest; oldest; slowest*
-ette	used to form nouns meaning: 1 small thing 2 female person	*kitchenette; cigarette* (originally thought of as a small cigar); *statuette* *usherette* = a woman who shows people to their seats in a cinema or theatre
-fold	used to form adjectives and adverbs meaning 'multiplied ___ times'	*fourfold; hundredfold*
-ful	1 used to form adjectives meaning 'having a certain characteristic or content' 2 used to form nouns meaning 'the contents of a ___, or the amount that would fill a ___'	*eventful* = having a lot of interesting things happening; *fearful* = afraid, full of fear; *forgetful* = tending to forget things; *painful; powerful; successful* *bagful; bucketful; cupful; handful; mouthful; spoonful*

Suffix	Meaning	Examples
-hood	used to form nouns meaning 'the state of being ___', 'something that is ___', or 'the ___ stage in life'	*likelihood* = likeliness, being likely; *falsehood*; *motherhood* = the state of being a mother; *knighthood* = the rank of knight; *childhood* = the time when one is a child
-i	used to form adjectives and nouns denoting nationality	*Iraqi; Israeli*
-ial	used to form adjectives meaning: 'relating to ___'	*finance → financial; editorial; managerial*
-ian	used to form nouns and adjectives meaning 'someone or something that relates to or is involved with ___', or 'relating to ___'	*Canadian; magician; musician; politician*
-ible	used to form adjectives meaning 'able to be ___ed'	*digestible* = able to be digested; *edible* = able to be eaten; *permissible* = able to be permitted; *reversible* = able to be reversed; *visible* = able to be seen Nouns formed from adjectives ending in **-ible** end in **-ibility**: *visible→ visibility; legible → legibility.*
-ic, -ical	used to form adjectives meaning 'of, like, or connected with ___'	*alcoholic* = containing alcohol; *historic* = important in history; *historical* = having happened or existed in history; *photographic*
-ice	forming nouns meaning 'the state of being ___'	*cowardice; injustice*
-ics	used to form nouns meaning: 1 a subject of study 2 something connected with a subject of study 3 an activity	*acoustics; mathematics; physics* *acoustics* = qualities of sound; *mathematics* = mathematical calculations *athletics*
-ide	used to form nouns denoting a chemical compound	*chloride* = a compound containing chlorine

Suffix	Meaning	Examples
-ie	used to form diminutive nouns, especially those used to or by young children	*auntie; budgie* = a budgerigar; *doggie*
-ify	used to form verbs meaning 'to make something or someone ___; to become ___'	*horrify* = to fill someone with horror; *pacify* = to make peaceful; *simplify* = to make simpler; *terrify* = to fill with terror Nouns formed from verbs ending in **-ify** end in **-ification**: *clarify* → *clarification; identify* → *identification; simplify* → *simplification*.
-ing	used to form present participles, and nouns derived from verbs	*betting; dancing; painting; singing; waiting*
-ion	used to form nouns from verbs	*adopt* → *adoption; create* → *creation; discussion; election; population; punctuation*
-ise (1)	used to form nouns meaning 'the state of being a ___'	*expertise*
-ise (2)	*see -ize*	
-ish	used to form adjectives meaning 'like ___; slightly ___'	*biggish; blackish; foolish; reddish; shortish; tallish; thinnish; yellowish; youngish*
-ism	used to form nouns meaning:	
	1 a belief in ___	*Buddhism; communism; socialism; Taoism*
	2 a prejudiced or hostile attitude	*racism; sexism*
	3 an example of ___; the fact of being ___	*colloquialism* = a colloquial expression; *heroism* = the state of being a hero, or a heroic act; *criticism* = an act of criticizing someone or something; *magnetism* = the fact of being magnetic
	4 an illness connected with ___	*alcoholism* = addiction to alcohol

Suffix	Meaning	Examples

Some common '-isms'

ageism = discrimination against someone on account of their age; *agnosticism* = doubt about whether it is possible to know whether or not there is a God; *anarchism* = the political theory that all forms of government are undesirable and that society can and should function without government; *anti-semitism* = discrimination against or hatred of Jewish people; *ascetism* = living in a very simple manner, especially for religious reasons; *atheism* = belief that there is no God; *Buddhism* = the system of beliefs based on the teaching of the Buddha; *capitalism* = the economic system based on private ownership of the means of production and on the need for profit; *communism* = an economic or social system on which there is a no private property, all property belonging to the community as a whole; *conservatism* = a political philosophy based on a belief that it is unnecessary to make radical changes to society, and generally favouring capitalism over socialism; *creationism* = the belief that the universe and everything in it was created by God rather than developing by evolution; *determinism* = the belief that there is no such thing as free will, all human actions and decisions being determined in advance by unchangeable causes; *egalitarianism* = the belief that all human beings should be socially, economically and politically equal; *egotism* = excessive belief in one's own importance; *élitism* = the belief that some people are better than others and therefore have special rights or deserve special treatment; *existentialism* = a philosophy based on the realization that human beings have to live in a world that does not make sense, and have a responsibility for their own actions and decisions; *fascism* = a right-wing nationalistic political philosophy advocating strong centralized government led by a dictator; *fatalism* = the belief that whatever is going to happen will happen and nothing can change it; *feminism* = a philosophy advocating increasing women's rights and the removal of inequalities between women and men; *Hinduism* = the main religion of India; *humanism* = a philosophy that rejects religious beliefs and asserts that human beings can make moral decisions without the aid of the supernatural; *Marxism* = the form of communism based on the economic and political principles advocate by Karl Marx; *pacifism* = opposition to war; *pantheism* = the belief that everything that exists is God; *racism* = discrimination against a person because of their race; *sexism* = discrimination against a person because of their sex; *Sikhism* = the religion based on the teachings of Nanak; *socialism* = the political and economic theory that advocates that the means of production of goods in society should be owned by the state or jointly by the community; *Taoism* = the religion and philosophy based on the teaching of Lao Zi, Zhuang Zi and others; *totalitarianism* = a political philosophy advocating complete control by the state over all aspects of its inhabitants' lives; *vegetarianism* = living on a diet that excludes meat, and sometimes also eggs, butter and milk

| -ist | used to form nouns and adjectives meaning 'related to, or a person connected with, an -ism' | *Buddhist; communist; racist; sexist; socialist; Taoist* |

Suffix	Meaning	Examples
-ite	1 used to form nouns denoting a chemical compound	*chlorite* = a compound containing chlorine and oxygen
	2 used to form nouns and adjectives meaning '(a person) from or connected with ___'	*Shi'ite* = a member of one branch of Islam; *Muscovite* = a person from Moscow
-itude	used to form nouns	*aptitude; gratitude; magnitude* = largeness, size; *servitude* = the state of being a slave
-ity	used to form nouns from adjectives	*absurdity; brutality; finality; rapidity; regularity; stupidity; validity*
-ive	used to form nouns and adjectives meaning '(someone or something) that ___s'	*aggressive* = showing aggression; *detective* = someone who detects crimes, etc; *explosive* = a substance that explodes; *persuasive* = able to persuade people
-ize, -ise	used to form verbs meaning 'to do something' or 'to become ___ or cause someone or something to become ___'	*criticize* = to make criticisms; *publicize* = to make something public, to draw attention to it; *modernize* = to make something modern or more modern; *fantasize* = to indulge in fantasies; *magnetize* = to make something magnetic
-less	used to form adjectives from nouns, meaning 'without ___'	*endless* = having no end, going on forever; *fearless* = showing no fear; *heartless* = unkind, cruel; *homeless; pointless* = having no point or purpose
-let	used to form nouns meaning 'a small or young ___'	*booklet; droplet; piglet*
-ling	used to form nouns meaning	
	1 a small or young ___	*duckling; gosling* = a young goose; *fledgling; nestling* = a young bird that cannot yet fly
	2 someone with a particular status or characteristic	*underling; weakling*

Suffix	Meaning	Examples
-long	used to form adjectives and adverbs meaning: 'in a __ way'	*headlong* = with one's head to the front; *sidelong* = sideways
-ly	1 used to form adverbs	*actively; foolishly; madly; quickly; sadly; slowly*
	2 used to form adverbs and adjectives meaning 'at certain intervals'	*hourly; monthly; weekly; yearly*
	3 used to form adjectives meaning 'showing a particular characteristic'	*cowardly; fatherly; friendly; godly*
-ment	used to form nouns	*development; encouragement; government; nourishment; statement*
-monger	used to form nouns denoting 'someone who sells or spreads __'	*fishmonger; ironmonger* = someone who sells tools, utensils and other household hardware; *scandalmonger* = someone who spreads scandalous stories about people
-most	used to form adjectives meaning 'nearest to __; most __'	*innermost* = furthest in; *northernmost* = most northerly; furthest north; *topmost* = nearest the top; *uppermost* = top, highest
-ness	used to form nouns meaning 'the state of being __'	*fearlessness, foolishness; happiness; rudeness; sadness*
-ock	used to form nouns meaning 'a young or small __'	*bullock* = a young bull; ; *hillock* = a little hill, a mound
-oid	used to form nouns and adjectives meaning 'like __, or someone or something that is like __'	*anthropoid* = resembling human beings; *humanoid; android* = a robot that looks like a human being (Also in *asteroid* = a small rocky body orbiting the Sun; *meteoroid* = a rocky body in space that would become a meteor if it entered the Earth's atmosphere)
-or	used to form nouns meaning 'someone or something that __s'	*actor* = a person who acts; *conductor; inspector; inventor; sailor; visitor*

Suffix	Meaning	Examples
-ose	used to form adjectives meaning 'having a certain characteristic or in a certain state'	*bellicose* = aggressive, warlike; *comatose* = in a coma
-ous	used to form adjectives meaning 'having a certain characteristic'	*adventurous; dangerous; glorious; ridiculous*
-s (1), -es	forming the plural of nouns	*books; boxes; churches; dogs; heroes; quizzes; radios*
-s (2), -es	forming the third person singular of the present tense of verbs	*builds; falls; makes; runs; stitches; swims; walks*
-ship	used to form nouns meaning:	
	1 a state or condition	*fellowship; friendship; membership; relationship*
	2 a skill	*musicianship; seamanship*
	3 a group	*fellowship; membership; readership*
	4 a position	*professorship*
-some (1)	used to form adjectives meaning:	
	1 causing or producing ___	*fearsome; troublesome*
	2 tending to ___	*quarrelsome*
-some (2)	used to form nouns meaning 'a group of ___ people'	*foursome; twosome*
-ster	used to form nouns meaning:	
	1 someone who is ___	*youngster*
	2 someone connected with ___	*gangster; trickster*
-th (1)	forming nouns	*warmth; growth; length; depth*
-th (2)	forming adjectives from numbers	*fourth, sixth; thousandth*

Suffix	Meaning	Examples
-ty	used to form nouns meaning 'the state of being ___; something that is ___'	*certainty; cruelty; safety*
-ual	used to form adjectives from nouns	*habitual; sexual; textual* (Also in *annual* = yearly; *manual* = done with the hands)
-uble	used to form adjectives meaning 'able to ___ or to be ___'	*soluble* = able to dissolve Nouns formed from adjectives ending in **-uble** end in **-ubility**: *soluble* → *solubility*
-ular	used to form adjectives from certain nouns	*glandular; tubular*
-ure	used to form nouns meaning 'the act of ___ing'	*closure; exposure; failure; seizure*
-ward/s	used to form adjectives and adverbs meaning 'in a particular direction'	*backward; homeward; inward*
-ways	used to form adjectives and adverbs meaning 'in a stated direction'	*lengthways; sideways*
-wise	used to form adjectives and adverbs meaning 'in a stated direction'	*clockwise; lengthwise*
-y (1)	used to form nouns	*butchery; expiry; jealousy*
-y (2), -ey	used to form adjectives meaning:	
	1 like ___	*feathery; snowy; thundery; clayey; wintry*
	2 covered with ___	*dirty; hairy; muddy*
-y (3)	used to form diminutive nouns, especially those used to or by young children	*daddy; doggy; mummy*

Combining Forms

> **Did You Know ?**
>
> Many combining forms can occur in several different forms, e.g.
> ***derm-, -derm, dermat-, dermato-***.

Combining form	Relating to	Examples
aero-	air or aircraft	*aeroplane; aerodrome* = a small airport; *aerobics* = exercises designed to improve breathing and blood circulation
Afro-	Africa	*Afro-American* = an American of black African origin
agri-, agro-	farming	*agriculture; agrochemicals* = chemicals used in agriculture
-algia, -alg-	pain	*neuralgia* = pain in a nerve; *analgesic* = a medicine that stops pain
ambi-	both, double	*ambidextrous* = able to use both hands equally well (Also in *ambiguous* = having more than one possible meaning)
amphi-	all round, on both sides	*amphitheatre* (from Greek *amphitheatron*) = an ancient arena in which the seats for the audience surround the central stage or sports area (Also in *amphibian* = a creature such as a frog or toad that can live both on land and in water)
andro-	man	*androgen* = a male hormone; *android* = a robot that looks like a human being
Anglo-	England, English, or Britain	*Anglo-American* = involving Britain and the United States; *anglophone* = speaking English
anthropo-	human beings	*anthropology* = the study of human beings, human cultures, etc; *anthropoid* = resembling human beings

Combining form	Relating to	Examples
aqua-	water	*aqualung* = apparatus for breathing under water (Also in *aquarium* = a tank in which fish and other water creatures are kept; *aquatic* = relating to or living in water; *aqueduct* = a bridge across which a canal is carried over a valley)
-arch, -archy	rule, ruler	*monarch* = a king or queen; *monarchy*; (Also in *anarchy* = the absence of government and law and order)
archaeo-	the past	*archaeology* = the study of things that date from the past; also in *archaic* = ancient
astro-	star, space	*astronomy* = the scientific study of the stars and planets; *astrology* = the study of the stars and planets as a guide to people's characters and future events; *astrophysics* = the branch of astronomy dealing with the physical nature of the stars and planets
audio-	sound or hearing	*audiovisual* = involving both sound and vision; *audiology* = the branch of science concerned with hearing (Also in *audible* = able to be heard, and *audience* = the people who listen to a performer, etc)
auto- (1)	self, by itself	*autobiography* = a book a person writes about their own life; *autofocus* = a device on a camera that focuses the camera automatically; *autograph* = a person's own signature; also in *automatic*.
auto- (2)	cars, vehicles	*autosport*
biblio-	book	*bibliophile* = someone who likes books; *bibliography* = a list of books
bio-	life	*biology* = the study of plants and animals; *biography* = the story of a person's life

Combining form	Relating to	Examples
broncho-, bronch-	the windpipe	*bronchitis* = inflammation of the tubes between the lungs and the throat
cardio-	heart	*cardiac* = relating to the heart; *cardiology* = the branch of medicine concerned with diseases of the heart
carni-	meat	*carnivore* = an animal that eats meat
centi-	1 one hundred	*centipede* = a creature with many legs (not necessarily one hundred); *centigrade* = having one hundred degrees (Also in *century* = a period of one hundred years)
	2 one hundredth	*centimetre* = one hundredth of a metre (Also in *centenary* = a hundredth anniversary)
chrono-	time	*chronometer* = a very accurate type of clock; *chronology* = a record of events in the order of their occurrence (Also in *chronic* = lasting for a long time)
-cide	killing; killer	*genocide* = the killing of a complete people; *insecticide* = a chemical that kills insects; pesticide; *suicide* = killing oneself, or someone who kills himself or herself
-cracy	rule, rulers; power	*aristocracy* = rule by nobles, or the nobles themselves; *bureaucracy* = rule by officials, or the officials themselves; *democracy* = rule by the people, or a state governed in this way
		Nouns that denote a person involved in or belonging to a '*-cracy*' end in *-crat*: *aristocrat; bureaucrat; democrat*. The related adjectives end in *-cratic*: *aristocratic*.
crypto-	secret	*crypto-Communist* = someone who is secretly a Communist but does not admit it

Combining form	Relating to	Examples
deca-, dec-	ten	*decagon* = a ten-sided figure; *decathlon* = a sports contest comprising ten events (Also in *decade* = ten years; *December* = the tenth month of the ancient Roman calendar)
deci-	tenth	*decilitre* = a tenth of a litre
derm-, dermo-, dermato-	skin	*dermatology* = the branch of medicine dealing with the skin; *hypodermic* = under the skin; *dermatitis* = a skin disorder
dia-	across, through	*diameter* = the distance across a circle
dys-	bad; difficult	*dyslexia* = a disorder that causes difficulty with reading; *dyspepsia* = indigestion
-ectomy	*see -tomy*	
electro-	electricity	*electrolysis* = chemical decomposition caused by an electric current (Also in *electrocute* = execute or kill by means of electricity)
entero-, enter-	gut, intestine	*enteritis* = inflammation of the intestine; *dysentery* = an infection in the intestine
equi-	equal	*equidistant* = at equal distances; *equilateral* = having equal sides
eu-	good; well	*eurhythmics* = a system of rhythmic physical exercises; *euthanasia* = the painless killing of someone who is suffering from an incurable disease and who wants to die
Euro-	Europe, the European Community	*Euro-American* = involving Europe and the United States; *Euro-MP* = a member of the European Parliament
Franco-	France, French	*Franco-German* = involving France and Germany
fratri-	brother	*fratricide* = murder of one's brother (Also in *fraternal* = brotherly; *fraternity* = brotherhood)

Combining form	Relating to	Examples
-gamy, -gam-	marriage	*bigamy* = marriage to two people at the same time; *monogamous* = married to one person
gastro-	stomach	*gastro-enteritis* = inflammation of the stomach and intestines; *gastric* = relating to the stomach
-gen	forming, producing	*hydrogen* (because hydrogen and oxygen form water)
-genarian	used to state people's ages in terms of decades	*octogenarian* = (someone who is) between eighty and eighty-nine years old
geo-	earth	*geology* = the science of rocks and minerals; *geography*
-gon	angle	*hexagon* = a figure with six sides and six angles
Graeco-, Greco-	Greece	*Greco-Roman* = involving ancient Greece and Rome
-graph, -graphy, -gram	writing or drawing; something written or drawn; a picture	*autograph* = a person's signature written by themselves; *photograph* = a picture made by means of light acting on a film; *seismography* = the use of instruments to record the force of earthquakes; *telegram* = a message sent a long distance along wires by telegraph
gynaeco-, -gyn-	woman	*gynaecology* = the branch of medicine that deals with women's health and diseases; *misogyny* = hatred of women
haemo-	blood	*haemoglobin* = the red protein in blood; *haemophilia* = a disorder of the blood
hecto-	hundred	*hectolitre* = 100 litres; *hectare* = 100 ares
-hedron	face of solid object	*octahedron* = a solid figure with eight faces
hemi-	half	*hemisphere* = half a sphere
hepta-	seven	*heptagon* = a seven-sided figure; *heptahedron*

Combining form	Relating to	Examples
herbi-	plant	*herbivore* = an animal that eats plants
hetero-	opposite	*heterosexual* = attracted to people of the opposite sex
hexa-	six	*hexagon* = a six-sided figure
homo-	same	*homosexual* = attracted to people of the same sex
hydro-, hydr-	water	*hydroelectricity* = electricity produced by the action of flowing water on a turbine; *hydrous* = containing water (in chemistry); *hydrogen* (because hydrogen and oxygen form water)
hyper-	above	*hypersensitive* = excessively sensitive; *hyperactive* = abnormally active; *hypermarket* = a large supermarket
hypo-	below, under	*hypodermic* = under the skin; *hypothermia* = the condition of being abnormally, and usually dangerously, cold
-iatry, -iatrics	medicine	*psychiatry; geriatrics* = the care of the elderly
Indo-	India	*Indo-Pakistan* = involving India and Pakistan
iso-	same	*isobar* = a line joining places having the same atmospheric pressure (Also in *isosceles* = denoting a triangle that has two sides of the same length)
Italo-	Italy	*Italo-German* = involving Italy and Germany
-itis	inflammation of a part of the body	*appendicitis; arthritis; tonsillitis*
kilo-	one thousand	*kilometre* = 1000 metres
-lith	stone	*Neolithic* = the Late Stone Age
-logy	a subject of study	*biology*

Combining form	Relating to	Examples
Some common '-ologies'		***anthropology*** = the study of human beings, human culture, etc; ***astrology*** = the study of the influence of the planets on human behaviour and personality; ***audiology*** = the branch of medicine concerned with the hearing system; ***biology*** = the study of living things; ***criminology*** = the study of crime and criminals; ***ecology*** = the relationship between living creatures and the environment, or the study of this; ***entomology*** = the study of insects; ***geology*** = the study of rocks and minerals; ***graphology*** = the study of handwriting; ***gynaecology*** = the branch of medicine concerned with diseases of women; ***hydrology*** = the science concerned with the Earth's water; ***ichthyology*** = the study of fish; ***meteorology*** = the study of weather and other atmospheric phenomena; weather-forecasting; ***neurology*** = the branch of medicine concerned with the nervous system; ***ornithology*** = the study of birds; ***parapsychology*** = the study of psychic phenomena such as telepathy which are unexplained by science and psychology; ***pathology*** = the branch of medicine concerned with the causes and effects of disease; ***pharmacology*** = the study of drugs and their effects; ***phonology*** = the study of speech sounds; ***physiology*** = the way living organs and tissues function, or the study of this; ***psychology*** = the study of the mind; ***seismology*** = the study of earthquakes; ***sociology*** = the study of human society; ***theology*** = the study of God; ***ufology*** = the study of unidentified flying objects or flying saucers; ***vulcanology*** = the study of volcanoes; ***zoology*** = the study of animals
macro-	large; great; long; over a long time	*macroeconomics* = the economics of large units, such as whole countries; *macrobiotic* = describing a diet intended to prolong life
-mania	mental abnormality; obsession	*kleptomania* A person suffering from a -***mania*** is a -***maniac***: *kleptomaniac*
matri-	mother	*matricide* = killing one's mother (Also in *matriarch* = the female head of a family or tribe)
mega-, megalo-	large	*megalith* = a large stone that forms part of a prehistoric construction; *megabyte* = 1,000,000 or 1,048,576 bytes; *megaton* = 1,000,000 tons; *megalomaniac* = a person with a delusion about their own importance or power
meso-	middle	*Mesolithic* = the middle period of the Stone Age

Combining form	Relating to	Examples
-meter	1 a measuring device	*barometer* = a device for measuring atmospheric pressure; *speedometer* = a device for measuring a vehicle's speed; *thermometer* = a device for measuring temperature
	2 a distance that can be measured	*diameter* = the distance across a circle; *perimeter* = the edge of an area
micro-	small	*microcomputer*; *microscope* = a device for looking at very small things
milli-	thousandth	*millimetre* = one thousandth of a metre
mono-, mon-	one, single	*monorail* = a railway with a single rail; *monarch* = king or queen, a 'sole ruler'; *monopoly* = the sole right to something; *monogamy* = marriage to one person
multi-	many	*multistorey* = having several storeys; *multicolour* = of many colours (Also in *multiple* = involving several parts, or many things)
neo-	new; later; modern	*Neolithic* = the later part of the Stone Age; *neologism* = a newly invented word or expression
neuro-, neur-	nerve	*neurology* = the branch of medicine that deals with the nervous system; *neuralgia* = pain in a nerve; *neural* = relating to a nerve
octo-, octa-, oct-	eight	*octopus* = a sea creature with eight legs; *octagon* = a figure with eight sides; *octet* = a band with eight players in it
omni-	all, everything	*omnivorous* = eating both meat and plants; *omniscient* = knowing everything; *omnipotent* = all-powerful
-osis	1 a diseased state	*neurosis* = a nervous disease; *cirrhosis* = a disorder of the liver
	2 a process	*metamorphosis* = a process of change; *osmosis* = a chemical process involving the movement of molecules

Combining form	Relating to	Examples
ortho-	correct	*orthodox* = having correct or conventional beliefs; *orthography* = conventional spelling
osteo-	bone	*osteopathy* = medical treatment involving manipulation of the bones; *osteoporosis* = degeneration of bones
palaeo-	ancient; early	*Palaeolithic* = the early part of the Stone Age
paedo-	child	*paediatrics* = the branch of medicine dealing with children's health and diseases
pan-	all, every	*pan-Asian* = involving the whole of Asia; *pantheism* = the belief that God is everything (Also in *panorama* = a wide unbroken view of an area, a view 'of everything')
para- (1)	1 beyond	*paranormal* = supernatural, beyond what is normal
	2 beside; auxiliary	*paramedic* = someone who is trained to give medical treatment but is not a fully trained doctor
	3 similar to	*paramilitary* = behaving like a military organization
para- (2)	parachute	*paragliding* = the sport of gliding through the air under a wide parachute
patho-, -path	disease	*pathology* = the branch of medicine that deals with the causes and effects of disease; *psychopath* = someone who has a severe disorder of the mind
patri-	father	*patricide* = the murder of one's father, or someone who has murdered their father (Also in *patriarch* = the male head of a family or tribe)
penta-, pent-	five	*pentagon* = a figure with five sides; *pentangle* = a five-pointed star; *pentathlon* = a sports contest comprising five events

Combining form	Relating to	Examples
philo-, phil-, -phile, -philia	love; lover	*philanthropist* = someone who 'loves people' and seeks to promote their welfare; *philosophy* = originally a 'love of wisdom'; *Anglophile* = someone who likes England or Britain; *Francophilia* = a love of France
-phobia, -phobe	fear or hatred; someone who has a fear or hatred	*claustrophobia* Related adjectives end in *-ic*: *claustrophobic*
Some common Phobias		**acrophobia** = fear of heights; **agoraphobia** = fear of open spaces; **ailurophobia** = fear of cats; **Anglophobia** = fear or hatred of England or Britain, the English or British, English or British culture, etc.; **arachnophobia** = fear of spiders; **astraphobia** = fear of thunder and lightning; **bathophobia** = fear of deep places; **batophobia** = fear of heights, or being close to high buildings, mountains, etc; **batrachophobia** = fear of frogs and toads; **belonephobia** = fear of pins and needles; **brontophobia** = fear of thunder; **canophobia or cynophobia** = fear of dogs; **claustrophobia** = fear of enclosed places; **cyberphobia** = fear of computers; **entomophobia** = fear of insects; **erythrophobia** = fear of blushing; **Francophobia** = fear or hatred of France, the French, French culture, etc; **haemophobia, haemaphobia or haematophobia** = fear of blood; **herpetophobia** = fear of reptiles; **hippophobia** = fear of horses; **homophobia** = fear or hatred of homosexuality or homosexual people; **hydrophobia** = fear of water; also used as another name for the disease rabies; **iatrophobia** = fear of doctors, or going to the doctor; **murophobia or musophobia** = fear of mice; **ochlophobia** = fear of crowds; **ophiophobia or ophidiophobia** = fear of snakes; **ornithophobia** = fear of birds; **pyrophobia** = fear of fire; **technophobia** = fear of technology; **triskaidekaphobia** = fear of the number 13; **xenophobia** = fear or hatred of foreigners or strangers; **zoophobia** = fear of animals
phono-, -phone	sound	*phonology* = the speech-sounds of a language; *telephone* = a device for carrying sound over a long distance; *anglophone* = English-speaking; *saxophone* = a musical instrument; *xylophone* = a musical instrument (Also in *phonetic* = relating to speech sounds)
photo-	1 light	*photography* (which uses light to make pictures); *photosensitive* = sensitive to light
	2 photography	*photocopy*

Combining form	Relating to	Examples
physio-	1 nature, natural things	*physiology* = the study of how the body works
	2 involving manipulation	*physiotherapy* = treatment involving movement and massage as opposed to drugs or surgery
poly-	many	*polygamy* = marriage to several partners at the same time; *polygon* = a figure with several sides
proto-	first; early; primitive	*protozoa* = tiny one-celled animals; *prototype* = an early form of something from which later models develop
pseudo-, pseud-	false	*pseudonym* = a false name; *pseudo-science* = something that appears to be a science but isn't
psycho-, psych-	mind	*psychology* = the study of the mind; *psychiatry* = medical treatment of mental disorders; *psychopath* = a person with a severe mental disorder
quadri-, quadra-	four	*quadriplegia* = paralysis of arms and legs (i.e. all four limbs); *quadraphonic* = relating to sound transmitted through four channels (Also in *quadrilateral* = a four-sided figure; *quadrangle* = a four-sided courtyard; *quadruped* = a four-footed animal)
quint-	five	*quintet* = a group of five musicians
radio-	1 radio	*radiotelescope* = a radio receiver that records radio waves from stars
	2 radiation	*radioactive; radiology* = the branch of medicine that uses radioactive substances in the diagnosis and treatment of disease; *radiotherapy* = the branch of medicine that uses radioactive substances to treat disease

Combining form	Relating to	Examples
retro-	backwards	*retroactive* = denoting legislation that applies to a time earlier than when it is passed (Also in *retrograde* = resulting in a worse state than before; *retroflex* = bent backwards)
Russo-	Russia	*Russo-Japanese* = involving Russia and Japan
-scope	a device for looking at something	*telescope; periscope; microscope; stethoscope* = the instrument doctors use to listen to what is happening inside a patient's body
sept-	seven	*septet* = a group of seven musicians (Also in *September*, which was the seventh month in the ancient Roman calendar)
sex-, sext-	six	*sexcentenary* = six-hundredth anniversary; *sextet* = a group of six musicians
Sino-	China	*Sino-Japanese* = involving China and Japan
socio-	society	*sociology* = the study of how society functions
-sphere	the air around the Earth	*atmosphere; stratosphere*
techno-	practical skills or practical science	*technology* = the use of science for practical purposes; *technophobia* = fear of new technology (Also in *technical, technician* and *technique*)
tele-	far away	*telescope* = a device for seeing things that are far away; *television* = a device for transmitting pictures over long distances; *telephone* = a device for sending sound over long distances
tetra-	four	*tetrahedron* = a solid object with four triangular faces
theo-, the-	god	*theology* = the study of religion; *theocracy* = a state ruled by God or priests; *atheist* = someone who does not believe there is a God

Combining form	Relating to	Examples
thermo-, therm-	heat	*thermometer* = an instrument for measuring temperature; *thermal* = relating to heat
-tomy	cutting; removal	*lobotomy* = an operation involving cutting into a lobe of the brain
		If what is meant is the act of cutting something out, the combining form is *-ectomy*: *appendicectomy* = the surgical removal of the appendix
uni-	one	*unisex* = denoting clothes designed to be suitable for both sexes; *unilateral* = involving one side only, or one group only (Also in *unicorn* = a mythical animal with one horn)
-vore, -vorous	eating	*carnivore* = an animal that eats meat; *herbivore* = an animal that eats plants; *omnivorous* = eating meat and plants
xeno-	foreign; foreigner	*xenophobia* = fear or dislike of foreigners
zoo-	animal	*zoology* = the study of animals

DO IT YOURSELF

A Identify the stems of the following words.

H i n t

*Remember that the
stem is what remains
when you take away the
last affix to have been
added in forming
the word.*

adventurous	forgetfulness	occurrence
annoying	frightened	piglet
closure	hopeful	poisonous
confusion	hopefully	scornfully
creation	hurriedly	strengths
duckling	illegible	symbolize
enjoyment	lazily	unforgettable
exploration	learning	unwritten
financial	lengthwise	wrongly
forgetful	muddy	wasteful

B Identify the roots of the following words.

H i n t

*Remember that the
root of a word is what
remains when all the
affixes have been
taken away.*

annoyingly	happenings	triumphantly
blamelessness	hopefulness	understandably
decentralize	hurriedly	unfortunately
discouragement	immovable	unreliable
enjoyably	indebtedness	unwritten
forgetfulness	limitations	weaknesses
frightened	thoughtfully	worldliness

C Say whether the following examples of word-formation involve derivation or inflection.

H i n t

*Remember that inflection
adds grammatical
information about a word,
whilst derivation results in
the formation of a
completely different word.*

amuses	kindness	runner
amusement	logical	running
announced	masterful	said
bigger	mathematical	smallest
conversation	misjudge	unnecessary
insisting	necessarily	valuable
joyful	redo	woven

D Using the prefixes *il-*, *im-*, *in-* and *ir-*, make the following words negative.

ability	considerate	possible
patient	humane	responsible
logical	expensive	sane
accurate	appropriate	attentive
polite	balance	literate
adequate	capable	mature
regular	moral	frequent
formal	liberal	perfect

E Complete the following sentences by selecting the correct word from the choice given within brackets.

1. An animal that eats meat is a (*herbivore, carnivore*).

2. An octagon is a figure with (*eight, ten*) sides.

3. A kilometre is equal to (*a thousand, a hundred*) metres.

4. Neurology is the branch of medicine that deals with functioning of the (*heart, nervous system*).

5. Fratricide is the murder of a person's own (*father, brother, mother*).

6. People who are Francophobic (*like, dislike*) the French.

7. Dermatitis is a disorder of the (*skin, hair*).

8. Omnivores eat (*fish, meat, anything*).

9. Zoology is the study of (*flowers, birds, animals*).

10. A polygamist is someone who is married to (*one person, several people at the same time*).

11. The Mesolithic period of the Stone Age came (*before, after*) the Neolithic period.

12. Hypothermia is the condition of being (*too cold, too hot*).

7 Word-Families

Word-families based on nouns

Noun	Verb	Adjective	Adverb	Related words
abuse	abuse	abusive	abusively	abuser
anger	anger	angry	angrily	
awe	awe	awed, awesome	awesomely	awful, awfully; awe-inspiring, awe-struck; overawe
beauty	beautify	beautiful	beautifully	beauteous; beautification
care	care	caring, careful, careless	carefully carelessly	carefulness, carelessness; uncaring
caution	caution	cautious, cautionary	cautiously	cautiousness; incautious
comfort	comfort	comfortable, comforting, comfortless	comfortably, comfortingly	comforter
courage	encourage	courageous	courageously	courageousness; encouraging, encouragingly, encouragement; discourage, discouragement, discouraging, discouragingly
critic	criticize	critical	critically	criticism
danger	endanger	dangerous	dangerously	endangerment
decor	decorate	decorated, decorative	decoratively	decorator, decoration, decorativeness
despair	despair	despairing	despairingly	desperate, desperately, desperation
disaster		disastrous	disastrously	
drama	dramatize	dramatic	dramatically	dramatist, dramatization
ease	ease	easy	easily	easiness; uneasy
effect	effect	effective	effectively	effectiveness; ineffective, ineffectual
energy	energize	energetic	energetically	

Noun	Verb	Adjective	Adverb	Related words
fault	fault	faulty	faultily	faultiness, faultless, faultlessly
fear	fear	fearful, fearless	fearfully, fearlessly	fearfulness, fearlessness; fearsome
force	force	forced, forcible, forceful	forcedly, forcibly, forcefully	forcedness, forcibleness, forcefulness
fury	infuriate	furious	furiously	furiousness; infuriating, infuriatingly
glory	glorify	glorious	gloriously	glorification; inglorious
grace	grace	graceful, gracious, graceless	gracefully, graciously gracelessly	gracefulness, graciousness, gracelessness; disgrace, disgraceful
grief	grieve	grievous	grievously	grievance; grievousness
harm	harm	harmful, harmless	harmfully, harmlessly	harmfulness, harmlessness
health		healthy	healthily	healthiness; unhealthy; heal, healer
honour	honour	honourable, honorary	honourably	dishonourable
hope	hope	hopeful, hopeless	hopefully, hopelessly	hopefulness, hopelessness
horror	horrify	horrendous, horrible, horrid, horrific, horrifying	horrendously, horribly, horridly, horrifically, horrifyingly	horrendousness, horridness, horrifyingness
joy		joyous, joyful, joyless	joyously, joyfully, joylessly	joyousness, joyfulness, joylessness; *see also* **enjoy**
length	lengthen	lengthy	lengthily lengthwise	*See also* **long** *on page 242*
light	light			lighter, lighting; enlighten, enlightenment; lightning
love	love	lovable, loveless, loving, lovely, loved	lovingly	lover, beloved, loveliness

Noun	Verb	Adjective	Adverb	Related words
mischief		mischievous	mischievously	mischievousness
misuse	misuse			
pain	pain	painful, painless	painfully, painlessly	painfulness, painlessness; pained, painkiller, painstaking
peace	pacify	peaceful, peaceable	peacefully, peaceably	peacefulness; peacemaker, pacification, pacifier; pacifism, pacifist
pity	pity	pitiful, pitiless, piteous, pitying	pitifully, pitilessly, piteously, pityingly	pitifulness, pitilessness, piteousness
poison	poison	poisoned, poisonous	poisonously	poisoner; non-poisonous
pride	pride	proud		*See also* proud *on page 242*
rage	enrage, rage	enraged		raging
reason	reason	reasonable	reasonably	unreasonable
slave	slave, enslave	slavish	slavishly	slavery
sleep	sleep	sleeping, sleepless, sleepy	sleepily, sleeplessly	sleeper; sleepiness; asleep
strength	strengthen	strong		*See also* strong *on page 243*
sympathy	sympathize	sympathetic	sympathetically	unsympathetic
terror	terrorize, terrify	terrible, terrifying	terribly, terrifyingly	terrorist, terrorism
thirst	thirst	thirsty	thirstily	
use	use	useful, useless	usefully, uselessly	usefulness, uselessness; *see also* abuse *on page 232*, misuse *on page 234*

Word-families based on verbs

Verb	Noun	Adjective	Adverb	Related words
abolish	abolition			abolitionist
absorb	absorption	absorbent		
abstain	abstainer, abstention			abstinence
acquire	acquisition	acquisitive	acquisitively	
act	act, action; acting, actor, actress	acting		*See also* active *on page 240*
add	addition	added, additional	additionally	additive
admire	admiration, admirer	admiring, admirable	admiringly, admirably	
admit	admission, admittance	admitted	admittedly	admissible, inadmissible
adore	adoration, adorer	adoring, adorable	adoringly, adorably	
agree	agreement	agreeable	agreeably	disagree, disagreeable, disagreeably
annoy	annoyance	annoying	annoyingly	
appeal	appeal	appealing	appealingly	
appear	appearance			apparent, apparently; disappear
apply	application	applied		applicable, inapplicable
approve	approval	approved, approving	approvingly	disapprove, disapproving, disapprovingly
attend	attention, attendance, attendant	attentive	attentively	attentiveness; inattentive
attract	attraction	attractive	attractively	attractiveness; unattractive
boast	boast, boaster, boasting	boastful	boastfully	boastfulness

Verb	Noun	Adjective	Adverb	Related words
cheer	cheer	cheerful, cheerless, cheery	cheerfully, cheerlessly	cheerfulness, cheerlessness
collect	collection, collector	collected		collective, collectively
compare	comparison	comparable, comparative	comparably, comparatively	incomparable, incomparably
conceive	concept, conception	conceivable	conceivably	inconceivable, inconceivably
confide	confidant, confidante	confidential, confiding	confidentially, confidingly	confidence, confident, confidently
continue	continuation continuance, continuity	continual, continuous, continued	continually, continuously	discontinue
consider	consideration	considerate, considered	considerately	inconsiderate, inconsiderately
create	creator, creation	creative	creatively	creativeness, creativity
deceive	deceiver, deception	deceptive	deceptively	deceptiveness
decide	decider, decision	decided, decisive	decidedly decisively	decisiveness; indecision, indecisive, undecided
deduce	deducer, deduction	deductive	deductively	
defend	defendant, defender, defence	defenceless, defensible, defensive	defensively	defencelessness, defensiveness; indefensible
delude	delusion	deluded		
demolish	demolition			
derive	derivation, derivative	derivative		
describe	description	descriptive	descriptively	indescribable
destroy	destroyer, destruction	destructive	destructively self-destruction	destructiveness;
differ	difference	different	differently	differentiate, differentiation

Verb	Noun	Adjective	Adverb	Related words
dread	dread	dreaded, dreadful	dreadfully	
enjoy	enjoyment	enjoyable	enjoyably	
excel	excellence	excellent	excellently	Excellency
expect	expectation, expectancy	expected, expecting, expectant	expectantly	unexpected, unexpectedly
fix	fix, fixer, fixture	fixed	fixedly	fixation
fool	fool, foolery	foolish, foolhardy	foolishly	foolishness, foolhardiness; foolproof
forget	forgetfulness	forgetful; forgotten	forgetfully	unforgettable
glare	glare	glaring	glaringly	
hate	hate, hatred	hated, hateful	hatefully	
help	help, helper; helping	helpful, helpless, helping	helpfully, helplessly	helpfulness, helplessness; unhelpful
hurry	hurry	hurried	hurriedly	unhurried
imagine	imagination	imaginable, imaginary, imaginative	imaginatively	imaginativeness; unimaginable, unimaginative
imitate	imitation, imitator	imitative	imitatively	imitativeness
induce	induction	inductive	inductively	
infect	infection	infectious, infected	infectiously	infectiousness
inform	informer, informant, information	informative, informed	informatively	informativeness; uninformative
injure	injury	injured, injurious	injuriously	
instruct	instruction, instructor	instructive, instructional	instructively	instructress
intend	intention, intent	intent, intended, intentional	intentionally, intently	

Verb	Noun	Adjective	Adverb	Related words
invite	invitation	invited, inviting	invitingly	uninvited, uninviting
know	knowledge	knowing, known	knowingly	knowledgeable; unknown
laugh	laugh, laughter	laughing, laughable	laughingly, laughably	
laze		lazy	lazily	laziness
marvel	marvel	marvellous	marvellously	
mistake	mistake	mistaken	mistakenly	unmistakable
move	move, mover, movement	moving, movable	movingly	motion; *see also* mobile *on page 242*
neglect	neglect	neglected, neglectful, negligent	neglectfully, negligently	negligence
obey	obedience	obedient	obediently	disobedient, disobedience
oblige	obligation	obligatory, obliged, obliging	obligatorily, obligingly	disobliging
pardon	pardon	pardonable	pardonably	unpardonable
perceive	perception	perceptive	perceptively	imperceptible
permit	permission, permit	permissive, permitted, permissible	permissively	permissiveness
persist	persistence	persistent	persistently	
persuade	persuasion	persuasive	persuasively	persuasiveness; dissuade, dissuasion
please	pleasure	pleased, pleasant, pleasing, pleasurable	pleasingly, pleasantly, pleasurably	displease; unpleasant
produce	producer, production	productive	productively	unproductive
prosper	prosperity	prosperous	prosperously	
receive	receiver, reception	receptive	receptively	

Verb	Noun	Adjective	Adverb	Related words
recognize	recognition	recognized, recognizable	recognizably	unrecognizable, unrecognized
reduce	reduction			
repeat	repetition	repeated, repetitive, repeatable	repeatedly, repetitively	repetitiveness; unrepeatable
reveal	revelation	revealing	revealingly	
satisfy	satisfaction	satisfying, satisfactory, satisfied	satisfyingly, satisfactorily	dissatisfy, dissatisfied; unsatisfactory
select	selector, selection	select, selective	selectively	
seem	semblance	seeming	seemingly	
shame	shame	shameful, shameless	shamefully, shamelessly	shamefulness, shamelessness; ashamed
solve	solution, solver	soluble		insoluble
study	study	studied		student, studious, studiously; studio
subscribe	subscriber, subscription			
succeed	success	successful	successfully	successive, successively; successor, succession
suspect	suspect, suspicion	suspected, suspicious	suspiciously	unsuspecting
think	thinker, thought	thinking, thoughtful, thoughtless	thoughtfully, thoughtlessly	thoughtfulness, thoughtlessness; unthinking
tire		tired, tireless, tiresome, tiring	tiredly, tirelessly, tiresomely	tiredness, tiresomeness, tirelessness; untiring
unite	unity,	united		unify, unification; disunity, disunited
will	will	willing	willingly	wilful, wilfully, wilfulness, willingness; unwilling, unwillingly

Word-families based on adjectives

Adjective	Noun	Verb	Adverb	Related words
able	ability	enable	ably	unable, inability; disable, disabled, disability
active	activeness, activity	activate	actively	activation, activator; activist; inactive, inactivity; *see also* act *on page 235*
bad	badness		badly	*See also* worse *on page 243*
black	blackness	blacken	blackly	
bold	boldness	embolden	boldly	
brave	bravery	brave	bravely	
bright	brightness	brighten	brightly	
broad	breadth, broadness	broaden	broadly	
busy	busyness	busy	busily	business; busybody
calm	calm, calmness	calm	calmly	
certain	certainty		certainly	certify, ascertain; uncertain
cheap	cheapness	cheapen	cheaply, cheap	
clean	cleanness	clean	cleanly, clean	cleanliness, cleanse, cleanser; cleanly /ˈklenli/
clear	clearness, clarity	clear, clarify	clearly	clarification; clearing, clearance
cool	coolness	cool	coolly	
correct	correctness, correction	correct	correctly	corrective; incorrect
dark	dark, darkness	darken	darkly	
dead	death	die; deaden	dead (*informal*), deadly	dying; deadly (*adjective*), deathly; undying
deep	depth, deep	deepen	deeply	deepening

Adjective	Noun	Verb	Adverb	Related words
dim	dimness	dim	dimly	
direct	directness	direct	directly	direction, director, directive, directory; indirect
dry	dryness	dry	dryly	drier, dryer
dull	dullness	dull	dully	
equal	equal, equality	equal, equalize	equally	equate, equation; unequal, inequality
false	falseness, falsehood	falsify	falsely	falsification
free	freedom	free	freely	
full	fullness	fill	fully, full	filled, filling; refill
glad	gladness	gladden	gladly	
hard	hardness	harden	hard	hardly (= *scarcely*)
high	height	heighten	high, highly	Highness
hot	heat	heat	hotly	heated, heatedly, heater, heating
humble	humility, humbleness	humble	humbly	
ideal	ideal	idealize	ideally	idealist, idealism, idealistic, idealistically, idealization
just	justice		justly	justify, justification, justifiable, justified, justifiably; unjustified
large	largeness	enlarge		largely (= *to a great extent*)
light (= *not heavy*)	lightness	lighten	lightly	
light (= *not dark*)	light, lightness	lighten		
lively	liveliness	enliven		

Adjective	Noun	Verb	Adverb	Related words
long	length	lengthen, elongate, prolong		*See also* **length** *on page 233*
loose	looseness	loosen	loosely	
mad	madness	madden	madly	maddening, maddeningly
mobile	mobility	mobilize		mobile (= *hanging decoration that moves*), mobilization
moist	moistness	moisten	moistly	
proud	pride		proudly	*See also* **pride** *on page 234*
pure	purity, pureness	purify	purely	purification, purist; impure, impurity
quick	quickness	quicken	quick, quickly	
ready	readiness	ready	readily	
regular	regularity	regularize	regularly	regulate, regulation, regulator; irregular
rich	rich, riches, richness	enrich	richly	roughage
rough	roughness	roughen	roughly	
sad	sadness	sadden	sadly	saddening
safe	safety	save	safely	saver, saviour, savings
secure	security	secure	securely	insecure
sharp	sharpness	sharpen	sharply	sharpener
short	shortness	shorten	shortly	shortage
sick	sickness	sicken		sickly, sickening
simple	simplicity	simplify	simply	simplification, simplified; simplistic, simplistically; simpleton
smooth	smoothness	smooth	smoothly	

Adjective	Noun	Verb	Adverb	Related words
soft	softness	soften	softly	softener
solid	solidness, solidity, solid	solidify	solidly	solidification, solidarity
special	speciality, specialty, specialist	specialize	specially	specialized, specialization
strong	strength	strengthen	strongly	*See also* **strength** *on page 234*
sweet	sweetness	sweeten	sweetly	sweetener
thick	thickness	thicken	thickly	thickener
tight	tightness	tighten	tightly	tights
tough	toughness	toughen	toughly	
warm	warmth	warm	warmly	
weak	weakness	weaken	weakly	weakling
white	whiteness	whiten	whitely	
wide	width	widen	widely	
worse		worsen	worse	

DO IT YOURSELF

Rewrite the following sentences using single words that have the same meaning as the words in italics.

> *Example:*
>
> They *made* the road **wider**.
> They *widened* the road.

Hint

Look at the word lists in this unit for the words that are in bold italics.

1. She arrived *when we were not* **expecting** her.

2. Opposition to the government's proposals has *become* **stronger**.

3. They fought *with great* **courage**.

4. You have behaved *like a* **fool**.

5. Their feelings of horror were *more than one can* **imagine**.

6. We could hear the *sound of people* **laughing** in the next room.

7. Is the stone *able to be* **moved**?

8. We are assured by many experts that eating genetically modified cereals will not *be a* **danger** *to* our health.

9. It was an experience *I will never* **forget**.

10. She had a rash on her leg *that caused her a lot of* **pain**.

11. After they captured the city, they *made* **slaves** of its inhabitants.

12. We are completely *unable to* **defend** ourselves.

13. I accept this award with feelings both of *being* **proud** and *being* **humble**.

14. She performed the concerto *without a single* **fault**.

15. Could you *make* your explanation **simpler**?

16. My mother was *in a* **fury** when she heard the news.

17. Handle the ornaments *with* **care**.

18. What's the name of the *person who wrote the* **drama**?

19. *I* **admit** there are still a few problems to be solved.

20. One of the *things that* **attract** *me* is the sheer simplicity of the proposal.

8 ▶ Irregular Verbs

Base form	Third person singular, present tense	Present participle	Past tense	Past participle
arise	arises	arising	arose	arisen
awake	awakes	awaking	awoke; *rarely* awaked	awoken; *rarely* awaked
be	is *Note also:* I am; we/you/they are	being	I was; he/she/it was; we/you/they were	been
bear	bears	bearing	bore	borne
beat	beats	beating	beat	beaten
become	becomes	becoming	became	become
begin	begins	beginning	began	begun
bend	bends	bending	bent	bent
bet	bets	betting	bet; *rarely* betted	bet; *rarely* betted
bid (= *offer money*)	bids	bidding	bid	bid
bid (= *ask someone to do something; say*)	bids	bidding	bade /bad, beɪd/; *less commonly* bid	bidden; *less commonly* bid
bind	binds	binding	bound	bound
bite	bites	biting	bit	bitten
bleed	bleeds	bleeding	bled	bled
blow	blows	blowing	blew	blown
break	breaks	breaking	broke	broken
bring	brings	bringing	brought	brought
broadcast	broadcasts	broadcasting	broadcast	broadcast
build	builds	building	built	built

Base form	Third person singular, present tense	Present participle	Past tense	Past participle
burn	burns	burning	burned, burnt	burned, burnt

burned, burnt
Burnt is commoner than **burned** when the verb is followed by an object, and **burned** commoner than **burnt** when there is no following object:
*The fire **burned** brightly. / I'm afraid I've **burnt** the toast.*
Burnt is the form used as an adjective: ***burnt** toast.*

Base form	Third person singular, present tense	Present participle	Past tense	Past participle
burst	bursts	bursting	burst	burst
buy	buys	buying	bought	bought
cast	casts	casting	cast	cast
catch	catches	catching	caught	caught
choose	chooses	choosing	chose	chosen
cling	clings	clinging	clung	clung
come	comes	coming	came	come
cost	costs	costing	cost, costed	cost, costed

cost, costed
When **cost** means 'calculate the cost of something', the past tense and past participle are both **costed**: *This project was never properly **costed**.*
In all other senses of the verb, the past tense and past participle are both **cost**: *How much did that car **cost**? / It must have **cost** a lot of money.*

Base form	Third person singular, present tense	Present participle	Past tense	Past participle
creep	creeps	creeping	crept	crept
cut	cuts	cutting	cut	cut
deal	deals	dealing	dealt /delt/	dealt
dig	digs	digging	dug	dug
do	does /dʌz/	doing	did	done /dʌn/
draw	draws	drawing	drew	drawn
dream	dreams	dreaming	dreamed, dreamt /dremt/	dreamed, dreamt

Base form	Third person singular, present tense	Present participle	Past tense	Past participle
drink	drinks	drinking	drank	drunk
drive	drives	driving	drove	driven
dwell	dwells	dwelling	dwelt; *less commonly* dwelled	dwelt; *less commonly* dwelled
eat	eats	eating	ate /et, eɪt/	eaten
fall	falls	falling	fell	fallen
feed	feeds	feeding	fed	fed
feel	feels	feeling	felt	felt
fight	fights	fighting	fought	fought
find	finds	finding	found	found
flee	flees	fleeing	fled	fled
fling	flings	flinging	flung	flung
fly	flies	flying	flew	flown
forbid	forbids	forbidding	forbade /fəˈbad, fəˈbeɪd/ or forbad /fəˈbad/	forbidden
forecast	forecasts	forecasting	forecast	forecast
forego *see* forgo				
forget	forgets	forgetting	forgot	forgotten
forgive	forgives	forgiving	forgave	forgiven
forgo	forgoes	forgoing	forwent	forgone
forsake	forsakes	forsaking	forsook	forsaken
freeze	freezes	freezing	froze	frozen
get	gets	getting	got	got; *also in US* gotten
give	gives	giving	gave	given
go	goes	going	went	gone

Base form	Third person singular, present tense	Present participle	Past tense	Past participle
grind	grinds	grinding	ground	ground
grow	grows	growing	grew	grown
hang	hangs	hanging	hung, hanged	hung, hanged

hung, hanged *see page 184 for comments on the use of these two words.*

have	has	having	had	had
hear	hears	hearing	heard	heard
hide	hides	hiding	hid	hidden
hit	hits	hitting	hit	hit
hold	holds	holding	held	held
hurt	hurts	hurting	hurt	hurt
keep	keeps	keeping	kept	kept
kneel	kneels	kneeling	knelt	knelt
knit	knits	knitting	knitted, knit	knitted, knit

knitted, knit
Knitted is the correct past tense and past participle to use when the verb is used in the sense of making clothes, etc with knitting needles and wool:
*I've **knitted** you a pair of socks.*
Knit is used in figurative senses:
*Adversity **knit** the family together. / a close-**knit** community*
Both forms are correct in the phrase **knit** one's brows (= frown):
*She **knit/knitted** her brows as she read what he had written.*

know	knows	knowing	knew	known
lay	lays	laying	laid	laid
lead	leads	leading	led	led
lean	leans	leaning	leaned, leant /lent/	leaned, leant
leap	leaps	leaping	leaped, leapt /lept/	leaped, leapt
learn	learns	learning	learned, learnt /lɜːnt/	learned, learnt

Base form	Third person singular, present tense	Present participle	Past tense	Past participle
leave	leaves	leaving	left	left
lend	lends	lending	lent	lent
let	lets	letting	let	let
lie	lies	lying	lay	lain

lie

In the sense 'to be in a flat or level position', the verb **lie** has **lay** and **lain** as its past tense and past participle: *The body must have **lain** undiscovered for months.*

The other verb **lie** (= *to tell lies*) is regular: *You have **lied** to me over and over again.*

light	lights	lighting	lit, lighted	lit, lighted

lighted, lit

Lit is more common than **lighted** except when the past participle is being used as an adjective. As an adjective, **lighted** is the usual form, except when the adjective is preceded by an adverb: *a **lighted** match / a well-**lit** room.*

lose	loses	losing	lost	lost
make	makes	making	made	made
mean	means	meaning	meant /ment/	meant
meet	meets	meeting	met	met
mistake	mistakes	mistaking	mistook	mistaken
mow	mows	mowing	mowed	mowed, mown
pay	pays	paying	paid	paid
prove	proves	proving	proved	proved; *less commonly* proven

proved, proven

Proved is the normal form of the past participle, but **proven** is the form used as an adjective: *a **proven** remedy for acne.*

put	puts	putting	put	put

Base form	Third person singular, present tense	Present participle	Past tense	Past participle
quit	quits	quitting	quit, quitted	quit, quitted
read	reads	reading	read	read
ride	rides	riding	rode	ridden
ring (= *make a ringing sound*)	rings	ringing	rang	rung
ring (= *form or put a ring round something*)	rings	ringing	ringed	ringed
rise	rises	rising	rose	risen
run	runs	running	ran	run
saw	saws	sawing	sawed	sawn, sawed
say	says	saying	said	said
see	sees	seeing	saw	seen
seek	seeks	seeking	sought	sought
sell	sells	selling	sold	sold
send	sends	sending	sent	sent
set	sets	setting	set	set
sew	sews	sewing	sewed	sewn, sewed
shake	shakes	shaking	shook	shaken
shear	shears	shearing	sheared	sheared, shorn
shine	shines	shining	shone, shined	shone, shined

shone, shined

Shined is only used in the sense of polishing something until it shines:
*He **shined** his shoes until they **shone**.*

shoot	shoots	shooting	shot	shot
show	shows	showing	showed	shown, showed

shown, showed

As a past participle, either form is possible, but in the passive use **shown**:
*I need to be **shown** what to do before I can do it.*

Base form	Third person singular, present tense	Present participle	Past tense	Past participle
shrink	shrinks	shrinking	shrank	shrunk
shut	shuts	shutting	shut	shut
sing	sings	singing	sang	sung
sink	sinks	sinking	sank	sunk
sit	sits	sitting	sat	sat
slay	slays	slaying	slew	slain
sleep	sleeps	sleeping	slept	slept
slide	slides	sliding	slid	slid
sling	slings	slinging	slung	slung
slink	slinks	slinking	slunk	slunk
slit	slits	slitting	slit	slit
smell	smells	smelling	smelt, smelled	smelt, smelled
sow	sows	sowing	sowed	sowed, sown
speak	speaks	speaking	spoke	spoken
speed	speeds	speeding	sped, speeded	sped, speeded

sped, speeded

Sped is the past tense and past participle of the simple verb **speed**: *The car sped along the road.* In the case of the phrasal verb **speed up**, the past tense and past participle are both **speeded**: *The car speeded up.*

spell	spells	spelling	spelt, spelled	spelt, spelled
spend	spends	spending	spent	spent
spill	spills	spilling	spilt, spilled	spilt, spilled
spin	spins	spinning	spun	spun
spit	spits	spitting	spat	spat
split	splits	splitting	split	split
spoil	spoils	spoiling	spoilt, spoiled	spoilt, spoiled
spread	spreads	spreading	spread	spread

Base form	Third person singular, present tense	Present participle	Past tense	Past participle
spring	springs	springing	sprang	sprung
stand	stands	standing	stood	stood
steal	steals	stealing	stole	stolen
stick	sticks	sticking	stuck	stuck
sting	stings	stinging	stung	stung
stink	stinks	stinking	stank, stunk	stunk
stride	strides	striding	strode	stridden
strike	strikes	striking	struck	struck
string	strings	stringing	strung	strung
strive	strives	striving	strove	striven
swear	swears	swearing	swore	sworn
sweep	sweeps	sweeping	swept	swept
swell	swells	swelling	swelled	swelled, swollen

swelled, swollen
Swelled is the normal past participle of **swell**. **Swollen** is normally used in passive constructions and as an adjective: *a **swollen** river.*

swim	swims	swimming	swam	swum
swing	swings	swinging	swung	swung
take	takes	taking	took	taken
teach	teaches	teaching	taught	taught
tear	tears	tearing	tore	torn
tell	tells	telling	told	told
think	thinks	thinking	thought	thought
throw	throws	throwing	threw	thrown
tread	treads	treading	trod	trodden
undergo	undergoes	undergoing	underwent	undergone

Base form	Third person singular, present tense	Present participle	Past tense	Past participle
understand	understands	understanding	understood	understood
undertake	undertakes	undertaking	undertook	undertaken
undo	undoes	undoing	undid	undone
uphold	upholds	upholding	upheld	upheld
upset	upsets	upsetting	upset	upset
wake	wakes	waking	woke	woken
wear	wears	wearing	wore	worn
weave	weaves	weaving	wove	woven

weaved

The irregular verb **weave** (past tense **wove**, past participle **woven**) means 'to make cloth, etc'.

A different verb **weave**, meaning 'to move in a winding course', has **weaved** as its past tense and past participle: *She **weaved** her way through the crowd.*

weep	weeps	weeping	wept	wept
wet	wets	wetting	wet, wetted	wet, wetted

wet, wetted

Wet is the normal past tense and past participle, except in the passive when **wetted** is more often used: *The jersey needs to be **wetted** before the dye is added.*

win	wins	winning	won	won
wind /waɪnd/	winds	winding	wound	wound
withdraw	withdraws	withdrawing	withdrew	withdrawn
withhold	withholds	withholding	withheld	withheld
withstand	withstands	withstanding	withstood	withstood
wring	wring	wringing	wrung	wrung
write	writes	writing	wrote	written

DO IT YOURSELF

A Rewrite the following sentences replacing the base form of the verbs in brackets with the appropriate past tense or past participle forms.

> *Examples:*
> The bird (*fly*) away.
> The bird **flew** away.
> The bird has (*fly*) away.
> The bird has **flown** away.

1. Who (*break*) the vase?

2. Who (*draw*) that picture on the wall?

3. Have you ever (*meet*) the Queen?

4. I (*know*) exactly what to do.

5. Who (*tell*) you that?

6. Have you (*see*) my pen anywhere?

7. Has the clock (*strike*) twelve yet?

8. The police (*begin*) to question witnesses to the accident.

9. You might at least have (*speak*) to him.

10. Her cutting remarks really (*upset*) me.

11. Who (*win*)?

12. I haven't (*write*) to my mother for weeks.

13. Has anyone ever (*tell*) you you're a pain in the neck?

14. This has (*become*) a serious problem now.

15. He's been (*bite*) by a snake.

16. I think the police (*deal*) with the matter very efficiently.

17. She was very angry but nevertheless she (*forgive*) him for what he had (*say*).

18. She turned and (*flee*).

19. I've (*sell*) my car.

20. Suddenly the bell (*ring*).

B Write down the past tenses of the following verbs.

bring	lay	stick
fight	meet	swim
fly	send	take
forbid	sew	wear
forgive	shine	wind
lie	shrink	write

C Write down the base forms corresponding to the following past participles.

chosen	lost
frozen	torn
led	wept
bled	bought
held	caught
laid	sought
lain	taught

Comparison of Adjectives, Adverbs and Determiners

9

Adjectives, adverbs and some determiners have three **degrees** of comparison:

positive (*bad, black, beautiful, often, little*),
comparative (*worse, blacker, more beautiful, more often, less*) and
superlative (*worst, blackest, most beautiful, most often, least*).

Comparison of Adjectives

One-syllable adjectives

▶ Most one-syllable adjectives form comparatives and superlatives by adding **-er** and **-est** to the positive form of the adjective:

black	*blacker*	*blackest*
long	*longer*	*longest*
new	*newer*	*newest*
rich	*richer*	*richest*
small	*smaller*	*smallest*
thick	*thicker*	*thickest*
warm	*warmer*	*warmest*

There are, however, a number of exceptions to this. Most one-syllable adjectives that are also past participles of verbs form their comparatives and superlatives with **more** and **most**:

bent	*more bent*	*most bent*
bored	*more bored*	*most bored*
torn	*more torn*	*most torn*
worn	*more worn*	*most worn*

but on the other hand:

drunk	*drunker* or	*drunkest* or
	more drunk	*most drunk*
tired	*tireder*	*tiredest*

▶ Some adjectives have irregular comparatives and superlatives:

bad	*worse*	*worst*
good	*better*	*best*
ill	*worse*	*worst*
well	*better*	*best*

▶ Some adjectives have more than one form of comparative and superlative:

far	*farther* or *further*	*farthest* or *furthest*
	(*See page 182 for comments on the uses of these forms.*)	
old	*older* or *elder*	*oldest* or *eldest*

▶ **Mere** has the superlative form **merest** but has no comparative form.

Spelling Tips

▶ When an adjective ends in a single consonant preceded by a single vowel, the consonant is doubled in the comparative and superlative forms:

big	*bigger*	*biggest*
fat	*fatter*	*fattest*
sad	*sadder*	*saddest*
slim	*slimmer*	*slimmest*
thin	*thinner*	*thinnest*

This is not the case, however, where the consonant is preceded by two or more letters representing a single vowel sound:

plain	*plainer*	*plainest*
proud	*prouder*	*proudest*
brown	*browner*	*brownest*
bright	*brighter*	*brightest*
calm	*calmer*	*calmest*

▶ If an adjective ends in **-e**, this **-e** is dropped before the **-er** and **-est** endings are added:

eerie	*eerier*	*eeriest*
free	*freer*	*freest*
rude	*ruder*	*rudest*
true	*truer*	*truest*
white	*whiter*	*whitest*

▶ If an adjective ends in a **-y** preceded by a consonant, this **-y** is in some cases changed to **-i-** before the **-er** and **-est** endings:

dry	*drier*	*driest*
shy	*shyer* or *shier*	*shyest* or *shiest*
sly	*slyer* or *slier*	*slyest* or *sliest*
spry	*spryer*	*spryest*
wry	*wryer* or *wrier*	*wryest* or *wriest*

▶ If the **-y** is preceded by a vowel, it does not change to **-i-**:

coy	*coyer*	*coyest*
grey	*greyer*	*greyest*

Two-syllable adjectives

▶ Most two-syllable adjectives form their comparatives and superlatives with **more** and **most**:

careless	*more careless*	*most careless*
foolish	*more foolish*	*most foolish*
modest	*more modest*	*most modest*
proper	*more proper*	*most proper*
senseless	*more senseless*	*most senseless*
special	*more special*	*most special*
tiring	*more tiring*	*most tiring*

▶ Two-syllable adjectives ending in **-y** form their comparatives and superlatives by adding **-er** and **-est** to the positive form:

busy	*busier*	*busiest*
dirty	*dirtier*	*dirtiest*
funny	*funnier*	*funniest*
happy	*happier*	*happiest*
pretty	*prettier*	*prettiest*

Spelling Tips

▶ As with one-syllable adjectives, a final **-y** preceded by a consonant changes to **-i-** before **-er** and **-est**:

cloudy	*cloudier*	*cloudiest*
friendly	*friendlier*	*friendliest*
happy	*happier*	*happiest*

▶ A final **-ey** also changes to **-i-**:

choosey	*choosier*	*choosiest*
clayey	*clayier*	*clayiest*
matey	*matier*	*matiest*

▶ Two-syllable adjectives ending in **-ow** and **-le** form comparatives and superlatives by adding **-er** and **-est** to the positive form:

hollow	*hollower*	*hollowest*
shallow	*shallower*	*shallowest*
noble	*nobler*	*noblest*
simple	*simpler*	*simplest*

Note also:

clever	*cleverer*	*cleverest*

▶ A number of two-syllable adjectives have both forms of comparative and superlative:

common	commoner or *more common*	commonest or *most common*
polite	politer or *more polite*	politest or *most polite*
secure	securer or *more secure*	securest or *most secure*
stupid	stupider or *more stupid*	stupidest or *most stupid*

Other adjectives in this group are:
cruel, eager, extreme, handsome, pleasant, quiet, remote, sincere, solemn, solid

Spelling Tips

▶ As with one-syllable adjectives, a final **-e** is dropped before adding **-er** or **-est**:

| remote | remoter | remotest |
| simple | simpler | simplest |

▶ If a two-syllable adjective ends in a single consonant preceded by a single vowel, the consonant is not doubled in the comparative and superlative forms unless it is an **l**:

common	commoner	commonest
stupid	stupider	stupidest
cruel	crueller	cruellest

Adjectives of three or more syllables

▶ Adjectives of three or more syllables form their comparatives and superlatives with **more** and **most**:

beautiful	more beautiful	most beautiful
convenient	more convenient	most convenient
sensitive	more sensitive	most sensitive

▶ The only exceptions to this rule are negative adjectives formed by adding the prefix **un-** to a two-syllable adjective that forms its comparative and superlative with *-er* and *-est*:

| unhappy | unhappier | unhappiest |
| untidy | untidier | untidiest |

Compound Adjectives

▶ Compound adjectives generally form their comparatives and superlatives with **more** and **most**:

bad-tempered	*more bad-tempered*	*most bad-tempered*
big-headed	*more big-headed*	*most big-headed*
hard-working	*more hard-working*	*most hard-working*
long-lasting	*more long-lasting*	*most long-lasting*

▶ If the 'core' of the compound adjective is a verb (e.g. **to work, to last**), then the comparative and superlative can be also formed by adding *-er* and *-est* to the first element of the compound:

hard-working	*harder-working*	*hardest-working*
long-lasting	*longer-lasting*	*longest-lasting*

▶ When the first element of the compound adjective is **good** or **well**, the comparatives and superlatives are usually formed with **better** and **best**:

good-looking	*better-looking*	*best-looking*
well-known	*better-known*	*best-known*

Comparison of Adverbs

▶ Adverbs formed by adding *-ly* to an adjective form their comparatives with **more** and **most**:

beautifully	*more beautifully*	*most beautifully*
foolishly	*more foolishly*	*most foolishly*
quickly	*more quickly*	*most quickly*
wisely	*more wisely*	*most wisely*

▶ Adverbs that have the same form as their corresponding adjectives make comparatives and superlatives with *-er* and *-est*:

fast	*faster*	*fastest*
hard	*harder*	*hardest*
loud	*louder*	*loudest*

So does the adverb **soon**:

soon	*sooner*	*soonest*

▶ Most other short adverbs also form their comparatives with **more** and **most**:

often   more often   most often
(**Oftener** and **oftenest** are acceptable in informal English.)

▶ Some adverbs have irregular comparatives and superlatives:

badly	*worse*	*worst*
ill	*worse*	*worst*
little	*less*	*least*
much	*more*	*most*
well	*better*	*best*

▶ As with the adjective, the adverb **far** has two forms for the comparative and superlative:

far   farther or *further   farthest* or *furthest (See page 183)*

Comparison of Determiners

▶ The determiners **little, many** and **much** have the following comparatives and superlatives:

little	*less*	*least*
many	*more*	*most*
much	*more*	*most*

Note

Do not confuse the determiner **little** (= *not much*) with the adjective **little** (= *small*).

The determiner **little** has the comparative form **less** and the superlative form **least**:

*That one costs very **little**.*
*That one costs even **less**.*
*Which one costs **least**?*

In Standard English, the adjective **little** has no comparative or superlative forms. Although **littler** and **littlest** are found in non-standard English, in Standard English comparatives and superlatives such as **smaller/smallest** and **younger/youngest** have to be used instead:

*A **little** dog was looking at me.*
*It was the **smallest** dog I had ever seen.*

DO IT YOURSELF

A Complete the following sentences with the correct comparative forms.

> *Example:*
> That suitcase is quite *light* but I'm looking for something even _____ .
> That suitcase is quite *light* but I'm looking for something even **lighter**.

1. That brand of soap is quite *gentle* but my skin needs something even _____ .

2. He's not very *choosey* about what he eats; his wife is far _____ .

3. A buffalo can run *quickly* but a cheetah can run much _____ .

4. 'Which end of the swimming pool is the *shallow* end?' 'I think it's _____ at this end.'

5. The morning lecture was pretty *boring* and the one in the afternoon was even _____ .

6. My French is *bad* but my Spanish is even _____ .

7. My suggestion got very *little* support but John's got even _____ .

8. I don't eat *much* red meat. Most people eat a lot _____ than I do.

9. Daffodils are *lovely* flowers but I think tulips are even _____ .

10. Men may think they are *clever* but women are far _____ than men.

11. I didn't used to come here very *often* but I come a lot _____ nowadays.

12. You may think that was a *silly* idea but I can come up with _____ ideas than that.

13. My sister is a *good* singer but my mother is even _____ .

14. I speak Chinese *badly* and Japanese even _____ .

15. 'Come back *soon*.' 'Oh, I'll be back _____ than you expect.'

16. 'You sing very *well*.' 'Thanks, but you sing far _____ than me.'

B Give the superlative forms of the following words.

narrow	odd	solemnly	tired
fat	peculiar	likely	tiring
helpful	many	unlucky	dry
ugly	energetic	unluckily	shy

10 ▶ Nouns and Related Adjectives

Nouns	Related adjectives
air	aerial
ape	simian
arm	brachial
ass	asinine (**Warning!** Nowadays normally used to mean 'stupid' rather than 'like an ass': *That was an asinine thing to say to her.*)
back	dorsal
bear	ursine
bird	avian (*for small perching birds:* passerine)
body	corporeal, corporal
brain	cerebral
cat	feline
chest	pectoral
cow	bovine
crow	corvine
dawn	crepuscular
deer	cervine
dog	canine
dove	columbine
dusk	crepuscular
eagle	aquiline
ear	aural

Nouns	Related adjectives
earth	terrestrial
elephant	elephantine
eye	ocular
farming	agricultural, agrarian
finger	digital
fish	piscine
flower	floral
foot	pedal
fox	vulpine
frog	amphibian
goat	caprine
goose	anserine
hand	manual
head	cephalic
heart	cardiac
heat	thermal
horse	equine
leg	crural
lion	leonine
lung	pulmonary
mental power	intellectual
mind	mental
money	monetary
moon	lunar

Nouns	Related adjectives
morning	matutinal
mouth	oral
nerve	neural
night	nocturnal
nose	nasal
picture	pictorial
pig	porcine
reptile	reptilian
sea	marine
sea/ship/sailing	nautical
sheep	ovine
skin	dermal
skull	cranial
snake	colubrine, serpentine

Nouns	Related adjectives
star	stellar, sidereal
stomach	gastric
sun	solar
tax	fiscal
thigh	femoral
thought/thinking	cognitive
throat	guttural, laryngeal
toad	amphibian
tongue	lingual
tooth	dental
tree	arboreal
water	aqueous (*in or on water:* aquatic)
wing	alar
wolf	lupine

DO IT YOURSELF

A State what nouns the following adjectives relate to.

anserine	equine	monetary
bovine	feline	neural
dental	floral	oral
digital	leonine	thermal
dorsal	mental	vulpine

B Complete the following sentences using the information given in the lists in this unit.

Example:

Owls generally come out at *night*. They are _____ birds.

They are ***nocturnal*** birds.

---

1. A doctor who specializes in diseases of the *heart* is a specialist in _____ medicine.

2. The liquids that break down food in the *stomach* are known as _____ juices.

3. _____ power is derived from the *sun*.

4. _____ plants grow in *water*.

5. The muscles in your *chest* are your _____ muscles.

6. Most of these monkeys are _____ and rarely come down from the *trees*.

7. The *brain* is divided into two _____ hemispheres.

8. My *nose* is blocked. Have you anything that would clear my _____ passages?

9. I love *sailing*. It's the _____ life for me!

10. The rocket landed on the *moon* and sent back pictures of the _____ landscape.

11. When I look at my *dog*, I often wonder what goes on in the _____ mind.

12. Although the government had managed to reduce *taxes*, its _____ policies were criticized by many experts.

Geographical Names

11 ▶

▽ Note

▶ Nouns ending in **-ese** can be used both as singular nouns and as plural nouns. However, such nouns are far more common in the plural than in the singular. When the reference is to a single person, it is more normal to use the **-ese** word as an adjective rather than a noun, e.g. *His wife is **Chinese*** rather than *His wife is **a Chinese***, or *A young **Japanese** boy asked him for directions* rather than *A young **Japanese** asked him for directions*.

▶ Countries whose names end in **-ia** have as the related adjectives and nouns words ending in **-ian**:

Armenia → *Armenian*   *Estonia* → *Estonian*
Georgia → *Georgian*   *Lithuania* → *Lithuanian*

Only some of these have been listed in this unit.

Country	Noun	Adjective
Afghanistan	Afghan, Afghani	Afghan, Afghani
Albania	Albanian	Albanian
Algeria	Algerian	Algerian
America	American	American
Angola	Angolan	Angolan
Argentina	Argentinian	Argentinian
Asia	Asian	Asian
Australia	Australian	Australian
Austria	Austrian	Austrian
Bangladesh	Bangladeshi	Bangladeshi
Belgium	Belgian	Belgian
Bhutan	Bhutanese	Bhutanese
Bolivia	Bolivian	Bolivian
Bosnia-Hercegovina	Bosnian	Bosnian
Brazil	Brazilian	Brazilian
Britain *see* United Kingdom		
Brunei	Bruneian	Bruneian
Bulgaria	Bulgarian	Bulgarian
Cambodia	Cambodian	Cambodian
Canada	Canadian	Canadian
Chile	Chilean	Chilean
China	Chinese	Chinese
Colombia	Colombian	Colombian
Congo	Congolese	Congolese
Croatia	Croat, Croatian	Croatian
Cuba	Cuban	Cuban
Czech Republic	Czech	Czech
Denmark	Dane	Danish
Ecuador	Ecuadorian	Ecuadorian
Egypt	Egyptian	Egyptian

Country	Noun	Adjective
England	Englishman, Englishwoman; *plural* the English	English
Eritrea	Eritrean	Eritrean
Ethiopia	Ethiopian	Ethiopian
Europe	European	European
Finland	Finn	Finnish
France	Frenchman, Frenchwoman; *plural* the French	French
Germany	German	German
Ghana	Ghanaian	Ghanaian
Great Britain *see* United Kingdom		
Greece	Greek	Greek
Hungary	Hungarian	Hungarian
Iceland	Icelander	Icelandic
India	Indian	Indian
Indonesia	Indonesian	Indonesian
Iran	Iranian	Iranian
Iraq	Iraqi	Iraqi
Ireland	Irishman, Irishwoman; *plural* the Irish	Irish
Israel	Israeli	Israeli
Italy	Italian	Italian
Japan	Japanese	Japanese
Jordan	Jordanian	Jordanian
Kenya	Kenyan	Kenyan
Korea	Korean	Korean
Kuwait	Kuwaiti	Kuwaiti
Laos	Laotian	Laotian
Lebanon	Lebanese	Lebanese
Liberia	Liberian	Liberian
Libya	Libyan	Libyan

Country	Noun	Adjective
Macao	Macanese	Macanese
Macedonia	Macedonian	Macedonian
Madagascar	Madagascan, Malagasy	Madagascan, Malagasy
Malawi	Malawian	Malawian
Malaysia	Malaysian	Malaysian
Mexico	Mexican	Mexican
Mongolia	Mongolian	Mongolian
Morocco	Moroccan	Moroccan
Mozambique	Mozambican	Mozambican
Myanmar	Myanmarese	Myanmarese
Nepal	Nepalese	Nepalese
the Netherlands	Dutchman, Dutchwoman; *plural* the Dutch	Dutch
New Zealand	New Zealander	—
Nigeria	Nigerian	Nigerian
Norway	Norwegian	Norwegian
Pakistan	Pakistani	Pakistani
Palestine	Palestinian	Palestinian
Paraguay	Paraguayan	Paraguayan
Peru	Peruvian	Peruvian
the Philippines	*masculine* Filipino, *feminine* Filipina	Filipino, Philippine
Poland	Pole	Polish
Portugal	Portuguese	Portuguese
Romania	Romanian	Romanian
Russia	Russian	Russian
Saudi Arabia	Saudi, Saudi Arabian	Saudi, Saudi Arabian
Scotland	Scot, Scotsman, Scotswoman	Scottish (Scotch *only when referring to things like whisky*)
Serbia	Serb, Serbian	Serbian
Singapore	Singaporean	Singaporean

Country	Noun	Adjective
Slovakia	Slovak, Slovakian	Slovakian
Slovenia	Slovene, Slovenian	Slovenian
Somalia	Somali	Somali
South Africa	South African	South African
Spain	Spaniard; *plural* the Spanish	Spanish
Sri Lanka	Sri Lankan	Sri Lankan
Sudan	Sudanese	Sudanese
Sweden	Swede	Swedish
Switzerland	Swiss	Swiss
Syria	Syrian	Syrian
Taiwan	Taiwanese	Taiwanese
Tanzania	Tanzanian	Tanzanian
Thailand	Thai	Thai
Tibet	Tibetan	Tibetan
Tunisia	Tunisian	Tunisian
Turkey	Turk	Turkish
Uganda	Ugandan	Ugandan
Ukraine	Ukrainian	Ukrainian
the United Kingdom	Briton	British
the United States of America	American	American
Ukraine	Ukrainian	Ukrainian
Uruguay	Uruguayan	Uruguayan
Venezuela	Venezuelan	Venezuelan
Vietnam	Vietnamese	Vietnamese
Wales	Welshman, Welshwoman; *plural* the Welsh	Welsh
Yugoslavia	Yugoslav, Yugoslavian	Yugoslavian
Zaire	Zairean	Zairean
Zambia	Zambian	Zambian
Zimbabwe	Zimbabwean	Zimbabwean

DO IT YOURSELF

A What is the name for a man who comes from the following countries?

Peru	Spain	France
Norway	Brunei	the Philippines
Iraq	Pakistan	Myanmar

B What countries do the following people come from?

the Danes	the Dutch	the Swiss
the Finns	the Turks	the Poles
the Swedes	the Thais	the Welsh

Occupations 12 and Professions

▶ The occupations and professions in this unit have been listed together in groups of related terms such as professions concerned with money and finance, professions involving medicine and healing, occupations relating to arts and crafts, and so on.

▶ Variant forms are separated by commas (**agriculturalist, agriculturist**), except masculine and feminine variants, which are separated by a solidus (**salesman / saleswoman**).

▶ In theory, any occupation or profession denoted by a word ending in **-man** can have an equivalent form that ends in **-woman**: **salesman / saleswoman**, **stuntman / stuntwoman**, etc. However, some of these **-woman** forms are extremely rare, either because the occupations they denote are rarely done by women or because nowadays it is considered preferable to use a word that can denote both men and women, e.g. **firefighter** rather than **fireman** or **firewoman**.

▶ Terms that are now out of date or are going out of date are marked *dated*.

Architecture and Building

architect
a person who draws plans of buildings, bridges, etc

bricklayer
a person who builds walls, houses, etc with bricks

builder
a person who builds houses, factories, etc or who owns a building company

carpenter
a person who makes and repairs wooden objects

decorator
a person who decorates rooms with paint, wallpaper, etc

glazier
a person who fits glass into windows and doors

electrician
a person who installs and maintains electrical wiring and equipment

joiner
a person who makes and repairs wooden objects, especially doors, windows and other wooden parts of buildings

interior designer,
interior decorator
a person who designs and often carries out the decoration and furnishing of a room or building

labourer
a person who does unskilled manual work

painter
a person who paints rooms, buildings, etc; *see also under* Arts and Crafts

plumber
a person who fits and repairs water pipes, baths, sinks, toilets, central heating systems, etc

quantity surveyor
a person who estimates the quantities and costs of materials needed for a building project

surveyor
a person who examines a building and gives a report on its condition and value; *also* a person who surveys an area of land in order to record its features on a map or plan

steeplejack
a person who carries out repairs on tall structures such as factory chimneys or church steeples

stonemason
a person who cuts and prepares stone for building and who builds with stone

town-planner
an official involved in the planning and control of the growth of a town or city

Arts and Crafts

artist

a person who paints pictures; *see also* page 178

painter

see artist; *see also under* Architecture and Building

blacksmith

a person who makes things out of iron, such as horse-shoes or gates

potter

a person who makes pots, cups, jugs, vases and similar items

cabinet-maker

a person who makes fine furniture

sculptor

a person who carves statues out of stone or wood or fashions them out of metal or plaster

calligrapher

a person who is an expert in beautiful artistic writing

silversmith

a person who makes articles out of silver

engraver

a person who cuts designs on stone or metal, especially an artist who cuts pictures into metal plates and uses the plates to print copies of the picture

taxidermist

a person who prepares and stuffs animal skins so that they look like living animals

glass-blower

a person who makes glass ornaments, etc by blowing down a tube which has a ball of molten glass at the end

upholsterer

a person who puts the padding and soft material on chairs, settees, etc

goldsmith

a person who makes articles out of gold

weaver

a person who makes cloth

Business and Shops

auctioneer
a person who sells goods to people at auctions

baker
a person who makes and sells bread and cakes

barber
a person who cuts men's hair and trims their beards

beautician, beauty therapist
a person who gives people, especially women, beauty treatments and advises them on cosmetic products

brewer
a person who makes beer

butcher
a person who sells meat

buyer
a person who buys goods for a shop, such as a large department store, to sell

clothier
a person who makes and sells clothing

cobbler
a person who makes and repairs boots and shoes

confectioner
a person who makes sweets and cakes

director
one of the senior managers of a business; *see also under* Music and Entertainment

distiller
a person who makes strong alcoholic drinks such as whisky

estate agent
a person who sells or rents out houses and other buildings on behalf of clients

fishmonger
a person who sells fish

florist
a person who sells flowers

fruiterer
a person who sells fruit

furrier
a person who makes clothing out of fur

greengrocer
a person who sells fruit and vegetables

grocer
a person who sells food and household supplies such as soap, matches, etc

gunsmith
a person who makes, sells and repairs guns

haberdasher
a person who sells thread, ribbon, buttons and other items used in making clothes

hairdresser
a person who cuts and styles men's and ladies' hair

hosier
a person who sells socks and stockings

hotelier
a person who runs or owns a hotel

ironmonger
a person who sells household goods such as pots and kettles, cleaning equipment, and tools

Business and Shops

jeweller
a person who makes and sells jewellery

locksmith
a person who makes or repairs locks, sells keys, etc

manager
a person who runs a business on behalf of another person or who supervises more junior staff; *see also* page 299

milkman
a person who delivers milk to customer's houses

miller
a person who grinds corn into flour

milliner
a person who makes ladies' hats

newsagent
a person who has a shop where newspapers and magazines are sold

newsvendor
a person who sells newspapers in the street

outfitter
a person who sells men's clothing

pedlar
a person who goes from place to place selling small goods

postman/postwoman
a person who delivers letters and parcels that have been sent by post

postmaster/postmistress
a person who is in charge of a post office

salesman/saleswoman
a person who works in a large shop; *also* a person who travels from place to place within an given area visiting potential customers on behalf of a company

sales representative
a person who visits potential customers on behalf of a business company in order to sell his or her company's products

shoemaker
a person who makes boots and shoes

shop assistant
a person who works in a shop

shopkeeper
a person who owns a shop

stationer
a person who sells pens, pencils, notepaper, envelopes, notebooks, etc

tailor
a person who makes or alters clothing, especially men's suits, jackets and trousers

tanner
a person who makes leather

tobacconist
a person who sells tobacco, cigars and cigarettes

vintner = wine merchant

wine merchant
a person who sells wine

Criminals

arsonist
a person who sets fire to buildings

assassin
a murderer, especially someone who murders a political leader

burglar
a person who enters a building illegally in order to steal something

drug dealer
a person who sells illegal drugs

forger
a person who makes imitations or copies of documents or banknotes and passes them off as genuine

gunrunner
a person who smuggles weapons and ammunition illegally into a country

pickpocket
a person who steals things from people's pockets

shoplifter
a person who steals goods from shops

smuggler
a person who brings goods into a country illegally, especially in order to avoid paying tax on them

Education and Training

coach
a person who gives training or instruction, especially to sportsmen and -women

driving instructor
a person who teaches other people how to drive

headmaster/headmistress
the senior teacher in a school

lecturer
a person who teaches at a college or university

personal trainer
a person who gives fitness instruction and training to one person at a time rather than in large classes

professor
the head of a university department (*Note:* In the United States, all university teachers are called professors.)

reader
a senior lecturer in a university department

teacher
a person who teaches, usually in a school

tutor
a person who gives instruction in a subject

Engineering and Technology

civil engineer
a person who builds roads, bridges etc

electrical engineer
a person concerned with the practical uses of electricity in machinery, etc

electronic engineer
a person who works on the design, manufacture and use of computers, telecommunications equipment and other electronic devices

engineer
a person involved with the science and technology of machinery

fitter
a person who assembles or repairs machinery such as household gas or electrical appliances

foreman/forewoman
a senior member of a workforce in a factory, etc who supervises the other workers; *see also under* Law and Order

industrialist
a person who owns one or more factories or who is a senior manager in a manufacturing industry

manufacturer
a person who owns or runs a factory or business in which some product, such as cars or paint, is made

mechanic
a person who maintains or repairs machinery, especially vehicles

mechanical engineer
a person who is involved with the design, construction and use of machines

miner
a person who digs in a mine for coal or metal ore

naval architect
a person who designs ships

shipbuilder
a person who builds ships

technician
a person who looks after technical equipment or who does practical work in a laboratory

welder
a person who joins metal by means of an apparatus that produces a very hot flame

Farming, Gardening and Similar Pursuits

agriculturalist, agriculturist
an expert in agriculture

agronomist
an expert in crop-production and soil-management

farmer
a person who grows crops or rears cattle, sheep, etc on a farm

fisherman
a person who catches fish

fish farmer
a person who rears fish or shellfish to sell, for example in special tanks or ponds

forester
a person who looks after woods and forests

gamekeeper
a person in charge of the breeding and protection of game animals and birds, such as deer or pheasants, on a private estate

gardener
a person who tends a garden

horticulturist
an expert in growing flowers, fruit and vegetables

landscape gardener
a person who designs beautiful gardens

market gardener
a person who grows fruit and vegetables to sell

planter
a person who owns or manages a plantation where, for example, tea, coffee or rubber is grown

rubber-tapper
a person who makes cuts in the bark of rubber trees in order to collect the sap from which rubber is obtained

shepherd
a person who looks after sheep on a farm (*NOTE*: The word shepherdess is now very old-fashioned. Women who look after sheep are shepherds.)

viniculturist
a person who grows grapes and makes wine

viticulturist
a person who grows grapes

Law and Order

advocate = barrister

barrister
a lawyer who is qualified to plead cases in a court of law

bodyguard
a person who is employed to protect someone

coastguard
a person who guards the coast of a country against smugglers, illegal immigrants, etc and who rescues people in difficulty at sea

coroner
an official whose duty is to hold an inquiry into any death that there is reason to believe may not have been due to natural causes

detective
a police officer who investigates crimes

executioner
a person who carries out executions of people condemned to death for crimes they have committed

foreman/forewoman
the senior member of a jury; *see also under* Engineering and Technology

jailer
a person in charge of prisoners in a jail (*dated*)

judge
a person who is in charge of a criminal trial and who passes sentence on those found guilty by the jury

lawyer
a member of the legal profession, especially a solicitor

magistrate
a judge who hears cases involving minor offences

police officer, policeman/policewoman
a member of a police force

prison officer
a person who is in charge of prisoners in a prison

private detective
a person, not a member of a police force, who is employed to investigate or prevent crimes

probation officer
a person who supervises people who have been put on probation

Queen's Counsel, QC
a senior barrister

sheriff
an elected law-enforcement officer in the United States

solicitor
a person who gives legal advice, draws up legal documents, and represents clients in some courts of law

warder/wardress (*dated*)
= prison officer

Medicine and Healing

acupuncturist
a person who treats medical disorders, relieves pain, etc by means of needles inserted into particular places in the body

anaesthetist
a doctor who gives anaesthetics to patients before and during surgical operations so as to make them unconscious or to prevent pain in a particular part of their body

anatomist
a person who studies the structure of the body and its parts

cardiologist
a doctor who specializes in the diseases of the heart

chemist = pharmacist

chiropodist
a person who treats minor disorders of the feet such as corns and bunions

chiropractor
a person who treats disease by manipulation of bones of the body

clinical psychologist
a psychologist who specializes in the diagnosis and treatment of mental illness

consultant
a senior doctor who is an expert in a particular branch of medicine

dental nurse
a person who assists a dentist in giving dental treatment, e.g. by mixing material for filling teeth

dental hygienist
a person who assists a dentist in the care and cleaning of teeth

dental technician
a person who makes false teeth

dentist, dental surgeon
a person who looks after people's teeth, filling cavities, extracting diseased teeth, etc

dermatologist
a doctor who deals with disorders of the skin

dietitian, dietician
a person who is an expert on diets and healthy eating

district nurse
a nurse who visits patients in their homes to give them medical care

doctor
a person who treats illness and disease

general practitioner
a doctor who treats patients for minor or general illnesses or if necessary refers them to specialists

gynaecologist
an expert in diseases specific to women and girls, especially the functioning and disorders of the reproductive system

herbalist
a person who specializes in the use of herbs to treat or prevent disease

house officer, houseman
a newly qualified doctor resident in a hospital

midwife
a nurse who is trained to assist women in childbirth

neurologist
an expert in the functions and diseases of the nervous system

Medicine and Healing

nurse
a person who looks after patients in a hospital

obstetrician
a doctor who specializes in childbirth

occupational therapist
a person who provides patients with activities that will help them recover from illness or mental illness

oculist (*dated*)
= ophthalmologist

ophthalmologist
a doctor who specializes in eye disorders and diseases

optician
a person who makes glasses and contact lenses; an ophthalmic optician is also qualified to test for eye defects and to prescribe glasses or contact lenses for a client

optometrist
a person who tests people's eyesight and can prescribe lenses or other treatment if defects are found

osteopath
a person who treats disease by manipulation of the joints and muscles of the body, especially the spine

paediatrician
a doctor specializing in children's diseases

pharmacist
a person who prepares medicines

pharmacologist
an expert in the uses and effects of medicinal drugs

physician
a doctor who treats diseases and disorders by any means other than surgery

physiotherapist
a person who treats disease, injuries or deformities by means of massage, exercise, etc

psychiatrist
a doctor who specializes in the diagnosis and treatment of mental illness

psychotherapist
a person who specializes in the treatment of mental disorders by psychological means such as discussion, drama, etc rather than by the use of medicines

radiographer
a person who takes X-rays

radiologist
a doctor who specializes in the use of X-rays and other forms of radiation in the diagnosis and treatment of disease

registrar
a senior doctor in a hospital, next below a consultant in rank

speech therapist
a person who treats speech and language disorders

surgeon
a doctor who specializes in the treatment of injuries to or disorders of the body by means of manipulation and especially cutting into or removing tissue from the body

vet, veterinary
a person who treats diseases and injuries of animals surgeon

Money and Finance

accountant
a person who deals with the financial records of a company or of an individual person

actuary
a person employed by an insurance company to calculate the risks and probabilities of fires, deaths, etc and who advises the company on the insurance premiums they should charge clients

auditor
a person who examines financial accounts and certifies that they are correct

banker
a person who owns, manages or is employed in a bank

bookkeeper
a person who keeps accounts

broker
a person who buys and sells stocks and shares

bursar
the person in charge of money in a school, etc

cashier
a person who is in charge of taking in and paying out money in a bank, shop, office, etc

economist
an expert in economics

money-lender
a person who lends money

pawnbroker
a person who lends money: a borrower gives the pawnbroker some valuable item of their property which the pawnbroker can then sell if the borrower does not repay the loan

stock-broker
a person who buys and sells shares on behalf of clients

teller
a person who takes money from customers or gives money to customers in a bank

treasurer
a person who looks after the finances of an organization

Music and Entertainment

acrobat
a person who performs gymnastic tricks, especially in a circus

actor/actress
a person who acts in plays and films (*NOTE*: Many women who act in plays and films nowadays prefer to be called actors than actresses.)

announcer
a person who makes announcements on radio and television

cameraman/camerawoman
a person who operates a television or cinema film camera

choreographer
a person who arranges dance routines

clown
a person who plays tricks to make people laugh

comedian/comedienne
a person who tells jokes and amusing stories or acts in amusing plays

Music and Entertainment

compère
a person who introduces the various acts in a show

composer
a person who writes music

conductor
a person who conducts a band or orchestra

conjuror, conjurer
a person who performs magic tricks

contortionist
a person who can twist their body into strange positions

director
a person who supervises and instructs the actors and other people involved in a play or film; *see also under* Business and Shops

disc jockey
a person who plays recorded music on radio or television, at a disco, etc

drummer
a person who plays a drum or a set of drums in a band

flautist
a person who plays the flute

guitarist
a person who plays the guitar

impressionist
a person who performs impersonations of other people

juggler
a person who performs the trick of throwing several objects such as balls or knives into the air and catching them again, in such a way that one or more of them are in the air at any time

lyricist
a person who writes the words of songs

magician = conjuror

organist
a person who plays the organ

pianist
a person who plays the piano

piano-tuner
a person who adjusts a piano to make it play in tune

producer
a person who is concerned with the practical and financial aspects of producing a play or film; *also* the director of a play

projectionist
a person who operates the projector for showing films in a cinema

ringmaster
the person in charge of a circus performance

stuntman/stuntwoman
a person who performs dangerous actions in films, such as climbing up or falling off high buildings, so that the actors do not have to perform them

ventriloquist
a person who is able to 'throw their voice', that is, to speak in such a way that it seems to be the dummy or puppet they are holding who is talking

violinist
a person who plays the violin

Office and Computing

clerk
a person who works in an office

computer
a person who writes and keys in the programs that operate on a programmer computer

copywriter
a person who writes advertisements or publicity material

data processor
a person who keys in and performs operations on data in a computer

draughtsman/draughtswoman
a person who makes technical plans or drawings

personnel manager
a person who is concerned with the hiring, firing, training and welfare of a company's or organization's employees

personal assistant, PA
a senior secretary who acts as assistant to one person

receptionist
a person who greets visitors or clients when they enter an office, surgery, hotel, etc and provides them with information, directs them to appointments, etc, and often also answers the telephone

secretary
a person who attends to office administration such as opening mail, typing letters and reports and filing information

systems analyst
a person who analyses a complex process by means of a computer in order to find ways of making the process more efficient

telephonist
a person who operates a telephone switchboard

typist
a person who types letters, reports, etc; an **audiotypist** types up material from a dictating machine; a **shorthand typist** types up material from notes taken in shorthand

People Performing Services

butler
the senior male servant in a house, who supervises other servants and especially attends to the serving of meals

caretaker
a person in charge of a building

char, charwoman
a person who cleans other people's houses

chauffeur/chauffeuse
a person who drives cars for other people

chef
a person who prepares meals, especially a senior cook in a hotel or restaurant

childminder
a person who looks after other people's children, for example while they are working

cook
a person who prepares meals for other people

People Performing Services

housekeeper
a person, usually a woman, who runs another person's house on their behalf

housemaid
a woman who cleans rooms in a house

maid
a female servant in a house, hotel, etc

masseur/masseuse
a person who gives massage

prostitute
a person who allows another person to have sexual intercourse with them in exchange for money

social worker
a person who tries to help underprivileged people, e.g. those suffering from poverty, poor housing, etc

undertaker
a person who organizes funerals

waiter/waitress
a person who serves customers in a café or restaurant

Public Service

ambassador
a diplomat who represents his or her country in another country

civil servant
a person employed in the administration of a state

consul
a person who is employed by a government to look after its interests and those of its citizens in a foreign country

councillor
a person elected to a local council that runs the affairs of a town or district

curator
a person who runs a museum or one department of a museum, or who looks after any similar collection of articles

diplomat
an official who represents his or her country in a foreign country

dustman
a person who removes household or office waste by emptying dustbins or collecting bags of rubbish

firefighter, fireman/firewoman
a person who puts out fires and rescues people from burning buildings

librarian
a person who looks after the books in a library, gives advice to users and borrowers of books, and supervises the lending and return of the books

lifeguard
a person who is employed, e.g. on a beach or at a swimming-pool, to help swimmers who get into difficulty

mayor
the elected head of a local council; *see also* councillor

Public Service

ombudsman/ombudswoman
an official who investigates complaints made by members of the public against government or other public bodies

politician
a person who is involved in politics, especially someone who has been elected to parliament

Religion

archbishop
a senior bishop

bishop
a senior member of the clergy, in charge of all the other clergy in a particular area

chaplain
a member of the clergy attached to a school hospital, the armed forces, etc

clergyman/clergywoman
a member of the clergy, that is, the priests and religious leaders of a religious body, especially of a Christian church

evangelist
a person who tries to convert people to Christianity

minister
a member of the clergy of a Protestant church

missionary
a person who goes to a foreign country to try to convert people to Christianity

monk
a man who devotes himself to religion and who lives with other men in a monastery

nun
a woman who devotes herself to religion and who lives with other women in a convent

pastor = minister

priest
a member of the clergy of the Roman Catholic, Orthodox or Anglican churches; *also* a person who performs religious ceremonies in a non-Christian religion (NOTE: In Christian churches in which women belong to the priesthood, they are known as **priests**; in non-Christian religions, female priests are referred to as **priestesses**.)

Science and Study

anthropologist
a person who studies the various peoples of the world and their physical characteristics, culture, etc

antiquary
an expert in, or collector of, relics of the past

archaeologist
a person who studies the remains of the past such as ancient buildings, ruins or sites where buildings have once been

astronomer
a person who studies the stars and planets and similar bodies found in space

Science and Study

astrophysicist
a person who studies the physical and chemical properties of the stars and planets

biochemist
a person who studies the chemical processes that occur within living creatures

biologist
an expert in the scientific study of living creatures

botanist
a person who studies plants and flowers

entomologist
a person who studies insects

chemist
a person who studies some branch of chemistry; *see also* Medicine and Healing

geographer
a person who studies and records the physical features such as lakes, mountains and cities and the effects that human beings have on the land

geologist
a person who studies rocks and minerals and the structure of the Earth

historian
a person who studies and writes about history

marine biologist
a person who studies the plants and animals that live in the sea

metallurgist
a person who studies the properties of metals and how to produce them from ores

meteorologist
a person who studies atmospheric phenomena, especially those connected with the weather

microbiologist
a person who studies very small living organisms, such as bacteria or viruses

mineralogist
a person who studies minerals

oceanographer
a person who studies all aspects of the seas and oceans

physicist
a person who studies physics

physiologist
an expert in the way the body functions

psychologist
a person who studies the functioning of the mind

scientist
a person who studies any branch of science

seismologist
a person who studies earthquakes

vulcanologist
a person who studies volcanoes

zoologist
a person who studies animals

Sports and Pastimes

caddie

a person who carries a golfer's clubs

croupier

the person who is in charge of a gambling table, taking bets and paying out money

groundsman

a person who looks after a sports ground or the grounds around a large building

jockey

a person who rides horses in races

linesman

a person who in certain sports acts as an assistant to the referee

referee

the person in charge of a sports match

Travel and Transport

air hostess

a female **flight attendant**

air traffic controller

a person who controls the movements of aircraft at take-off, in the air and when landing, and who instructs pilots about their height, speed and direction of flight

astronaut

a person who takes part in space travel

aviator

a person who flies an aeroplane (NOTE: the feminine form of this word is **aviatrix**, but it is not much used nowadays.)

bus conductor

a person who collects fares from passengers in a public bus (NOTE: A female bus conductor is usually called a **bus conductress**, but may also be called a **bus conductor**.)

bus driver

a person who drives a bus

captain

the person in charge of a ship

cosmonaut = astronaut

driver

a person who drives a vehicle or train, e.g. a **lorry driver**, a **taxi driver** or an **engine driver**

flight attendant

a member of the crew of a passenger aircraft who serves food to passengers and attends to their needs

pilot

a person who flies an aeroplane; *also* a person who guides ships into harbour

porter

a person who carries people's luggage at a railway station

purser

the officer on a ship in charge of financial accounts; on a passenger ship, the purser is also in charge of the staff concerned with the service and welfare of the passengers

stewardess

a female **flight attendant**

Travel and Transport

stoker

a person who puts fuel into the furnace that drives the engine of a ship or railway engine

traffic warden

an official who notes the numbers of vehicles that are parked where they should not be

Writing, Publishing and Journalism

author

a person who writes books (*Note*: The word authoress is not much used nowadays: female writers are authors.)

biographer

a person who writes a book about another person's life

compositor

a person who arranges the type from which something will be printed or who keys text into a machine that produces type for printing

copy editor

a person who checks and edits text that is to be printed

correspondent

a person who produces reports for newspapers or radio or television news programmes

critic

a person who writes their opinions of plays, films, books, music, etc for a newspaper, magazine, etc

editor

a person who is in charge of a newspaper or magazine

journalist

a person who writes for a newspaper or magazine or who produces news reports for radio or television

lexicographer

a person who writes dictionaries

novelist

a person who writes novels

playwright

a person who writes plays

poet

a person who writes poetry (*Note*: The word poetess is not much used nowadays: female writers are poets.)

printer

a person who prints books, leaflets, magazines, newspapers, etc

proofreader

a person who checks text that has been set for printing to make sure it is free from errors

publisher

a person who publishes books, etc or who owns a publishing company

reporter

a person who produces news reports for newspapers radio or television

typesetter

a person who arranges the type from which something will be printed

Other Professions and Occupations

archivist
a person who looks after documents

astrologer
a person who predicts that future by studying the positions of the stars and planets

bookmaker
a person who takes bets on horse-races, etc

cartographer
a person who makes maps

courier
a person who carries documents or goods for someone else

groom
a person who looks after horses at a stable

interpreter
a person who translates what people are saying if they do not speak the same language

model
a person who clothes in order to show them to potential buyers at fashion shows or in magazines and catalogues

photographer
a person who takes photographs of people, places, events, etc

public relations officer, PRO
a person who acts on behalf of an organization or someone famous in order to create public interest or goodwill towards them

stevedore
a person who loads and unloads ships in a port

translator
a person who translates texts from one language into another

zookeeper
a person who looks after animals in a zoo

DO IT YOURSELF

A Are the following statements true or false?

1. An *ironmonger* makes horse-shoes.

2. A *taxidermist* drives a taxi for a living.

3. A *chauffeur* drives cars.

4. A *bookmaker* writes books.

5. A *lexicographer* writes dictionaries.

6. An *acrobat* performs gymnastic tricks.

7. A *caretaker* looks after other people's children.

8. A *forger* makes illegal imitations of documents and banknotes.

9. An *astronomer* foretells the future by means of the movements of the planets.

10. An *undertaker* organizes funerals.

11. A *greengrocer* sells fruit and vegetables.

12. A *bookkeeper* works in a library.

13. A *meteorologist* studies meteors.

14. A *botanist* studies insects.

15. A *metallurgist* makes things out of metal.

B For those statements in Exercise A that are false, write two sentences giving the correct answers.

Example:

A *ventriloquist* is a person who can twist their body into strange shapes and positions. *(False)*

A **ventriloquist** is a person who is able to speak so as to make a dummy or puppet appear to be talking.

A **contortionist** is a person who can twist their body into strange shapes and positions.

C Complete the following sentences.

> *Example:*
>
> If you need new glasses, you need to consult an o_____ .
> If you need new glasses, you need to consult an **optician**.

1. A nurse who helps women in childbirth is a m_____ .

2. The person in charge of a museum is a c_____ .

3. If you have problems with your feet, you should consult a
   c_____ .

4. If you break the glass in a window you need to call in a
   g_____ .

5. If you want to sell your house, you can go to an e_____
   a_____ .

6. If you want to discuss this further with me, phone my
   p_____ a_____ to arrange a meeting.

7. When you come to my office, the r_____ will tell you
   how to find my room.

8. Someone who plays a flute is a f_____ .

9. I never buy fish in the supermarket, I prefer to go to our
   local f_____ .

10. When she had a sore back, she went to consult an
    o_____ .

13 Males, Females and Young

How to use the lists

▶ In theory, any occupation or profession denoted by a word ending in **-man** can have an equivalent form that ends in **-woman**: **salesman / saleswoman**, **stuntman / stuntwoman**, etc. However, some of the **-woman** forms are very rare, either because the occupations they denote are rarely done by women or because nowadays it is considered preferable to use a word that can refer equally well to both men and women, e.g. **firefighter** rather than **fireman** or **firewoman**, **police officer** rather than **policeman** or **policewoman**. Sometimes forms ending in **-person** are used (**chairperson**, **postperson**, **stuntperson**, etc) but apart from **chairperson** none of these are very common.

▶ Words that are out of date and rarely or never used nowadays are labelled *dated*.

People

Male	Female
abbot	abbess
actor	actress

> **Did You Know ?**
> Many female actors prefer to be called **actors** rather than **actresses**.

Male	Female
adulterer	adulteress
ambassador	ambassadress

> **Did You Know ?**
> A female ambassador is often referred to simply as an **ambassador**, and an **ambassadress** may be the wife of an ambassador.

Male	Female
author	authoress (*dated*)

> **Did You Know ?**
> Nowadays female writers are normally referred to as **authors**, not **authoresses**.

Male	Female
aviator	aviatrix (*dated*)

> **Did You Know ?**
> Nowadays woman fliers would normally be referred to as **aviators**.

Male	Female
bachelor	spinster
baron	baroness
boy	girl
boyfriend	girlfriend
brave	squaw
bridegroom	bride

Male	Female
brother	sister
cameraman	camerawoman
comedian	comedienne
chairman	chairwoman

> **Did You Know ?**
> Strictly speaking, a woman who is chairing a meeting should be referred to as the **chairman** and addressed as 'Madam Chairman'. However, **chairwoman** is now accepted as correct. To avoid all reference to the sex of the person chairing a meeting, many people prefer **chairperson**, or even simply **chair**.

Male	Female
chauffeur	chauffeuse
clergyman	clergywoman
conductor	conductress

> **Did You Know ?**
> A woman who conducts an orchestra is a **conductor**. The word **conductress** may be used to refer to a female bus conductor, but one may equally say that a woman is a **bus conductor**.

Male	Female
count	countess
Cub Scout/Cub	Brownie Guide/Brownie
draughtsman	draughtswoman
duke	duchess
earl	countess
emperor	empress
enchanter	enchantress
father	mother

Male	Female
father-in-law	mother-in-law
fiancé	fiancée
foreman	forewoman
gentleman	lady
god	goddess
godfather	godmother
godson	goddaughter
granddad, grandpa	grandma
grandfather	grandmother
grandson	granddaughter
headmaster	headmistress
heir	heiress
hero	heroine
horseman	horsewoman
host	hostess
hunter	huntress (*dated*)

Did You Know ?

Huntress is now only used in mythology to refer to a woman or a goddess who is a hunter.

Male	Female
husband	wife
instructor	instructress (*dated*)

Did You Know ?

A female instructor is more often referred to as an **instructor** now.

Male	Female
king	queen

Male	Female
knight	lady; dame
lad, laddie	lass, lassie
landlord	landlady
lord	lady
maharajah	maharani
man	woman
manager	manageress

Did You Know ?

While **manageress** is used to refer to a woman who manages a shop, in other situations both men and women are **managers**.

Male	Female
manservant (*dated*)	maidservant (*dated*)
marquess	marchioness
masseur	masseuse
master	mistress
Master	Miss, Ms
mayor	mayoress

Did You Know ?

Strictly speaking, a **mayoress** is the wife of a **mayor**, but the word is also now used to refer to a woman who is a mayor.

Male	Female
monk	nun
Mr	Mrs
murderer	murderess (*dated*)

Did You Know ?

A female murderer would nowadays normally be referred to as a **murderer**.

Male	Female
nephew	niece

Male	Female
ombudsman	ombudswoman
papa	mama
patriarch	matriarch
patron	patroness

> **Did You Know ?**
> **Patroness** is now rather dated but is still used.

Male	Female
poet	poetess (*dated*)

> **Did You Know ?**
> Like authoress, **poetess** has now dropped out of use.

Male	Female
policeman	policewoman
postman	postwoman
postmaster	postmistress
priest	priestess

> **Did You Know ?**
> In Christian churches in which women belong to the priesthood, they are known as **priests**; in non-Christian religions, female priests are referred to as **priestesses**.

Male	Female
prince	princess
prior	prioress
proprietor	proprietress, proprietrix

> **Did You Know ?**
> A woman may also be referred to as a **proprietor**.

Male	Female
rajah	rani
salesman	saleswoman
schoolmaster	schoolmistress

Male	Female
Scout	Guide, Girl Scout
shepherd	shepherdess (*dated*)

> **Did You Know ?**
> **Shepherdesses** are only found in old-fashioned songs and stories. Women who look after sheep are shepherds.

Male	Female
singer, songster	songstress

> **Did You Know ?**
> Neither **songster** nor **songstress** are very common now.

Male	Female
sir	madam
son	daughter
son-in-law	daughter-in-law
sorcerer	sorceress
stepfather	stepmother
stepson	stepdaughter
stepbrother	stepsister
steward	stewardess
stuntman	stuntwoman
sultan	sultana
uncle	aunt
waiter	waitress
warder (*dated*)	wardress (*dated*)
widower	widow
wizard	witch

> **Did You Know ?**
> The word **witch** is sometimes also applied to men.

Animals

Where there is a gap in the lists, there is no special word for the male or female. In such cases, the words 'male' and 'female' are used.

Animal	Male	Female	Young
antelope	buck	doe	calf, kid
ass	jackass, jack	jenny-ass, jenny	foal
bear	boar	sow, she-bear	cub
bee	drone	queen, worker	larva, grub
bird	cock	hen	chick, fledgling, nestling
butterfly	–	–	caterpillar
camel	bull	cow	calf
cat	tom-cat	tabby-cat, tabby, queen	kitten
cattle	bull	cow	calf; heifer (= *a young cow*)
deer	buck, stag	doe, hind	fawn
dog	dog	bitch	puppy, pup
donkey	jack	jenny	foal
duck	drake	duck	duckling
eagle	–	–	eaglet
elephant	bull	cow	calf
fox	dog fox	vixen	cub
frog	–	–	tadpole
goat	billy-goat	nanny-goat	kid
goose	gander	goose	gosling
hare	buck	doe	leveret
horse	stallion	mare	foal; filly (= *a young female horse*)
insect	–	–	larva, grub, caterpillar, maggot, nymph
kangaroo	buck, jack, boomer	doe, jill, flier	joey

Animal	Male	Female	Young
leopard	leopard	leopardess	cub
lion	lion	lioness	cub
moth	–	–	caterpillar
owl	–	–	owlet
peacock, peafowl	peacock	peahen	peachick
pig	boar	sow; gilt (= *a young sow*)	piglet
pigeon	–	–	squab
poultry	cock; cockerel (= *a young cock*); rooster (*mainly US*)	hen	chicken, chick; pullet (= *a young hen*)
rabbit	buck	doe	kitten
seal	bull	cow	calf
sheep	ram	ewe	lamb
swan	cob	pen	cygnet
tiger	tiger	tigress	cub
toad	–	–	tadpole
whale	bull	cow	calf
wolf	wolf	she-wolf	cub
zebra	stallion	mare	foal

DO IT YOURSELF

A Give the female or male equivalents of the following words.

The female of: duke, earl, god, hero, king, master, monk, nephew, rajah, waiter

The male of: aunt, bride, empress, fiancée, lady, madam, matriarch, widow, witch

B What is the name for a male, a female or the young of the following creatures?

The male of: cattle, deer, duck, goose, horse, pig, sheep

The female of: cattle, deer, dog, fox, horse, lion, pig, sheep, tiger

The young of: duck, eagle, frog, leopard, sheep, swan, wolf

14

Groups
and
Quantities

Noun	Group or Quantity
acrobats	troupe
actors	company, troupe; *also* cast (of a play)
aircraft	formation, flight (of aircraft flying together); fleet (of aircraft owned by one person or company); squadron (e.g. in the armed forces)
angels	host
antelope	herd
arrows	hail, shower; quiver (of arrows being carried)
bacon	rasher (= *slice*)
bananas	bunch; *more technical* hand; comb (*in SE Asia*)
banknotes	wad
beads	string
beauties	bevy
bees	hive, nest, swarm
birds	flock, flight
bread	loaf, slice, piece; crumb (= *a tiny piece*)
buses	fleet (belonging to one company)

Noun	Group or Quantity
butter	pat (= *a small piece*), slab (= *a large piece*)
cake	slice, piece; wedge (= *a triangular piece cut from a round cake*); crumb (= *a tiny piece*)
cars at a funeral	cortege
cattle	herd; drove (of cattle being driven from one place to another)
chickens	brood (= *chicks born to the same mother at the same time*)
chocolate	bar, slab; square (= *one of the small square sections that together form a bar*); bit, piece
cigarettes	packet
cloth	bale, roll (= *a large amount rolled up*); length, piece (= *an amount cut off a roll*)
clothes	suit (if the clothes, e.g. jacket and trousers or skirt, are intended to be worn together)
corn	sheaf
cotton	bale (as picked from the cotton plants); wad (processed and formed into a pad); reel (of cotton thread)

Noun	Group or Quantity
dancers	troupe
data	batch, collection, file
deer	herd
directors	board
dogs	pack
dolphins	pod, school
ducklings	brood (= *ducklings born to the same mother at the same time*)
earth	clod (= *lump*)
eggs	clutch (in a nest)
elephant	herd (NOTE: *two elephants* but *a herd of elephant*)
events	chain, series
experts	panel
film	roll (in a camera); reel (on a projector)
fish	shoal, school
flats	block
flies	swarm
flowers	bouquet, bunch; posy (= *small bunch of small flowers*)

Noun	Group or Quantity
fruit	piece; segment (of a fruit such as an orange that splits into separate pieces)
furniture	suite
geese	flock; gaggle (if on the ground); skein (if in flight)
glass	pane, sheet; splinter, sliver (= *very small sharp piece*)
goats	flock, herd
grapes	bunch
gunfire	volley
hair	tuft; wisp (= *very small amount, a few hairs*)
hay	bale; *also* haystack
horses	string (of horses owned by one person)
hounds	pack
insects	cloud, swarm
judges	panel (if amateur judges e.g. at a contest); bench (in a lawcourt)
keys	bunch

Noun	Group or Quantity
kittens	litter (= *kittens born to the same mother at the same time*)
labourers	gang
lies	pack, tissue
lions	pride
loaves	batch (= *a number of loaves baked at the same time*)
locusts	cloud swarm
magistrates	bench
monkeys	troop
mountains	chain, range
musicians	band, group, orchestra
paper	piece, sheet; quire (= *24 or 25 sheets*), ream (= *480, 500 or 516 sheets*)
papers	bundle, sheaf
partridges	covey
pearls	rope, string (= *necklace*)
people	body, crowd, group, horde, multitude, party
people at a show	audience

Noun	Group or Quantity
performers	troupe
pig	herd
piglets	litter (= *piglets born to the same mother at the same time*)
playing cards	pack; hand (= *the cards held by one player in a game*)
poems	anthology
porpoises	pod, school
pupils	class
puppies	litter (= *puppies born to the same mother at the same time*)
restaurants	chain (= *a number of restaurants owned by the same person or company*)
rioters	mob
robbers	band
rooms	suite
rope	coil, hank, length
rubber	bale
sailors	crew
seals	pod

Noun	Group or Quantity
sheep	flock
ships	fleet, flotilla
shops	chain (= *a number of shops owned by the same person or company*)
singers	choir
snow	fall (= *the amount that falls at one time*); flake (= *one single little piece of snow*)
soap	bar, cake
soldiers	army, battalion, brigade, platoon, regiment, squad, troop
spectators	crowd
sports players	team; eleven (in sports in which there are eleven players in a team), fifteen (in sports in which there are fifteen players in a team), and so on for other sports
stairs	flight
stars	cluster, constellation, galaxy
steps	flight
stone	block
students	class
teeth	set

Noun	Group or Quantity
thieves	gang
thread	ball, reel
tools	set; *also* tool-kit
trees	clump, grove; wood, forest
whales	pod, school
witches	coven
wolves	pack
wood	block, lump, piece, plank; log (of wood from a tree); splinter (= *a very small sharp piece that gets stuck in your skin*)
wool	ball, hank, skein
workmen	gang
worshippers in church	congregation

Did You Know ?

There are many other special words for groups of animals and birds, but they are not very common. Among these are *a **clowder** of cats, a **crash** of rhinoceroses, an **exaltation** of larks, a **leap** of leopards, a **murder** of crows, a **pandemonium** of parrots, a **parliament** of owls, a **sloth** of bears, and an **unkindness** of ravens.*

Although these words do exist and are found in dictionaries, they are not part of everyday English – in fact, they mostly appear in crossword puzzles and quizzes! – and they should not be used in normal conversation. Use a more general word such as *herd, flock, group,* etc.

Noun	Group or Quantity	Noun	Group or Quantity
There are of course a number of general words that describe groups or quantities:			
batch	a group or quantity of something dealt with or produced at one time	lump	a large piece or quantity of something
bundle	a number of things or a quantity of something tied together	pile	a number of things placed one on top of another
chip	a small piece of something such as stone	pinch	the amount of something that can be held between one's finger and thumb
chunk	a large piece or quantity of something	queue	a number of people or vehicles lined up one behind another waiting to do something or to move on
clump	a small group of something, such as flowers, grass or trees, that sticks up prominently	row	a number of people or things standing or placed side by side
cluster	a number of things forming a group	series	a number of things following one after another
collection	a number of things that are gathered together	set	a number of things that belong together or that are used together
cube	a small block	shower	a number of things falling like rain; a large number of things coming together
flood	a large number or quantity of something		
grain	a single tiny piece (e.g. of sand or salt); a very small quantity of something	slice	a thin piece cut off something larger
		speck	a very small piece (e.g. of dust)
group	a number of people or things together	stack	a number of things placed one on top of another; a large number of things
handful	a small amount, as much as can be held in one hand; a small number		
heap	a number of things placed one on top of another	tuft	a small amount of something, such as grass or feathers, that sticks up prominently
hunk	a large piece or quantity of something		

Pairs

Many things come in **pairs**.

▶ Some pairs consist of two identical or very similar things that are normally used together:

a pair of gloves   *a pair of shoes*
a pair of socks   *a pair of clogs*

Also in this category are:

boots   *slippers*
earrings   *trainers*
sandals   *wellingtons*

Words in this category can be used in the singular:

*Have you seen my other **glove**?*
*I've found one **sock** but I can't find the other one.*

▶ Some pairs are objects that consist of two parts that are fastened together to form a single object:

a pair of scissors   *a pair of binoculars*
a pair of trousers   *a pair of sunglasses*

Also in this category are:

briefs   *goggles*
denims   *glasses*
jeans   *pliers*
pants   *secateurs*
shorts   *tongs*
tights   *tweezers*
pyjamas   *wire-cutters*
spectacles   *shears*

These words cannot be used in the singular. When referring to two or more of such things, the word **pair** is used:

***two pairs** of scissors*
*Why do you need **four pairs** of trousers?*

▶ The word **pair** is also used to refer to parts of the body that come in twos, such as eyes, feet or hands:

***Two pairs** of eyes were watching him.*

Notice also that when playing cards, two cards of the same type are referred to as a **pair**:

a pair of nines
a pair of black queens

DO IT YOURSELF

A What is the name for a group of the following people or things?

acrobats	dancers	grapes
bananas	deer	kittens
birds	dogs	robbers
cattle	directors	sheep

B What would you find in groups with the following names?

bouquet	covey	shoal
constellation	gang	suite
coven	pride	swarm

C Join the words denoting units or quantities given in the first of the following lists to form a phrase with the items in the second list.

> *Example:*
> bunch + keys
> a bunch of keys

bar	arrows
coil	butter
fleet	cards
flight	chocolate
pack	cigarettes
packet	glass
pane	paper
pat	rope
quiver	ships
ream	steps

15 ▶ Animal Homes and Shelters

Animal	Home or shelter	Animal	Home or shelter
ant	nest, anthill	leopard	den
badger	sett, earth	lion	den
bear	den, lair	mouse	hole, mousehole, nest
beaver	lodge	otter	holt, den
bee	hive (= *box for honeybees*); nest (of wild bees)	pig	sty
bird	nest; roost, perch; cage; aviary (= *a large cage where many birds are kept*)	pigeon	dovecote, pigeon loft
		poultry	coop, hen-house, hen-run
		rabbit	burrow, hole, warren; hutch
cattle	byre, cowshed, pen	rat	nest
dog	kennel	sheep	fold, pen
dove	dovecote	snake	nest
eagle	eyrie (= *nest*)	squirrel	drey, nest
fox	den, lair, earth	termite	nest, mound, anthill
hare	form	tiger	den, lair
hawk	eyrie (= *nest*)	wasp	nest
horse	stable; paddock (= *field*)		

DO IT YOURSELF

A What animal or bird would you find in the following places?

aviary	kennel	stable
byre	lodge	sty
coop	paddock	warren

B What do you call the place where the following animals or birds live?

eagle	lion	squirrel
honeybee	otter	wasp

16 ▶ Sounds and Movements

How to use the lists

▶ Where there is a blank in the list of sounds, the animal or object does not normally make a sound.

▶ Where there is a blank in the list of movements, either the animal or object does not move, or else there is no special word for its movement.

	Sound	**Movement**
aeroplane	roars	flies, zooms, takes off, lands
alarm	goes off, rings, sounds	
ape	gibbers	lumbers
arrow	whizzes	flies
ass	brays	
bear	growls	lumbers
bee	buzzes, hums	flies, flits
bell	chimes, peals, rings, tinkles, tolls	
bird	sings, cheeps, chirps, twitters	flies, flaps, flutters; hops
bow (*for firing arrows*)	twangs	
brakes	screech	
breeze	murmurs	blows
brook	babbles, murmurs	flows, trickles
bull	bellows	lumbers, charges
butterfly		flies, flits, flutters
cat	mews, miaows, purrs	
caterpillar		crawls
chains	clank, jangle, rattle	
clock	ticks, chimes	
cock	crows	struts
coins	jingle	

	Sound	Movement
cork	pops	
cow	moos, lows	
crow	caws	flies
cymbals	clash	
dishes	clatter, rattle	
dog	barks, growls, snarls, yaps, yelps	
donkey	brays	
door	bangs, creaks, slams	
dove	coos	flies, flutters
duck	quacks	waddles, flies, swims
eagle	screams	flies, swoops
elephant	trumpets	walks, runs, charges
feet	patter, shuffle, stamp, tramp	
fire	crackles	
fish		swims
fox	barks, yelps	walks, runs, trots
frog	croaks	hops, jumps
glass	tinkles (when broken)	
goose	cackles, hisses, honks	waddles, flies
goat	bleats	
guitar	twangs	
guns	boom, roar	

	Sound	Movement
hawk	screams, yelps, whistles	flies, swoops
hen	cackles, clucks	
hinge	creaks	
hooves	clatter, pound, thunder	
horn	honks, hoots, peeps, toots	
horse	neighs, whinnies	canters, trots, gallops
hound	barks, bays	
lamb	bleats	gambols
leaves	rustle	flutter
lion	growls, roars	prowls
monkey	chatters, screeches	climbs, swings
mouse	squeaks	runs, scampers, scurries
owl	hoots	flies, glides
paper	rustles	
parrot	chatters, screams, screeches, squawks	
pig	grunts, squeals	trots
pigeon	coos	flies, flutters
rabbit		hops, jumps, runs, scampers
raindrops	patter	fall
river	gurgles	flows
seal	bellows	
sheep	bleats, baas	
siren	wails	

	Sound	Movement
snail		crawls
snake	hisses	crawls, slithers
sparrow	chirps	flies, flutters
spider		crawls, runs
steam	hisses	
stream	babbles, gurgles, murmurs	flows
tears		fall, flow, trickle
telephone	rings	
thunder	rolls, rumbles	
traffic	roars, rumbles	moves, crawls, flows
train	rattles, roars, rumbles	runs
trumpet	blares	
turkey	gobbles	
tyres	screech	
watch	ticks	
wasp	buzzes	flies
water		drips, flows, laps, runs, splashes, trickles
whip	cracks	
whistle	blows	
wind	howls, moans, sighs, whispers	blows
wolf	howls, growls, snarls	lopes, runs
worm		crawls, wiggles, wriggles

DO IT YOURSELF

A Fill in the blanks in the following story with suitable words for animal sounds and movement.

Lying in the garden in the sunshine, I could hear the bees b_____ing as they f_____ from flower to flower. Sparrows were c_____ing on the roof of the house, and a blackbird was s_____ing in the apple tree beside me. Brown and orange butterflies f_____ed among the blossom. A gentle breeze was b_____ing, so it wasn't too hot.

I could hear the clock t_____ing quietly in the lounge, and Emma, my cat, was p_____ing gently on my lap. In the distance, traffic r_____ along the motorway and the siren on a police car was w_____ing, but they were far enough away not to disturb me. There was nothing to disturb the peace of the afternoon.

Suddenly everything changed. Two dogs started b_____ing loudly outside in the street. A jet plane r_____ed overhead as it t_____ o_____ from the nearby airfield. A hawk s_____ed down on an unsuspecting sparrow and carried it off. And then the telephone r_____ and I had to get up and go into the house to answer it.

B Complete the following sentences.

1. A frog c_____s.
2. A duck q_____s.
3. A wolf h_____s.
4. A snake h_____s.
5. An elephant t_____s.
6. A donkey b_____s.
7. A whistle b_____s.
8. A horse n_____s.
9. A mouse s_____s.
10. An owl h_____s.
11. A pigeon c_____s.
12. A crow c_____s.

17 ▶ Phrasal Verbs

Phrasal verbs are phrases that consist of a verb and either an adverb e.g. *away* or *down* or a preposition e.g. *for* or *with*, or sometimes both. In many cases, the meaning of the phrase is quite clear, e.g. **go in**, **run away**, **fall off**, but some phrasal verbs are idiomatic, that is, they have meanings that cannot be understood from the meanings of the individual words that form them, e.g. **put up with** (= to tolerate), **butter up** (= to flatter), and many of these are listed and explained in this unit.

abide

To *abide by* a rule or law is to do what it says; to *abide by* a decision is to do what has been decided.

account

If you can *account for* something, you are able to explain it, give a reason for it, or say what has happened to it: *He was unable to account for his mistake. / There's still $35 not accounted for.*

If something *accounts for* a proportion of something, it forms that part of it: *Reading manuscripts accounts for a large part of my work.*

add

If something does not *add up*, it does not make sense: *Why would she leave without telling anyone? It just doesn't add up.*

agree

You may *agree with* somebody, or *with* what they say, but you *agree to* a proposal or suggestion, and you *agree*, or *agree on*, a date or an agenda. Two or more people may *agree about* something.

If food does not *agree with* you, it makes you ill.

aim

If you *aim at* somebody, or *aim* a gun, etc *at* them, you point a gun at them or try to hit them: *She aimed a blow at his head.* You may also *aim for* something: *I was aiming for that tree.*

Something that is *aimed at* somebody is intended for them or intended to be heard by them: *Her remarks were clearly aimed at us.*

If you *aim to* do something, you intend to do it. If you *aim for* something, you intend to have it, to do it or to reach it: *I'm aiming for an income of $100,000 a year by the time I'm thirty.*

allow

If you *allow for* something, you take it into consideration when you are making plans or decisions: *We must allow for the possibility that it will rain on the day of the fair.*

answer

If you have to *answer to* somebody *for* something, you have responsibility for it and have to explain to some person if things go wrong and perhaps be punished by them: *If anything happens to the children, you'll have me to answer to.* If somebody *answers for* something wrong they have done, they are punished for it: *One day he will answer for his crimes.*

If you say you can *answer for* somebody or something, you are saying that you believe they or it can be relied on.

Somebody who *answers*, or *answers to*, a description matches that description: *The police have arrested a man answering to the description of the burglar.*

approve

If somebody in authority *approves* a plan, etc, they give their formal agreement that it should go ahead. If somebody *approves of* a plan, they are in agreement with it and think it is a good idea.

ask

If you *ask for* something, you are making a request for it. You say that somebody *is asking for it*, or *is asking for trouble*, if you think that they are behaving in a way that is certain to get them into trouble.

If you *ask* somebody *out*, you invite them to go somewhere with you, such as a cinema or restaurant or a party or dance.

back

If you *back away* or *back off*, you move back slowly, e.g. when faced with a threat or danger.

If you *back down*, you abandon your opinion, claim, demands, etc: *She knew she was in the wrong, but she just would not back down.*

A building, garden, etc *backs onto* something if the back of it is next to something or faces it.

If somebody *backs out*, or *backs out of* something, they try to avoid doing something they have said they would do: *He said he would teach me to drive but now he's trying to back out of it.*

If you *back* somebody *up*, you give them your support. If something *backs up* what you are saying, it supports or confirms it.

If you *back up* data on a computer, you make a copy of it, e.g. on a floppy disk or a tape.

bail / bale

If a person who has been arrested is *bailed out*, it means that somebody has paid money to a court of law in order for the accused person to be released from prison until the time of their trial. In a more general sense, to *bail* somebody *out* is to help somebody who is in difficulties.

If you *bail out* or *bale out* a boat, you scoop up water that has got into it and pour it out of the boat again. If you *bail out* or *bale out* of an aircraft in an emergency, you jump out of it with a parachute on.

bank

If you *bank on* something happening, you are expecting it to happen or relying on it: *I wouldn't bank on him helping you out.*

bear

To *bear* something *out* is to confirm or support it: *Her theories are not borne out by the results of our research.* If you *bear* somebody *out*, you support them or confirm what they are saying.

If you manage to remain strong in difficult or sad circumstances, you are said to be *bearing up*: *She bore up remarkably well after her husband's death.*

If you *bear with* somebody, you remain patient and tolerate what they are doing: *Bear with me a moment and I'll show you how this works.*

beat

If rain *beats down*, it falls heavily; if the sun *beats down*, it shines very strongly: *The sun was beating down on them as they walked along the beach.*

If you try to *beat* somebody *down*, or *beat* a price *down*, you try to get somebody to reduce the price of something: *I wanted $2000 for my car but he tried to beat me down to $1800.*

If you *beat off* an attacker, a challenger, or an opponent, you prevent them from defeating you. You can also *beat off* an attack or a challenge.

If you *beat* somebody *up*, you hit or kick them violently and repeatedly.

beaver

Somebody who is *beavering away* at something is working very hard at it.

believe

If you *believe* something or somebody, you accept that it is true or that what they are saying is true. To *believe in* something is to believe that it exists.

To *believe in* somebody is to have confidence in them and their ability, sense, judgement, etc: *The people support him because they believe in him.* To *believe in* something is to be in favour of it: *I don't believe in smacking children.*

belong

If something *belongs to* you, it is your property. If you *belong to* a town or country, that is where you come from. And somebody who *belongs to* an organization is a member of it.

If one thing *belongs with* another or others, the things should be together, e.g. because they form a pair or set.

blow

If you *blow out* a candle, you puff air at it so that it stops burning.

If a storm *blows* itself *out*, it becomes weaker until it disappears altogether. If a storm *blows over*, it passes over and goes away. If a threat or scandal *blows over*, it goes away: *Once the papers lose interest in it, the whole affair will soon blow over.*

If something *blows up* or *is blown up*, it explodes or is destroyed by an explosion. If you *blow up* a balloon, you blow air into it to make it expand, and if you *blow up* a photograph, you enlarge it.

In informal language, if somebody *blows up*, it means that they become very angry and start shouting: *When she was late for work yet again, I just blew up at her.* In this sense you can also *blow* somebody *up*.

bottle

If you *bottle up* your feelings and emotions, you keep them to yourself and do not express them openly.

break

To *break away* is to escape suddenly from somebody's control or to leave a group or body you have been part of: *Two protesters managed to break away from the police and run towards the parade.* / *Several states broke away to form independent countries.*

If a car or a piece of machinery *breaks down*, it stops working properly. If negotiations *break down*, they come to an end because no agreement can be reached. And if a person *breaks down*, they are overcome by their emotions: *When he asked her to marry him, she just broke down and cried.*

If you *break* something *down*, you split it or break it into smaller or separate parts: *We could break down his argument into three basic points.* / *This process breaks down carbohydrates in the stomach.*

If somebody *breaks in*, or *breaks into* a building, they force a way into a building illegally, e.g. through a window, usually intending to steal something. To *break in* is also to interrupt somebody when they are speaking: *If I could just break in here, I'd like to disagree with your last remark.*

If you *break in* shoes, you make them less stiff by wearing them.

If you *break into* something, you begin to do it: *The horse suddenly broke into a gallop.*

To *break* something *off* is to bring it to a sudden end: *The talks were abruptly broken off.* If you *break off*, you abruptly stop talking: *She broke off and started to polish her glasses.*

If something *breaks out*, it appears or starts suddenly. If you *break out in* a rash, you become covered in it.

When something *breaks up*, or if you *break* it *up*, it breaks, or you break it, into pieces. If you *break up* a fight, you stop it.

When a meeting *breaks up*, it comes to an end. When a school *breaks up*, or its pupils and teachers *break up*, term ends and the holidays begin. If two people *break up*, they cease to have a close relationship: *John and his girlfriend broke up last week.*

If somebody *breaks with* somebody else, they end their association with them: *She finally broke with the Communist Party in 1968.* If you *break with* tradition, you do something different to what has generally been done in the past.

bring

If you *bring* something *about*, you make it happen.

Something that *brings back* memories makes you remember something from the past.

To *bring down* prices, etc is to lower or reduce them. To *bring* somebody or something *down* is to cause them or it to fall to the ground: *They didn't have powerful enough guns to bring down the enemy planes.*

To *bring* something *off* is to manage or achieve it.

If an illness or other condition is *brought on* by something, it is caused by it: *Being near cats brings on my hay fever.*

If you *bring* somebody *round* or *bring* them *to*, you restore them from unconsciousness. To *bring* somebody *round* also means to persuade them to agree with you.

If you *bring up* children, you raise them and educate them on how to behave: *I was brought up to respect the law.* If you *bring up* a matter, you mention it or introduce it for discussion.

brush

If you *brush* something *up*, or *brush up on* it, you refresh your knowledge of it: *I must brush up on my Japanese before I go on holiday.*

butter

If you *butter* somebody *up*, you flatter them in order to get them to do something for you.

call

If you *call for* something, you ask loudly for it. If a situation *calls for* something, it requires it: *The economic crisis calls for stringent measures by the government.* If you say you will *call for* somebody, you mean you will come to where they are to collect them.

To *call in* somewhere is to pay a brief visit there.

If a meeting, strike, etc is *called off*, it is abandoned or cancelled.

If you *call on* or *upon* somebody to do something, you appeal to them to do it. And to *call on* or *upon* your strength is to bring it into use: *She had to call on all her emotional strength to get through these black days.*

To *call on* somebody is to pay a short visit to them.

To be *called up* is to be ordered to join the armed forces of your country.

care

If you *care about* somebody, you are fond of them and are concerned for their welfare. If you *care for* somebody, you look after them: *She has an elderly mother to care for.*

If you *care about* something, you are concerned about it and want to preserve it or protect it: *I care about my reputation.*

If you say that you do not *care for* something, you mean you do not like it: *I don't care much for her poetry.*

carry

If a person gets *carried away*, they lose control of their emotions, e.g. because of excitement or over-enthusiasm: *She got quite carried away at the match and started screaming at the referee.*

To *carry off* a prize is to win it. If an eagle *carries off* a lamb, it seizes it and takes it away.

To *carry on* is to continue doing something: *It's all right, don't stop. Just carry on with what you're doing.* To *carry on* is to behave in a foolish or disruptive manner: *That was a dreadful way to carry on. Carry on* also means to complain or fuss noisily about something: *The neighbours are carrying on about our untidy hedge again.*

To *carry out* a task is to accomplish it. To *carry out* instructions is to follow them.

catch

If something *catches on*, it becomes popular: *Who was it who said that Walkmans would never catch on?*

You *catch on*, or *catch on to* something, when you begin to understand it.

If you *catch* somebody *out*, you cause them to make a mistake or show their ignorance, often by a trick: *That last question in the exam caught most of you out.*

If you *catch up with* somebody or *catch* somebody *up*, you come up from behind them and draw level with them: *She left five minutes ago, but if you run quickly you might catch up with her. / I'd missed a lot of classes through illness and I had to work hard to catch up with the other students.* If you are *catching up on* or *with* something that should have been done or finished but has not been, you are working to finish it or bring it up to date: *I'll work late tonight to catch up on all this paperwork.*

If the police, for example, *catch up with* somebody who has done wrong, it means that they have finally found them: *You may think you've got away with not paying your taxes but the authorities will catch up with you eventually.* And if your past *catches up with* you, then something that you have done or been in the past begins to affect your life in the present in a bad way: *When he was recognized by a man he had known in prison, the mayor knew his criminal past was about to catch up with him.*

chalk

To *chalk up* a victory or a success is to achieve it.

chicken

If you *chicken out*, or *chicken out of* something dangerous, you decide not to do it because you are scared to: *He says he's going to ask for a pay rise, but I bet he chickens out.* This is an informal expression.

come

If something *comes about*, it happens.

If you *come across* something, you discover it by chance; if you *come across* somebody, you meet them by chance.

To *come across* in a certain way is to give a certain impression of oneself to other people: *He comes across as a caring man.*

When an opportunity *comes along*, it arrives or happens: *A chance like that doesn't come along very often.* When you ask somebody to *come along*, you are inviting them to come somewhere: *We're going to the zoo. Would you like to come along with us? Come along* is also used to encourage somebody to do something: *Come along now, it won't hurt.* And if you ask how somebody or something is *coming along*, you want to how well that person or thing is progressing: *How's the book coming along?*

To *come by* something is to obtain it.

If you *come down on* somebody, you criticize them or punish them severely. If you *come down with* an illness, you catch it: *I think I'm coming down with a cold.*

If you *come in for* attention or criticism, you receive it. To *come into* a fortune is to inherit it.

To *come of* something is to have a result: *I've applied for promotion but I don't suppose anything will come of it.* To *come off* is to succeed: *It was a good plan and it nearly came off.*

Come on is used to encourage someone to do something, especially to hurry up: *Come on, you can do it if you try. / Come on, will you! We haven't got all day to finish this. Come on* is also used to suggest that somebody's behaviour or comments are inappropriate or unreasonable: *Oh, come on! That's a stupid thing to say.*

When the sun or moon or stars *come out*, they appear in the sky. When a flower *comes out*, it opens up.

If a book or magazine *comes out*, it is published. If a person *comes out in* spots, it means that spots have appeared on their body.

To *come over* or *come round* is to visit a person or place: *Why don't you come over to my house tomorrow and we can discuss the plans then.*

To *come round* also means to regain consciousness, as does *come to*: *When she came to, she was lying at the side of the road.*

If something *comes up*, it occurs or happens.

To *be coming up for* a time or an event is to be approaching it: *It must be coming up for half past seven.*

If you *come up with* an idea, you produce it: *I'm sure we can come up with a solution to the problem.*

conform

Somebody or something usually *conforms to* a rule or regulation and *conforms with* or *to* a specification or requirement: *Members are reminded that they must conform to the dress code in the clubhouse: ties must be worn. / Well, that wall over there certainly doesn't conform with the architect's drawings.*

consist

To *consist of* something is to be made of it or to include it: *Concrete consists of a mixture of cement, sand, small stones, and water.*

To *consist in* something is to be it or come from it: *True happiness consists in being content with what you have.*

cook

To *cook* something *up* is to invent it or create it: *We'll have to cook up some excuse for why we weren't there.*

cross

If you *cross* something *out*, you put a line through it to show that you do not want to include it or want to change it: *You'll need to go through the report again and cross out any reference to Bill Jones, since he is leaving the firm.* Similarly, you may *cross* somebody or something *off* a list.

cut

If you *cut across* somewhere, such as a field, you take a short-cut across it to get somewhere else more quickly.

If you *cut* something *back*, or *cut back on* it, you reduce it or do less of it: *The Government has promised not to cut back on spending on education.*

To *cut* something *down*, or *cut down on* something, is also to reduce it or do less of it: *You really must cut down on your smoking. It's bad for your health.*

To *cut in* is to interrupt when somebody else is speaking. If a vehicle *cuts in*, it moves in front of another one in a dangerous or inconsiderate way: *He overtook at a bend in the road and had to cut in to avoid a lorry coming the other way.*

If you are *cut off* when you are talking on the telephone, it means that the connection between you and the person you are talking to has been broken; and if a power supply is *cut off*, it is stopped or disconnected.

If people find themselves *cut off* by a flood or earthquake, they are unable to move from where they are or get to some other place because the route is blocked; and if soldiers move to *cut off* the enemy, they move to where they an intercept them and stop them escaping.

If you say that somebody is not *cut out for* something or *cut out* to do or be something, you mean that they are not suited to it: *I'm just not cut out to be a teacher.*

If an engine *cuts out*, it stops working.

If you *cut* something *out*, you stop doing it, taking it, eating it, etc: *Starting today, I'm going to cut out snacks between meals. / I'm tired of all these silly remarks, so just cut it out, OK?*

To be *cut up* about something is to be upset about it: *She was really cut up at not getting the job.*

deal

If you *deal in* something, that is what you do business in, what you buy and sell: *He made his fortune dealing in diamonds.*
To *deal* or *deal out* playing cards is to give some cards to each of the players in a game. To *deal out* punishment to somebody is to punish them; to *deal out* justice is to administer it.

If a book *deals with* a subject, that is what the book is about: *a book that deals with the problems of growing up in the late twentieth century.*

If you say that you are going to *deal with* a problem, complaint, etc, then you are going to take whatever action is necessary with regard to it, e.g. to solve the problem, settle the complaint, etc. If you say that you are going to *deal with* somebody, you probably mean you are going to punish them for doing something wrong: *I'll deal with you when we get home.*

die

If a sound *dies away*, it grows fainter and fainter until it disappears. If something else *dies away*, it gradually weakens and disappears.

To *die down* is to decrease in strength or intensity: *I think the wind is dying down at last. / The Government will just wait until all the fuss dies down.*

To be *dying for* something is to have a strong desire for it: *I'm dying for a cup of coffee.*

A person may *die from* or *of* a disease, starvation, cold, a drug overdose, etc.

If people or animals *die off*, they die quickly or in large numbers, and perhaps all die: *Throughout the region the cattle were dying off because of the drought.*

If animals or peoples *die out*, they become extinct. If a custom *dies out*, it goes out of practice: *Men of this tribe used to file their teeth to sharp points, but the custom is dying out nowadays.*

disagree

You *disagree with* somebody or their opinions or actions. If you say that food *disagrees with* you, you mean it upsets your stomach or makes you ill.

do

To *do away with* something is to abolish it: *The company can't just decide to do away with tea breaks. It's against the law.*

If you *do away with* somebody, you kill them; to *do away with* oneself is to commit suicide: *He was so depressed after his wife died that he tried to do away with himself.*

To *do* somebody *down* is to talk about them in a way that makes them seem stupid, unimportant, incompetent, etc: *No matter what I do, she's always doing me down.*

If somebody is *done for*, they are, or are going to be, ruined or in serious trouble: *If I don't get this finished by the end of the week, I'm done for.* An informal expression. *Do for* also means to kill somebody or put an end to something: *Television almost did for the cinema.*

To *do* somebody *in* is to kill them. An informal expression.

To *do* somebody *out of* something is to do something unfair or dishonest to stop them having it: *This is just a ploy by the company to do us out of a day's wages.*

To *do up* shoe laces, buttons, etc is to fasten them: *He hasn't learned to do up buttons yet. / The dress does up at the back.* If you *do* something *up*, you wrap it up as a parcel or make it into a bundle: *The wedding presents were all done up in silver paper.* If a woman's hair is *done up* in a particular style, it is put into that style and fixed by some means, e.g. a ribbon or hairpins.

If you *do up* a room or a house, you redecorate it, repair it, or modernize it.

If you ask what something has to *do with* something else, you are wanting to know how the two things are related: *I don't see how the weather has anything to do with how she behaves.* If you say that something has nothing to *do with* somebody, you mean that you do not think they have any right to get involved or pass an opinion: *The way they bring up their children has nothing to do with you.*

If you ask somebody what they have *done with* something, you want to know where they have put it, perhaps because you cannot find it: *What have you done with my grey socks? They're not in the drawer.*

If you say you *could do with* something, you mean that you want it or need it: *I could do with some help here.* But if you *can't be doing with* something, you mean you cannot tolerate it or do not like it: *I can't be doing with noisy parties at my age.*

To *do without* something is to manage or exist without it: *We could do without our car if we had to.* You also say you *could do without* something when you have got it and you do not want it: *I could do without all these silly comments, thank you very much.*

drag

To *drag on* is to continue for a long time in a boring or tiring way: *The discussion dragged on for hours before a vote was finally taken.*

To *drag* something *out* is to make it go longer than necessary or reasonable: *I don't know why they want to drag out the discussion.*

draw

To *draw back* is to move back or away from somebody or something frightening or unpleasant: *She drew back from him in disgust.* You also *draw back* from something if you decide against it after coming close to doing it or agreeing to it.

If a vehicle *draws in*, it moves to the side of the road it is on and stops. A train *draws into* a station when it goes in and stops to let passengers on or off.

When nights are *drawing in*, days are getting shorter.

To *draw out* a process is to prolong it. If you *draw* money *out* at a bank, you take it out of your account.

A vehicle *draws out* when it moves out from the side of the road towards the centre; a train *draws out* when it leaves a station.

If you encourage a shy person to talk, you are *drawing* them *out*.

If a vehicle *draws up* somewhere, it comes to a stop there. If people or things are *drawn up*, they are arranged in an orderly manner: *The foot soldiers were drawn up in three lines along the hill, with the cavalry to one side of them.* If you *draw up* a piece of furniture, you bring it near something or somebody: *They drew up their chairs and warmed their hands at the fire.*

If you *draw up* a plan or a contract, you prepare it and, usually, set it down on paper.

If you *draw* yourself *up*, you stand as straight and tall as you can be: *She drew herself up to her full height and looked at him with contempt.*

dream

You *dream about* things when you are asleep; when you are awake and thinking of something in your imagination, you are *dreaming of* it, though *dreaming about* is also correct in this sense. When you say you *wouldn't dream of* doing something, you mean you would not consider doing it for any reason.

If somebody *dreams up* an idea or a plan, they create it in their mind.

drop

If you *drop by*, *drop in*, or *drop round*, you pay a casual visit to somebody or somewhere: *Feel free to drop in on us any time.*

To *drop off* is to fall asleep.

If somebody in a car *drops* you *off* somewhere, they take you there and let you out of the car: *I can drop you off at the station on my way to work if you like.*

If you *drop out*, you withdraw from an activity, or from your studies at school or college.

egg

If you *egg* somebody *on*, you encourage them to do something, especially something foolish or wrong.

fall

If ground *falls away*, it slopes downward, usually steeply. If something *falls away*, it becomes less in amount: *Demand for barbecues and lawnmowers falls away at the end of the summer. / After the recent scandals, support for the government has fallen away.*

To *fall back* is to move back from somebody or something or to retreat. If you are forced to *fall back on* something, you use it or do

it when you are in difficulty or when some other alternative no longer exists: *If I lose my job, I can always fall back on my savings.*

To *fall behind* is to progress less rapidly than others, or to fail to maintain a schedule of work or payments: *He's been ill so often, he is falling behind the rest of the class. / We mustn't fall behind with the rent.*

If a plan or theory *falls down*, it fails in some respect in which it is false or inadequate.

If you *fall for* a trick, you are deceived by it. If you *fall for* a person, you are strongly attracted to them or you fall in love with them.

If soldiers *fall in* for a parade or inspection, they get into lines.

If you *fall in with* a proposal, you agree to it or comply with it.

To *fall off* is to decrease in number: *Applications to join have been falling off lately. Fall off* also means to deteriorate or worsen: *The level of candidates has fallen off recently.*

If people *fall out*, they quarrel. If soldiers on parade are told to *fall out*, they are being given permission to leave the parade.

If plans *fall through*, then what was planned does not happen.

fan

If people or things *fan out*, they spread out in the shape of a fan.

fill

You can either *fill in* or *fill out* a form by putting in the information that is asked for.

fly

If you *fly into* a rage, you become very angry very quickly.

fork

To **fork out** is to pay money, usually unwillingly: *I've just paid for two new tyres for the car and now I'm having to fork out for a new exhaust pipe.*

frown

If something is **frowned on**, it is disapproved of: *Smoking is not actually banned in the office, but it's certainly frowned on.*

get

If someone is able to **get about**, they can move or travel from place to place. If a story or rumour **gets about**, it spreads: *I don't know how the rumour got about that I was leaving the company. There's no truth in it whatsoever.*

If you try to **get** something **across** to someone, you try to make them understand it.

To **get ahead** is to make progress or be successful. To **get along** is to manage or progress: *I could do with more detailed information, but I can get along without it.* If you **get along with** someone, or if you and other people **get along**, then you are friendly towards each other and don't argue or fight.

If you can't **get at** something, you can't reach it. If you **get at** someone, you criticize them or make fun of them.

To **get away with** something is to do something, usually something bad, without getting caught or punished.

To **get back at** someone is to have revenge on them for something they have done to you.

To **get by** is to manage satisfactorily: *We don't have much money but we get by nonetheless.*

To **get down to** something is to start work on it, or to start working on something seriously rather than without effort.

get on = get along

If you **get over** an illness or disappointment, you recover from it. If you say that you **can't get over** something, you mean you can hardly believe it or cannot understand it why it has happened: *I just can't get over her leaving her husband like that.*

If you **get round** someone, you persuade them to allow something or do something. If you **get round** a problem or difficulty, you solve it or find a way of avoiding it. To **get round** to or **get around to** doing something is to finally do it after some delay: *I was always meaning to mend the fence, but I just never got round to it.*

To **get through** work is to do it. To **get through to** someone is to make contact with them by telephone. It also means to make someone understand something: *I just can't get through to her how important this is to me.* To **get through** a quantity of food or drink is to eat it or drink it. To **get through** an exam is to pass it.

When people **get together**, they meet by arrangement.

To **get up** is to get out of bed or get on to your feet. If the wind **gets up**, it starts to blow hard. To **get up to** something is to do something surprising or undesirable.

give

If you **give** something **away**, you give it or sell it for nothing or very cheaply. To **give away** a secret is to let it become known, usually unintentionally.

To **give in** is to admit that you are beaten by someone or something: *I refuse to give in to their threats. / I give in. I can't solve this problem at all.*

If a fire **gives off** smoke, it produces smoke.

If something **gives out**, it stops working or comes to an end.

Like **give in**, **give up** means to admit that you are beaten: *I give up. I don't know where* *you've hidden my shoe.* If you *give* yourself *up*, you surrender. If you *give* something *up*, you stop eating it, drinking it, using it, etc: *This year I really am going to give up smoking.*

go

To *go about* a job is to do it or to find some way of doing it: *How does one go about changing the way people think?*

To *go after* someone is to chase them; to *go after* a job or a prize is to try to get it or win it.

If something *goes against* your principles, it conflicts with them: *It goes against my conscience to tell lies.*

If you *go ahead* with something, you do it.

If you *go along with* a person, you agree with them; if you *go along with* an idea, you support it.

If you *go back on* a promise or your word, then you fail to keep your promise.

To *go down with* a disease is to catch it. If you say that something did not *go down* well with somebody, you mean that they didn't like it or approve of it.

If a person *goes for* something, they go somewhere to get it. To *go for* someone is to attack them: *I was walking along the road when this little dog suddenly went for me.* If you say 'That *goes for* him, too', you mean that whatever has been said is true for or applies to him as well.

To *go in for* a competition is to take part in it. To *go in for* something is to do it as a hobby, habit, etc. If you *go in for* something, then that is the career you have chosen: *Why on earth did you go in for dentistry?*

To *go into* something its to examine it or investigate it.

If a bomb *goes off*, it explodes; if an alarm *goes off*, it rings.

To *go on* is to continue. If you *go on at* someone, you criticize or scold them, especially repeatedly or at length.

If a light or a candle *goes out*, it stops shining or burning.

If you *go over* something, you look at it, study it, rehearse it or check it: *Always leave time at the end of an exam to go over your answers for careless mistakes. / If you like, I'll go over your lines with you before the rehearsal.* If someone *goes over to* something, they change in loyalty or habit from one thing to another: *I used to smoke cigarettes, but I've recently gone over to cigars.*

To *go through* something is to suffer in some way: *You have no idea what I went through while you were away.* If you *go through* something, you examine it or search in it: *You can't have lost the keys. Go through all your pockets again.* If you *go through with* something, you carry it out right to the end.

If two or more things *go together*, they look well together or belong together.

grow

If something *grows on* you, you gradually begin to like it when you didn't like it at first.

hand

If a precious object or a belief has been *handed down* over the years, it has been passed from the people of one generation to those of the next generation, and the next, and so on.

To *hand* something *on* is to pass it on to someone else, especially to hand it down to people of the next generation.

To *hand* something *out* is to give it to someone, especially to give things to many people: *They were handing out leaflets to everyone who entered the shop.*

To *hand* something *over* is to give or send it or them to someone else: *Hand over all your money!*

hang

To *hang about* or *hang around* is to stand somewhere doing nothing: *Why are all these people hanging around outside the supermarket?*

If you say to somebody to *hang on*, you mean you want them to wait. To *hang on to* something is to hold on to it. If you decide to *hang on to* something, you decide to keep it.

If you *hang* something *up*, you put it on a hook or hang it on something. If you *hang up* when you are on the phone, you finish the phone call and put down the receiver or switch off the phone.

hinge

If something *hinges on* something else, it depends on it: *The whole plan hinges on how fast we can get to the door.*

hold

If something *holds* you *back*, it stops you making progress or getting a job done. If you *hold back* before doing something, you wait or hesitate before doing it.

To *hold down* a job is to manage to keep it or stay in it.

If rain *holds off*, it stays away. If you *hold off* an attack or an attacker, you successfully resist the attack.

If you ask someone to *hold on*, you want them to stop or wait a bit.

To *hold out* in a difficult or dangerous situation is to manage to survive until help comes: *Although outnumbered by the enemy, the soldiers in the fort managed to hold out for three weeks.*

If something *holds* you *up* or *holds up* the job you are doing, it stops you or makes you late or slows your progress. If someone *holds up* a bank or a train, they rob it.

If you say you don't *hold with* something, you mean you don't approve of it.

jump

To *jump at* an opportunity is to take it or accept it eagerly: *I'd jump at a chance to study in the United States.*

keep

To *keep at* something is to continue doing it steadily, often in spite of problems or difficulties.

To *keep in with* someone is to be friendly with them.

To *keep on* doing something is to do it repeatedly. To *keep on at* someone is to urge them repeatedly to do something: *Don't keep on at me to take you to the circus. We're not going and that's final.*

If you *keep to* a plan, a path, etc, you don't leave it.

If you can't *keep up* with someone else, it means that you can't go as fast as them. To *keep up* some activity is to continue with it: *The soldiers kept up the bombardment of the fort. / There's no point in buying a new car as I wouldn't be able to keep up the payments on it.* To *keep up* something such as a garden is to keep it in good condition.

laugh

To *laugh at* jokes or clowns is to be amused by them. If you *laugh at* a person, however, you may be making fun of them: *If I said I was going to ballet lessons, all my friends would laugh at me.* If you *laugh about* a situation, you see that it has an amusing aspect: *Setting fire to the house was a bit of a catastrophe, but maybe one day we'll be able to laugh about it.*

lay

If rules or procedures are *laid down*, then they are given as instructions to be followed.

If you *lay into* someone, you attack them either physically or in words. This is an informal phrase.

If staff have to be *laid off*, then they have to be dismissed from work temporarily because there is not enough work for them to do. If you tell someone to *lay off*, you mean you want them to stop doing what they are doing. This is an informal usage. To *lay on* food, etc is to provide it.

let

If you *let* somebody *down*, you fail them in some way: *There's no point in asking Tony to help on Saturday. He always lets us down.*

To *let* somebody *in on* a secret is to share it with them.

To *let* someone *off* is to allow them to go without punishment or without having to do something they do not want to do. If you *let off* a gun or a firework you make it fire or explode.

If something *lets up*, it stops or becomes less strong or violent.

look

To *look after* someone is to take care of them.

If you *look ahead*, then you are thinking about what will happen at some time in the future. If you *look back*, you are thinking about the past.

To *look down on* someone is to despise them.

If you are *looking for* someone or something, you are searching for them or for it. If you are *looking for* something, you may be expecting it: *I was looking for a bit more enthusiasm than that.*

To *look forward to* something is to anticipate it or expect it with pleasure.

If you *look in on* someone, you make a short visit: *The doctor said he would look in again tomorrow.* If you *look into* something, you investigate it closely.

To *look on* is to be a spectator, to watch while someone does something. If you *look on* something in a certain way, you have a certain opinion about it: *I look on her as my aunt even though we aren't related.*

To *look out* is to be careful. If you *look out for* someone, you watch for them.

To *look over* something is to examine it.

If you *look* something *up* in a book, such as a dictionary, then you search for it in the book. If you *look* someone *up*, you visit them. To *look up to* someone is to feel respect for them.

make

To *make for* a place is to go towards it, to try to reach it.

To *make off with* something is to run away with it, to steal it.

To *make* something *out* is to see it, read it, hear it or understand it: *Can you make out what is written on this stone?* To *make out* is also to manage in spite of difficulties.

If someone *makes up* a story or excuse, they invent it. If two people *make up*, they become friends again after having a fight. If something *makes up for* a loss or disappointment, it compensates for it.

nod

If you *nod off*, you fall asleep. This is an informal phrase.

own

To *own up* to something is to admit that you have done it.

pack

If an engine *packs in*, it stops working. If a person *packs* something *in*, they stop doing it. These are informal expressions.

pass

To *pass away* is to die.

If someone could *pass for* or *pass as* something, they could be mistaken for it or be accepted as it: *He's nearly sixty but he could pass for a forty-year-old.*

If you *pass* something *off* as something, you represent it falsely as being that thing.

To *pass out* is to faint or become unconscious.

If you *pass over* a mistake, you overlook it or ignore it. If you *pass over* somebody, you ignore them, for example for promotion or an opportunity to do something.

To *pass up* an opportunity is to fail to take it.

pay

To *pay for* something is to bear the expenses of it. *Pay for* also means to be punished for something or to suffer because of it: *I'll make him pay for his treachery.*

If a plan *pays off*, it yields good results. If you *pay off* a debt, you pay it in full. If a company has to *pay off* its workers, it pays them what they are due and then discontinues their employment.

If you have to *pay up*, you have to pay what you owe, often unwillingly.

pull

To *pull down* a building is to demolish it.

If a train *pulls in* at a station, it arrives there. If a car *pulls in*, it moves close to the side of the road and stops.

To *pull* something *off* is to succeed in doing it.

If a train *pulls out* of a station, it leaves it. If a car *pulls out*, it moves away from the side of the road or into a faster-moving lane of traffic, for example in order to overtake a vehicle in front of it. If people *pull out* of something , they leave it or no longer take part in it.

If someone who has been very ill *pulls through*, they recover from their illness and get well again. If you *pull through*, you survive in spite of difficulties: *Life may be hard now that I don't have a job, but we'll pull through.*

If a car *pulls up*, it stops.

push

In informal English, to *push off* is to go away.

put

To *put* a story *about* is to spread it.

To *put* an idea or message *across* to people is to communicate it to them.

To *put* work *aside* is to leave it until later on. To *put* money *aside* is to save for the future.

To *put* something *down* on paper is to write it down. If a rebellion is *put down*, it is suppressed by force. If an animal has to be *put down*, it is killed, usually because it is very ill. If an aircraft *puts down* somewhere, it lands there. If you *put* someone's behaviour *down to* something, you say that is what caused that behaviour: *I put his bad temper down to lack of sleep.*

If someone is *put off* by something, they are discouraged by it. If you *put* something *off* or *put off* doing it, you postpone it till a later time.

To *put on* weight is to become fatter and heavier.

To *put out* a fire is to stop it burning. To

put out to sea is to go out to sea in a boat, to set off from the shore or a harbour. If you *put* yourself *out* for somebody, you go to some trouble for their sake.

If you *put* someone *up*, you provide them with food and lodging. If you *put up* a building, you build it. If you *put up* money for something, you provide it: *A local millionaire has put up the money for a small library in the village.* If there is something you will not *put up with*, it means you will not allow it or tolerate it.

rule

If you *rule* something *out*, you forbid it or say that it is impossible.

run

To *run across* someone is to meet them by accident.

If you say to someone to *run along*, you mean they are to go away. This is an informal expression.

If someone is *run down* by a car, they are knocked over by it. If you *run* someone *down*, you say bad things about them, for example criticizing them or saying that they are not very clever.

If you *run into* someone, you meet them unexpectedly.

If you *run out of* something, you don't have enough of it or any more of it. If something *runs out*, there isn't enough of it or any more if it. If a contract or agreement has *run out*, it is no longer valid.

If someone is *run over* in the street, then a vehicle has knocked them down and driven over them.

To *run through* a script is to go over it or rehearse it. To *run through* a series of points in a discussion or argument is to read them or look at them or discuss them: *OK, let's just run through what we want to say at the meeting once more.*

To *run up* expenses is to create them or accumulate them: *My wife has run up an enormous bill for shoes.*

see

To *see about* something is to do whatever needs to be done about it.

If you *see* someone *off*, you accompany them to the station, airport, etc when they are going away. To *see* someone *off* is also to chase them away; this is an informal use of the phrase.

To *see* someone *out* is to conduct them to the door when they are leaving: *Thank you for coming. My secretary will see you out.*

To *see over* or *see round* a building is to visit it and look at all its rooms, etc.

If you can *see through* someone or *see through* what they are saying or doing, then you can understand their true nature or aims which they are trying to keep hidden. To *see* a job *through* is to complete it in spite of difficulties.

To *see to* something is to look after it or do what is necessary about it: *You bring the wine and I'll see to the food. / Who will see to the goldfish while we're on holiday?*

set

To *set about* doing something is to begin doing it. If you *set about* someone, you attack them.

If something *sets* someone *apart* from other people, it makes them different from them or special in some way.

If you *set* money *aside* for some purpose, you keep it specially for that purpose. If an agreement or decision is *set aside*, it is rejected.

If something *sets* you *back* a certain amount of money, it costs you that amount. If a building is *set back* from a road, it has been built at a slight distance away from the road rather than being right on the edge of it. If a difficulty *sets* a project *back*, it delays it.

If something *sets in*, it begins: *Winter set in early that year and the snow was soon thick on the ground.*

If you *set off*, you start on a journey. If something *sets off* an alarm, it starts it ringing. If something *sets off* something else, it makes it look particularly attractive: *Her green dress set off her red hair perfectly. / The curtains set off the carpet.*

To *set out* is to start on a journey.

To *set* something *up* is to build it or erect it: *We could set up our tent over there.* If someone *sets up* an organization, they start it.

show

If you *show up*, you arrive or appear somewhere. If something *shows up*, it becomes visible or obvious. If you *show* someone *up*, you embarrass them by your bad behaviour, or you do something that reveals their mistakes or inadequacies or their true character.

stand

If you *stand by* someone, you support them in times of difficulty. If you *stand by* your principles, you keep to them. If you *stand by* in case you are needed, you keep yourself in readiness. But if someone *stands by* while something bad is happening, they watch it happening without taking any action.

To *stand down* is to withdraw from a contest.

If you *stand for* election, you are a candidate in an election. If something *stands for* something else, it represents it: *What do these little crosses on the map stand for?* If you won't *stand for* something, you won't tolerate it.

If you *stand in for* someone, you take their place when they are unable to be somewhere or do something: *I can't be at both meetings at the same time. Will you stand in for me at one of them?*

To *stand out* is to be noticeable or prominent.

If you *stand up for* something, you support it. If you *stand up to* someone, you resist them.

step

To *step down* is to resign from a job.

If you *step in*, you intervene or become involved, in order to help someone or stop something.

If something, such as output or effort, is *stepped up*, it is increased.

stick

To *stick around* is to remain in a place. This is an informal expression.

If you *stick by* someone, you support them in times of difficulty.

If you say you'll *stick* it *out*, you mean you will stay on in a situation you do not like or want to be in until it is over or until there is an appropriate time to leave: *We're having a dreadful holiday here, but we'll stick it out in any case.*

To *stick up for* someone is to speak or act in their defence.

strike

To *strike at* someone is to try to hit them. To *strike back* is to return a blow. To *strike at* something is to attack it, threaten it or harm it: *Replacing the pound by the euro would strike at British independence.*

If a band *strikes up*, it begins to play. If you *strike up* a conversation, you begin to talk to someone.

take

To *take after* someone is to resemble them or behave like them.

If you *take back* something you have said, you admit that it was not true.

If you *take down* a building, you demolish it. If you *take down* something someone says, you write it down.

If you *take* someone *in*, you provide lodgings for them. To *take* someone *in* is also to make them believe something false, to trick them. If you *take in* an item of clothing, you reduce the size of it.

If an aircraft *takes off*, it leaves the ground for a flight.

If you *take on* a job, you undertake to do it.

To *take* something *over* is to assume control of it.

If you *take to* someone or something, you become fond of them or it.

If you *take up* a profession or a hobby, you start doing it: *I think I'll take up the violin.*

think

To *think about* something is to have it in your mind. To *think about* doing something is to consider whether or not you should do it.

To *think of* doing something is to consider doing it or to intend to it. If you ask someone what they *think of* something, you want their opinion about it. If you are surprised at what someone has done, you may ask them what they were *thinking of* when they did it.

To *think out* a solution to a problem is to think until you find the solution.

To *think* something *over* is to consider it.

If you *think up* an idea, you create it in your mind.

throw

If you *throw* something *at* someone, you mean to hit them. If you *throw* something *to* someone, you intend them to catch it.

If you *throw away* an opportunity, you fail to take advantage of it. If you say that someone is *throwing away* their money, you mean they are just wasting it.

If you *throw in* something, you add it as an extra.

To *throw* something *off*, such as a cold, is to get rid of it.

To *throw out* an idea is to reject it. If you *throw* someone *out*, you force them out of a room, an association, etc.

touch

If an aircraft *touches down* somewhere, it lands there.

To *touch on* a subject is to mention it in passing while mainly talking about something else.

To *touch up* something such as a painting is to improve it by small touches of paint.

turn

To *turn* someone *away* is to refuse to let them into a meeting, concert, etc.

To *turn back* is to turn round and go back towards the place you have come from. To *turn* somebody *back* is to make them do this.

If you *turn down* an offer or a proposal, you reject. If you *turn down* the light, you make it dimmer; if you *turn* a radio *down*, you reduce the level of noise it produces.

To *turn in* is to go to bed. This is an informal expression.

To *turn into* something is to become it by a gradual process of change: *A tadpole eventually turns into a frog.*

If you *turn off* water, electricity, etc, you stop it flowing; if you *turn off* a television, a tap, etc, you stop it working. To *turn* something *on* is the opposite of to turn it off.

To *turn out* is to come to a place: *People turned out in their thousands to see the Pope.* If a factory *turns* something *out*, it produces it.

If you *turn* something *over* in your mind, you think about it carefully.

To *turn to* someone is to go to them for help, advice, comfort, etc.

To *turn up* is to appear or arrive. If you say that something that has been lost will *turn up* again, you mean it will be found again. To *turn up* light, sound, etc is to increase its brightness, loudness, etc.

work

To *work off* something unpleasant or unwanted is to do something to get rid of it: *He went for a long walk to work off his bad mood.*

To *work on* someone is to try to influence them.

To *work* something *out* is to calculate it. Something that *works out at* a certain figure or amount is the result of a calculation: *The bill comes to £35, so that works out at £7 each.* If you say that things will *work out*, you mean they will develop or happen in a desirable way.

To *work up* an appetite is to create it or stimulate. To *work* someone *up* into a particular state is to cause them to get into that state: *He worked himself up into a fury.*

DO IT YOURSELF

A Insert the correct preposition or adverb into the following sentences to make phrasal verbs with the same meaning as the words in brackets.

1. There are some things about his story that don't *add* _____ . (make sense)

2. Does your little sister still *believe* _____ Santa Claus? (think he exists)

3. We're all going to watch the old bridge being *blown* _____ . (destroyed in an explosion)

4. Looking at these photos *brings* _____ happy memories. (brings them to mind)

5. I must *brush* _____ the Highway Code before I sit my driving test. (improve my knowledge of it)

6. I expect my orders to be *carried* _____ exactly. (obeyed)

7. The police admit that they do not know how it *came* _____ that the thieves got away in a police car. (happened)

8. You really ought to *cut* _____ the amount of coffee you drink. (reduce)

9. I may have bought you a car but I have no intention of *forking* _____ for one for your boyfriend. (paying money)

10. I'm sorry, I can't *go* _____ you on that. (agree with)

11. Every child needs someone to *look* _____ . (respect)

12. *Pull* _____ along there and we'll have another look at the map. (stop the car)

13. A fire started in the kitchen but fortunately the staff were able to *put* it _____ before it spread. (stop it burning)

14. He accused her of lying to the police, but he was forced to *take* _____ what he had said. (admit it was not true)

15. I'm very tired this evening. I think I'm going to *turn* _____ now. (go to bed)

B Rewrite the following sentences, replacing the words in italics with phrasal verbs that have the same meaning. The verbs in brackets following the sentences indicate where the phrasal verbs will be found in the lists in this unit.

Example:
The rain was *falling heavily*. (beat)
The rain was **beating down**.

---

1. She was *working very hard* when I went into the room. (beaver)

2. I *discovered* the book *by chance* in the library last week. (come)

3. Suddenly the alarm *started ringing.* (go)

4. It was so hot in the shop, she nearly *fainted.* (pass)

5. They buy old houses, *redecorate* them, and then sell them again for a huge profit. (do)

6. We don't want to listen to your silly stories. Why don't you just *go away.* (push)

7. What does that tree-shaped mark *represent?* (stand)

8. It will be no easy task to *accomplish* our plan. (carry)

9. I'll *start my journey* sometime after breakfast. (set)

10. I hope the rain will *stay away.* (hold)

11. Sadly her mother *died* last week. (pass)

12. Perhaps she will be able to tell us what happened when she *regains consciousness.* (come)

13. A hole has appeared in the road outside them library. The police are *investigating* the matter. (look)

14. The speaker did *mention* the election in his speech. (touch)

15. I *had a strong desire* for a glass of water. (die)

16. The shop *doesn't have any more* bread. (run)

17. I think the fish I ate last night *upset my stomach.* (disagree)

18. If I were you, I would *be eager to accept* a chance of a free holiday in New Zealand. (jump)

19. Just *continue* with what you're doing. (carry)

20. I always have the feeling that she *despises* me because I don't have a university education. (look)

C Supply the correct prepositions for the following phrasal verbs.

1. abide _____ (= obey)
2. fall _____ (= be deceived by)
3. get _____ (= reach)
4. go _____ (= attack)
5. grow _____ (= begin to be liked)
6. hinge _____ (= depend on)
7. keep _____ (= not leave)
8. look _____ (= try to find)
9. make _____ (= go towards)
10. see _____ (= do what is needed)
11. stand _____ (= support)
12. strike _____ (= attack)

18 ▶ Common Idioms

An **idiom** is a phrase or compound word
whose meaning cannot be guessed from
the meanings of the words that form
it, e.g. *from the bottom of your heart*
(= *sincerely*) or *the green-eyed
monster* (= *jealousy*).

How to use the lists

▶ The idioms in the following lists are entered in order of their first main word.
For example, **with flying colours** is at *flying*, and **in the red** is at *red*.
Words in brackets may be omitted: thus **once (and) for all** means that you
can say either **once and for all** or **once for all**. Alternatives are shown by
a solidus: thus **bear / keep in mind** means that you can say **bear in mind** or
keep in mind.

▶ Phrases with *like*, such as **like a fish out of water** or **sell like hot cakes**, or
with *as*, such **as good as gold**, are to be found in the lists of Similes in Unit
19. Some idioms are based on well-known proverbs, and are fully explained in
Unit 20 on Proverbs and Sayings.

from A to Z

from beginning to end

absent-minded

not paying attention; thinking about something else

above board

honest, fair or legal: *I don't think the arrangement was entirely above board.*

above yourself

conceited; having too high an opinion of your importance: *She's getting a bit above herself these days.*

have an ace up your sleeve

to have a secret advantage that you can use to beat an opponent unexpectedly

alive and kicking

in a healthy condition: *Unfortunately, racism is still alive and kicking. / She's alive and kicking and living in New York.*

all ears

listening attentively: *We were all ears as she told her story.*

all eyes

watching attentively; keeping a careful watch

all in

1 exhausted: *They were all in after the walk.*
2 with everything included: *The trip will cost $1200 all in.*

all set

ready: *Are we all set? OK, let's go.*

the apple of somebody's eye

something or somebody much loved.

armed to the teeth

heavily or elaborately armed; with many weapons

up in arms

protesting angrily: *We were up in arms when we found out that the council was going to cut down all the trees.*

have an axe to grind

to have a strong personal opinion about something or a strong reason for doing something or for wanting it done: *I've no particular axe to grind. I just don't think programmes like that should be on television.*

backbiting

saying unkind things about somebody or criticizing them when they are not present

back-breaking

very hard: *Digging is back-breaking work.*

a back-handed compliment

words that seem to be expressing admiration but are to some extent, and may well be intended as, an insult: *She said I was the best teacher she'd had as I wasn't as intellectual as all the others, which I thought was rather a back-handed compliment.*

the back of beyond

somewhere far away from town and people: *I'm not spending a month on holiday on a farm in the back of beyond.*

behind somebody's back

without somebody knowing or being asked for their permission, especially when they should: *I didn't say they could go. They did it behind my back.*

back-scratching

doing favours for one another. *See also* You scratch my back ... *in Unit 20, page 394*

bad blood

angry or hostile feelings: *There's bad blood between them.*

be in somebody's bad books

to be the subject of somebody's displeasure: *She's in her mother's bad books because she broke a valuable vase.*

a bad debt

a debt that will never be paid, for example because the people who owe it have no money

bad language

swearing; vulgar language

badly off

not having enough of something you need, especially money: *We're not rich but we're not badly off. / We don't need to go shopping today; we're not badly off for food.*

get / set / start the ball rolling

to get some activity started: *Would anyone like to bid something to start the ball rolling?* Once an activity has started, to keep the ball rolling is to keep it going: *I'll bid $10 to keep the ball rolling.*

a baker's dozen

thirteen. Formerly, when bakers were fined for giving goods that weighed less than they should, they would give thirteen items instead of twelve in order to ensure that they were giving no less than the correct weight.

a bare-faced lie

a lie made openly, with no attempt to disguise it. A person can be a bare-faced liar.

with your bare hands; bare-handed

without any weapons or tools: *He claims to have killed a lion with his bare hands.*

bare-headed

without a hat on

be barking up the wrong tree

to be mistaken. The idea comes from raccoon-hunting: when a raccoon is chased by a dog, it runs up a tree, but the dog may be confused and bark beside the wrong tree.

bear / keep in mind

to remember or consider something; not to forget it: *Do bear in mind that I shall be on holiday next week.*

beat about the bush

to talk about something in an indirect way: *Don't beat about the bush. Just say exactly what you think.*

a bed of roses

any easy or comfortable place, position, occupation, etc: *Being a teacher is no bed of roses these days.*

have a bee in your bonnet

to be obsessed about something: *She's got a bee in her bonnet about people dyeing their hair.*

the best bet

the most sensible thing to do, or the thing that is most likely to succeed: *I think your best bet would be to go home and wait for her to phone you.*

bite off more than you can chew

to undertake to do something which is too much or too difficult for you to manage

in black and white

in writing or in print

the black market

buying and selling of goods in a way that is against the law, for example because the goods are illegal or rationed

the black sheep (of the family)

a member of a family, or other group, who does disgraceful things and makes the others feel ashamed

blaze a trail

to be the first in some new area of activity or research: *She's hoping to blaze a trail in new methods in psychiatry.* A person can be referred to as a trailblazer.

a blind alley

1 a street closed at one end.
2 an approach or activity that will not lead to success: *I think all talk of strike action is just leading us down a blind alley.*

a blind date

an arranged romantic meeting to go out with somebody you have never seen before, or the person you are to go out with

blood-curdling

horrible and terrifying: *blood-curdling screams / a blood-curdling story.*

bloody-minded

deliberately awkward or unco-operative: *This bloody-minded approach taken by the union leadership is damaging trade unionism throughout the country.* This is an informal expression.

blow your own trumpet

to praise yourself

a bolt from the blue

an unexpected event: *Her resignation came as a bolt from the blue.* A 'bolt' is a flash of lightning. The idea is that no-one expects lightning from a blue sky. You can also say that something comes out of the blue when it is totally unexpected.

a bone of contention

something that causes trouble or disagreement between people, just as dogs may fight over a bone

a bosom friend / pal / buddy

a close friend

from the bottom of your heart

sincerely: *I thank you from the bottom of my heart for all you have done.*

on the breadline

very poor. The 'breadline' was formerly a queue of poor people waiting to be given free food.

break somebody's heart

to upset somebody very much: *It broke his mother's heart when he was jailed for fraud.* Compare heart-broken and broken-hearted.

break the ice

to put an end to feelings of shyness or formality, for example at a party: *They played a game in which they had to find partners by making animal noises. Silly, but it broke the ice and had everyone laughing.*

break your word

to fail to keep a promise

a breath of fresh air

somebody or something that brings a new invigorating or exciting influence or feature to something

bright-eyed and bushy-tailed

lively and well rested, ready to get into action: *You'd better go to bed now. You have to be up early tomorrow, bright-eyed and bushy-tailed.*

broad-minded

tolerant of other people's attitudes and behaviour

broken English

badly spoken ungrammatical English

a broken home

the home of children whose parents have separated or are divorced

broken-hearted

overcome by grief; very sad. Compare break somebody's heart.

a bull in a china shop

1 somebody who is very clumsy or rough, knocking things over and causing damage
2 somebody who is not very sensitive or tactful

burn a hole in your pocket

If money is burning a hole in your pocket, you are eager to spend it.

burn the candle at both ends

to exhaust yourself by working or indulging in pleasure to an excessive amount

burn your fingers; get your fingers burnt

to suffer the unpleasant consequences of interfering in something, taking a risk, or acting foolishly: *I warn you, if you invest in those shares you'll get your fingers burnt.*

burn the midnight oil

to study late into the night

bury the hatchet

to become friends again after a quarrel

have butterflies (in your stomach)

to feel nervous

call it a day

1 to stop what you are doing even though it is incomplete: *I'm tired. Let's call it a day and finish the job tomorrow.*
2 to put an end to something: *You don't want to marry me and I don't want to marry you, so let's just call it a day.*

call a spade a spade

to say exactly what you mean, even if it gives offence, without trying to find more pleasant and less offensive ways of saying it.

call the tune

to have control over something. *See also He who pays the piper … in Unit 20, page 392*

a carbon copy

an exact copy. Originally, a carbon copy was a copy of a document made by means of a sheet of 'carbon paper', a type of ink-covered paper.

carry the can

to take the blame and suffer the punishment for something, even if you are not responsible for it or solely to blame

castles in the air

ambitious projects that are unlikely to succeed

catch somebody's eye

to be noticed by somebody; to attract somebody's attention: *I was just looking in the shop window when this necklace caught my eye. / We need more milk. Try and catch the waiter's eye.*

catch somebody red-handed

to catch a person in the very act of doing something wrong

change your mind

to change your opinion, intention or decision: *I was going to buy that dress, but I've changed my mind.*

chickenfeed

something of little value, especially a small amount of money: *$2000 may be a lot of money to you but it's just chickenfeed to her.*

child's play

something that is very easy to do

a chip off the old block

a man or boy who resembles his father in character, interests, etc.

have a chip on your shoulder
to have a feeling of resentment about something: *He's got a chip on his shoulder about people who have been to university.*

clear the air
to release the tension in a situation, e.g. by giving people a chance to express their opinions: *We had a furious row last night, but at least it cleared the air.*

clear-cut
clear and unambiguous: *a clear-cut decision.*

clear-headed
able to think clearly: *I'm not drinking any wine now. I want to be absolutely clear-headed when the meeting starts.*

round the clock
all day and all night without stopping: *This is the only radio station to bring you round-the-clock news bulletins.*

behind closed doors
in secret; not in public All the discussion has been behind closed doors.

a close shave
a narrow escape from danger or disaster

under a cloud
in trouble, disgrace or disfavour

on cloud nine
very happy

a cock-and-bull story
an unbelievable story: *He made up some cock-and-bull story about his dog having eaten his homework.*

in cold blood
cruelly, without any feelings of pity: *murdered in cold blood.* You can talk of a cold-blooded murder, or a cold-blooded killer.

get / have cold feet
to suddenly become, or be, afraid to do something: *I was going to ask her out, but I got cold feet.*

cold-hearted
lacking feelings of kindness or consideration

a cold war
a severe struggle, especially between countries, by all means short of actual fighting

come of age
1 to reach the age at which you are legally considered an adult
2 to reach a state of maturity: *With this new album, her music has come of age.*

come to blows
to begin to fight with fists or weapons: *They may disagree with one another but I'd never have expected them to come to blows over it.*

come clean
to confess; to tell the truth after trying to hide it: *Why don't you just come clean and admit you did it?*

come to grief
to meet with disaster, mishap, or loss

come to light
to be revealed or discovered: *The theft only came to light when staff opened the shop on Monday morning.*

come to nothing
to fail; to have little or no result or effect

come to your senses
to realize that you have been behaving foolishly and begin to have sensibly instead.

come what may
no matter what happens: *I'll be there on Thursday, come what may.*

common-or-garden

of an ordinary type: *I don't want some fancy carpet-care machine, just a common-or-garden vacuum cleaner.*

cool-headed

not easily excited; capable of acting calmly in a difficult situation

cool one's heels

to be kept waiting

cost a bomb

to be very expensive. This is an informal expression.

till the cows come home

forever: *You can keep on asking till the cows come home. The answer will still be 'No'.*

crocodile tears

insincere expressions of sadness. Crocodiles were once believed to sigh and moan in order to attract victims, or to weep while eating them.

as the crow flies

measured in a straight line: *The village is about three miles away as the crow flies.*

not your cup of tea

not the sort of thing you like: *Modern art really isn't her cup of tea.*

a dark horse

a person who keeps his or her opinions, plans, abilities, etc secret

in the dark

not knowing about something that you should have been told about: *The staff complained that the directors were keeping them in the dark about the future of the company.*

daylight robbery

charging an unreasonable price for something: *$50 for that pot? That's daylight robbery!*

a dead end

1 a road or path that is closed at one end: *We went down a country lane but it was a dead end, so we just had to turn and come back.*
2 a situation, action, etc that will not make progress or lead to success: *The police said that their inquiries had unfortunately come to a dead end. / a dead-end job.*

a dead heat

a race in which two or more competitors finish at exactly the same time, or any similar situation in which two or more people are equal in merit, points, or some other respect: *'Well, which of the candidates do you think is best?' 'It's a dead heat, I think.'*

a dead letter

1 a law that is no longer enforced
2 a letter that remains undelivered or unclaimed at the post office

a dead loss

somebody or something that is totally useless or worthless: *I'm a dead loss at tennis. / I'm giving up on this project. It's a dead loss.*

at death's door

so ill as to be in danger of dying

a dog's life

a wretched or miserable life: *It was a dog's life for miners in those days.*

down-hearted

sad; disappointed; depressed

draw the line at something

to be unwilling to do something: *I'm willing to speak to my ex-wife but I draw the line at dancing with her.*

drop somebody a line

to write a brief letter to somebody

drop the subject

to stop discussing something

ear-piercing, ear-splitting

loud and shrill: *She let out an ear-piercing shriek.*

earth-shattering

of great importance

eat humble pie

to have to be humble and apologetic about something you have said or done. Originally this had nothing to do with being humble: a 'humble pie' or 'umble pie' was a pie made with the entrails of a deer and was given to servants while important people got the better-quality meat.

eat your words

to admit that something you said was wrong: *I said she'd never pass her exams, but I was forced to eat my words.*

elbow grease

hard physical work

in your element

in a situation, job, activity, etc that you enjoy and are well suited to: *She's in her element working as a gardener.*

at the eleventh hour

just before it is too late; at the last possible moment

empty-handed

without bringing or getting anything: *I didn't want to come to your party empty-handed. / The union negotiators said they couldn't go back to their members empty-handed.*

empty-headed

lacking wisdom and intelligence

not the end of the world

not very bad; not as bad as it seems: *It's a pity we didn't get tickets for the concert, but it's not the end of the world.*

up to one's eyes

extremely busy with something: *I've no time for a holiday. I'm up to the eyes in work at the moment.*

face the music

to accept criticism for, or the unpleasant consequences of, something you have done

faint-hearted

lacking courage

a fair-weather friend

somebody who is a friend only in good or prosperous times

a fat chance

no chance at all: *A fat chance I have of getting into the movie business!* This is an informal expression.

a feather in your cap

an achievement you deserve to be proud of. In many cultures in the past, warriors would put feathers in their hats or caps when they had killed an enemy.

fight a losing battle

to continue to try to do something that you know is not going to succeed: *I try to get my daughters to keep their rooms tidy, but I'm fighting a losing battle.*

a fighting chance

a small chance of success, but one that definitely exists; a definite possibility: *If I can only get to meet her, I've got a fighting chance of persuading her to help us. / There's a fighting chance that she made up the whole story herself.*

a finger in every pie

involvement in many activities

have something at your fingertips

to know something very well and be able to produce facts and information about it immediately when asked

flat out

as quickly as possible: *We're going flat out to finish this by Friday.*

fly off the handle

to become very angry very quickly

a fly in the ointment

some slight flaw which spoils a thing of value or something that makes your situation less pleasant than it could be.

with flying colours

with great success

foot a bill

to pay a bill

have one foot in the grave

to be near death; to be very old

a foregone conclusion

something that is bound to happen, such as a decision that is bound to be made: *The result of the government inquiry into political corruption is a foregone conclusion. No-one will be found guilty.*

forty winks

a short sleep. An informal expression.

foul-mouthed

using vulgar or obscene language

foul play

a criminal act, especially murder: *The police say they suspect foul play.*

have a frog in your throat

to have something in your throat that makes you talk hoarsely and want to cough

full of beans

lively and cheerful: *She was feeling a bit under the weather yesterday but she's full of beans today.*

the generation gap

the difference in attitudes, interests and behaviour between one generation and another, especially adults and young people

get on somebody's nerves

to irritate somebody: *Her voice really gets on my nerves.*

get out of bed on the wrong side

to start the day in a bad mood

the gift of the gab

a talent for talking persuasively: *You should be a salesman. You really have got the gift of the gab.*

give somebody the cold shoulder

to deliberately ignore somebody and refuse to speak to them

give the game away

to reveal a secret

give somebody a hand

1 = lend a hand
2 give somebody a big hand = to give them enthusiastic applause

give somebody a piece of your mind

to express your anger or disapproval openly to somebody because of something they have done: *Why on earth was she so careless? I'll give her a piece of my mind when I next see her.*

go all out

to try or work as hard as possible: *We're going all out to finish this by Friday.*

go back on one's word

to not do something you have promised to do

go cap in hand

to go begging to somebody for something

go to the dogs

to get into a bad condition: *I'm exhausted all the time and I have no concentration. I'm really going to the dogs.*

go Dutch

to each pay for oneself, for example at a restaurant

go over / through something with a fine-tooth comb

to examine something very carefully

go to your head

to allow something to make you very proud or conceited: *Her promotion has gone to her head and she won't talk to me now.*

go for a song

to be for sale at a very low price: *I couldn't resist buying the car. It was going for a song.*

go up in the world

to become increasingly successful in society, business, etc

a golden opportunity

an excellent opportunity: *Since I was in London on business, I thought it was a golden opportunity to see a couple of shows.*

do somebody a good turn

to do something helpful for someone

grasp the nettle

to deal with a problem or difficulty firmly and resolutely. A nettle is a plant with stinging leaves; if you touch it hesitantly, you will get stung, but if you grasp it firmly, the leaves do not sting you.

grease somebody's palm

to bribe somebody

the green-eyed monster

jealousy

a grey area

a matter or situation in which people are not sure what is right or true and what is wrong or false: *Whether boxing causes brain damage is still a bit of a grey area.*

hair-brained

See hare-brained

hair-raising

frightening; terrifying: a hair-raising experience

hair-splitting

See split hairs

half-hearted

with little enthusiasm or effort: *She made a half-hearted attempt to catch the dog as it ran past her.*

ham-fisted, ham-handed

clumsy

at hand

conveniently near; within easy reach

a hard act to follow

somebody who sets such a high standard that others will find it hard to achieve the same standard: *He's been a brilliant president. He'll be a hard act to follow.*

hard cash

money in the form of coins or bank-notes

a hard nut to crack

a difficult problem to solve

hard of hearing

quite deaf

hard-hearted

cruel; not feeling sympathy or pity

hard-pressed, hard put to it

only able to do something with great difficulty: *I'd be hard put to it to buy a new car at the moment.*

hare-brained, hair-brained

foolish: *That was a hare-brained idea if ever I heard one!*

hear things

to imagine that you are hearing something that in fact you cannot hear: *Am I hearing things? Did you just volunteer to wash the dishes?*

with your heart in your mouth

nervous or frightened: *With her heart in her mouth, she cautiously opened the door.*

have a heart of stone

to have no feelings of kindness or sympathy

heart-broken

overcome by grief; very sad. Compare break somebody's heart. Something can be said to be heart-breaking if it causes great grief: *It was heart-breaking to see all those starving children on television.*

heart-rending

causing intense sadness; *a heart-rending story.*

heart-searching

examination of your feelings, motives, etc: *After the poor exam results, the headmaster said that the staff all needed to do some heart-searching.*

heart-warming

causing emotional pleasure: *a heart-warming story of a little boy's love for his dog*

hen-pecked

controlled by your wife: *a hen-pecked husband.*

high-handed

done, or acting, without considering other people's feelings, rights or opinions: *She accuses the government of censorship, high-handed behaviour, lies, and a cover-up.*

high living

luxurious living

hit somebody below the belt

to attack somebody unfairly. Boxers are not allowed to hit their opponents below the belt.

hit the jackpot

to win the top prize in a game or competition, or to have any big success

hit the nail on the head

to identify a problem, etc exactly: *You've hit the nail on the head. Our problem is a lack of money.*

hold the fort

to take charge temporarily: *I'll hold the fort while you go for lunch.*

hold / stand your ground

to remain firm in your beliefs, etc and not give in to pressure or persuasion

by hook or by crook

by some means or another

hopping mad

very angry

(straight) from the horse's mouth

from a very reliable source

hot air

boastful words or promises the speaker has no intention of keeping: *Half of what politicians say is just hot air.*

hot and bothered

flustered and agitated, for example from having too much work to do, being anxious, being in a hurry, etc: *There's no point in getting all hot and bothered about missing the bus. We can always get the next one.*

hot under the collar

showing irritation or annoyance, or sometimes embarrassment, in an excited, often slightly aggressive manner

be in, or get into, hot water

to be in, or get into, trouble

have several / too many irons in the fire

See **Don't have too many irons in the fire** in Unit 20, page 388

have a job

to have some difficulty doing something: *By all means ask her but I think you'll have a job persuading her to come.*

join the club

I have the same feelings, or I've had the same experience: *'I'm tired of teachers telling me what to do.' 'Join the club! I can't wait to leave school.'*

beyond a joke

quite unacceptable; more than you are prepared to put up with: *I didn't mind them having a party next door, but loud music playing till four o'clock in the morning was beyond a joke.*

jump the gun

to act before the time is right. In a race, runners have to wait for the starter's gun to go off before they start running.

keep somebody at arm's length

not to show friendliness towards somebody, or not become involved with them

keep body and soul together

to just manage to live: *I'm not rich, but I earn enough to keep body and soul together.*

keep your chin up

to try to be cheerful and unworried in spite of being in a difficult or unpleasant situation: *Keep your chin up! It's not long till the holidays now.*

keep an eye on somebody / something

to watch somebody or something to ensure that they do not come to harm or do anything wrong: *We'll keep an eye on your house while you're away.*

keep an eye out for somebody / something

to watch for somebody or something while doing something else: *Keep an eye out for John and Mary. They said they might be at the concert too.*

keep your fingers crossed

to hope for success or good luck

keep in mind

See **bear in mind**

keep your word

to do what you have promised

keep the ball rolling

See **get/set/start the ball rolling**

keep up with the Joneses

to maintain equality with your neighbours, for example by buying expensive goods or going on expensive holidays because they do. 'Jones' is a common surname.

a kettle of fish

1 a fine/pretty kettle of fish = a difficult situation: *This is a pretty kettle of fish we're in now.*
2 a quite different person or thing: *He's very pleasant but his brother's a different kettle of fish.*

kick the bucket

to die. This is a slang expression.

kill two birds with one stone

to achieve two results while doing one thing: *I was in town in any case, so I thought I would kill two birds with one stone and buy some new shoes.*

have kittens

to be very upset, worried or angry: *When she didn't turn up for the meeting, the boss had kittens.*

the last straw

one thing more than a person, etc can bear. *See* It is the last straw that breaks the camel's back *in Unit 19.*

have the last word

1 to have the final remark in a conversation
2 to make the final decision: *Well, you've got the last word. You decide what to do.*

a laughing stock

somebody who is laughed at because of something foolish they have done: *I'm not wearing these shorts in public. I'd be a laughing stock.*

lay / put your cards on the table

to reveal your intentions or resources

lay down your arms

to stop fighting; to surrender

lay down your life

to die in battle, etc: *We honour those who have laid down their lives for their country.*

lay hands on something

1 to obtain or find something: *Do you know where I could lay my hands on a copy of 'The History of Western Philosophy'?*
2 to catch or capture somebody: *The police had been trying to lay hands on them for months.*

by leaps and bounds

quickly and by large amounts: *Her English has improved by leaps and bounds over the past few weeks.*

leave somebody holding the baby or be left holding the baby

to leave somebody to deal with a problem *or* responsibility themselves, *or* to be left to do so

leave no stone unturned

to do everything that can be done to do something, especially to get information: *The government said it would leave no stone unturned in its search for the truth.*

lend an ear

to listen to what somebody has to say: *She's always lent a sympathetic ear to all my tales of woe.*

lend a hand

to help somebody: *Do you think they can manage on their own, or should we offer to lend a hand?*

let the cat out of the bag

to reveal a secret. Formerly, people who went to market to buy a pig were sometimes cheated by being given a cat in a sack instead. If they opened the sack, then the trick was revealed and they had 'let the cat out of the bag'. Compare a pig in a poke.

let your hair down

to completely relax and enjoy yourself freely

level-headed

sensible; having common sense

lift a finger

to make even the slightest effort: *I wouldn't lift a finger to help them.*

light-fingered

inclined to steal things

like anything

a great deal, very much, or with great effort: *It was so funny, we were laughing like anything.* An informal expression.

like-minded

having similar opinions, values, etc

the lion's share

the largest share: *Well, I did the lion's share of the work, didn't I?*

live from hand to mouth

to live with always just enough food and money to satisfy your immediate needs

not by a long chalk

not at all: *This work just isn't good enough. Not by a long chalk.*

a long face

a sad or gloomy look on your face

the long and the short of it

a summary of the facts or situation in a few words: *The long and the short of it is, I need more money.*

long-winded

boringly long; using too many words: *The subject of the talk was interesting enough, but the speaker was so long-winded I fell asleep.*

lose face

to lose other people's respect; to be shamed or humiliated

no love lost

no liking for one another: *There's no love lost between them, even though they're brothers.*

make an ass of yourself

to behave foolishly

make a beeline for something / somewhere

to go straight to it: *When he arrived at the party, he made a beeline for the kitchen.*

make believe

to pretend: *Let's make believe you're mummy and I'm daddy and the teddies are our children.*

make the best of something

to do the best with what you have, or accept an unpleasant or undesirable situation as well as you can: *Well, it's a pity it's raining but we'll just have to make the best of it.*

make somebody's blood boil

to make somebody very angry

make a clean breast of it / everything

to make a full confession

make ends meet

to manage to live on the money you have or earn

make somebody's flesh crawl / creep

to give somebody a feeling of disgust or horror: *That film really made my flesh creep.*

make the grade

to succeed

make somebody's hair stand on end

to terrify somebody: *I could tell you stories that would make your hair stand on end.*

make up your mind

to make a decision: *There's so many to choose from, I can't make up my mind.*

make your mouth water

to make you desire or anticipate something: *I saw some dresses that would make your mouth water.* The underlying idea is that the smell of food can make you produce saliva in your mouth. Something can be said to be **mouth-watering**: *a mouth-watering display of food.*

the man in the street
the ordinary man

meet your Waterloo
to be utterly defeated. The French emperor Napoleon was beaten by combined British and German forces at the battle of Waterloo in Belgium in 1815.

mind your own business
not to interfere in other people's affairs

mind-blowing
impressive; causing feelings of exhilaration: *a mind-blowing experience.* This is an informal expression.

mind-boggling
amazing. This is an informal expression.

a month of Sundays
a very long time

over the moon
absolutely delighted

mouth-watering
See make your mouth water

move heaven and earth
to do everything possible to achieve something

the naked eye
looking at something without the aid of a microscope, telescope, etc: *These insects are so small, they are barely visible to the naked eye.*

name-dropping
casually mentioning the names of famous people you know, or claim to know, in order to impress the people you are talking to: *As I was saying to the Prime Minister just the other day, I do hate name-dropping.*

narrow-minded
unable to accept ideas that are different from your own

neck of the woods
area; district: *You won't find any posh restaurants in this neck of the woods.* Originally an American term, a 'neck of the woods' was a settlement in the forest.

in the nick of time
just in time

under your nose
so close to you that you should see it: *I don't know how she managed to steal clothes from the shop right under my nose.*

there is nothing to it
it is very easy: *Look, there's nothing to it. You just twist the rope like this and pull.*

in a nutshell
briefly; to sum up a situation or story: *'So she was lying all the time!' 'That's it in a nutshell.'*

the odd one out
the thing or person that does not fit in with the rest of the group: *Which of the following words is the odd one out: cat, dog, horse, table?*

an old hand
an experienced person: *Don't worry. I'm an old hand at painting.*

once (and) for all
finally and definitely (allowing no further discussion or argument, or requiring no further action): *Once and for all, I'm going to the meeting and you're not! / This shampoo should get rid of your dandruff once and for all.*

once in a blue moon
once in a very long time. Very occasionally, the moon seems to have a bluish tinge.

with open arms
sincerely and with obvious pleasure: *We were welcomed with open arms.*

open-minded

willing to consider new ideas; not narrow-minded

open-mouthed

amazed: *They watched open-mouthed as the jugglers tossed swords to one another.*

the other day

a day not long ago: *I met him just the other day.*

out of date

not in the latest style; old-fashioned

out of hand

not under control: *The riot was getting out of hand.*

part and parcel

a necessary, and usually annoying or unpleasant, aspect of something: *I'm afraid having spots is part and parcel of being a teenager.*

pass the buck

to pass the responsibility for causing or dealing with a problem to somebody else. The 'buck' is an object passed from player to player in the game of poker.

pass the hat round

to take up a collection of money; to ask for contributions

pick somebody's brains

to ask for information from somebody about something they know a lot about

a piece of cake

something that is very easy to do

pig-headed

foolishly stubborn

a pig in a poke

1 something you have bought without seeing it first and which may turn out not to be as good as you expect. *See the note at* **let the cat out of the bag.**

2 a commitment made to something as yet not fully known: *This project is a bit of a pig in a poke. I know how much they're paying me, but I don't know how long it will take me to do it.*

pins and needles

a tingling feeling in a part of the body where the blood is beginning to flow freely after being constricted: *I've got pins and needles in my hand.*

in the pipeline

in preparation; being planned: *There are some major changes in the pipeline.*

play it by ear

to deal with a situation in a way that responds to what is happening at the time rather than by following a fixed plan you have made beforehand: *I don't know what I'm going to say to her. I'll just have to play it by ear.*

play with fire

to do something that is more risky than you think

play the game

to behave fairly

point-blank

1 direct; straightforward: *a point-blank refusal.*

2 directly; absolutely: *She refused point-blank to help.*

a poison-pen letter

an anonymous letter expressing hatred, threats, etc

poker-faced

with no expression on your face to give away your thoughts or feelings. A person playing poker must not allow the other players to see from the look on his face whether or not he has a good hand of cards

pour cold water on something

See throw cold water on something

a practical joke

a trick played on someone for amusement.

pros and cons

reasons for and against; benefits and drawbacks. The words come from Latin 'pro' meaning 'for' and 'contra' meaning 'against'.

pull your socks up

to try to do better than you have been doing: *If you don't pull your socks up, you'll fail your exams.*

pull somebody's leg

to tease somebody, or playfully make fun of them: *That can't be true. Surely he was pulling your leg.*

put somebody's back up

to annoy somebody: *What really put my back up was her claiming to have done most of the work.*

put your best foot forward

to make your best effort

put your cards on the table

See lay your cards on the table

put your foot down

to insist on something: *They weren't going to come but I put my foot down and said that they had to.*

put your foot in it

to say something foolish or embarrassing. 'It' refers to your mouth.

put the cart before the horse

See Don't put the cart before the horse in Unit 20.

put two and two together

to draw a conclusion from various facts

rain cats and dogs

to rain heavily

for a rainy day

for a time in the future when something, especially money, might be needed: *I'm not going to spend all this money now. I'll save some for a rainy day.*

read between the lines

to draw conclusions from what is not clearly stated

in the red

having spent more money than you have, and therefore, for example, owing money to your bank: *I can't take any money out of the bank because my account's in the red.* Formerly, when this happened, the sum you owed the bank was written in red ink on your bank statement.

red-carpet treatment

See roll out the red carpet

red-faced

blushing from embarrassment or shame

a red-letter day

an important or memorable day. Formerly, important church celebrations were indicated in red on church calendars.

red tape

official rules or procedures that are strictly adhered to

a right-hand man

a trusted assistant

rock the boat

to cause trouble for yourself or others: *I wasn't happy about the decision, but I certainly wasn't going to rock the boat by complaining.*

roll out the red carpet

to make a great effort to entertain a visitor very well. A red carpet is sometimes put out for an important visitor to walk on. You can also talk of giving somebody **the red-carpet treatment**.

roll up your sleeves

to get ready to make a great effort

through rose-coloured / rose-tinted glasses / spectacles / lenses

in a too optimistic way: *She looks at the world through rose-tinted spectacles*

a rude awakening

a sudden and unpleasant experience that forces you to see the truth about something: *You think you can pass your exams without doing any work. Well, one of these days you'll get a rude awakening!*

a rule of thumb

an approximate rule that can be used as a rough guide: *As a rule of thumb, I allow three cups of water for every cup of rice.* This phrase refers to the use of your thumb to make approximate measurements.

run a mile

to run away; to try to escape from a situation: *She'd run a mile if anyone suggested she should sing a solo at the concert.*

in the same boat

in the same awkward or unpleasant situation: *There's no point in complaining about paying income tax. We're all in the same boat.*

not a sausage

nothing at all

save face

to avoid shame or humiliation

scatterbrained

forgetful and disorganized: *a scatterbrained person.* You can say that somebody is a scatterbrain.

scot-free

free from expense, injury, punishment, etc

from scratch

from the very beginning: *If the plans are wrong, we'll have to start from scratch again.* The 'scratch' was a line scratched in the ground from which runners in a race started.

second childhood

childish behaviour in old age: *My husband has started playing with toy trains. Must be his second childhood.*

second thoughts

reconsideration; a change of plan or opinion: *On second thoughts, perhaps we shouldn't go after all. / I think she's having second thoughts.*

second-hand

that has been owned and used by somebody else: *a second-hand car.*

see the back of somebody / something

to get rid of them/it: *I've had friends staying with me for two weeks now. I love them dearly but I'll be glad to see the back of them on Saturday.*

see eye to eye

to think alike; to agree

see the light

to suddenly understand, accept or believe something after not doing so: *One day her boss will see the light and realize how much she does for him.*

see red

to become very angry

see things

to imagine that you are seeing something that in fact is not there: *'There's a man walking about in the garden!' 'Don't be silly , there's no-one there. You're just seeing things.'*

a sharp tongue

a tendency to say bad-tempered or sarcastic things

on a shoe-string

with very little money

short-handed

having fewer people to do the work than is normal or necessary

a shot in the dark

a wild guess: *In a sense, every marriage is a shot in the dark.*

show a clean pair of heels

to escape by running away quickly; to move ahead and way from somebody quickly

show your face

to appear somewhere where you would be unwelcome or unexpected: *He wouldn't dare show his face around here again after the way he behaved the last time.*

a sight for sore eyes

somebody or something you are very glad to see

single-handed

on your own; without help or company: *He's intending to sail round the world single-handed.*

single-minded

with only one aim or purpose in mind: *She's very single-minded. She intends to be a success, and everything she does, she does with that in mind.*

sit on the fence

to avoid taking sides in a dispute; to avoid making a decision.

sixth sense

the power of intuition, or some sense or awareness that you cannot explain: *Her sixth sense told her she was being followed.* The five senses are sight, hearing, smell, taste and touch.

a skeleton in the cupboard / closet

a shameful secret from your past: *Americans are beginning to wonder if they can find any president who doesn't have some skeletons in his closet.*

by the skin of your teeth

very narrowly; only just: *I got away by the skin of my teeth.*

a slip of the tongue

a mistake made in speaking

small fry

a person or people of little importance: *What makes you think she'd be concerned about small fry like you?*

the small hours

the hours immediately after midnight

small talk

conversation about matters of little importance

smell a rat

to have a suspicion that something about a situation is not quite right: *He's being nice to us. I smell a rat. He wants us to do something for him.*

smooth-tongued

flattering or persuasive

a snake in the grass

somebody who cannot be trusted

soft-hearted

kind and generous

something else

special; notable: *Their house is something else.* This is an informal expression.

in the soup

in trouble: *If she catches you in her office, you'll really be in the soup.*

sour grapes

saying that you don't want something or that it isn't very good simply because you can't have it in any case: *She says she wouldn't have wanted to go to the party anyway, but that's just sour grapes because she wasn't invited.* In an ancient Greek story, a fox who cannot reach some juicy grapes he wants to eat walks away saying that he can see that the grapes are sour anyway.

spine-chilling

frightening: *a spine-chilling story of murder in a remote village*

the spitting image of somebody

an exact likeness of a person: *He's the spitting image of his father.* This odd phrase comes from an earlier phrase 'spit and image', in which 'spit' means somebody so like another that it is as if he had been spat out of the other person's mouth.

split hairs

to argue over small details or make trivial distinctions between things that are essentially the same: *Arguing about whether his remarks were really racist or not is just splitting hairs.*

a square meal

a good satisfying meal

square one

the beginning or starting-point: *We thought we'd got our house sold, but the deal fell through and we found ourselves back at square one.*

a square peg in a round hole

somebody unsuited to the particular position they occupy or job they are doing

stand your ground

See hold your ground

a stone's throw

a short distance: *Their house is just a stone's throw from the beach.*

a storm in a teacup

a great deal of fuss about something unimportant

a straight face

a serious expression, not smiling or laughing: *It was hard to say that with a straight face. / I don't know how you managed to keep a straight face.*

suit somebody down to the ground

to suit somebody perfectly: *That dress suits her down to the ground, doesn't it?*

sweep the board

to win everything

take the biscuit

to be the best, worst, strangest, etc example of something: *I've heard some ridiculous suggestions this morning, but that one really takes the biscuit.*

take the bull by the horns

to grapple boldly with danger or a difficulty

take something with a grain / pinch of salt

not to believe something entirely; to be sceptical about it: *He says his father was a war hero, but I'd take that with a pinch of salt.*

a tall order

something difficult to achieve; an unreasonable request: *'He wants us to finish this by tomorrow night.' 'That's a bit of a tall order.'*

a tall story

an unbelievable story; a lie

tender-hearted

kind; feeling pity and sympathy

through thick and thin

no matter what happens; in both good times and bad times: *He has supported this company through thick and thin.*

thick-skinned

not easily upset by insults or criticism

thin air

nowhere: *My wallet just disappeared into thin air (= completely disappeared). / The magician seemed to produce the rabbit out of thin air.*

the thin end of the wedge

a small detail or action that may be leading to something much greater, especially something undesirable: *Building a small dam is just the thin end of the wedge. They're clearly intending to flood the whole valley eventually.*

thin on the ground

not very common; scarce: *Good accountants are thin on the ground these days.*

thin-skinned

easily upset by insults or criticism

throw / pour cold water on something

to be discouraging about a proposal, plan, etc

throw the book at somebody

to reprimand somebody severely for doing wrong: *If he finds out you've not been filling out these forms correctly, he'll throw the book at you.*

throw caution to the wind

to take a risk; to decide not to be cautious

throw in the sponge / towel

to give up; to surrender. In boxing, throwing the boxer's towel or sponge into the ring means that the boxer is admitting defeat.

tight-fisted

mean with money: *You won't get any money out of him, the tight-fisted old miser.*

tight-lipped

refusing to speak; refusing to give information: *No matter how much they threatened her, she remained tight-lipped about what she knew of the plot.*

a tight spot / corner

a difficult situation

tighten your belt

to reduce the amount you spend: *Now that your father has been made redundant, we'll all have to tighten our belts.*

behind the times

not aware of changes; old-fashioned

tongue-tied

unable to speak because of shyness, embarrassment, etc. In a more technical sense, to be tongue-tied is to be unable to speak properly because your tongue cannot move freely in your mouth.

a tough customer

a difficult person to deal with or please

tread on somebody's toes

to offend somebody by doing something that they consider to be their responsibility

turn a blind eye to something

to pretend not to see something; to ignore it: *The management turn a blind eye to minor pilfering by the staff.*

turn a deaf ear to something

to ignore something you hear; not to listen to it: *He turns a deaf ear to all our complaints.*

not turn a hair

to show no surprise, fear or dismay when something happens: *When some crazy guy rushed into the room waving a sword, she didn't turn a hair.*

turn over a new leaf

to start behaving in a better way than before

turn tail

to turn around (and run away): *When the police arrived, the rioters turned tail and fled.*

in the twinkling of an eye

in a moment; very quickly

two-faced

hypocritical

under somebody's thumb

under somebody's control

up and about

to be out of bed and able to walk, for example after a period of illness: *The doctor says you'll be up and about again by next week.*

get / have the upper hand

to gain/have control

ups and downs

good and bad parts, times of success and failure or of happiness and unhappiness: *Life has its ups and downs.*

upset the apple-cart

to throw plans into confusion

walk on air

to be very happy: *After her engagement, she was walking on air for weeks.*

warm-hearted

kind and sympathetic

wash your hands of somebody / something

to refuse to take responsibility for somebody/something: *If you won't listen to my advice, I wash my hands of the whole affair.*

under the weather

not very well; slightly ill

a wet blanket

a person who spoils other people's fun or dampens their enthusiasm by being boring or unenthusiastic or over-cautious: *'There's no point in going for a walk. It's bound to rain.' 'Oh, don't be such a wet blanket!'*

a white elephant

something useless, unused or unwanted, especially if it is also expensive to keep: *They built a large new office for the company but it's a bit of a white elephant because they've now had to sack half their staff.* It is said the kings of Siam (Thailand) would give white elephants to courtiers they wished to ruin, since such elephants were expensive to look after.

whole-hearted

sincere and enthusiastic: *You can count on my whole-hearted support.*

a wild-goose chase

any foolish or useless attempt to find or fetch someone or something

wipe the slate clean

to make a fresh start, ignoring past mistakes, problems, etc: *I know we've been enemies up till now, but let's wipe the slate clean and see if we can work together.*

by word of mouth

by somebody telling you when speaking to you, and then you telling someone else: *The story spread by word of mouth.*

DO IT YOURSELF

A Rewrite the following sentences using idioms that have the same meaning as the phrases in italics. The idioms will be found in entries for the words in brackets.

Example:

He went through the procedure from *beginning to end*. (A)

He went through the procedure from A to Z.

---

1. Life was not *easy* in those days. (bed)

2. The two girls agreed to *stop quarrelling*. (bury)

3. When she was invited to meet the Queen, she was *very happy*. (cloud)

4. She's got a superb car but it must have been *very expensive*. (cost)

5. She told me what the car cost. I thought it was a *ridiculous price* to pay. (daylight)

6. I told her she would never pass her driving test, but I had to *admit I'd been wrong* when she did pass. (eat)

7. It was a very expensive restaurant so my girlfriend insisted that we *each paid for our own food*. (go)

8. I only meant to buy one new suit, but they were *being sold at a very low price*, so I ended up buying three. (go)

9. There is no avoiding the question of money, so we are just going to have to *deal with it firmly*. (grasp)

10. Exactly! You have *pinpointed the problem*. (hit)

11. When we reached the shop, my wife *went straight* to the cosmetics counter. (make)

12. My daughter was *very pleased* when she heard she had got into university. (moon)

13. Writing computer programs is *very easy*. (piece)

14. You can't go outside to play. It's raining *very heavily*. (rain)

15. My father taught me always to put some of my salary in a bank account *in case I needed it some day*. (rainy)

16. When he suggested I was mistaken, I *became very angry*. (see)

B Choose the correct phrase from the alternatives given.

1. If you are the *apple of someone's eye*, they (envy you, love you, dislike you).

2. If you have *a bee in your bonnet* about something, you are (very concerned about it, very fond of it).

3. If something is *child's play*, it is (boring, childish, easy).

4. *Till the cows come home* means (until tomorrow, until this evening, forever).

5. *As the crow flies* means (in a circle, in a straight line).

6. To *fly off the handle* is to (burst out laughing, burst into tears, become very angry).

7. To *get out of bed on the wrong side* is to be (in a bad mood, slightly confused, very sleepy)

8. To *give someone a piece of your mind* is to (give them some advice, give them a scolding, give them some information).

9. If you *let the cat out of the bag*, you (give away a secret, give someone a present, allow someone to leave).

10. If you do something *once in a blue moon*, you do it (frequently, very rarely, once a month, once a year).

11. If you tell someone to *pull their socks up*, you mean you want them to (get dressed, improve their performance).

12. If you *see eye to eye* with someone, you are (quarrelling, in agreement).

13. To *sit on the fence* is to (relax, worry, be undecided).

14. If you are *in the soup*, you are (in trouble, safe, pleased).

15. A *wild-goose chase* is (a children's game, a hunting expedition, a pointless attempt at finding something).

16. If you are *under the weather*, you are feeling (very ill, slightly ill).

19 ▶ Similes

A **simile** is an expression that makes a comparison between two things using the words **as** or **like**.

While similes are fairly fixed phrases, some variations are possible. For example, in some cases, when the simile refers to one person or thing, the noun following the second **as** will be singular while if it refers to more than one person or thing, the noun will be plural: *The little boy was **as busy as a bee** all morning* but *The children were **as busy as bees** all morning*. This is of course not the case where the noun following the **as** refers to a general substance, for example, *The cake was **as hard as iron*** and *The cakes were **as hard as iron***.

Note also that the first **as** may often be omitted: ***Cool as a cucumber**, she took out a knife and cut the string.*

Similes with *as*

as agile as a cat / as a monkey
    very agile

as ancient as the hills / as the stars
    very old

as bald as a coot
    totally bald. A coot is a water bird rather like a duck. It is not bald, but has a patch of white skin above its bill that contrasts vividly with its dark plumage.

as black as the ace of spades / as coal / as hell / as ink / as midnight / as night / as pitch / as soot / as a starless night
    black in colour

as black as thunder
    black in colour (the sky becomes very dark when a thunderstorm is brewing); *also* showing anger: *Her face was as black as thunder when she heard the news.*

as blind as a bat / as a mole / as an owl
    completely blind, or not able to see very well. In fact, none of these creatures is blind.

as bold as a lion
    very brave

as bold as brass
    without fear, but also showing an element of impudence: *He went up to her as bold as brass and kissed her on the cheek.*

as bright as a button / as a new penny
    clever, lively: *Our little granddaughter's as bright as a button, and copies everything we do.*

as bright as day / as a star
    not dark

as bright as a new penny / as a new pin
    shiny, clean

as brittle as glass
    very brittle; easily broken

as brown as a berry
    very brown; suntanned: *The whole family came back from their holiday as brown as berries.*

as busy as an ant / as a beaver / as a bee
    very busy: *The children have been as busy as bees this morning, decorating the classroom for the party.* These creatures are traditionally considered to work very hard.

as calm as a cat / as death
    not worried

as calm as a millpond
    with a smooth surface: *The sea was as calm as a millpond.* Formerly, a millpond was a pond that held the water needed to make the wheel of a mill go round.

as changeable as the weather
    very changeable. In some parts of the world, weather conditions are very unpredictable and change frequently.

as cheap as dirt
    very cheap: *Good-quality carpets are as cheap as dirt in some North African markets.* You can also say that something is dirt-cheap.

as cheerless as the grave
    sad or depressing: *The view was as cheerless as the grave.*

as clean as a new pin / as a whistle
very clean, with no trace or dirt or dust: *The whole house was spotless, as clean as a new pin.*

as clean as a whistle
bare, with no trace of anything else: *He scraped the meat off the bones until they were as clean as a whistle.* Also with no ragged parts: *The axe cut through the branch as clean as a whistle.*

as clear as a bell
not muffled: *The sound rang out as clear as a bell.*

as clear as crystal / as day / as daylight
obvious or clearly understood.

as clear as crystal / as glass
transparent

as clear as mud
not at all clear: *Even with his diagrams, the procedure is still as clear as mud to me.*

as cold as charity / as death / as ice / as marble / as the grave
not hot

as cold as charity / as ice
not friendly

as common as dirt
existing in large numbers; easy to find

as common as dirt / as muck
not polite or well brought up; coarse: *He's a real gentleman but his wife's as common as muck.*

as cool as a cucumber
completely cool. 'Cool' usually in the sense of 'calm', but also in the sense of 'not hot'.

as countless as the desert sands / as the hairs on one's head / as the sands on the shore / as the stars
more than can be counted

as crafty as a fox
very crafty. Foxes are traditionally thought to be very cunning animals.

as cross as two sticks
very cross. Perhaps a play on words, from two sticks forming the shape of a cross.

as cunning as a fox
see as crafty as a fox

as daft as a brush
foolish, or insane. The original phrase was as soft as a brush, 'soft' in this sense meaning 'foolish' or 'silly' in English dialect.

as dead as a dodo / as the dodo / as a doornail / as mutton
completely dead. The dodo is an extinct species of bird.

as deaf as an adder / as a post
very deaf. An adder is a type of snake. Snakes have no sense of hearing.

as different as chalk and cheese
totally different from one another. Chalk and cheese are very different in texture. You can also say that two people or things are like chalk and cheese.

as drunk as a lord / as an owl / as a skunk
very drunk. A nobleman, being rich, could afford to drink as much alcohol as he wanted, and so get drunk. 'Skunk' is probably used just because it rhymes with 'drunk'. It is not clear why owls should have been taken as an example of drunkenness, though.

as dry as a bone / as dust
not wet

as dry as paper
unhealthily or uncomfortably dry: *My mouth's as dry as paper.*

as dry as dust
boring: *His speech was as dry as dust.*

as dull as ditch-water
very boring: *The show was as dull as ditch-water.* Water in a ditch is usually muddy and brown.

as easy as ABC / as falling off a log / as one two three / as pie / as winking
very easy

as fat as a pig
very fat, too fat

as fierce as a lion / as a tiger
very fierce

as firm as a rock
absolutely firm

as fit as a fiddle
completely fit; in good health

as flat as a board / as a pancake
completely flat

as free as a bird
completely free

as fresh as new paint / as paint
not old, or not dirty

as fresh as a daisy
not tired: *In spite of having had only two hours sleep, she was as fresh as a daisy in the morning.*

as gentle as a lamb
very gentle

as good as gold
very well-behaved

as graceful as a swan
very graceful, as swans are when they are swimming.

as green as you are cabbage-looking
Always with 'not'. 'Green' in this sense means 'not wise or experienced'. If somebody is 'not as green as they're cabbage-looking', they are cleverer or wiser than they seem.

as happy as the day is long / as a lark / as Larry / as a pig in clover / as a pig in muck / as a sandboy
very happy. A sandboy was a boy who sold sand. It is not recorded who Larry was.

as hard as iron / as nails / as rock / as steel / as stone
very hard

as harmless as a baby / as a dove
totally harmless

as heavy as an elephant / as lead
very heavy

as helpless as a baby / as a child / as a newborn babe
completely helpless: *If the car broke down, she'd be as helpless as a baby.*

as high as the sky
not low, not near the ground

as high as a kite
very excited: *The children were all as high as kites on the day of the party.*

as honest as the day as long
totally honest

as hot as a furnace / as hell
very hot

as hungry as a bear / as a hunter / as a wolf
very hungry

as innocent as a baby / as a child / as a dove / as a lamb / as a newborn babe

totally innocent, both in the sense of 'not guilty' or in the sense of 'naïve'.

as keen as mustard

very enthusiastic

as large as life

actually present: *We were just talking about him, and in he came as large as life.*

as light as air / as a fairy / as a feather / as thistledown

not heavy

as light as day

bright

as like as two peas in a pod

very alike

as lively as a cricket

very lively. A cricket is an insect like a grasshopper.

as loud as thunder

very loud

as mad as a hatter / as a March hare

crazy. A hatter is a person who makes hats. A chemical once used in hat-making caused brain damage, and hatters were known for being slightly mad. Male hares in springtime seem to behave rather madly as well when they are looking for a mate.

as mad as a hornet

very angry. A hornet is a large wasp.

as meek as a lamb

very meek

as merry as a cricket / as a grig / as a lark

very merry or happy. As merry as a grig is rather old-fashioned. 'Grig' is an old word for a grasshopper.

as mischievous as a monkey

rather mischievous.

as miserable as sin

very unhappy: *He was looking as miserable as sin as he went into the exam room.*

as neat as a button / as a pin

very neat

as nice as pie

very friendly: *He can be as nice as pie and then suddenly bite your head off.*

as nutty as a fruitcake

crazy. There is a play on words here based on the nuts you find in a fruitcake.

as obstinate as a mule

very obstinate. Mules are traditionally thought of as stubborn animals.

as old as the hills / as Methuselah / as time

very old. According to the story in the Bible, Methuselah (pronounced /məˈθjuːzələ/) was Noah's grandfather and lived for 969 years.

as pale as ashes / as death / as a ghost

very pale

as patient as Job

very patient. Job (pronounced /dʒoʊb/) was a man who according to a story in the Bible suffered great misfortune, including losing all his possessions and his children, and bore his sufferings with great patience.

as plain as the nose on your face / as a pikestaff

very obvious. A pikestaff was a long thin pole with a sort of spear at the end, formerly used as a weapon.

as plain as a pikestaff

very plain in appearance; not beautiful or handsome: *I don't know why he's marrying her. She's as plain as a pikestaff.*

as playful as a kitten / as a puppy

very playful, as young animals are.

as pleased as Punch / as a dog with two tails

very pleased. Punch is a character in a puppet show who is always very pleased with himself.

as poor as a church mouse / as Job

very poor. A mouse that lives in a church will not have so much to eat as a mouse that lives in a house or a barn. For a note on 'Job', *see* as patient as Job.

as pretty as a picture

very pretty

as proud as a peacock

very proud. Peacocks seem to strut around proudly when they are displaying to female birds.

as pure as the driven snow

morally pure; often used ironically to mean just the opposite: *Her? She's as pure as the driven snow.*

as quiet as a lamb

peaceful

as quiet as the grave / as a mouse

silent

as quick as a flash / as lightning

very quickly

as rare as hen's teeth

very rare. Hens, of course, being birds, have no teeth.

as regular as clockwork

completely regular

as rich as Croesus

very rich. Croesus (pronounced /ˈkriːsəs/) was a rich and powerful king of Lydia, in what is now Turkey, in the 6th century BC.

as right as rain

all right; not ill or harmed: *Despite her fall, she was as right as rain next day.*

as safe as houses

completely safe: *Investments like that are as safe as houses.*

as sharp as a needle / as a razor

having a sharp point or sharp edge

as sharp as a needle / as a tack

very clever or cunning

as sick as a cat / as a dog

physically sick; vomiting

as sick as a parrot

disappointed or upset. An informal expression

as silent as the grave

completely silent

as simple as ABC / as one two three

very simple

as slippery as an eel / as ice

very slippery

as slow as death / as a snail / as a tortoise

very slow

as sly as a fox

very sly. Compare as crafty as a fox.

as smart as paint

very clever or quick to understand things: *He's as smart as paint, that one. He always sees exactly what needs to be done.*

as smooth as a baby's bottom / as a billiard ball / as glass / as satin / as velvet

completely smooth.

as snug as a bug in a rug

very comfortable: *Don't worry about me. I'll be as snug as a bug in a rug in this tent.*

as sober as a judge

completely sober; not drunk; *also* very solemn or serious: *I wonder if he ever laughs. He's always as sober as a judge when you speak to him.*

as solemn as an owl

very solemn. Owls look very serious.

as soft as butter / as a kiss / as a sigh / as silk / as a whisper

very soft

as solid as a rock

absolutely solid

as sound as a bell

in good condition: *I've been to see the doctor and he says I'm as sound as a bell.*

as sour as vinegar

very sour

as steady as a rock

completely steady, both in the sense of 'not moving or rocking' and 'firm of mind, loyal, sensible, not liable to panic': *That's fixed the table. It's as steady as a rock now. / Others were beginning to lose their nerve, but she remained as steady as a rock.*

as stiff as a board / as a poker / as a ramrod

rigidly upright in posture. A ramrod is a pole used for cleaning a gun or for pushing explosive charges down a gun barrel.

as stiff as a poker

formal in manner; not relaxed and friendly: *He was clearly not comfortable at the party and remained as stiff as a poker all evening.*

as still as death / as the grave / as a post / as a statue

not moving or making a sound; without anything moving or making a sound: *The streets were as still as the grave. / She stood as still as a statue, not wanting to frighten the bird away.*

as straight as an arrow / as a die / as a ramrod

absolutely straight. For a note on 'ramrod', *see* as stiff as a ramrod.

as straight as a die

honest. A 'die' in this sense is a dice you use in playing various games.

as strong as a bull / as a horse / as a lion / as an ox

very strong

as stubborn as a mule

very stubborn. Compare as obstinate as a mule.

as sure as death / as eggs is eggs / as fate / as night follows day

absolutely certain. As sure as eggs is eggs is rather informal, as shown by the non-standard English 'eggs is eggs'.

as sweet as honey / as sugar
very sweet

as swift as an arrow
very fast

**as thick as a brick /
as two short planks**
not intelligent. This is an informal expression.

as thick as thieves
very friendly with one another.

as thin as a rake
very thin, as the long handle of a rake is.

as timid as a mouse
very timid, as mice are.

as tough as leather / as old boots
not tender; hard to chew

as tough as nails / as old boots
strong in mind or body: *She looks frail but she's really as tough as nails.*

as ugly as sin
very ugly

as vain as a peacock
very vain. Compare *as proud as a peacock.*

as warm as toast
comfortably warm: *Outside it was snowing but we were as warm as toast in the hut.*

as weak as a baby / as a kitten
very weak

**as white as marble / as milk /
as snow**
pure white; very white

**as white as chalk / as a ghost /
as a sheet**
very pale, for example from illness or shock: *Suddenly she turned as white as a sheet and collapsed on the floor.*

**as wise as an owl / as a serpent /
as Solomon**
very wise. Solomon was a king of Israel in the 10th century BC who was reputed to be very wise. Owls and snakes are both traditionally thought of as wise animals.

as wriggly as a worm
wriggling a lot: *It's hard changing the baby's nappy. She's as wriggly as a worm.*

Similes with *like*

like ants
If people swarm like ants round something, they move around it in large numbers.

like something out of the ark
very old-fashioned. The ark is Noah's ark in the Bible.

like a baby
If you sleep like a baby, you sleep very soundly. If you cry like a baby, you cry intensely.

like the back of your hand
If you know something like the back of your hand, you know it very well.

like a bad penny
If you say that somebody will turn up like a bad penny, you mean that they will be sure to appear when or where they are not wanted. A 'bad penny' is a counterfeit coin: the expression comes from the idea that if you use such a coin to pay for something, you may get it back again one day from somebody else.

like a bat out of hell

very quickly: *They got such a fright, they were out of the house like a bat out of hell.*

like a bear with a sore head

bad-tempered; in a bad mood: *Careful! The boss is like a bear with a sore head this morning.*

like bees round a honey-pot

enthusiastically and in great numbers: *Photographers swarmed round her like bees round a honey-pot.*

like a bird

If you eat like a bird, you eat very little.

like getting blood out of a stone / like trying to get blood out of a stone

Said of something that is very difficult or almost impossible: *Getting the facts out of them was like getting blood out of a stone.*

like a bolt from the blue

suddenly and unexpectedly. *See also* a bolt from the blue under *Common Idioms* on page 344.

like a bomb

If something goes like a bomb, it goes very fast, very well, or very successfully.

like a book

If you can read somebody like a book, you understand what they are thinking and feeling.

like a bull in a china shop

very clumsy or rough, or clumsily or roughly; *also* insensitive(ly) or tactless(ly). *See also* a bull in a china shop under *Common Idioms* on page 345.

like a candle

as easily and completely as when a candle is extinguished: *The roof suddenly collapsed and her life was snuffed out like a candle.*

like cat and dog

If two people fight like cat and dog, they are always fighting or arguing.

like a cat on hot bricks / like a cat on a hot tin roof

excited or anxious; unable to relax or sit still

like the cat that got the cream

very pleased with yourself

like something the cat brought in

looking very untidy: *Go and comb your hair. You look like something the cat brought in.*

like chalk and cheese

completely different from one another. Compare as different as chalk and cheese on page 367.

like a charm

If something works like a charm, it works perfectly.

like a Cheshire cat

If you are grinning like a Cheshire cat, you have a wide grin on your face. The Cheshire cat is a smiling cat character in Lewis Carroll's book *Alice in Wonderland* that gradually disappears until all that is left of it is its smile.

like a chimney

If you smoke like a chimney, you smoke a great deal: *He smokes like a chimney. You never see him without a cigarette.*

like the clappers

If you go like the clappers, you go very quickly or do something very energetically. This is an informal expression.

like clockwork

perfectly; as planned; without problems.

like the dead

To sleep like the dead is to sleep soundly.

like death warmed over or up

awful; very ill or very tired: *You look like death warmed over. What's the matter with you?*

like the devil / the dickens

very quickly or very energetically: *You'll need to run like the devil to catch the bus now.*

like dirt

If somebody treats you like dirt, they treat you very badly, without respect or consideration.

like a dog

If you work like a dog, you work very hard. If somebody treats you like a dog, they treat you very badly.

like a dog with two tails

very pleased or proud: *He was like a dog with two tails when the elected him chairman.* Compare as pleased as a dog with two tails on page 370.

like a dog's dinner

If you are dressed up like a dog's dinner, you are dressed in clothes that are too smart or fancy.

like a dream come true

as exciting or pleasing as getting something you have been dreaming of: *Meeting the Queen was like a dream come true.*

like a duck to water

If you take to something like a duck to water, you learn it very quickly or show a natural aptitude for it, or you fit in very quickly to a new situation such as a new job: *She took to teaching like a duck to water.*

like fighting cocks

If you live like fighting cocks, you live very well, with the best of everything.

like a fish

Somebody who drinks like a fish drinks a great deal, especially alcoholic drinks.

like a fish out of water

If you feel or look like a fish out of water, you feel or look very uncomfortable because you are in an unaccustomed situation or somewhere where you do not fit in or think that you do not: *I felt like a fish out of water at the party.*

like a galley slave

Somebody who works like a galley slave works very hard.

like a glove

If something, for example a piece of clothing, fits like a glove, it fits perfectly.

like greased lightening

very quickly.

like grim death

If you hang on or hold on like grim death, you hold on very tightly.

like a headless chicken

Somebody who is running around like a headless chicken is rushing around frantically doing things without any system or order, for example because they have too many things to do.

like a horse

If you work like a horse, you work very hard; if you eat like a horse, you eat a great deal.

like hot cakes

If things are selling or going like hot cakes, they are selling in large numbers or very quickly.

like a hot potato

If you drop somebody or something like a hot potato, you abandon them or it very quickly and abruptly: *When the Government realized how much opposition there was to the bill, they dropped it like a hot potato.*

like a house on fire

very well: *I was getting on like a house on fire with this project until my computer crashed. / I'm very fond of Jane. We get on like a house on fire.*

like Kilkenny cats

People who fight like Kilkenny cats fight very bitterly. This expression is now rather dated. Kilkenny (pronounced /kɪlˈkeni/) is a town in Ireland. The story is told that two cats in Kilkenny were once tied together by their tails and left to fight each other.

like a knife through butter

smoothly and cleanly: *The saw went through the wood like a knife through butter.*

like a lamb

meekly and obediently, without complaining or protesting.

like a lead balloon

If a remark or suggestion goes down like a lead balloon, it is not very popular or well received: *His jokes about mothers-in-law went down like a lead balloon.*

like a leaf

If somebody is shaking like a leaf, they are trembling or shaking a lot, like a leaf does when blown in the wind.

like a log

If you sleep like a log, you sleep very soundly.

like magic

If something works like magic, it works very well: *Two aspirins cleared my headache like magic.*

like a mill pond

calm and smooth: *There was no wind and the sea was like a mill pond.* Compare as calm as a millpond on page 366.

like nobody's business

very hard, very well, or very frequently: *The phone's been ringing like nobody's business all morning.*

like rabbits

To breed like rabbits is to have large numbers of babies.

like a red rag to a bull

If something is like a red rag to a bull to someone, it is likely to provoke great resentment or a violent reaction from them: *With John, any mention of socialism was like a red rag to a bull.*

like sardines

If people or things are packed in like sardines, they are crowded very close together: *There were so many people at the meeting that we were packed into the hall like sardines.* Sardines are small fish that are usually sold in tins in which they are packed very tightly together.

like a scalded cat

very quickly, especially because of fear or pain: *He was off like a scalded cat when he thought he saw a ghost.*

like sheep

To follow like sheep is to follow blindly, without thinking.

like a shot

very quickly or eagerly: *When the cat saw the dog approaching, it was off like a shot. / If they asked me to go, I'd do it like a shot.*

like a sieve

To have a memory like a sieve is to be very forgetful.

like a sore thumb

Somebody or something that sticks out like a sore thumb is very noticeable.

like a stone

To drop like a stone is to drop heavily and straight down, as a stone does.

like a ton of bricks

very heavily or severely. If you come down on somebody like a ton of bricks, you reprimand them severely: *If I didn't get you to sign this bit of paper, the boss would be down on me like a ton of bricks.*

like a top

If you sleep like a top, you sleep soundly. Something that spins like a top spins round and round very fast.

like a Trojan

Somebody who works like a Trojan (pronounced /ˈtroʊdʒən/) works very hard. The Trojans were the people of Troy, an ancient city in what is now Turkey that was destroyed by the Greeks in the 13th century BC.

like a trooper

Somebody who swears like a trooper uses a lot of swearwords.

like water

If you spend money like water, you spend a great deal of money very quickly.

like water off a duck's back

making no impression at all on somebody: *I keep on telling him to tidy his room, but it's like water off a duck's back.*

like wildfire

Something that spreads like wildfire spreads very quickly. Panic and rumours, for example, may spread like wildfire.

like the wind

If you run like the wind, you run very quickly.

DO IT YOURSELF

A Complete the similes in the following sentences.

1. If a person is bald, they are *as bald as a c_____* .

2. If a person can't see very well, they are *as blind as a b_____* .

3. If the sea is very flat, it can be said to be *as calm as a m_____* .

4. If someone is very cunning, you can say that they are *as cunning as a f_____* .

5. You can say that someone who is very deaf is *as deaf as a p_____* .

6. Two people who are very unlike each other can be said to be *as different as c_____ and c_____* .

7. If you are in good health, you may say that you feel *as fit as a f_____* .

8. A well-behaved child may be said to be *as good as g_____* .

9. If you are very happy, you may be said to be *as happy as L_____* .

10. If you are very enthusiastic, someone may say that you are *as keen as m_____* .

11. Two people that are very alike are *as like as two p_____ in a p_____* .

12. Someone who is very old may be said to be *as old as the h_____* .

13. If you are very pleased about something, you are *as pleased as P_____* .

14. If something happens very quickly, it happens *as quick as a f_____* .

15. Something that is very safe is *as safe as h_____* .

16. If you are very obstinate, someone may say that you are being *as stubborn as a m_____* .

17. Someone who is not very intelligent may be described as being *as thick as t_____ s_____ p_____* .

18. Someone who is very wise may be said *as wise as S_____* .

B Complete the similes in the following sentences.

1. If you know something very well, you know it *like the
    b_____ of your h_____ .*

2. If you are in a bad mood, someone may say that you are
    going round *like a b_____ with sore h_____ .*

3. If you are very clumsy and are forever knocking things over,
    you may be told that you are *like a b_____ in a
    c_____ s_____ .*

4. If you have a big smile on your face, you are grinning *like a
    C_____ c_____ .*

5. If things go as planned, they *go like c_____ .*

6. If you find an occupation that suits you very well, you may
    take to it *like a d_____ to w_____ .*

7. Something that is very popular and sells very quickly *goes
    like h_____ c_____ .*

8. Someone who is trembling may be said to be shaking *like a
    l_____ .*

9. If you work very hard, you work *like a T_____ .*

10. If something spreads very quickly over a wide area, it
    spreads *like w_____ .*

20 ▶ Proverbs and Sayings

Proverbs are traditional sayings that give advice or moral opinions, make comments about the world, or state general truths. Many come from the Bible or well-known poems.

How to use the lists

▶ There are three things to note about proverbs:

- Since many proverbs are traditional sayings dating back many centuries, the words used are sometimes rather old-fashioned or have out-of-date meanings, for example, **Handsome is as handsome does** (in which **handsome** means 'gracious', not 'good-looking') or **There's many a slip 'twixt cup and lip** (in which **twixt** means 'between').

- Many proverbs are found in more than one form. It is impossible to give all the variant forms in a book of this size, but some are noted below. If a word is given in brackets, it can be omitted from the proverb. Thus **A bad workman (always) blames his tools** means that you can say either **A bad workman blames his tools** or **A bad workman always blames his tools**. Slashes separating words also indicate possible variants, for example, **A little knowledge / learning is a dangerous thing** means that you can say either **A little knowledge is a dangerous thing** or **A little learning is a dangerous thing**.

- Since proverbs are well-known sayings, it is not always necessary to quote them in full when you are using them. For example, instead of saying **It's an ill wind that blows nobody any good**, you could just say **It's an ill wind**, because you expect the people you are talking to to know the full saying and to understand what you mean.

▶ Since proverbs may occur in different forms, for example, **A barking dog seldom bites** or **Barking dogs seldom bite**, they have been entered in the lists in order of their first main word rather than just the first word. Where necessary, cross-references have been added.

Absence makes the heart grow fonder

When you have to be away from somebody for a while, you love them all the more.

Accidents will happen

It is to be expected that accidents will happen from time to time. Usually said to forgive somebody who has caused an accident or to excuse oneself for having done so.

There is no accounting for taste

One cannot explain why different people like different things. This proverb usually means that the speaker is referring to something that he or she does not like: *You're not going to put salt in your coffee, are you? Well, there's no accounting for taste.*

Actions speak louder than words

Doing something is more important or more effective than just talking about doing it or promising to do it. Judge people by what they do rather than what they say.

An apple a day keeps the doctor away

Eating fruit keeps you healthy.

A bad workman (always) blames his tools

Said of incompetent people who make excuses for their own failings by blaming something else, such as the equipment they are using.

A barking dog seldom / never bites

Also Barking dogs seldom bite. People who utter loud threats rarely carry them out, or those who boast a lot rarely do much.

His bark is worse than his bite

He is not as bad-tempered, unkind or unpleasant as he appears to be from the way he speaks.

If you can't beat them, join them

Often in the more informal form If you can't beat 'em, join 'em. It means that if an opposing group is more successful than your own, it is better to join with them than to go on opposing them.

Beauty is / lies in the eye of the beholder

What you find beautiful, another may not. There is no absolute standard of beauty beyond a person's own likes and dislikes.

Beauty is only skin deep

You cannot judge a person or thing's real quality from appearances alone. The pleasing appearance of a person or thing may not be as important as their inner qualities.

Beggars can't be choosers

If you are asking for or getting a favour, you have to accept what you are given.

Better late than never

It is better to do something late than not do it at all, or it is better to get something after some delay than never to get it at all. Sometimes said as an apology for lateness, or to forgive somebody for being late: *'I'm sorry I'm late.' 'Better late than never.'*

Better (to be) safe than sorry

It is better to be cautious, even over-cautious, than to take risks which may cause harm or lead you into danger or which you may regret later: *'You don't need your umbrella, do you?' 'Better safe than sorry. It might rain later.'*

Better the devil you know than the devil you don't (know)

It is better to put up with an unpleasant person or situation that you know and understand than to change the situation at the risk of ending up with somebody or something that may be even worse: *I don't get on with my boss and I had been thinking of looking for a new job, but then I thought 'Well, better the devil you know', so I'm staying.*

A bird in the hand is worth two in the bush

What you have is worth more than something better that you do not have and might never get. Be content with what you have, and do not risk losing it for the possibility of something better.

Birds of a feather flock together

People with similar interests, backgrounds, or characters will often be found together. Sometimes people are said to be birds of a feather: *I think my brother and his boss are very much birds of a feather – they do their jobs, they go home to their wives, and they play golf at the weekend.*

The blind leading the blind

Often said when commenting on somebody who lacks ability, knowledge or experience trying to guide or advise somebody else who knows no more than they do. This saying is taken from the Bible: '*… if the blind lead the blind, both shall fall into the ditch*'.

There are / There's none so blind as those who will not see

People who do not want to believe something will refuse to accept any evidence or arguments that challenge their belief. 'Will not' in this sense means 'are not willing to' or 'refuse to'. There is a similar proverb that runs There are none so deaf as those who will not hear.

Blood is thicker than water

Family loyalties are stronger than anything else.

You can't get blood from / out of a stone

Said of something impossible, or almost impossible, especially trying to get something from somebody. Often found in other forms: *Getting him to smile is like trying to get blood out of a stone.*

Be born with a silver spoon in one's mouth

To be born into a wealthy family.

Boys will be boys

This saying means that that is the sort of thing one would expect boys to do. Said indulgently as an excuse for bad or foolish behaviour, or as a comment on such behaviour. Less commonly Girls will be girls.

You cannot make bricks without straw

Nothing can be done unless you have the tools, materials, information, etc to do it with: *Writing the report without adequate research would be like making bricks without straw.* Straw was used in brick-making in ancient times as it made the bricks stronger.

If it ain't broke, don't fix it

If something is functioning perfectly well, do not try to change it or improve it. Originally an American saying, but now common in Britain also. Note the colloquial word form 'ain't broke' (= *isn't broken*).

Let bygones be bygones

Forget people's past mistakes or offences, or old quarrels or disagreements. 'Bygones' ('baɪgɒnz) are things that have happened in the past.

If the cap fits, wear it

Said of criticism or advice. If what is being said is applicable to you, then you should apply it to yourself without complaining or arguing: '*I think it was a bit unfair of the manager to say the staff are lazy.' 'Well, if the cap fits, wear it; if it doesn't, then he wasn't criticizing you.*'

You cannot have your cake and eat it

Also **You cannot eat your cake and have it**. This means that sometimes you have to make a choice and be happy with one thing or the other when it is not possible to have both, or that if you want one thing, you may have to put up with something else as well: *You won't be able to go out with your friends so often when you're married, but you can't have your cake and eat it.* Often found in other forms, such as trying / wanting to have your cake and eat it.

Don't put the cart before the horse

Do things in the right order. The saying often occurs in other forms: *'Let's start building the garage now.' 'Hang on. You're putting the cart before the horse. First we have to draw some plans.'*

A cat may look at a king

This saying is used to suggest to an arrogant or haughty person that you are as good as they are, or that even though they are more powerful or important than you, you still have the right to be treated politely and considerately: *She thought it was beneath her dignity to talk to someone like me, but a cat may look at a king, so I went over and spoke to her.*

Charity begins at home

You should help people close to you, such as your family and friends, and then help people you do not know, such as beggars in the street or starving people in other countries. Often said as an excuse for doing nothing at all to help the needy.

The child is father to the man

Also **The child is the father of the man**. This saying means that what sort of person you are when you are grown up is determined to a large extent by what you were as a child.

Cleanliness is next to godliness

Originally this meant that cleanliness is a consequence of godliness, i.e. keeping oneself clean derives from a reverence for God. Now the saying is generally understood to mean that cleanliness is next in importance to godliness.

It is too late to close the stable door once the horse has bolted

see It is too late to shut the stable door ...

Every cloud has a silver lining

There is something good in every situation, no matter how bad it seems.

All things come to those who wait

Also **Everything comes to him who waits**. Said as an encouragement to be patient: *'I don't think I'm ever going to be promoted!' 'Just be patient. Everything comes to him who waits.'*

Too many cooks spoil the broth

If there are too many people involved in doing something, it will not be done properly (e.g. because there will be too many different opinions about how it should be done).

Don't count your chickens before they are hatched

Do not make plans on the basis of something that has not yet happened and which might not happen: *'I'm going to university to study accountancy so that I can make lots of money when I'm older.' 'Don't count your chickens before they're hatched. You haven't passed your exams yet.'*

Don't cross your bridges until you come / get to them

Do not waste time worrying about difficulties or trying to solve them until you actually come to them. Often found in other forms, such as **We'll cross that bridge when we come to it.**

There is no use crying over spilt milk

What's done is done, and cannot be changed. There is no point in having regrets about something that has happened in the past, even if you wish it hadn't happened: *'If I hadn't sprayed the flowers to kill the insects on them, I wouldn't have killed the flowers.' 'Well, there's no use crying over spilt milk. The flowers are dead now.'*

Curiosity killed the cat

People who are too curious and pry into things may come to harm. Usually said to somebody, especially a child, who is being too inquisitive.

Don't cut off your nose to spite your face

Do not do something that will harm or disadvantage you simply in order to harm or disadvantage or take revenge on somebody else: *I'm tempted not to accept her gift after she was so rude to me, but that would just be cutting off my nose to spite my face.*

Cut your coat according to your cloth

You should do whatever is appropriate in the situation you find yourself in. This saying is used especially to suggest that you must accept the limitations imposed by the limited resources you have available, e.g. that you should not spend more money than you can afford.

There are / There's none so deaf as those who will not hear

see There are / There's none so blind as those who will not see

The devil finds work for idle hands to do

This proverb means that people who have nothing useful to do will get up to mischief.

A similar saying is An idle brain is the devil's workshop.

Give the devil his due

Give even a bad person or a person you dislike due credit for any good things they do or any good aspects of their character: *I never liked him, but to give the devil his due, he treated me very kindly when my wife died.*

Discretion is the better part of valour

'Valour' is another word for courage. The saying means that it is foolish to take unnecessary risks or get into dangerous situations, no matter how courageous you are: *I was going to argue with her but, discretion being the better part of valour, I said nothing.*

Distance lends enchantment to the view

It is very easy to have an idealized and unreal picture of faraway places or of events in the distant past, without seeing or remembering their unpleasant or disagreeable side. The saying comes from a poem by Thomas Campbell.

Do unto others as you would they should do unto you

In rather old-fashioned language ('would' here means 'want' or 'would like'), this saying means that you should treat other people the way you would want them to treat you. It is adapted from words of Jesus in the Bible. There is another simpler form of this saying, Do as you would be done by.

Every dog has his / its day

Everybody will have their time of success, wealth, happiness, etc.

A drowning man will clutch at a straw

This means that people will grasp at the slightest chance or cling to the slimmest hope when they are desperate. A straw floating on water will not be enough to keep a person afloat, but if you are drowning you will grab hold of anything to try to stop yourself sinking. Often simply used as an idiom, **to clutch / grasp at straws**: *The opposition claim that recent polls show they have a chance of winning the election but most political commentators say this is just grasping at straws.*

The early bird catches the worm

The person who acts promptly or who takes the trouble to get somewhere before other people is the one who will succeed or get what they are wanting: *There aren't many tickets so I'm going to start queuing now. It's the early bird that catches the worm.*

Easier said than done

Used to point out that it may be more difficult to do what is being suggested than the person making the suggestion seems to realize: *'We can borrow the money from my father.' 'Easier said than done. How are we going to persuade him to lend us any money?'*

Easy come, easy go

This means that if something has been acquired very easily or quickly, it may just as quickly and easily be lost again. Often said to show that you don't care when something, e.g. money, has been lost or wasted: *I won over $1000 playing roulette and then lost it all playing poker. Oh well, easy come, easy go.*

Don't put all your eggs in one basket

Do not risk all your assets in one single venture or business, or rely on only one thing which may let you down: *I've got money in several different pension funds. I don't like to put all my eggs in one basket. / We have a good product that is selling well, but we must come up with new ideas. It would be foolish to put all our eggs in one basket.*

Empty vessels make the most noise / sound

Foolish empty-headed people are often the ones who talk most or boast a lot, while people with common sense or ability remain quiet. A 'vessel' in this sense is a dish.

The end justifies the means

Said to justify using unscrupulous or immoral ways of achieving something on the grounds that what has been or is to be achieved is so good or desirable that it does not matter how you achieve it.

Enough is as good as a feast

If you have as much as you need, you do not require any more; you should be satisfied with what you have.

To err is human

It is natural for human beings to make mistakes and behave badly. Often said to excuse bad or foolish behaviour: *I know I shouldn't have lost my temper with her, but to err is human.* A longer version of this saying – **To err is human, to forgive, divine** – comes from a poem by Alexander Pope.

The exception proves the rule

This saying means that the fact that you have found an exception to some general rule confirms the overall accuracy of the rule: an exception cannot actually *prove* a rule, but merely draws attention to it. This saying is often misused to justify prejudices in the face of contrary evidence: *'Scotsmen are supposed to be mean, but he has always been very generous.' 'Well, he's the exception that proves the rule.'*

Experience is the best teacher

The best way to learn anything is by doing it, and we learn by our mistakes.

All's fair in love and war

Used to justify unscrupulous or unfair behaviour, especially something that gives somebody an advantage over a rival.

Fair exchange is no robbery

Also A fair exchange is no robbery. Said when taking one thing and leaving something else in its place, and very often when the exchange is anything but fair: *Well, I'm taking her new bike and she can have my old one. Fair exchange is no robbery, as they say.*

Familiarity breeds contempt

This saying means that we tend to lose our respect for, appreciation of, or interest in somebody we have known a long time or something we have experienced frequently.

It ain't over till the fat lady sings

Also The opera isn't / ain't over till the fat lady sings. This is a modern saying of American origin. It means that you cannot be sure of the final outcome of anything until it is all over: *United are two–nil down with ten minutes to go, but remember it ain't over till the fat lady sings and they could still win.* The underlying idea is that an opera is not finished until the leading female singer – often a rather large woman – has sung her final aria. Note the informal form 'ain't'.

Like father, like son

Used to remark on a man who has the same interests, failings, etc as his father. A similar saying is Like mother, like daughter.

Finders keepers, losers weepers

Used, especially by children, to justify keeping something they have found even when they know who it really belongs to: *'That's my ring! I dropped it on the way to school.' 'Well, I found it and I'm keeping it. Finders keepers.'*

Fine feathers make fine birds

Beautiful clothes impart beauty and dignity to the person wearing them. Often said ironically of somebody who is overdressed.

Fire is a good servant but a bad master

This means that something may bring benefits so long as it is used wisely and carefully, but be harmful if used foolishly or immoderately.

There are as good fish in the sea as ever came out of it

Said to encourage or cheer up somebody who has missed an opportunity: even if you have missed this chance, another will come along. The saying may also be used to imply that somebody who has been passed over is as good as another person who has been promoted or rewarded. Another version of the saying is There are plenty more fish in the sea, said especially to somebody who has been rejected in love: *I know you think she was the only girl for you, but there are plenty more fish in the sea. You'll find someone else.*

There is no use flogging a dead horse

There is no point in making efforts to achieve something that cannot be done, e.g. in trying to arouse interest in something that people have already rejected or already accepted: *He'll never get people interested in a campaign to save an obscure species of South American toad. He's just flogging a dead horse. / You'll never get him to stop smoking after all these years. It's flogging a dead horse.* The underlying idea of this saying is that if a horse is dead, no amount of beating will get it to move.

A fool and his money are soon parted

If you are foolish, you will soon lose your money by spending it unwisely or by letting other people cheat you.

There is no fool like an old fool

Said of somebody who is behaving foolishly when they are old enough to know better.

Fools rush in where angels fear to tread

A foolish person will act hastily whilst a wise person will stop and consider carefully before acting: *It looks like a good scheme, but I'm not putting any money into it until I've checked it out thoroughly. Fools rush in, you know.*

Forewarned is forearmed

If you are aware of problems ahead, you are in a better position to deal with them.

There's no such thing as a free lunch

Originally an American saying. It means that no matter what anyone says or promises, you don't get something for nothing; there is always a catch: *'The boss is lending me his yacht this weekend.' 'I wonder what he wants from you. There's no such thing as a free lunch.'*

A friend in need is a friend indeed

A true friend is somebody who helps you when you are in trouble. You know who your real friends are when you need help.

Girls will be girls

see Boys will be boys

All that glitters is not gold

The old word 'glisters' is also used in this proverb. The saying means that you must not rely on appearances, as people and things may not be as good as they look or be what they seem to be.

All good things must come to an end

Good fortune and happiness cannot last forever.

One good turn deserves another

If somebody does you a favour, it is only right that you should do something for them in return.

What goes around, comes around

A modern saying of American origin. It means that whatever a person does, whether good or bad, will affect them similarly in the future: *Go out and do something nice for somebody. Remember, what goes around, comes around.*

God helps those / them that help themselves

Do not wait for outside help: try to solve your own problems or work for your own success. You must make an effort yourself before expecting God to come to your assistance. Said to encourage people who are lazy or discouraged, and sometimes cynically to suggest that a person should always look after their own interests first.

The grass is always greener on the other side of the fence

This proverb describes feelings of dissatisfaction with what you have and yearnings for what you do not have, just as to a cow in a field, for example, the grass on the opposite side of the fence may seem greener and tastier than the grass on its own side of the fence.

Great oaks from little acorns grow

Things that begin in a small way may become great in the end: *Opening a small café is hardly the same as becoming a famous restaurateur, but great oaks from little acorns grow.*

Half a loaf is better than no bread

It is better to have something, even if it is less than you would like, than to have nothing at all.

Many hands make light work

The more people that help with a job, the less work any one person needs to do and the job is therefore easier for everyone.

Handsome is as handsome does

'Handsome' here means 'gracious', an old sense of the word. The proverb means that a person can only be considered as good as their actions. Appearances and promises do not count.

As well be hanged for a sheep as a lamb

If you are going to get into trouble, you might as well get into trouble for doing something really bad as for doing something only slightly bad, or if you are involved in something for which you will be punished anyway, you might as well see it through to the end rather than pull out part way through. The origin of the proverb lies in the fact that most crimes of stealing were once punished by hanging, regardless of how much or how little was stolen.

More haste, less speed

This means that if you try to do something too quickly, you will probably make mistakes and therefore have to do it over again, which will take more time than if you had worked more slowly and carefully in the first place. Another form of this proverb is Make haste slowly.

Don't put your head into the lion's mouth

Do not take unnecessary risks or put yourself in danger. The saying may appear in other forms: *He decided to complain to the police, which for a burglar was rather like putting his head in the lion's mouth.* Some circus performers put their heads into lions' mouths as part of their act, but they can never be sure that the lions won't bite them.

Two heads are better than one

This means that if two people try to solve a problem together, they are more likely to come up with a solution than one person trying to solve it alone.

If you can't stand the heat, get out of the kitchen

Another form is If you don't like the heat .... This saying means that if you cannot cope with the pressures and responsibilities of a situation you find yourself in, such as your job, you should leave: *If you find it too stressful being a schoolteacher nowadays, then look for another job. If you can't stand the heat, get out of the kitchen – it's as simple as that.*

He who hesitates is lost

Indecision and hesitation may lead to disaster or failure. You need to act decisively if you want to succeed.

Hitch your wagon to a star

Do not set limits to your ambitions.

Honesty is the best policy

It is better to be honest, e.g. because it is morally the right thing to do or because you might get into trouble if people find out that you have been dishonest.

Hope springs eternal

This saying means that people have a natural tendency to hope that their situation will get better or that something good will happen, even when this is very unlikely: *He says he's going to keep on asking her to marry him even though she has turned him down three times already. Hope springs eternal, as they say.* The saying comes from a poem by Alexander Pope: *Hope springs eternal in the human breast.*

Don't stir up a hornets' nest

Hornets are a type of large wasp, and if you disturb a hornets' nest you are liable to get badly stung. This proverb means that you should not do anything that will create trouble for yourself, or lead people to criticize or argue with you, or cause other people to fight or argue: *For a bishop to say that it is not always wrong to steal was bound to stir up a hornets' nest*. The saying is also found in other forms: *The question of whether it is right to smack children has become a real hornets' nest*.

You can lead / take a horse to water but you cannot make it / him drink

You can give people good advice or offer them good opportunities, but there is nothing you can do to make them take the advice or make use of the opportunities: *Her father got her a good job with an insurance company but she quit after a few weeks. It just shows that you can take a horse to water but you can't make it drink*.

An idle brain is the devil's workshop

see **The devil finds work for idle hands to do**

Ignorance is bliss

This proverb means that it is often better not to know something if the truth is unpleasant. It is sometimes used ironically: *If I had known how long the job would take, I would never have agreed to do it. But ignorance is bliss*. It may be used to imply that somebody is deliberately avoiding the truth because they do not want to know: *I tried to tell her that her husband is having an affair but she wouldn't listen. I suppose she thinks that ignorance is bliss*. The full form of the saying comes in a poem by Thomas Gray: *Where ignorance is bliss, 'tis folly to be wise*. A similar saying is **What you don't know can't / won't hurt you**.

It's an ill wind that blows nobody any good

'Ill' here means 'bad'. This proverb really means that one person's misfortune or bad luck may nevertheless bring benefits to somebody else, but nowadays it is most often used to remark on a good or beneficial aspect of one's own misfortune: *It was a nuisance having a broken arm, but it's an ill wind, as they say – at least I didn't have to do PE any more*.

Imitation is the sincerest form of flattery

If you follow somebody's example, then you must really admire them and are not just flattering them by pretending that you admire them.

In for a penny, in for a pound

This saying means that you are willing to go further with something than you had originally intended because you recognize that it is necessary, wise or helpful to do so: *I wasn't meaning to get very involved with the committee this year, but in for a penny, in for a pound – if you want me to be chairman, I will. / We only meant to buy new curtains for the lounge, but once we'd bought them, we decided it was a case of 'in for a penny, in for a pound', and we bought a new carpet as well*.

Don't have too many irons in the fire

This saying means that it is unwise to be involved in too many things or to have too many responsibilities at the one time, as you may end up doing everything badly or unsuccessfully. The underlying image is that of a blacksmith who has too many horse-shoes heating at one time. It is also common to speak of **having several irons in the fire**, meaning that a person has a number of responsibilities or interests, but not too many.

Jack of all trades and master of none

This saying means that somebody knows a little about many things but is not very knowledgeable or skilful in any of them. It is often said disapprovingly. However, if you refer to somebody as simply being a Jack of all trades, it is usually a compliment, emphasizing that they have a wide range of skills: *I have a friend who is a bit of a Jack of all trades. He can do electrical work, plumbing, plastering, carpentry, and goodness knows what else.*

You can't judge / tell a book by its cover

You cannot judge somebody or something by their appearance.

Why keep a dog and bark yourself?

Why do something yourself if you already employ somebody to do it? For example: *My wife expects me to do all the housework. As she says, why keep a dog and bark yourself?*

What you don't know can't / won't hurt you

see Ignorance is bliss

The labourer is worthy of his hire

A person should be paid properly for the work they do: *Nurses have been poorly paid for too long. They deserve a pay rise: the labourer is worthy of his hire.* The saying comes from the Bible.

It is the last straw that breaks the camel's back

This saying means that after you have faced a series of problems, difficulties, insults, etc, just one more, no matter how small in itself, may be too much to cope with or put up with. The underlying image is of a camel carrying a heavy load and collapsing when even a little weight is added to it. Nowadays the proverb is less common than the phrase the last straw: *I'd missed the bus, had to walk in the rain, and got splashed by a car, so the heel coming off my shoe was simply the last straw – I just turned round and went home again.*

He who laughs last laughs longest

This saying means that the person who succeeds in the end or who is finally proved right can laugh at those who laughed at him or her earlier when he or she seemed to be wrong or likely to fail. You can talk simply about having the last laugh: *My brothers all laughed at me for having to run errands for my grandmother, but I had the last laugh – she gave me $5.* Another form of this proverb is He laughs best who laughs last.

Learn to walk before you run

Learn to do simple things before attempting more difficult ones.

Least said, soonest mended

This proverb means that it is often better not to talk about something, especially something bad that has happened, because if you don't talk about it, it will soon be forgotten, whereas if you do talk about it, you may make things worse or get into difficulties: *I wouldn't try to apologize for what you did. Just forget about it. Least said, soonest mended.*

Leave / Let well alone

This saying means that you should not interfere with something that is already satisfactory: *'Do you think I should tell her what he said?' 'No, I'd just leave well alone if I were you.'*

The leopard does not change his spots

People do not change their character or habits: *I wouldn't give him that job. He always was a careless worker, and the leopard doesn't change his spots, does it?* The saying comes from the Bible: *Can the Ethiopian change his skin, or the leopard his spots?*

Where / While there is life there is hope

This is a saying of encouragement, meaning 'never give up hope, no matter how difficult things may be or how unlikely it seems that you will survive or succeed': *I know I may never become Managing Director, but, well, where there's life, there's hope.'*

A little knowledge / learning is a dangerous thing

This saying means that somebody who knows only a little about something may get into trouble or difficulties because they overestimate their knowledge or expertise. The saying comes from a poem by Alexander Pope.

Live and let live

This means that you should tolerate other people's behaviour and lifestyles just as you expect them to tolerate yours: *I don't really approve of couples living together without getting married, but, well, live and let live is my motto.*

People / Those who live in glass houses shouldn't throw stones

You should not criticize or speak badly about other people if you are vulnerable to similar criticism yourself, because people who are criticized or slandered will hit back.

It is too late to lock the stable door once the horse has bolted

see It is too late to shut the stable door once the horse has bolted

Don't look a gift horse in the mouth

This saying means that if you are given something for nothing, you should not ask about the quality or value of it: *My aunt is giving me her old piano. I don't know whether it's much good, but I'm certainly not going to look a gift horse in the mouth.* You can tell the age of a horse by looking at its teeth.

It's a long lane that has no turning

This proverb offers encouragement by suggesting that bad luck or misfortune will not last for ever.

Look before you leap

This means that you should check the situation carefully before making a decision or taking action: *The job looks good, but I want to know more about the firm before I decide to take it. It's always best to look before you leap.*

It is like looking for a needle in a haystack

This is said when something is very hard to find, as a needle would be in a large pile of hay: *Trying to find my wife on the beach was like looking for a needle in a haystack.*

What you lose on the swings, you gain on the roundabouts

This saying means that things tend to even out in life and that if you lose out somewhere, compensations may come somewhere else or in another way: *Being married means I'm not as free as I once was, but on the other hand , it's nice not to be living alone. As they say, what you lose on the swings, you gain on the roundabouts.* It may refer to a specific situation in which a loss in one respect may produce a gain in another respect: *If we lower our prices, we'll make less profit, but we may get more customers, so what we lose on the swings we'll gain on the roundabouts.* Sometimes people talk simply about swings and roundabouts.

Love is blind

This means that a person in love cannot see the faults of the person they are in love with.

As you make your bed, so you must lie in / upon it

If you have got yourself into a situation you regret, you simply have to accept it. The saying comes in various forms: *I warned her not to marry him, but she went ahead anyway. Well, she's made her bed, so she'll just have to lie in it.*

Make hay while the sun shines

Make use of opportunities when you have them.

Don't make mountains out of molehills

This means you should not exaggerate difficulties or problems. The saying comes in various forms: *There's no need to make a mountain out of a molehill. You've only got a slight cold, not pneumonia.*

One man's meat is another man's poison

People have different likes and dislikes, i.e. there's no accounting for taste.

A miss is as good as a mile

A failure is a failure, no matter whether you fail by a lot or only by a little: *I only failed one thing in my driving test, but a miss is as good as a mile, isn't it?*

Money is the root of all evil

This is the usual form of this proverb nowadays, but in fact the original saying in the Bible is that it is the *love* of money that is the root of all evil.

Money talks

Money brings power, influence and preferential treatment, or that it can be the deciding factor in a situation: *They told me the restaurant was full, but when this guy drove up in a big car, they soon found a table for him. Money talks, doesn't it?*

Like mother, like daughter

see Like father, like son

Necessity is the mother of invention

This means that when you are faced with a problem, you will find some way of solving it: *As a First Aider you must always remember that necessity is the mother of invention. If you haven't got the right equipment, use what you can find.*

Needs must when the devil drives

This means that sometimes the situation you are in forces you to do something you don't like or don't want to do: *I hate speaking in public, but I'm the father of the bride so I suppose I'll have to make a speech. Needs must, as they say.* 'Needs' here means 'of necessity', and 'needs must' is short for 'one needs must go', i.e. when the Devil is driving, you have to go where he takes you.

Never say die

Never give up hope.

It is never too late to mend

This saying means that it is never too late for a person to change their ways and attitudes, no matter how long they have been that way: *I've always been bad-tempered in the morning.' 'Well, you could try not to be. It's never to late to mend, you know.'*

A new broom sweeps clean

Also New brooms sweep clean. When a new person takes charge of something, they will make a lot of changes: *'The new manager is driving us all crazy, changing the way we do everything in the office.' 'Well, what do you expect? A new broom always sweeps clean.'*

No news is good news

This means that if you haven't heard any news about somebody or something, then everything must be all right because if the news had been bad, then you would have been told: *I've never heard whether her husband has got cancer or not, but I suppose no news is good news.*

A nod's as good as a wink to a blind horse

This rather nonsensical saying means that a mere hint is often enough to convey your meaning to somebody else: *She was glaring at me and I realized that she wanted me to leave them alone. A nod's as good as a wink, as they say.*

Nothing venture / ventured, nothing gain / gained

This saying means that if you never attempt something, you will never succeed.

Once bitten, twice shy

This means that a person who has had a bad experience will be more careful or wary in future, in order not to let the same thing happen again.

The opera isn't over till the fat lady sings

see It ain't over till the fat lady sings

Opportunity knocks but once

Also Opportunity never knocks twice at any man's door. This means you should grasp any opportunity that presents itself to you, for you may not get the chance again: *'He's asked me to go to America with him. Do you think I should?' 'You'd be crazy not to. Opportunity never knocks twice, you know.'*

Out of the frying-pan and into the fire

You say this when someone has got out of one difficult or dangerous situation only to find themselves in an equally bad or even worse situation.

Out of sight, out of mind

If you are away from somebody, you forget all about them.

Paddle your own canoe

This means that you should depend on your own efforts and make your own decisions: *Once my children had left school, as far as I was concerned they were free to paddle their own canoes.*

He who pays the piper calls the tune

If you are paying for something, you have the right to say what is done and how it is done.

The pen is mightier than the sword

This means that for all the destructive power of armed force, the greatest changes in the world come through education, persuasion and legislation, that is, through words rather than weapons.

Take care of the pence / pennies and the pounds will take care of themselves

This means that if you are careful to save or not waste small amounts of money, then by so doing you will save large amounts: *My mother always looks for special offers and bargains at the supermarket. Take care of the pennies and the pounds will take care of themselves, she says.*

A penny saved is a penny earned / gained

If you manage to save a penny then it is as good as earning a penny.

Penny wise and pound foolish

This proverb means that you save a small amount of money at the risk of having to spend a larger sum at a later date, or you are careful to make small savings but spend larger amounts foolishly: *He doesn't seem to realize that if he doesn't give his fence a coat of paint, it'll rot and he'll have to replace it. Penny wise and pound foolish, I'd say.*

Practice makes perfect

This means that if you keep on practising something, you will become good at it: *She's not a very good guitarist, but practice makes perfect, or so they say.*

Practise what you preach

This means that a person should do what they tell other people to do: *Practise what you preach. If you want me to stop smoking, then you give it up too.*

Prevention is better than cure

It is better to take steps to prevent something bad happening than to have to do something about it once it has happened.

Pride comes / goes before a fall

This is said to somebody, or about somebody, who is very proud about their ability, importance etc, as a warning that they may one day suffer some disaster or failure (or sometimes as a hope that they will): *She kept telling us how she would win all the prizes, but in the event she went to pieces and failed all her exams. Well, pride comes before a fall.* The saying comes from the Bible.

Procrastination is the thief of time

'Procrastination' means 'not doing something that you ought to do now, but leaving it till some time in the future'. This proverb means that if you put off doing something, then you may be wasting time or missing an opportunity or leaving it until too late. This saying comes from an 18th-century poem. A similar proverb is **Don't put off till tomorrow what you can do today.**

The proof of the pudding is in the eating

In this saying, 'proof' means 'test', not 'proving something'. You can only see how good something is by using it or experiencing it, just as you can only see how good a pudding is by eating it: *They seem to have fixed the car all right, but the proof of the pudding is in the eating. Let's see how it goes.*

It never rains but it pours

Misfortunes never come singly: *It never rains but it pours, does it? First my car broke down, then my cooker set the kitchen on fire, and then last night we had burglars!*

All roads lead to Rome

This proverb means that there can be more than one way of achieving an objective or reaching a position: *It doesn't matter how we persuade him to do it just so long as he does it. All roads lead to Rome.* Rome was the capital and centre of the ancient Roman empire, and it was felt that no matter what road you travelled on, it would eventually take you to Rome.

A rolling stone gathers no moss

A person who never settles down in one place or one job will never become rich or make good friends. Sometimes a person can be referred to as a rolling stone.

Rome was not built in a day

It takes time to achieve something worthwhile: *I know it's taking a long time to write this book, but Rome wasn't built in a day.*

When in Rome, do as the Romans do

When you are visiting a place, do as the local people do, or, in general, when you are with any group of people, fit in with their habits and lifestyle even if it involves doing things you would not normally do: *I don't normally go to church, but my brother and his family are committed Christians, so when in Rome, I do as the Romans do.*

There's safety in numbers

A group of people is stronger or less likely to come to harm than a single person: *If we're going to complain to the manager, I think we should all go together. There's safety in numbers.*

What is sauce for the goose is sauce for the gander

A gander is a male goose. This saying means that what is right or suitable for one person is equally right or suitable for another: *If girls have to learn to cook, so should boys. What's sauce for the goose is sauce for the gander.*

You scratch my back and I'll scratch yours

This means 'You do me a favour and I'll do something for you'.

Seeing is believing

This means that you can, or will, believe something only if you see it for yourself, or that you know something is true because you have seen it yourself: *I'd never imagined she could paint like that, but seeing is believing – she's a very talented artist.*

Silence is golden

It is often better to say nothing and keep your thoughts and opinions to yourself. A longer form of this proverb is Speech is silver but silence is golden.

You can't make a silk purse out of a sow's ear

You cannot make something good out of poor-quality materials: *He wants to become a doctor but he hasn't got the brains for it. You can't make a silk purse out of a sow's ear.*

Let sleeping dogs lie

Do not stir up trouble or difficulty where there isn't any, for example by asking awkward questions or trying to make changes: *'Do you think I should tell him what I saw?' 'No. What he doesn't know won't hurt him. I'd just let sleeping dogs lie.'*

There is many a slip 'twixt / between cup and lip

'Twixt' is short for 'betwixt', an old word meaning 'between'. This proverb means much the same as Don't count your chickens before they're hatched. You cannot be sure you have got something or achieved something until you actually have got it or have achieved it, because something could always go wrong with your plans even at the last moment. The underlying idea is that you might have something nice to drink in your cup, but it might get spilt before it reaches your mouth.

Slow and steady wins the race

This proverb means that somebody who works away slowly and carefully may succeed while another who rushes at something may fail.

There is no smoke without fire

A rumour or story must have some basis of truth: *The Government denies that the minister was sacked for corruption, but I say there's no smoke without fire.*

Sow the wind and reap the whirlwind

This saying means that if you act unwisely, you may have to face unpleasant consequences. A similar proverb is As you sow, so shall you reap. Both these sayings have their origin in the Bible.

It is too late to shut / close / lock the stable door once / after / when the horse has bolted

This means that once something you didn't want to happen has happened, it is too late to do anything about it. The saying is found in various forms: *'Now that my car has been stolen, I realize I ought to have it insured.' 'Isn't that rather like locking the stable door after the horse has bolted?'*

Still waters run deep

This means that people who are very quiet may nevertheless be very wise, clever, emotional or cunning: *She was always such a quiet, reserved woman, and yet she was having an affair with the man next door. Still waters run deep, it seems.*

A stitch in time saves nine

If you act promptly to deal with a problem, it will save you having to take more trouble later on when the problem has become worse: *You ought to weed the garden before the weeds make seeds. A stitch in time saves nine, you know.*

Strike while the iron is hot

This proverb means that you should act when the opportunity arises. The underlying image is that of a blacksmith making horseshoes, which he has to beat into shape while the iron is hot enough to shape.

If at first you don't succeed, try, (try,) try again

Do not give up just because you have failed at your first or second attempt. Keep on trying.

One swallow doesn't make a summer

Swallows are birds that arrive in Britain in summer. This proverb means that you cannot be sure that something has happened or is going to happen just because you have seen one indicator of it, any more than you can be sure that summer has come just because you have seen one swallow. You should not jump to hasty conclusions.

It takes all sorts to make a world

This saying means that there are many different types of people in the world, with different lifestyles, different characters, different likes and dislikes, etc. Usually said when commenting on somebody who has different tastes and habits to your own.

Talk of the Devil and he will appear

Also Talk of the Devil and he is bound / sure to appear. This saying means that when you are talking about somebody, they are sure to turn up. The first form of this saying is often used on its own when a person just being spoken about appears unexpectedly: *Talk of the devil, here comes John now.*

You can't teach an old dog new tricks

This means that you cannot get people who are set in their ways, especially older people, to change their opinions, habits, ways of working, etc: *I know I should get a computer, but I prefer my typewriter. I'm an old dog, and I'm not going to learn new tricks now.*

Don't teach your grandmother to suck eggs

This means that you should not try to tell somebody how to do something when they already know how to do it, possibly better than you do: *The new girl in the office tried to tell the computer officer how to set up a new computer system. Talk about trying to teach your grandmother to suck eggs!*

You can't tell a book by its cover

see You can't judge a book by its cover

Set a thief to catch a thief

This means that the best people to catch criminals or prevent crimes are those who have done such things themselves, as they know better than anyone else how to do them and therefore how to prevent them: *Some companies have been employing convicted computer hackers to advise them on how to stop people hacking into their files, a case of 'set a thief to catch a thief' if ever there was one.*

Don't throw out the baby with the bathwater

Do not discard something valuable when getting rid of something worthless: *Perhaps the plan isn't perfect, but let's not throw out the baby with the bathwater – some of the ideas are good.*

Don't throw good money after bad

Do not waste money trying to make up for the loss of money already wasted when it can only result in further losses to no purpose: *Having been stupid enough to buy a wreck of a car, I was tempted to get it completely overhauled, but that would just have been throwing good money after bad, because it would never have been fit to drive.*

Time and tide wait for no man

This means that you should seize an opportunity when it arises, or the chance may never come again.

Time flies

Time passes very quickly: *Doesn't time fly! They've been married three years already.*

Time is money

If you use your time wisely, you can make money, and if you waste time, you will lose money: *Well, I can't stand here chatting all morning. I've got work to do. Time is money.*

A trouble shared is a trouble halved

If you tell somebody else about a problem or worry that you have and let them help or advise you, then you will not have to carry the burden of it alone and it will not seem so bad.

Truth is stranger than fiction

Things that are true are sometimes more unbelievable than what you read in stories.

Variety is the spice of life

Life is more enjoyable when there is some variety in what one is doing. The saying comes from a poem by William Cowper.

Don't wash your dirty linen in public

Do not make public your private quarrels or scandals: *'That's a family matter,' she said, 'and we're keeping it that way. We're certainly not going to wash our dirty linen in public.'*

Waste not, want not

'Want' here means 'be in need'. This saying means that if you are thrifty and do not waste what you have, you will never be short of money, food, possessions, etc. Often said when a person is using something up, such as food, or taking the last of it: *'No-one wanting that last slice of ham? Oh well, waste not, want not,' he said, helping himself.*

A watched pot never boils

This means that if you are waiting for something to happen, you always seem to have to wait a long time because the time passes so slowly.

Well begun is half done

If you make a good start to a job, you are well on the way to completing it successfully.

All's well that ends well

Even if there have been difficulties or worries, if something comes out all right in the end, that is all that matters.

Where there's a will, there's a way

If you want to do something badly enough, you will find a way of doing it: *I don't know how I will ever get her autograph, but where there's a will, there's a way.*

All work and no play makes Jack a dull boy

This means that it is not good for a person to spend all their time working, with no time off for enjoyment. Often said to justify doing something other than working when you should be working: *I know I should be swotting for my exam, but it's Saturday night. All work and no play makes Jack a dull boy, you know.*

Two wrongs don't make a right

Doing something that is morally wrong in order to make up for another wrong or in revenge does not make the situation as a whole morally right: *Even if he did hit you, you shouldn't have hit him back. Two wrongs don't make a right.*

DO IT YOURSELF

A Complete the following proverbs.

1. A_____ makes the heart grow fonder.

2. A_____ speak louder than words.

3. A b_____ in the hand is worth two in the bush.

4. If the c_____ fits, wear it.

5. You cannot have your c_____ and eat it.

6. There is no use c_____ over spilt milk.

7. Don't put all your e_____ in one basket.

8. Two h_____ are better than one.

9. Ignorance is b_____ .

10. He who laughs last l_____ longest.

B Complete the proverbs in the following sentences.

1. If you want to excuse yourself for having broken something accidentally you may say that *a_____ will happen.*

2. If you ask a friend for a loan of his car and he offers you his bicycle instead, you may accept the offer of the bike even though it is not what you wanted, with the thought that *b_____ can't be choosers.*

3. If you arrive late for an appointment, you may apologise for being late but add '*Better late than n_____*'.

4. *Every c_____ has a silver lining.* If I had got the job in Japan that I applied for, I would never have met the girl who became my wife.

5. 'What are we going to do if she won't talk to us?' 'We'll *cross that b_____ when we come to it.*'

6. If you do something to lessen a rival's chance of success and increase your own chances, even though you know that what you are doing is wrong, you may try to justify your actions by telling yourself that *all is fair in l_____ and w_____ .*

7. The more helpers we can get on the day, the quicker the job will be done. *Many hands make l_____ work.*

8. I don't object to her copying my hairstyle. *Imitation is the sincerest form of f_____ .*

9. I don't mind if the man next door is a homosexual. *L_____ and let live*, I say.

10. The key to winning is not to give up hope when you're losing. *Never say d_____ , that's the thing.*

11. Fleeing from the ravenous lions, he found himself facing an enraged elephant. *Out of the frying-pan, into the f_____ .*

12. To think that my little granddaughter is three years old already! *Doesn't time f_____ !*

13. I know the plane is supposed to leave at half past three but I'm going to check the departure time again just to be sure. *Better s_____ than sorry!*

14. I think I'll leave John to make all the arrangements himself. *Too many c_____s spoil the broth.*

15. If you want to be president some day, go for it. Never be afraid to *hitch your w_____ to a star.*

21 ▶ British and American English

Notes

There are many differences between the English of the United Kingdom and that of the United States. This unit describes the main differences in spelling and vocabulary.

British and American Spelling

■ British English **-our**: *colour, favourite, flavour, humour, mouldy, saviour*
American English **-or**: *color, favorite, flavor, humor, moldy, savior*

> ### Did You Know ?
> **Savior** and **savor** may be spelt with a *u* in American English.
>
> **Glamour** is the correct spelling in both British and American English.

■ British English **-re**: *centre, millimetre, theatre*
American English **-er**: *center, millimeter, theater*

> ### Did You Know ?
> When the **-re** is preceded by the letter **c** in British English, American English also has **-cre**: **acre, massacre, mediocre**.
>
> Note also American English **macabre** and **ogre**.

■ British English **-ae-**, **-oe-**: *amoeba, anaemia, archaeology, diarrhoea, foetus, haemoglobin*
American English **-e-**: *ameba* or *amoeba, anemia, archeology, diarrhea, fetus, hemoglobin*

British English **-ise**, **-ize**: *criticise* or *criticize, modernise* or *modernize, systematise* or *systematize*
American English **-ize**: *criticize, modernize, systematize*

> ### Did You Know ?
> This rule applies only to verbs that are formed by adding the **-ise/-ize** suffix to roots and stems (see page 212).
>
> Note also **analyse** and **paralyse** in British English but **analyze** and **paralyze** in American English.

■ British English *-ll-*, *-pp-*, *-tt-*: *cancelled, carburettor, councillor, dishevelled, equalled, kidnapped, traveller, woollen, worshipped*
  American English *-l-*, *-p-*, *-t-*: *canceled, carburetor, councilor, disheveled, equaled, kidnapped* or *kidnaped, traveler, woolen, worshiped* or *worshipped*

Did You Know ?

As a general rule, where the final consonant of a stem (see page 194) is doubled when a suffix is added in British English, the consonant is generally not doubled in American English. The exception is a final *-l*, which is doubled in American English if the preceding syllable contains a single stressed vowel: ***canceled, traveled*** but ***propelled, rebelled***.

Handicapped is the only correct spelling in both British and American English.

Note also British English ***chilli***, American English ***chili*** or ***chilli***.

■ British English *-l*, *-l-*: *appal, distil, enrol, fulfil, instil; skilful, wilful*
  American English *-ll*, *-ll-*: *appall, distill, enroll, fulfill, instill; skillful, willful*

Did You Know ?

In American English, the spellings ***appal***, ***distil***, ***enrol***, etc are also acceptable, but only ***skillful*** and ***willful***.

■ British English *-logue*: *analogue, catalogue, dialogue*
  American English *-logue*, *-log*: *analogue* or *analog, catalogue* or *catalog, dialogue* or *dialog*

■ British English *-ce*: *defence, offence, pretence*
  American English *-se*: *defense, offense, pretense*

Did You Know ?

In British English, ***practice*** is a noun and ***practise*** a verb. In American English, both the noun and the verb are spelled ***practice***. Similarly, in British English, ***licence*** is a noun and ***license*** a verb, while in American English, both the noun and the verb are spelled ***license***.

Differences in Vocabulary

British English	American English
aeroplane	airplane
aluminium	aluminum
anticlockwise	counterclockwise
aubergine	eggplant
autumn	fall
axe	ax *or* axe
baby milk	formula
barman	bartender
bath	bathtub
biscuit	cookie
bonnet (of car)	hood
bookshop	bookstore
boot (of car)	trunk
braces	suspenders
camp bed	cot
candy floss	cotton candy
car park	parking lot
caravan	trailer
chemist	druggist
chemist's	drugstore
chips	french fries
cigarette	cigarette *or* cigaret
cinema	movie theater

British English	American English
cheque	check
cobweb	cobweb *or* spiderweb
cooker	stove
cosy	cozy
cot	crib
courgette	zucchini
crisps	chips
curriculum vitae	résumé
dialling tone	dial tone
doll's house	doll house
draught	draft
draughts (game)	checkers
drawing-pin	thumbtack
driving licence	driver's license
dustbin	garbage can *or* trashcan
film (e.g. at cinema)	movie
first floor	second floor
flat (to live in)	apartment
garden	yard
goods	freight
grey	gray
ground floor	first floor

British English	American English	British English	American English
guard (on train)	conductor	past (in telling the time)	after
hockey	field hockey	pavement	sidewalk
holiday	vacation	pay rise	raise
jelly	jello	pedestrian crossing	crosswalk
jewellery	jewelry	petrol	gas or gasoline
jug	pitcher	plough	plow or plough
jumper (clothing)	sweater	pocket money	allowance
kerb	curb	post	mail
lift	elevator	postcode	zip code
maize	corn	postman	mailman
manoeuvre	maneuver	pram	baby carriage
mark (e.g. for an exam)	grade	primary school	elementary school
maths	math	programme	program
mince (meat)	ground beef	pyjamas	pajamas
mollusc	mollusk	railway	railroad
motorway	superhighway	roundabout (on road)	traffic circle
moustache	mustache *or* moustache	rowing boat	rowboat
Mum	Mom	rubber (for rubbing out writing)	eraser
nappy	diaper	sceptic	skeptic
(pound) note	(dollar) bill	self-raising flour	self-rising flour
office block	office building	sledge	sled
a packet of cigarettes	a pack of cigarettes	spanner	wrench
paraffin	kerosene	storey (of a building)	story
parcel	package	subway	underpass

British English	American English
sulphur	sulfur
sweetcorn	corn
sweets	candy
tap (for water)	tap *or* faucet
tights	pantyhose
tin (container)	can
to (in telling the time)	of
torch	flashlight
trainers (shoes)	sneakers
treacle	molasses

British English	American English
trousers	pants
tyre	tire
underground	subway
vest	undershirt
waistcoat	vest
wastepaper basket	waste basket *or* wastepaper basket
windscreen	windshield
zebra crossing	crosswalk
zip	zipper

DO IT YOURSELF

A The following words are spelled according to the conventions of American English. Rewrite them as they would be spelled in British English.

analyze	gray	pajamas
ax	honor	plow
behavior	jewelry	prolog
defense	liter	skeptic
fiber	marvelous	skillful

B Give the British English equivalents of the following American English words.

airplane	eggplant	movie
baby carriage	elevator	parking lot
cookie	fall	sidewalk
corn	ground beef	thumbtack
crosswalk	math	undershirt

Foreign Words
and **Phrases**
22 Used in English

Some of the foreign words and phrases
used in English are pronounced very
much as if they were English words and
phrases, while others are pronounced in
a way that closely reflects their pronunciation
in the original language. In many cases more
than one pronunciation is accepted.

In German, nouns are always written with an
initial capital letter, but when German nouns are
used in English they are often written with a small
letter.

a cappella (Italian) /a kəˈpelə/
  sung without accompaniment

à deux (French) /a ˈdø/
  for or involving two people

ad hoc (Latin) /ad ˈhɒk/
  for this, or a, particular purpose

adieu (French) /əˈdjuː/
  goodbye (*plural adieus, adieux* /-z/)

ad infinitum (Latin) /ad ɪnfɪˈnaɪtəm/
  forever

ad interim (Latin) /ad ˈɪntərɪm/
  for the meantime

adiós (Spanish) /adiːˈɒs/
  goodbye

a fortiori (Latin) /eɪ fɔːtɪˈɔːraɪ/
  for an even stronger reason

aficionado (Spanish) /afɪʃɪəˈnaːdoʊ/
  a fan; an ardent follower (*plural aficionados*)

agent provocateur (French) /aʒɑ̃ prɒvɒkaˈtœr/
  somebody employed to infiltrate a group and persuade them to commit illegal acts (*plural agents provocateurs* /aʒɑ̃ prɒvɒkaˈtœr/)

aide-de-camp (French) /eɪd də ˈkɑ̃/
  an officer acting as assistant to a general (*plural aides-de-camp* /eɪd/)

aide-mémoire (French) /eɪd meɪˈmwɑː/
  a note or summary to help you remember something (*plural aide-memoire, aide-mémoires* /-z/)

à la (French) /a la/
  in the manner of

à la carte (French) /a la ˈkɑːt/
  allowing diners to choose dishes from a large menu and pay for each dish individually

à la mode (French) /a la ˈmoʊd/
  in fashion

aloha (Hawaiian) /əˈloʊhɑː/
  hello; goodbye

alma mater (Latin) /ˈalmə ˈmeɪtə/
  the school, college or university you attend or attended

alter ego (Latin) /ˈɔːltər ˈiːgoʊ, ˈaltər ˈegoʊ/
  1 an alternative personality
  2 a close friend (*plural alter egos*)

ambience (French) /ɑ̃biːˈɑ̃s/
  atmosphere: *I like the ambience in this restaurant.*

angst (German, Danish) /ɑːŋst/
  a feeling of anxiety caused by awareness of the uncertainties of life

anno Domini (Latin) /ˈanoʊ ˈdɒmɪnaɪ/
  in the year of our Lord, counting years after the birth of Christ

à point (French) /a ˈpwɛ̃/
  cooked to perfection

a posteriori (Latin) /eɪ pɒsterɪˈɔːraɪ/
  reasoning from experience, from particular cases to general principles

apparatchik (Russian) /apəˈratʃɪk/
  a party official, especially of a Communist party (*plural apparatchiks*)

appellation contrôlée (French) /apeˈlasjɔ̃ kɒnˈtroʊleɪ/
  a guarantee of the quality of a French wine

après-ski (French) /apreˈskiː/
  activities after a day's skiing

a priori (Latin) /eɪ praɪˈɔːraɪ/
  arguing from general principles to their effects and consequences

apropos (French) /aprəˈpoʊ/
  relevant

arrivederci (Italian) /ariːvəˈdeətʃiː/
  goodbye

au contraire (French) /oʊ kɒnˈtreə/
  on the contrary

au fait (French) /oʊ ˈfeɪ/
well acquainted with a matter; well informed

auf Wiedersehen (German) /aʊf ˈviːdəzeɪn/
goodbye

au natural (French) /oʊ natjəˈrel/
cooked plainly; uncooked; served without dressing

au pair (French) /oʊ ˈpeə/
a foreign girl living with a family and doing light housework, looking after children, etc
(*plural* **au pairs** /-z/)

au revoir (French) /oʊ rəˈvwaː/
goodbye

avant-garde (French) /avãˈgaːd/
1 innovative and unconventional
2 people such as artists who produce innovative and unconventional works

beau geste (French) /boʊ ˈʒest/
a gracious gesture

beaux arts (French) /boʊ ˈzaː/
the fine arts

belles-lettres (French) /bel ˈletrə/
elegant literature, e.g. poetry, novels, etc

bête noire (French) /bet ˈnwaː/
a person or thing you particularly dislike or are afraid of (*plural* **bêtes noires** /bet ˈnwaːz/)

blancmange (French) /bləˈmãʒ/
a type of milk pudding (*plural* **blancmanges** /-ˈmãʒɪz/)

blasé (French) /ˈblaːzeɪ/
not much impressed by or interested in something because you are too familiar with it

Blitzkrieg (German) /ˈblɪtskriːg/
a sudden overwhelming attack in war

bona fide (Latin) /ˈboʊnə ˈfaɪdiː/
genuine

bona fides (Latin) /ˈboʊnə ˈfaɪdiːz/
genuineness; sincerity; good faith

bon mot (French) /bɔ̃ ˈmoʊ/
a witty saying (*plural* **bons mots** /bɔ̃ ˈmoʊ/)

bon vivant, bon viveur (French)
/bɔ̃ viːˈvã, bɔ̃ viːˈvɜː/
somebody who enjoys good food, and is a good table companion (*plural* **bons vivants, bons viveurs** /bɔ̃ viːˈvã, bɔ̃ viːˈvɜː/)

bon voyage (French) /bɒn vɔɪˈaːʒ, bɔ̃ vwaɪˈaːʒ/
have a good journey

bouillon (French) /ˈbuːjɒn/
a thin clear soup, or a meat or vegetable stock

bourgeois (French) /ˈbʊəʒwaː/
1 middle-class; conventional in morals and materialistic in outlook
2 a member of the middle class with such an outlook

bourgeoisie (French) /bʊəʒwaːˈziː/
the middle class

café au lait (French) /kafeɪ oʊ ˈleɪ/
white coffee

café noir (French) /kafeɪ ˈnwaː/
black coffee

carte blanche (French) /kaːt ˈblãʃ/
freedom to do as you please

carte du jour (French) /kaːt djuː ˈʒʊə/
the menu of the day

cause célèbre (French) /koʊz səˈlebrə/
a controversial issue that attracts a great deal of attention (*plural* **causes célèbres** /koʊz səˈlebrə/)

c'est la vie (French) /se la ˈviː/
that's life

chacun à son gout (French) /ʃakœ̃ a sɔ̃ ˈguː/
everyone to his/her own taste

chaise-longue (French) /ʃez'lõg/
a type of settee (*plural **chaises-longues*** /ʃez'lõg, ʃez'lõgz/)

chambré (French) /'ʃãbreɪ/
(said of wine) brought to room temperature

chargé d'affaires (French) /ʃɑːʒeɪ dɑ'feə/
a diplomat lower in rank than an ambassador (*plural **chargés d'affaires*** /ʃɑːʒeɪ/)

chef d'oeuvre (French) /ʃeɪ 'dɜːvrə/
a masterpiece (*plural **chefs d'oeuvre*** /ʃeɪ/)

chilli con carne (Spanish) /'tʃɪlɪ kɒn 'kɑːneɪ/
a beef and bean stew flavoured with chilli peppers

ciao (Italian) /tʃaʊ/
hello; goodbye

cinéma vérité (French) /'sɪnəmə 'veriteɪ/
a cinema technique giving fiction the appearance of real life

circa (Latin) /'sɜːkə/
about; around

cliché (French) /'kliːʃeɪ/
an overused phrase (*plural **clichés*** /'kliːʃeɪz/)

comme il faut (French) /kɒm iːl 'foʊ/
as it should be; proper; correct

compos mentis (Latin) /'kɒmpəs 'mentɪs/
of sound mind; able to think sensibly

compte-rendu (French) /kõtrã'djuː/
an official report (*plural **comptes-rendus*** /kõtrã'djuː/)

cordon bleu (French) /kɔːdã 'blɜː/
a cook or cookery of the highest standard

corps diplomatique (French) /kɔː dɪplouma'tiːk/
diplomatic corps

coup de grâce (French) /kuː də 'grɑːs/
a decisive blow that puts an end to something (originally a blow that puts an end to suffering): *Montgomerie delivered the coup de grâce with a 20-foot putt at the*

seventeenth hole. (*plural **coups de grâce*** /kuː də 'grɑːs/)

coup d'état (French) /kuː deɪ'tɑː/
the violent overthrow of a government (*plural **coups d'état*** /kuː/)

coupé (French) /kuː'peɪ/
a type of car (*plural **coupés*** /-z/)

crème de la crème (French) /krem də la 'krem/
the very best

cul-de-sac (French) /'kʌldəsak/
a street blocked at one end (*plural **cul-de-sacs*** /-s/)

curriculum vitae (Latin) /kə'rɪkjʊləm 'viːtaɪ/
a brief outline of your life, career, etc (*plural **curricula vitae***)

de facto (Latin) /deɪ 'faktoʊ/
actual, if not by right: *a de facto ruler*

Dei gratia (Latin) /'diːaɪ 'greɪʃɪə, 'deɪiː 'grɑːtɪə/
by the grace of God

déjà vu (French) /'deɪʒɑ 'vuː/
the experience of thinking you have experienced something before when you are in fact experiencing it for the first time

de jure (Latin) /deɪ 'dʒʊəreɪ/
by right; according to the law

deluxe (French) /də'lʌks/
luxury: *a deluxe model.*

Deo gratias (Latin) /'deɪoʊ 'grɑːtɪəs/
thanks be to God

Deo volente (Latin) /'deɪoʊ və'lentɪ/
God willing

de rigueur (French) /də ri'gɜː/
obligatory; necessary

détente (French) /deɪ'tɒnt, deɪ'tãt/
a relaxation in relations between unfriendly countries

de trop (French) /də 'troʊ/
in the way; superfluous: *I felt a bit de trop and left the two of them alone.*

deus ex machina (Latin) /ˈdeɪʊs eks ˈmakɪnə/
a very unlikely happening that saves an otherwise hopeless situation, especially in a play or novel

distingué (French) /dɪˈstaŋgeɪ/
distinguished, especially in appearance

dolce far niente (Italian) /ˈdɒltʃiː fɑː niːˈenti:/
the pleasantness of doing nothing

la dolce vita (Italian) /la ˈdɒltʃiː ˈviːtə/
the sweet life

doppelgänger (German) /ˈdɒpəlgaŋə, -geŋə/
a ghost or double of a living person (*plural **doppelgängers** /-z/*)

double entendre (French) /duːbəl ɑ̃ˈtɑ̃drə/
a word or phrase that can be interpreted in two ways, usually one in which one meaning is indecently sexual (*plural **double entendres** /-z/*)

doyen (French) /ˈdɔɪən, ˈdwajɛ̃/
the senior member of a group or organization

éclat (French) /eɪˈklɑː/
brilliance

élan (French) /eɪˈlɑ̃, eɪˈlɑːn/
energy and style

embarras de richesses (French) /ɒmˈbarɑː də riːˈʃes/
having so many options it is difficult to choose one

éminence grise (French) /ˈemɪnɑ̃s ˈgriːz/
somebody who exercises power unofficially through somebody else who has the official power (*plural **éminences grises** /ˈemɪnɑ̃s ˈgriːz/*)

en bloc (French) /ɑ̃ ˈblɒk/
as one unit; all together

encore (French) /ˈɒŋkɔː/
an extra or repeated item at the end of a programme of song or music (*plural **encores** /-z/*)

en famille (French) /ɑ̃ faˈmiːj/
at home; casually

enfant terrible (French) /ɑ̃fɑ̃ teˈriːblə/
somebody who acts unconventionally or controversially (*plural **enfants terribles** /ɑ̃fɑ̃ teˈriːblə/*)

en garde (French) /ɑ̃ ˈgɑːd/
on guard (a command in fencing)

en masse (French) /ɑ̃ ˈmas/
all together

ennui (French) /ˈɒnwiː/
bored dissatisfaction

en passant (French) /ɑ̃ paˈsɑ̃/
in passing

en route (French) /ɑ̃ ruːt/
on the way

entente (French) /ɒnˈtɒnt, ɑ̃ˈtɑ̃t/
an agreement between countries or groups

entrecôte (French) /ˈɒntrəkoʊt/
a cut of steak

entre nous (French) /ɑ̃ˈtrə ˈnuː/
between ourselves

ersatz (German) /ˈeəzats/
artificial

esprit de corps (French) /eˈspriː də ˈkɔː/
a feeling of pride or loyalty felt by members of a group

et alia (Latin) /et ˈalɪə/
and other things

et aliae (Latin) /et ˈalɪaɪ/
and others (feminine)

et alii (Latin) /et ˈalɪiː/
and others (masculine)

et cetera (Latin) /et ˈsetərə/
and so on

eureka (Greek) /jʊəˈriːkə/
I've got it!

ex cathedra (Latin) /eks kəˈθiːdrə/
(said of the Pope) speaking in his official capacity when defining church doctrine

ex gratia (Latin) /eks ˈɡreɪʃə/
done as a favour rather than out of obligation: an ex-gratia payment.

ex officio (Latin) /eks əˈfɪʃɪəʊ/
by virtue of your official position

exposé (French) /eksˈpəʊzeɪ/
an newspaper article, etc that exposes a crime or scandal (*plural exposés* /-z/)

fait accompli (French) /feɪt əˈkɒmpliː/
something that has been done or decided and which just has to be accepted (*plural faits accomplis* /feɪz əˈkɒmpliː, feɪts əˈkɒmpliː, feɪt əˈkɒmpliːz/)

faute de mieux (French) /fəʊt də ˈmjɜː/
for lack of something better; because there is no better option

faux ami (French) /fəʊ zaˈmiː/
a word in one language that resembles a word in another language but has a different meaning (*plural faux amis* /fəʊ zaˈmiː/)

faux pas (French) /fəʊ ˈpɑː/
a social blunder; doing or saying something inappropriate or embarrassing (*plural faux pas* /-pɑːz/)

femme fatale (French) /fam fəˈtɑːl/
an irresistibly attractive and seductive woman (*plural femmes fatales* /fam fəˈtɑːl/)

flambé (French) /ˈflɒmbeɪ/
(said of food) covered with a strong alcoholic drink and set alight

force majeure (French) /fɔːs maˈʒɜː/
superior power

Frau (German) /frau/
Mrs

Fräulein (German) /ˈfrɔɪlaɪn/
Miss

Führer (German) /ˈfjʊərə/
leader (a title adopted by Adolf Hitler)

gauche (French) /ɡəʊʃ/
socially awkward or uncomfortable

gendarme (French) /ˈʒɒndɑːm, ˈʒɑ̃dɑːm/
a French police officer (*plural gendarmes* /-z/)

gestalt (German) /ɡəˈʃtalt/
in psychology, a whole that is more than the sum of its parts

gestapo (German) /ɡəˈstɑːpəʊ/
the Nazi secret police

glasnost (Russian) /ˈɡlaznɒst/
openness in government

gnocchi (Italian) /ˈnjɒkiː/
small dumplings

grande dame (French) /ɡrɑ̃d ˈdam/
a dignified lady with great social influence (*plural grandes dames* /ɡrɑ̃d ˈdam/)

grand prix (French) /ɡrɑ̃ ˈpriː/
an important motor-racing or motorcycle race (*plural grands prix* /ɡrɑ̃ ˈpriː/)

gratis (Latin) /ˈɡratɪs/
for nothing; free

habeas corpus (Latin) /ˈheɪbɪəs ˈkɔːpəs/
a writ requiring that a prisoner be brought to court in order that the reason for his or her detention can be verified

harakiri (Japanese) /harəˈkɪəriː/
a Japanese form of suicide by cutting open the stomach

hasta la vista (Spanish) /astə la ˈviːstə/
until we meet again

haute couture (French) /əʊt kʊˈtjʊə/
the designing and making of expensive, fashionable clothing

haute cuisine (French) /əʊt kwɪˈziːn/
high-quality cookery

Herr (German) /heə/
Mr

hoi polloi (Greek) /hɔɪ pəˈlɔɪ/
the ordinary people: He says he would
never read the sort of newspapers that the
hoi polloi read.

Homo sapiens (Latin) /ˈhoʊmoʊ ˈsapɪenz,
ˈhɒmoʊ –, – ˈseɪpɪenz/
human beings

hors-d'oeuvre (French) /ɔː ˈdɜːv, ɔː ˈdɜːvrə/
savoury food eaten at the start of a meal
as an appetizer (plural **hors d'oeuvres**
/ɔː ˈdɜːv, ɔː ˈdɜːvrə/)

ibidem (Latin) /ˈɪbɪdem, ɪˈbaɪdem/
in the same place

idée fixe (French) /ˈiːdeɪ ˈfiːks/
a fixed idea; an obsession (plural **idées fixes**
/ˈiːdeɪ ˈfiːks/)

idem (Latin) /ˈɪdem, ˈaɪdem/
the same

in absentia (Latin) /ɪn əbˈsentɪə, ɪn əbˈsenʃɪə/
in his, her, their, etc absence: She was
condemned in absentia.

in camera (Latin) /ɪn ˈkamərə/
not in public

in flagrante delicto (Latin) /ɪn fləˈgrantɪ;
dɪˈlɪktoʊ/
while committing the offence

infra (Latin) /ˈɪnfrə/
below

in loco parentis (Latin) /ɪn ˈloʊkoʊ pəˈrentɪs/
in place of a parent; with the role and
authority of a parent

in memoriam (Latin) /ɪn mɪˈmɔːrɪəm/
in memory of

in situ (Latin) /ɪn ˈsɪtjuː/
in its place: The statue looks OK here, but we'll
have to see what it looks like in situ.

inter alia (Latin) /ˈɪntər ˈeɪlɪə/
among other things

in toto (Latin) /ɪn ˈtoʊtoʊ/
totally; completely

in vitro (Latin) /ɪn ˈviːtroʊ/
in a test-tube or other dish

in vivo (Latin) /ɪn ˈviːvoʊ/
in the body

ipse dixit (Latin) /ˈɪpsɪ ˈdɪksɪt/
an unsupported statement (plural **ipse
dixits**)

ipso facto (Latin) /ˈɪpsoʊ ˈfaktoʊ/
because of that very fact

joie de vivre (French) /ʒwɑː də ˈviːvrə/
enjoyment of life

kamikaze (Japanese) /kamɪˈkɑːzɪ/
denoting a Japanese suicide bomber in
World War II

kaput (German) /kaˈpʊt/
ruined; broken

kibbutz (Hebrew) /kɪˈbʊts/
a collective farm (plural **kibbutzes,
kibbutzim** /kɪbʊˈtsiːm/)

kitsch (German) /kɪtʃ/
poor-quality sentimental art or literature

laisser-faire, laissez-faire (French) /ˈleseɪˈfeə/
non-interference, especially by
governments in economic matters

lasagna, lasagne (Italian) /ləˈzanjə/
flat strips of pasta

leitmotif (German) /ˈlaɪtmoʊtiːf/
a recurring theme in a book, piece of music,
etc (plural **leitmotifs**)

loco citato (Latin) /ˈloʊkoʊ sɪˈtɑːtoʊ/
in the place already mentioned

macaroni (Italian) /makəˈroʊniː/
pasta in the form of hollow tubes

machismo (Spanish) /məˈtʃɪzmoʊ, məˈkɪzmoʊ/
aggressive masculinity

macho (Spanish) /ˈmatʃoʊ/
aggressively masculine

Madame (French) /ˈmadəm, maˈdam/
Mrs

Mademoiselle (French) /madəmwəˈzel/
Miss

magnum opus (Latin) /ˈmagnəm ˈoʊpəs/
an important, or the most important, work produced by a writer, artist, composer, etc (*plural* **magnum opuses, magna opera** /ˈmagnə ˈoʊpərə/)

maître d'hôtel (French) /meɪtrə doʊˈtel/
a head waiter (*plural* **maîtres d'hôtel** /meɪtrəz/)

mañana (Spanish) /manˈjaːnə/
tomorrow, usually meaning 'sometime'

mea culpa (Latin) /ˈmeɪə ˈkʊlpə/
an admission of guilt

Messieurs
see monsieur

modus operandi (Latin)
/ˈmoʊdəs ɒpəˈran diː, – ɒpəˈrandaɪ/
a way of working

modus vivendi (Latin)
/ˈmoʊdəs vɪˈvendiː, – vɪˈvendaɪ/
a way of living; a compromise that allows people who disagree to get on together

monsieur (French) /məˈsjɜː/
Mr (*plural* **Messieurs** /məɪˈsjɜː, ˈmesəz/)

Monsignor (Italian) /mɒnˈsiːnjə/
a high-ranking Roman Catholic churchman (*plural* **Monsignors**)

mot juste (French) /moʊ ˈʒuːst/
the exact word; the appropriate word

moussaka (Greek) /mʊˈsaːkə/
a Greek dish containing meat, tomatoes and aubergines

mutatis mutandis (Latin) /muˈtaːtɪs muˈtandɪs/
making any necessary changes

ne plus ultra (Latin) /neɪ plʊs ˈʊltrə/
the perfect example of something, or the most extreme example

née (French) /neɪ/
born; used to state a married woman's maiden name

nemine contradicente (Latin)
/ˈneməniː kɒntrədɪˈsentiː/
with no-one disagreeing

noblesse oblige (French) /noʊˈbles oʊˈbliːʒ/
having noble rank imposes an obligation on a person to be honourable, etc

nom de plume (French) /nɒm də ˈpluːm/
a pen-name; a writer's pseudonym (*plural* **noms de plume** /nɒm/)

nota bene (Latin) /ˈnoʊtə ˈbenɪ/
note well

nouveau riche (French) /ˈnuːvoʊ ˈriːʃ/
a person who has acquired wealth but often not good taste (*plural* **nouveaux riches** /ˈnuːvoʊ ˈriːʃ/)

nouvelle cuisine (French) /ˈnuːvel kwɪˈziːn/
a simple style of cooking and presenting food

numero uno (Italian) /ˈnuːməroʊ ˈuːnoʊ/
number one, i.e. oneself. This is an informal expression.

objet d'art (French) /ˈɒbʒeɪ ˈdaː/
an article such as a vase that has artistic value (*plural* **objets d'art** /ˈɒbʒeɪ ˈdaː/)

opere citato (Latin) /ˈɒpərɪ sɪˈtaːtoʊ/
in the work already named

opus (Latin) /ˈoʊpəs/
an artistic work, especially a musical composition (*plural* **opuses, opera** /ˈɒpərə/)

outré (French) /ˈuːtreɪ/
unusual and rather shocking

pace (Latin) /ˈpɑːtʃeɪ, ˈpeɪsɪ/
with due respect to: *Pace your teacher, I don't think you're working hard enough* (Your teacher may think you are working hard enough, but I disagree).

par excellence (French)
/pɑːr ˈeksələns, pɑːr eksəˈlɑ̃s/
better than all the others; eminently

pâté (French) /ˈpateɪ/
a meat or vegetable paste

pâté de foie gras (French) /ˈpateɪ də fwɑː ˈɡrɑː/
a rich paste made with the livers of specially fattened geese or ducks

per annum (Latin) /pər ˈanəm/
each year; yearly

per capita (Latin) /pə ˈkapɪtə/
each; for or of each person

perestroika (Russian) /perəˈstrɔɪkə/
economic reconstruction

per se (Latin) /pə ˈseɪ/
in itself; essentially

persona non grata (Latin) /pɜːˈsoʊnə nɒn ˈɡrɑːtə/
somebody who is unacceptable or unwelcome somewhere (*plural* **personae non gratae** / pɜːˈsoʊniː nɒn ˈɡrɑːtiː/, but the singular form may be used when referring to more than one person: *They're both persona non grata at the moment*)

pièce de résistance (French) /pɪˈes də reɪˈzɪstɑ̃s/
a masterpiece (*plural* **pièces de résistance** /pɪˈes/)

pied-à-terre (French) /pɪːeɪdɑːˈteə/
a flat or house you use only occasionally: I live in Birmingham but I have a little pied-à-terre in London too. (*Plural* **pieds-à-terre** /pɪːeɪdɑːˈteə/)

plus ça change (French) /pluː sa ˈʃɑ̃ʒ/
things never really change. The full French saying has the meaning 'The more things change, the more they stay the same'.

prêt-à-porter (French) /pretaˈpɔːteɪ/
denoting ready-to-wear designer clothing

prima ballerina (Italian) /ˈpriːmə baləˈriːnə/
the chief female dancer in a ballet company (*plural* **prima ballerinas**)

prima donna (Italian)/ˈpriːmə ˈdɒnə/
1 the leading female singer in an opera company (*plural* **prima donnas**)
2 a temperamental self-important woman

prima facie (Latin) /ˈpraɪmə ˈfeɪʃiː/
at first sight; as it first seems

prix fixe (French) /priː ˈfiːks/
a fixed price (for a meal)

pro bono publico (Latin)
/proʊ ˈboʊnoʊ ˈpʊblɪkoʊ/
for the public good

pro rata (Latin) /proʊ ˈrɑːtə/
in proportion

pro tempore (Latin) /proʊ ˈtempərɪ/
temporarily

putsch (German) /pʊtʃ/
a political revolt; a coup d'état

quiche (French) /kiːʃ/
an open savoury tart

quid pro quo (Latin) /ˈkwɪd proʊ ˈkwoʊ/
a favour given in return (*plural* **quid pro quos**)

quod erat demonstrandum (Latin)
/kwɒd ˈerat demənˈstrandəm/
which was the thing to be demonstrated or proved

raison d'être (French) /ˈreɪzɔ̃ ˈdetrə/
the reason for existing (*plural* **raisons d'être** /ˈreɪzɔ̃/)

rara avis (Latin) /ˈreərə ˈeɪvɪs/
an exceptional person or thing (*plural* **rarae aves** /ˈreəriː ˈeɪviːz/)

ravioli (Italian) /ravɪˈoʊliː/
small square pasta parcels containing meat, etc

realpolitik (German) /reɪˈɑːlpɒlɪˈtiːk/
politics based on expediency rather than morality

répondez s'il vous plaît (French)
/reɪˈpɔ̃deɪ siːl vuː ˈpleɪ/
please reply; often abbreviated to **RSVP**

requiescat in pace (Latin)
/rekwɪˈeskat ɪn ˈpaːtʃeɪ/
may he or she rest in peace (*plural **requiescant in pace***)

rigor mortis (Latin) /ˈrɪgə ˈmɔːtɪs/
the stiffening of a body after death

risotto (Italian) /rɪˈzɒtoʊ/
a dish of rice, vegetables, meat, etc (*plural **risottos***)

risqué (French) /ˈrɪskeɪ/
slightly indecent: *a risqué joke.*

sangfroid (French) /sɒŋˈfrwɑː/
calmness; self-possession

savoir-faire (French) /savwɑːˈfeə/
the ability to know what is the right thing to do in any situation

Schadenfreude (German) /ˈʃɑːdənfrɔɪdə/
pleasure at other people's misfortune

schmaltz (Yiddish) /ʃmɔːlts, ʃmɒlts/
excessive sentimentality

scilicet (Latin) /ˈsaɪlɪset/
that is to say; namely

Señor (Spanish) /senˈjɔː/
Mr

Señora (Spanish) /senˈjɔːrə/
Mrs

Señorita (Spanish) /senjɔːˈriːtə/
Miss

sic (Latin) /siːk/
thus; in this way

Signor (Italian) /ˈsiːnjə/
Mr

Signora (Italian) /siːnˈjɔːrə/
Mrs

Signorina (Italian) /siːnjɔːˈriːnə/
Miss

sine die (Latin) /ˈsɪneɪ ˈdiːeɪ, ˈsaɪnɪ ˈdaɪiː/
for an indefinite time

sine qua non (Latin) /ˈsɪneɪ kwɑː ˈnɒn/
something absolutely essential (*plural **sine qua nons***)

sotto voce (Italian) /ˈsɒtoʊ ˈvoʊtʃeɪ/
in a quiet voice; in a whisper

soufflé (French) /ˈsuːfleɪ/
a light spongy baked dish of eggs and other ingredients (*plural **soufflés** /-z/*)

spaghetti (Italian) /spəˈgetiː/
long thin strings of pasta

status quo (Latin) /ˈsteɪtəs ˈkwoʊ/
the current state of affairs

supra (Latin) /ˈsuːprə, ˈsjuːprə/
above

table d'hôte (French) /ˈtɑːbəl ˈdoʊt/
a menu offering a meal at a fixed price and with few choices

tagliatelle (Italian) /taljəˈteleɪ/
thin strips of pasta

terminus ad quem (Latin) /ˈtɜːmɪnəs ad ˈkwem/
a finishing point

terminus a quo (Latin) /ˈtɜːmɪnəs ɑː ˈkwoʊ/
a starting point

terra firma (Latin) /ˈterə ˈfɜːmə/
solid ground

tête-à-tête (French) /tetəˈtet, teɪtəˈteɪt/
a conversation between two people (*plural **tête-à-têtes** /-s/*)

tortilla (Spanish) /tɔːˈtiːjə/
a flat pancake made with maize flour (*plural* **tortillas** /-z/)

touché (French) /tuːˈʃeɪ/
1 in fencing, an acknowledgement that your opponent has hit you
2 an acknowledgement of a clever remark made at your expense

tour de force (French) /tʊə də ˈfɔːs/
a masterly achievement or skilful performance (*plural* **tours de force** /tʊə/)

ultra vires (Latin) /ˈʌltrə ˈvaɪəriːz/
going beyond somebody's legal power

vice versa (Latin) /vaɪs ˈvɜːsə/
the other way round

vide (Latin) /ˈviːdeɪ, ˈvaɪdiː/
see

videlicet (Latin) /vɪˈdiːlɪset, vɪˈdelɪset, vaɪ–/
that is to say; in other words

vin de pays (French) /vɛ̃ də peɪˈiː/
a classification of French wines (*plural* **vins de pays** /vɛ̃/)

vis-à-vis (French) /viːzaːˈviː/
in relation to

viva 1 (Italian) /ˈviːvə/
long live …

viva 2 (Latin) /ˈvaɪvə/
an oral examination (*plural* **vivas**)

vive (French) /viːv/
long live …

volte-face (French) /vɒltˈfaːs/
a sudden change to an opposite opinion from the one held before (*plural* **volte-face, volte-faces** /ɪz/)

Weltanschauung (German) /ˈveltanʃaʊʊŋ/
a particular view of life

zabaglione (Italian) /zabaˈljoʊniː/
a dessert made with whipped egg yolks, sugar and wine

zeitgeist (German) /ˈtsaɪtgaɪst/
the general mood typical of a particular period of history

DO IT YOURSELF

A Give the meaning of the following Latin phrases.

ad hoc	bona fide	mea culpa
ad infinitum	de facto	mutatis mutandis
anno Domini	gratis	per annum
a priori	inter alia	sine qua non

B Give the meaning of the following French phrases.

bête noire	crème de la crème	faux pas
bon voyage	cul-de-sac	pièce de résistance
carte blanche	déjà vu	tête-à-tête
coup d'état	fait accompli	tour de force

C Select the correct English phrase from the choice in brackets to give the meaning of the phrases in italics.

1.   An *aficionado* of football (likes, dislikes) the game.

2.   If you have a feeling of *angst*, you are feeling (happy, sad, anxious).

3.   Something that is *ersatz* is (genuine, imitation).

4.   You shout *eureka* when you have (lost, found) something.

5.   The *hoi polloi* are the (aristocracy, ordinary people) of a country.

6.   If your washing-machine is *kaput*, it is (broken, brand new).

7.   A *leitmotif* in a story is (a recurring theme, an unexpected ending).

8.   If you are asked to do a job and you say *mañana*, you mean you are going to do it (right away, tomorrow, sometime, never).

9.   If you say you are going to look after *numero uno*, you mean you are going to look after (your wife, your boss, yourself).

10.   If you are speaking *sotto voce*, you are (speaking quietly, talking loudly).

Answers to Do-It-Yourself Exercises

Unit 1: Synonyms

1. Can't you see my mother is in *agony*?
2. Are you going to *drive* there?
3. I think I need a *nap/snooze*.
4. We're having a *house-warming* next Saturday.
5. The car was *filthy*.
6. There were *footprints* all over the garden.
7. It started to rain and by the time we got home we were *soaking/drenched*.
8. She hit the *bull's-eye* with every arrow.
9. Unfortunately we had to leave before the *finale*.
10. When the bomb went off, everyone *fled*.
11. When the bomb went off, everyone ran away in *panic/terror*.
12. My sister *adores* strawberries.
13. The police examined the doors and windows for *fingerprints*.
14. It's not polite to *gobble* your food like that.
15. What an *obnoxious/horrible/nasty* person she is!
16. My boss is extremely *meticulous/thorough*.
17. We need more soap powder, so I bought *an economy-size* packet.
18. He built a *lean-to* at the bottom of the garden.

1. Why don't you *invite* Mary to the party?
   After the earthquake, the government *appealed* for international aid.
2. That was a *delightful/beautiful* meal!
   That's a *beautiful/attractive/pretty* hat!
3. The *following* day we went back into town.
   The television was on in the *adjacent/adjoining* room.
4. The concert was *extremely/highly/immensely* successful.
   She was *dreadfully/awfully/extremely/terribly* upset at his personal remarks.
5. The concert was a *huge/great/colossal* success.
   The house is surrounded by a *large/extensive* garden.
6. He was in *great/intense/acute* pain.
   A good teacher knows when to be lenient and when to be *strict*.
7. A *little/young* child was looking at us intently.
   There's only a *limited/slight/slim* chance of success, you realize.
8. I earned far more in my *last* job than I do now.
   An *elderly* woman was sitting begging at the corner of the street.
9. Please write *distinctly* in black ink.
   She was *evidently/manifestly/obviously* very upset.
10. I *presume/suppose/think* she'll be along later.
    Try to *picture/visualize* what the finished house will look like.
11. Have you had a *reply/response* to your letter?
    Have you found the *solution* to your problem?
12. *Spicy/creamy* food doesn't agree with me.
    She hopes her daughters will find *wealthy/prosperous* husbands.
13. There's a *strange/odd/peculiar* smell in the house.
    My brother keeps all the children amused with his *amusing* stories.
14. What a *wonderful/marvellous/excellent/brilliant* idea!
    She rents a *luxurious/magnificent/impressive* apartment in a fashionable part of the city.
15. It's not my *job/responsibility* to look after her.
    I set up this *company/firm* four years ago.
16. Her mother was *angry/blazing/fuming/livid/wild* when she heard the news.
    A *fierce* battle then began.
17. We'll need to find some *convincing/compelling/persuasive* arguments to back our case.
    A *fierce/violent* wind was blowing from the east.
18. I can remember when I was a *penniless/hard-up/impoverished* student with hardly enough money to buy food.
    Thanks to the team's *dismal/feeble/pathetic/lamentable/deplorable/pitiful* performance last week, we're certainly not going to come top of the League this year.

19. It's a *tough/hard/arduous* climb to the top of that hill.
    We get some really *awkward/demanding/fussy* people to deal with at the shop.
20. Is this a *suitable/opportune* time for me to have a talk with you?
    Mrs Chen is very *kind/nice* to her grandchildren.
21. Sheila was really *angry/blazing/livid/furious* when the bus didn't stop for her.
    Their proposal is completely *crazy/absurd/insane/stupid*, you know.
22. It was a *balmy/peaceful* summer's evening.
    We need someone who will remain *composed/unflustered/cool/relaxed* under pressure.
23. I only had time to give your report a *brief/cursory* read before the meeting.
    I'm sorry to rush you but we need a *prompt* reply to our offer.
24. Digging the garden is *backbreaking/tiring/exhausting* work.
    That's a *difficult* question to answer.
25. No matter what happened, I would never *leave/desert* my children.
    Due to unforeseen circumstances, the company has had to *give up/drop* its plans for expansion.

1. The story is that he *murdered* his wife.
2. We need to keep everything *legal*.
3. This plan does have a few *defects*.
4. I think we've been *cheated*!
5. She's extremely *vain*.
6. I saw a terrible *accident* on the road on the way here.
7. Mrs Grant was *astonished* when she heard the news.
8. We live a very *boring* life these days.
9. As the saying goes, my *energy* seems to have got up and gone.
10. She is just being *obstinate*.
11. I just love visiting *distant* corners of the earth.
12. Outside, she heard a *frightening* scream.
13. I was feeling slightly *ill* yesterday.
14. It was a *sad* tale that the old woman told.
15. My sister was *delighted* when she learned she had got second prize in the poetry competition.

1. Suddenly there was an *ear-piercing* shriek.
2. She was *heart-broken* when she didn't get the job at the local radio station.
3. I do wish someone would write a really *user-friendly* guide to computer programming.
4. I was sitting watching one of those *run-of-the-mill* gardening programmes on television last night when the phone rang.
5. The boys had a *hair-raising* journey over the mountains.
6. It was *heart-breaking* to see the children begging in the streets.
7. When the bomb went off, there was a *panic-stricken* rush to get out of the stadium.
8. There are a few *spine-chilling* moments in the film.
9. They put forward some *half-baked* scheme involving raising money by collecting old envelopes.
10. Being found out like that left me rather *red-faced/shamefaced*.

Unit 2: Hyponyms

1. A *salmon* is a type of *fish*.
2. A *parsnip* is a kind of *vegetable*.
3. A *monsoon* is a kind of *wind*.
4. A *lance* is a *weapon*.
5. A *balaclava* is a *hat*.
6. A *chateau* is a kind of *building*.
7. An *iris* is a kind of *flower*.

8. A *barrow* is a kind of *garden tool*.
9. A *bear* is a kind of *animal*.
10. A *downpour* is a period of *wet* weather.
11. *Dividers* are a tool for *drawing* with.
12. A *mussel* is a *shellfish*.
13. A *trowel* is a *tool*.
14. A *chrysanthemum* is a kind of *flower*.
15. An *axle* is a *part of a vehicle*.
16. A *hubcap* is part of a *vehicle*.
17. *Rum* is the name of a *drink*.
18. A *porch* is part of a *building*.
19. A *pointer* is a *dog*.
20. A *femur* is a *bone*.
21. A *lemur* is an *animal*.
22. A *moccasin* is a *shoe*.
23. A *water moccasin* is a *snake*.
24. A *flask* is a type of *bottle*.
25. A *foxtrot* is a *dance*.

 B

1. I need a new *table*. Do you know where there's a good *furniture* shop?
2. I want to buy a *goldfish*. Do you know where there's a good *pet* shop? (A fish-shop or fishmonger is where you buy fish to eat.)
3. I must buy some *scones*. Where's the nearest *bakery*?
4. I need some *money*. Where's the nearest *bank*? (A cash-and-carry is a large shop.)
5. We need more *sugar*. Pop along to the *grocer's* for me, will you? (Greengrocers sell fruit and vegetables.)
6. I bought some lovely *flowers* at the *florist* on the way home.
7. I can't eat this. It has *pecans* in it and I'm allergic to *nuts*.
8. Lots of people keep *birds* as pets. My mother has a *budgerigar/cockatoo*. (A didgeridoo is an Australian Aborigine musical instrument.)

 C

1. *Indigo* is a variety of *blue*.
2. *Ebony* is a variety of *black*.
3. *Vermilion* is a variety of *red*.
4. *Lilac* is a variety of *purple*.
5. *Crimson* is a variety of *red*.
6. *Fawn* is a variety of *brown*.
7. *Tan* is a variety of *brown*.
8. *Lavender* is a variety of *purple*.
9. *Maroon* is a variety of *red*.
10. *Auburn* is a variety of *brown*.

Unit 3: Antonyms

 A

inability	misbehave	unnatural	irregular
unable	discourteous	unnecessary	unreliable
inaccurate	unexpected	abnormal	insane
inadequate	inexpensive	impatient	atypical
disagree	unfortunate	unpleasant	misunderstand
disappear	unfriendly	impolite	unwelcome
unavoidable	dishonest	impossible	

 B

1. a *blunt/dull* knife
2. the *stern* of a ship
3. *concentrated* orange juice
4. *fresh* bread
5. furniture of *inferior* quality
6. a *professional* football team
7. *deep* water
8. an *interesting/exciting/stimulating* story
9. at the *exit*
10. their *descendants/offspring*
11. My hands are *dirty/filthy*.

12. I *adore/like/love* cabbage.
13. *Ignorance* can be a dangerous thing.
14. She looked down at the little boy with a *frown*.
15. She's the *senior* partner in the firm.

 C

1. I wasn't *angry* at what she said. In fact, I was quite *pleased*.
2. I don't *agree* with you. In fact, I totally *disagree* with you.
3. I'm not a *pessimist*. In fact, I'm really quite an *optimist*.
4. There has been no *increase* in crimes of violence over the past twelve months. In fact, there has been a slight *decrease/drop/fall/reduction*.
5. 'Athletics' may look like a *plural* noun, but in fact it is *singular*.
6. I took over a failing company from my *predecessor*, but I intend to hand over a highly successful company to my *successor*.
7. He is always looking for the *maximum* profit with the *minimum* of risk.
8. Our *imports* are other countries' *exports*.
9. I didn't say I would meet you *before* the concert, I said I would meet you *after* it.
10. She refuses to *admit* that she was his accomplice. In fact, she totally *denies* ever having met him.
11. *Drunk* or *sober*, he's a brilliant musician.
12. Somehow they always manage to turn *defeat* into *victory*.

Unit 4: Homonyms, Homographs and Homophones

 A

1. There were *hordes* of people in town this afternoon.
2. My son has just been elected to the town *council*.
3. Is it wrong to *steal* food when your family is starving?
4. Looking after pigs is a real *bore*.
5. A bucket is the same thing as a *pail*.
6. My daughter decided to *dye* her hair red.
7. I bought a bottle of perfume for my wife. It cost me 23 dollars and 50 *cents*.
8. Of *course* I'll come and help you start your car.
9. There's no need to *alter* your plans on my account.
10. I've got a terrible *pain* in my stomach, doctor.
11. Passengers should not alight until the train is *stationary*.
12. Can you smell gas? There must be a *leak* somewhere.
13. The driver had to *brake* sharply when a little girl ran out in front of his car.
14. I bought this boat cheap in the end-of-season *sale*.
15. The children were feeding buns to the *bears* at the zoo.
16. The prisoners were locked up in tiny *cells*.
17. The crowd *raised* a cheer as the procession drove *past*.
18. I was *born* 50 years ago today. I was the eighth child that my mother had *borne*.
19. The band consisted of a drummer, pianist, saxophonist and a *bass* guitarist.
20. The *principal* benefit of this method is its simplicity.
21. I love wandering down country *lanes* on warm summer evenings.
22. A man was killed this afternoon when several *bales* of hay fell off a lorry onto his car.

 B

1. A river *bank*.
2. *Scales*.
3. They both have *ears*.
4. Because they're her *hind* legs.
5. Because it's a *date* palm.
6. A *mole*.
7. It was a *grave* mistake.
8. Because she was the *belle* of the ball.
9. A traffic *jam*.
10. A *boxer*.
11. It was a *rash* decision.
12. An elastic *band*.

Unit 5: Words that Are Often Confused or Misused

1. We're all here *except* John.
2. These are particularly *fragrant* roses.
3. His lack of experience was not the only thing that *militated* against him being chosen for the job.
4. I don't drink much, but I'm not *averse* to an occasional glass of sherry.
5. Alcohol *affects* the functioning of the brain.
6. How long are you going to leave these dirty clothes *lying* there?
7. My mother is very ill, but she's in the hands of an *eminent* doctor, so we are hopeful she will make a full recovery.
8. I bought a new watch today to *replace* the one I lost last week.
9. You won't be *eligible* to join the club until you're twenty-one.
10. After a *momentary* hesitation, she decide to go with them.
11. The hens have *laid* more than a dozen eggs today.
12. The boats in the round-the-world race have all been *affected* by *adverse* weather conditions.
13. Scientific progress often comes via *fortuitous* discovery rather than deliberate experimentation.
14. The trouble with doctors is that when they *prescribe* drugs, their writing is often *illegible*.
15. After the flooding there was an *imminent* danger of an outbreak of cholera.
16. In spite of her weakness, she tried to *rise* from the bed to answer the telephone.
17. It is *especially* nice to be here because it gives me the opportunity to meet so many old friends.
18. Saying that is *tantamount* to calling him a liar.

1. The pole was sticking out at a 90-degree *angle* to the wall.
2. One of my front teeth is *loose*.
3. The police said they knew of no *motive* for the killing.
4. Britain and America were *allies* during the war.
5. I've thrown out my old armchairs and bought a new three-piece *suite*.
6. If you are interested in working for this company, please apply in writing to the *personnel* manager.
7. The union held a *ballot* to elect a new president.
8. She popped the cheque into the *envelope* and carefully sealed it.
9. I intend to go to art *college* when I leave school.
10. I have no *illusions* about him – I know he can't be trusted.
11. Her father is an *eminent* surgeon.
12. The garden was full of *fragrant* flowers.

Unit 6: Prefixes, Suffixes and Combining Forms

adventure	finance	lazy	scornful
annoy	forget	learn	strength
close	forgetful	length	symbol
confuse	frighten	mud	forgettable
create	hope	occur	written
duck	hopeful	pig	wrong
enjoy	hurried	poison	waste
explore	legible		

B

annoy	fright	debt	fortune
blame	happen	limit	rely
centre	hope	thought	write
courage	hurry	triumph	weak
enjoy	move	understand	world
forget			

amuses – inflection	misjudge – derivation
amusement – derivation	necessarily – derivation
announced – inflection	redo – derivation
bigger – inflection	runner – derivation
conversation – derivation	running – inflection
insisting – inflection	said – inflection
joyful – derivation	smallest – inflection
kindness – derivation	unnecessary – derivation
logical – derivation	valuable – derivation
masterful – derivation	woven – inflection
mathematical – derivation	

D

inability	irregular	imbalance	insane
impatient	informal	incapable	inattentive
illogical	inconsiderate	immoral	illiterate
inaccurate	inhumane	illiberal	immature
impolite	inexpensive	illegal	infrequent
inadequate	inappropriate	irresponsible	imperfect

E

1. An animal that eats meat is a *carnivore*.
2. An octagon is a figure with *eight* sides.
3. A kilometre is equal to *a thousand* metres.
4. Neurology is the branch of medicine that deals with functioning of the *nervous system*.
5. Fratricide is the murder of a person's own *brother*.
6. People who are Francophobic *dislike* the French.
7. Dermatitis is a disorder of the *skin*.
8. Omnivores eat *anything*.
9. Zoology is the study of *animals*.
10. A polygamist is someone who is married to *several people at the same time*.
11. The Mesolithic period of the Stone Age came *before* the Neolithic period.
12. Hypothermia is the condition of being *too cold*.

Unit 7: Word-Families

1. She arrived *unexpectedly*.
2. Opposition to the government's proposals has *strengthened*.
3. They fought *courageously*.
4. You have behaved *foolishly*.
5. Their feelings of horror were *unimaginable*.
6. We could hear *laughter* in the next room.
7. Is the stone *movable*?
8. We are assured by many experts that eating genetically modified cereals will not *endanger* our health.
9. It was an *unforgettable* experience.
10. She had a *painful* rash on her leg.
11. After they captured the city, they *enslaved* its inhabitants.
12. We are completely *defenceless*.
13. I accept this award with feelings both of *pride* and *humility*.
14. She performed the concerto *faultlessly*.
15. Could you *simplify* your explanation?
16. My mother was *furious* when she heard the news.
17. Handle the ornaments *carefully*.
18. What's the name of the *dramatist*?
19. *Admittedly* there are still a few problems to be solved.
20. One of the *attractions* is the sheer simplicity of the proposal.

Unit 8: Irregular verbs

1. Who *broke* the vase?
2. Who *drew* that picture on the wall?
3. Have you ever *met* the Queen?
4. I *knew* exactly what to do.

5. Who *told* you that?
6. Have you *seen* my pen anywhere?
7. Has the clock *struck* twelve yet?
8. The police *began* to question witnesses to the accident.
9. You might at least have *spoken* to him.
10. Her cutting remarks really *upset* me.
11. Who *won*?
12. I haven't *written* to my mother for weeks.
13. Has anyone ever *told* you you're a pain in the neck?
14. This has *become* a serious problem now.
15. He's been *bitten* by a snake.
16. I think the police *dealt* with the matter very efficiently.
17. She was very angry but nevertheless she *forgave* him for what he had *said*.
18. She turned and *fled*.
19. I've *sold* my car.
20. Suddenly the bell *rang*.

brought	laid	stuck
fought	met	swam
flew	sent	took
forbade OR forbad	sewed	wore
forgave	shone	wound
lay	shrank	wrote

choose	hold	tear	catch
freeze	lay	weep	seek
lead	lie	buy	teach
bleed	lose		

Unit 9: Comparison of Adjectives, Adverbs and Determiners

A

1. That brand of soap is quite *gentle* but my skin needs something even *gentler*.
2. He's not very *choosey* about what he eats; his wife is far *choosier*.
3. A buffalo can run *quickly* but a cheetah can run much *more quickly*.
4. 'Which end of the swimming pool is the *shallow* end?' 'I think it's *shallower* at this end.'
5. The morning lecture was pretty *boring* and the one in the afternoon was even *more boring*.
6. My French is *bad* but my Spanish is even *worse*.
7. My suggestion got very *little* support but John's got even *less*.
8. I don't eat *much* red meat. Most people eat a lot *more* than I do.
9. Daffodils are *lovely* flowers but I think tulips are even *lovelier*.
10. Men may think they are *clever* but women are far *cleverer* than men.
11. I didn't used to come here very *often* but I come a lot *more often/oftener* nowadays.
12. You may think that was a silly idea but I can come up with *sillier* ideas than that.
13. My sister is a *good* singer but my mother is even *better*.
14. I speak Chinese *badly* and Japanese even *worse*.
15. 'Come back *soon*.' 'Oh, I'll be back *sooner* than you expect.'
16. 'You sing very *well*.' 'Thanks, but you sing far *better* than me.'

narrowest	most	most unluckily
fattest	most energetic	tiredest
most helpful	most solemnly	most tiring
ugliest	most unlikely	driest
oddest	unluckiest	shyest/shiest
most peculiar		

Unit 10: Nouns and Related Adjectives

A

anserine: goose	*equine*: horse	*monetary*: money
bovine: cow	*feline*: cat	*neural*: nerve
dental: tooth	*floral*: flower	*oral*: mouth
digital: finger	*leonine*: lion	*thermal*: heat
dorsal: back	*mental*: mind	*vulpine*: fox

B

1. A doctor who specializes in diseases of the *heart* is a specialist in *cardiac* medicine.
2. The liquids that break down food in the *stomach* are known as *gastric* juices.
3. *Solar* power is derived from the *sun*.
4. *Aquatic* plants grow in *water*.
5. The muscles in your *chest* are your *pectoral* muscles.
6. Most of these monkeys are *arboreal* and rarely come down from the *trees*.
7. The *brain* is divided into two *cerebral* hemispheres.
8. My *nose* is blocked. Have you anything that would clear my *nasal* passages?
9. I love *sailing*. It's the *nautical* life for me!
10. The rocket landed on the *moon* and sent back pictures of the *lunar* landscape.
11. When I look at my *dog*, I often wonder what goes on in the *canine* mind.
12. Although the government had managed to reduce *taxes*, its *fiscal* policies were criticized by many experts.

Unit 11: Geographical Names

A

a Peruvian	a Spaniard	a Frenchman
a Norwegian	a Bruneian	a Filipino
an Iraqi	a Pakistani	a Myanmarese

B

Denmark	the Netherlands	Switzerland
Finland	Turkey	Poland
Sweden	Thailand	Wales

Unit 12: Occupations and Professions

A

1. False.	5. True.	9. False.	13. False.
2. False.	6. True.	10. True.	14. False.
3. True.	7. False.	11. True.	15. False.
4. False.	8. True.	12. False.	

B

1. An *ironmonger* sells household goods such as pots and kettles, cleaning equipment, and tools.
   A *blacksmith* makes horse-shoes.
2. A *taxidermist* arranges and stuffs the skins of dead animals so that they look like the animals did when they were alive.
   A *taxi driver* drives a taxi for a living.
4. A *bookmaker* takes bets on horse-races, etc.
   An *author* writes books.
7. A *caretaker* looks after a building.
   A *childminder* looks after other people's children.
9. An *astronomer* studies the stars and planets.
   An *astrologer* foretells the future by means of the movements of the planets.

12. A *bookkeeper* keeps financial accounts.
    A *librarian* works in a library.
13. A *meteorologist* studies atmospheric phenomena, especially those affecting the weather.
    An *astronomer* studies meteors.
14. A *botanist* studies plants and flowers.
    An *entomologist* studies insects.
15. A *metallurgist* studies the properties of metals and how to produce them.
    A *blacksmith*, a *goldsmith*, and a *silversmith* all make things out of metal.

 C

1. A nurse who helps women in childbirth is a *midwife*.
2. The person in charge of a museum is a *curator*.
3. If you have problems with your feet, you should consult a *chiropodist*.
4. If you break the glass in a window you need to call in a *glazier*.
5. If you want to sell your house, you can go to an *estate agent*.
6. If you want to discuss this further with me, phone my *personal assistant* to arrange a meeting.
7. When you come to my office, the *receptionist* will tell you how to find my room.
8. Someone who plays a flute is a *flautist*.
9. I never buy fish in the supermarket, I prefer to go to our local *fishmonger*.
10. When she had a sore back, she went to consult an *osteopath*.

Unit 13: Males, Females and Young

 **A**

duchess	queen	niece
countess	mistress	rani
goddess	nun	waitress
heroine		
uncle	fiancé	patriarch
bridegroom	gentleman OR lord	widower
emperor	sir	wizard

B

bull	gander	boar
stag OR buck	stallion	ram
drake		
cow	vixen	sow
hind OR doe	mare	ewe
bitch	lioness	tigress
duckling	cub	cygnet
eaglet	lamb	cub
tadpole		

Unit 14: Groups and Quantities

 A

a *troupe* of acrobats	a *pack* of dogs
a *bunch/comb/hand* of bananas	a *board* of directors
a *flock/flight* of birds	a *bunch* of grapes
a *herd* of cattle	a *litter* of kittens
a *troupe* of dancers	a *band* of robbers
a *herd* of deer	a *flock* of sheep

 B

a *bouquet* of *flowers*	a *pride* of *lions*
a *constellation* of *stars*	a *shoal* of *fish*
a *coven* of *witches*	a *suite* of *furniture/rooms*
a *covey* of *partridges*	a *swarm* of *bees/flies/insects/locusts*
a *gang* of *thieves/labourers /workmen*	

 C

a *bar* of *chocolate*	a *packet* of *cigarettes*
a *coil* of *rope*	a *pane* of *glass*
a *fleet* of *ships*	a *pat* of *butter*
a *flight* of *steps*	a *quiver* of *arrows*
a *pack* of *cards*	a *ream* of *paper*

Unit 15: Animal Homes and Shelters

 A

bird	dog	horse
cow	beaver	pig
poultry	horse	rabbit

 B

eyrie	den	nest OR drey
hive	holt OR den	nest

Unit 16: Sounds and Movements

 A

Lying in the garden in the sunshine, I could hear the bees *buzzing* as they *flew* from flower to flower. Sparrows were *chirping* on the roof of the house, and a blackbird was *singing* in the apple tree beside me. Brown and orange butterflies *flitted* among the blossom. A gentle breeze was *blowing*, so it wasn't too hot.

I could hear the clock *ticking* quietly in the lounge, and Emma, my cat, was *purring* gently on my lap. In the distance, traffic *rumbled/roared* along the motorway and the siren on a police car was *wailing*, but they were far enough away not to disturb me. There was nothing to disturb the peace of the afternoon.

Suddenly everything changed. Two dogs started *barking* loudly outside in the street. A jet plane *roared* overhead as it *took off* from the nearby airfield. A hawk *swooped* down on an unsuspecting sparrow and carried it off. And then the telephone *rang* and I had to get up and go into the house to answer it.

 B

1. A frog *croaks*.
2. A duck *quacks*.
3. A wolf *howls*.
4. A snake *hisses*.
5. An elephant *trumpets*.
6. A donkey *brays*.
7. A whistle *blows*.
8. A horse *neighs*.
9. A mouse *squeaks*.
10. An owl *hoots*.
11. A pigeon *coos*.
12. A crow *caws*.

Unit 17: Phrasal Verbs

 A

1. There are some things about his story that don't *add up*.
2. Does your little sister still *believe in* Santa Claus?
3. We're all going to watch the old bridge being *blown up*.
4. Looking at these photos *brings back* happy memories.
5. I must *brush up on* the Highway Code before I sit my driving test.

6. I expect my orders to be *carried out* exactly.
7. The police admit that they do not know how it *came about* that the thieves got away in a police car.
8. You really ought to *cut down on* the amount of coffee you drink.
9. I may have bought you a car but I have no intention of *forking out* for one for your boyfriend.
10. I'm sorry, I can't *go along with* you on that.
11. Every child needs someone to *look up to*.
12. *Pull in* along there and we'll have another look at the map.
13. A fire started in the kitchen but fortunately the staff were able to *put it out* before it spread.
14. He accused her of lying to the police, but he was forced to *take back* what he had said.
15. I'm very tired this evening. I think I'm going to *turn in* now.

1. She was *beavering away* when I went into the room.
2. I *came across* the book in the library last week.
3. Suddenly the alarm *went off*.
4. It was so hot in the shop, she nearly *passed out*.
5. They buy old houses, *do them up*, and then sell them again for a huge profit.
6. We don't want to listen to your silly stories. Why don't you just *push off*.
7. What does that tree-shaped mark *stand for*?
8. It will be no easy task to *carry out* our plan.
9. I'll *set out* sometime after breakfast.
10. I hope the rain will *hold off*.
11. Sadly her mother *passed away* last week.
12. Perhaps she will be able to tell us what happened when she *comes round* OR *comes to*.
13. A hole has appeared in the road outside them library. The police are *looking into* the matter.
14. The speaker did *touch on* the election in his speech.
15. I *was dying for* a glass of water.
16. The shop *has run out of* bread.
17. I think the fish I ate last night *disagreed with me*.
18. If I were you, I would *jump at* a chance of a free holiday in New Zealand.
19. Just *carry on* with what you're doing.
20. I always have the feeling that she *looks down on* me because I don't have a university education.

1.	*abide by*	5.	*grow on*	9.	*make for*
2.	*fall for*	6.	*hinge on*	10.	*see to*
3.	*get at*	7.	*keep to*	11.	*stand by*
4.	*go for*	8.	*look for*	12.	*strike at*

Unit 18: Common Idioms

1. Life was not *a bed of roses* in those days.
2. The two girls agreed to *bury the hatchet*.
3. When she was invited to meet the Queen, she was *on cloud nine*.
4. She's got a superb car but it must have *cost a bomb*.
5. She told me what the car cost. I thought it was *daylight robbery*.
6. I told her she would never pass her driving test, but I had to *eat my words* when she did pass.
7. It was a very expensive restaurant so my girlfriend insisted that we *went Dutch*.
8. I only meant to buy one new suit, but they were *going for a song*, so I ended up buying three.
9. There is no avoiding the question of money, so we are just going to have to *grasp the nettle*.
10. Exactly! You have *hit the nail on the head*.

11. When we reached the shop, my wife *made a beeline for* the cosmetics counter.
12. My daughter was *over the moon* when she heard she had got into university.
13. Writing computer programs is *a piece of cake*.
14. You can't go outside to play. It's raining *cats and dogs*.
15. My father taught me always to put some of my salary in a bank account *for a rainy day*.
16. When he suggested I was mistaken, I *saw red*.

1. If you are *the apple of someone's eye*, they *love you*.
2. If you have *a bee in your bonnet* about something, you are *very concerned about it*.
3. If something is *child's play*, it is *easy*.
4. *Till the cows come home* means *forever*.
5. *As the crow flies* means *in a straight line*.
6. To *fly off the handle* is to *become very angry*.
7. To *get out of bed on the wrong side* is to be *in a bad mood*.
8. To *give someone a piece of your mind* is to *give them a scolding*.
9. If you *let the cat out of the bag*, you *give away a secret*.
10. If you do something *once in a blue moon*, you do it *very rarely*.
11. If you tell someone to *pull their socks up*, you mean you want them to *improve their performance*.
12. If you *see eye to eye with* someone, you are *in agreement*.
13. To *sit on the fence* is to *be undecided*.
14. If you are *in the soup*, you are *in trouble*.
15. A *wild-goose chase* is *a pointless attempt at finding something*.
16. If you are *under the weather*, you are feeling *slightly ill*.

Unit 19: Similes

1. If a person is bald, they are *as bald as a coot*.
2. If a person can't see very well, they are *as blind as a bat*.
3. If the sea is very flat, it can be said to be *as calm as a millpond*.
4. If someone is very cunning, you can say that they are *as cunning as a fox*.
5. You can say that someone who is very deaf is *as deaf as a post*.
6. Two people who are very unlike each other can be said to be *as different as chalk and cheese*.
7. If you are in good health, you may say that you feel *as fit as a fiddle*.
8. A well-behaved child may be said to be *as good as gold*.
9. If you are very happy, you may be said to be *as happy as Larry*.
10. If you are very enthusiastic, someone may say that you are *as keen as mustard*.
11. Two people that are very alike are *as like as two peas in a pod*.
12. Someone who is very old may be said to be *as old as the hills*.
13. If you are very pleased about something, you are *as pleased as Punch*.
14. If something happens very quickly, it happens *as quick as a flash*.
15. Something that is very safe is *as safe as houses*.
16. If you are very obstinate, someone may say that you are being *as stubborn as a mule*.
17. Someone who is not very intelligent may be described as being *as thick as two short planks*.
18. Someone who is very wise may be said to be *as wise as Soloman*.

1. If you know something very well, you know it *like the back of your hand*.
2. If you are in a bad mood, someone may say that you are going round *like a bear with sore head*.
3. If you are very clumsy and are forever knocking things over, you may be told that you are *like a bull in a china shop*.

4. If you have a big smile on your face, you are grinning *like a Cheshire cat.*
5. If things go as planned, they go *like clockwork.*
6. If you find an occupation that suits you very well, you may take to it *like a duck to water.*
7. Something that is very popular and sells very quickly goes *like hot cakes.*
8. Someone who is trembling may be said to be shaking *like a leaf.*
9. If you work very hard, you work *like a Trojan.*
10. If something spreads very quickly over a wide area, it spreads *like wildfire.*

Unit 20: Proverbs and Sayings

1. *Absence* makes the heart grow fonder.
2. *Actions* speak louder than words.
3. A *bird* in the hand is worth two in the bush.
4. If the *cap* fits, wear it.
5. You cannot have your *cake* and eat it.
6. There is no use *crying* over spilt milk.
7. Don't put all your *eggs* in one basket.
8. Two *heads* are better than one.
9. Ignorance is *bliss.*
10. He who laughs last *laughs* longest.

1. If you want to excuse yourself for having broken something accidentally you may say that *accidents will happen.*
2. If you ask a friend for a loan of his car and he offers you his bicycle instead, you may accept the offer of the bike even though it is not what you wanted, with the thought that *beggars can't be choosers.*
3. If you arrive late for an appointment, you may apologise for being late but add *'Better late than never'.*
4. *Every cloud has a silver lining.* If I had got the job in Japan that I applied for, I would never have met the girl who became my wife.
5. 'What are we going to do if she won't talk to us?' 'We'll *cross that bridge when we come to it.'*
6. If you do something to lessen a rival's chance of success and increase your own chances, even though you know that what you are doing is wrong, you may try to justify your actions by telling yourself that *all is fair in love and war.*
7. The more helpers we can get on the day, the quicker the job will be done. *Many hands make light work.*
8. I don't object to her copying my hairstyle. *Imitation is the sincerest form of flattery.*
9. I don't mind if the man next door is a homosexual. *Live and let live,* I say.
10. The key to winning is not to give up hope when you're losing. *Never say die,* that's the thing.
11. Fleeing from the ravenous lions, he found himself facing an enraged elephant. *Out of the frying-pan, into the fire.*
12. To think that my little granddaughter is three years old already! *Doesn't time fly!*
13. I know the plane is supposed to leave at half past three but I'm going to check the departure time again just to be sure. *Better safe than sorry.*
14. I think I'll leave John to make all the arrrangements himself. *Too many cooks spoil the broth.*
15. If you want to be president some day, go for it. Never be afraid to *hitch your wagon to a star.*

Unit 21: British and American English

analyse	grey	pyjamas
axe	honour	plough
behaviour	jewellery	prologue
defence	litre	sceptic
fibre	marvelous	skilful

aeroplane	aubergine	film
pram	lift	car park
biscuit	autumn	pavement
sweetcorn	mince	drawing pin
pedestrian/zebra crossing	maths	vest

Unit 22: Foreign Words and Phrases Used in English

ad hoc = for a particular purpose
ad infinitum = forever, without an end
anno Domini = in the year of our Lord
a priori = arguing from general principles to particular cases or examples
bona fide = genuine
de facto = actual, in fact
gratis = free
inter alia = among other things
mea culpa = my fault
mutatis mutandis = changing what must be changed
per annum = every year
sine qua non = something absolutely necessary

bête noire = someone or something disliked or feared
bon voyage = have a good journey
carte blanche = freedom to do what you want
coup d'état = the violent overthrow of a government
crème de la crème = the best, the elite
cul-de-sac = a street that is closed at one end
déjà vu = the feeling of having experienced something before when that is not possible
fait accompli = something that cannot be changed
faux pas = a mistake
pièce de résistance = a masterpiece
tête-à-tête = a conversation
tour de force = a great achievement or performance

1. An *aficionado* of football *likes* the game.
2. If you have a feeling of *angst*, you are feeling *anxious.*
3. Something that is *ersatz* is *imitation.*
4. You shout *eureka* when you have *found* something.
5. The *hoi polloi* are the *ordinary people* of a country.
6. If your washing-machine is *kaput*, it is *broken.*
7. A *leitmotif* in a story is *a recurring theme.*
8. If you are asked to do a job and you say *mañana*, you mean you are going to do it *tomorrow* OR (more likely) *sometime.*
9. If you say you are going to look after *numero uno*, you mean you are going to look after *yourself.*
10. If you are speaking *sotto voce*, you are *speaking quietly.*